BUILDING TRUSTWORTHY SEMANTIC WEBS

OTHER AUERBACH PUBLICATIONS

BUILDING
TRUSTWORTHY
SEMANTIC WEBS

Bhavani Thuraisingham

CRC Press
Taylor & Francis Group
Boca Raton   London   New York

CRC Press is an imprint of the
Taylor & Francis Group, an **informa** business

CRC Press
Taylor & Francis Group
6000 Broken Sound Parkway NW, Suite 300
Boca Raton, FL 33487-2742

First issued in paperback 2019

© 2008 by Taylor & Francis Group, LLC
CRC Press is an imprint of Taylor & Francis Group, an Informa business

No claim to original U.S. Government works

ISBN-13: 978-0-8493-5080-1 (hbk)
ISBN-13: 978-0-367-38808-9 (hbk)

Library of Congress Cataloging-in-Publication Data

Thuraisingham, Bhavani M.
    Building trustworthy semantic webs / Bhavani Thuraisingham.
        p. cm.
    Includes bibliographical references and index.
    ISBN-13: 978-0-8493-5080-1 (alk. paper)
    ISBN-10: 0-8493-5080-8 (alk. paper)
    1. Semantic Web. 2. Database security. I. Title.

TK5105.88815T59 2008
025.04--dc22   2007027962

Visit the Taylor & Francis Web site at
http://www.taylorandfrancis.com

and the Auerbach Web site at
http://www.auerbach-publications.com

Dedication

In Memory of My Parents

Nitchingam
3 October 1913 – 30 October 1971
and
Gnanam
25 September 1919 – 28 October 1984

Although your time with me was short,
you gave me the strength to be brave and take on challenges.

Contents

Chapter 3 Secure Data, Information, and Knowledge Management 47

Preface

Background

Recent developments in information-systems technologies have resulted in computerizing many applications in various business areas. Data has become a critical resource in many organizations, and therefore, efficient access to data, sharing the data, extracting information from the data, and making use of the information has become an urgent need. As a result, there have been many efforts on not only integrating the various data sources scattered across several sites, but also extracting information from these databases in the form of patterns and trends. These data sources may be databases managed by database-management systems, or they could be data warehoused in a repository from multiple data sources.

The advent of the World Wide Web (WWW) in the mid-1990s has resulted in even greater demand for managing data, information, and knowledge effectively. There is now so much data on the Web that managing it with conventional tools is becoming almost impossible. New tools and techniques are needed to effectively manage this data. Therefore, to provide interoperability as well as to ensure machine-understandable Web pages, the concept of a semantic Web was conceived by Tim Berners Lee who heads the World Wide Web Consortium (W3C).

As the demand for data and information management increases, there is also a critical need for maintaining the security of the databases, applications, and information systems. Data and information have to be protected from unauthorized access as well as from malicious corruption. With the advent of the Web it is even more important to protect the data and information as numerous individuals now have access to this data and information. Therefore, we need effective mechanisms to secure semantic Web technologies.

This book will review the developments in semantic Web technologies and describe ways of securing these technologies. The focus will be on confidentiality, privacy, trust, and integrity management for the semantic Web. We will call such a semantic Web a trustworthy semantic Web. We will also discuss applications of trustworthy semantic Webs in secure Web services, secure interoperability, secure knowledge management, secure E-business, and secure information sharing.

We have written a series of books for Taylor & Francis on data management, data mining, and data security.

Book 1 (*Data Management Systems Evolution and Interoperation*) focused on general aspects of data management and also addressed interoperability and migration.

Book 2 (*Data Mining: Technologies, Techniques, Tools and Trends*) discussed data mining. It essentially elaborated on Chapter 9 of Book 1.

Book 3 (*Web Data Management and Electronic Commerce*) discussed Web database technologies and E-commerce as an application area. It essentially elaborated on Chapter 10 of Book 1.

Book 4 (*Managing and Mining Multimedia Databases for the Electronic Enterprise*) addressed both multimedia database management and multimedia data mining. It elaborated on both Chapter 6 of Book 1 (for multimedia database management) and Chapter 11 of Book 2 (for multimedia data mining).

Book 5 (*XML, Databases, and the Semantic Web*) described XML technologies related to data management. It elaborated on Chapter 11 of Book 3.

Book 6 (*Web Data Mining Technologies and Their Applications in Business Intelligence and Counterterrorism*) elaborated on Chapter 9 of Book 3.

Book 7 (*Database and Applications Security: Integrating Data Management and Information Security*) examines security for technologies discussed in each of our previous books. It focuses on the technological developments in database and applications security. It is essentially the integration of information security and database technologies.

One can regard our Book 7 to be the start of a new series in data security. Our current book (Book 8) is an elaboration of Chapter 25 of Book 7. It also integrates security with the contents of Book 5. The relationships between our texts will be illustrated in Appendix A.

Developments and Directions for Trustworthy Semantic Webs

As stated by Tim Berners Lee, the semantic Web consists of a collection of technologies that enable machine-understandable Web pages. The idea is for agents acting on behalf of users to collaborate with one another, invoke Web services, understand the Web pages, and carry out activities such as make airline reservations, plan for a surgery, or design a vehicle. The technologies that consist of the semantic Web include markup languages such as eXtensible Markup Language (XML), semantics-based languages such as Resource Description Framework (RDF), and ontology languages such as Web Ontology Language (OWL). Agents use these technologies, negotiate contracts with each other, and carry out activities. To ensure the security of operation, the semantic Web needs to enforce policies for confidentiality, privacy, trust, and integrity, among others, that is, policies specify the types of access that agents have to the Web resources and also the extent to which the agents trust one another. To carry out negotiations, various inferencing systems have been developed. Although numerous developments have been reported on semantic Web technologies, it is only recently that security is getting some attention. Therefore, one of the major directions for the semantic Web is to ensure the security of operation. We discuss some of the security issues in the next few paragraphs.

Consider the XML layer of the semantic Web. One needs secure XML, that is, access must be controlled to various portions of the document for reading, browsing, and modifications. There is research on securing XML and XML schemas. The next step is securing RDF. Now, with RDF not only do we need secure XML, we also need security for the interpretations and semantics. For example, under certain contexts, portions of the document may be unclassified, whereas under certain other contexts the document may be classified. As an example, one could declassify an RDF document once the war is over.

Once XML and RDF have been secured, the next step is to examine security for ontologies; that is, ontologies may have security levels attached to them. Certain parts of the ontologies could be secret, whereas certain other parts may be unclassified. The challenge is, how does one use these ontologies for applications such as secure information integration? Researchers have done some work on the secure interoperability of databases, and the use of ontologies is being explored.

We also need to examine the inference problem for the semantic Web. Inference is the process of posing queries and deducing new information. It becomes a problem when the deduced information is something the user is unauthorized to know. With the semantic Web, and especially with data mining tools, one can make all kinds of inferences. Recently there has been some research on controlling unauthorized inferences on the semantic Web.

Security should not be an afterthought. We have often heard that one needs to insert security into the system right from the beginning. Similarly, security cannot be an afterthought for the semantic Web. However, we cannot also make the system inefficient if we must guarantee 100 percent security at all times. What is needed is a flexible security policy. During some situations we may need 100 percent security, whereas during some other situations some security (e.g., 60 percent) may be sufficient.

Closely related to security is privacy. The challenge here is protecting sensitive information about individuals. Other challenges include trust management and negotiation. How do we determine the trust that agents place in one another? Is it based on the reputation of the agents? Another challenge is maintaining integrity. For example, when XML documents are published by third parties, we need to ensure that the documents are authentic and are of high quality. We hope that many of these challenges will be clearer in this book. As more progress is made on investigating these various issues, we hope that appropriate standards will be developed for securing the semantic Web. Note that although security is essentially about confidentiality, we use the term trustworthiness to include not only confidentiality, but also privacy, trust, and integrity.

Organization of this Book

This book is divided into five parts, each describing some aspect of trustworthy semantic Webs. Part I, consisting of three chapters, discusses concepts in trustworthy-information systems. Note that the supporting technologies for trustworthy semantic Webs are trustworthy-information systems and semantic Webs. Trustworthy-information systems consist of many aspects. We will focus on three aspects. Chapter 2 discusses concepts in trustworthy systems including secure systems as well as features such as integrity, trust, and privacy. Chapter 3 discusses secure data, information, and knowledge management. We discuss topics such as secure database systems, secure information systems such as secure multimedia systems, and secure knowledge management. Chapter 4 discusses concepts in semantic Webs.

Part II, consisting of five chapters, discusses secure semantic Webs. Note that this part is the heart of the book. In Chapter 5 we provide an overview of secure semantic Webs. In Chapter 6 we discuss XML security. In Chapter 7 we discuss RDF security. Security and ontologies including security for OWL are discussed in Chapter 8. Integrating security into Web rules is the subject of Chapter 9.

Part III, which consists of six chapters, discusses dependability of the semantic Web. Note that whereas security (i.e., confidentiality) has been our main focus, we also address other features such as trust management and privacy. Chapter 10 discusses trust management for the semantic Web. We discuss trust policies and describe how automatic trust management may be included in the operation of the semantic Web. Note that trust is already discussed in the definition of the semantic Web by Tim Berners Lee. For example, how can we trust the statements? Logicians are working on proof systems to determine trust. However, the security community has also investigated trust extensively. For example, if A trusts B and B trusts C, then should A trust C? Chapter 11 discusses privacy for the semantic Web. We examine the Platform for Privacy Preferences Project (P3P) and discuss ways to extend it. We also examine the privacy problems that arise through semantic Web mining and discuss approaches for privacy-preserving semantic Web mining. Chapter 12 discusses integrity and data quality for the semantic Web. How do we ensure that the information that is exchanged is of high quality? Multilevel security for the semantic Web is the subject of Chapter 13. Note that multilevel security is an aspect of confidentiality. However, we decided not to include it in Part II to give

Part II more focus. Managing the policies is an important aspect. Therefore, policy engineering is discussed in Chapter 14. Finally, in Chapter 15 we elaborate on the developments about the semantic Web from research, standards, products, and applications points of view. We decided to include Chapter 15 in Part III mainly for completion.

Part IV discusses applications that utilize trustworthy semantic Webs. Chapter 16 discusses secure Web services that utilize semantic Web technologies. Semantic Web technologies for managing secure databases is the subject of Chapter 17. Secure semantic interoperability for heterogeneous information sources is discussed in Chapter 18. Chapter 19 discusses a semantic Web for secure E-business applications. Chapter 20 discusses a semantic Web for secure digital libraries. Chapter 21 discusses semantic Web technologies for an important applications area called assured information sharing.

Part V consists of three chapters and describes specialized and domain-specific semantic Webs. In Chapter 22 we discuss domain-specific semantic Webs for defense, financial, and medical domains, among others. Trustworthy semantic Webs for geospatial data as well as for sensor data are discussed in Chapter 23. In particular, the work carried out on Geography Markup Language (GML) as well as the interoperability work of the Open Geospatial Consortium (OGC) is discussed. Chapter 24 discusses pervasive computing applications including secure mobile sensor semantic Webs as well as pervasive semantic Webs.

Chapter 25 summarizes the book and discusses future directions. We have included three appendices. Appendix A provides an overview of data management and discusses the relationship between the texts we have written. A summary of data and applications security (which is our Book 7) is given in Appendix B to give the reader a better understanding as to where we are coming from. Various standards efforts related to the semantic Web are detailed in Appendix C. This book ends with a bibliography and an index. Each of Chapters 1 through 25 includes references for that chapter as well as exercises that will be useful for students.

Data, Information, and Knowledge

In general, data management includes managing the databases, interoperability, migration, warehousing, and mining. For example, the data on the Web has to be managed and mined to extract information, patterns, and trends. Data could be in files, relational databases, or other types of databases such as multimedia databases. Data may be structured or unstructured. We repeatedly use the terms data, data management, and database systems and database-management systems in this book. We elaborate on these terms in Appendix A. We define data-management systems to be systems that manage the data, extract meaningful information from the data, and make use of the information extracted. Therefore, data-management systems include database systems, data warehouses, and data-mining systems. Data could be structured data such as that found in relational databases, or it could be unstructured such as text, voice, imagery, and video.

There have been numerous discussions in the past to distinguish between data, information, and knowledge. In some of our previous books on data management and mining, we did not attempt to clarify these terms. We simply stated that data could be just bits and bytes, or it could convey some meaningful information to the user. However, with the Web and also with increasing interest in data, information, and knowledge management as separate areas, in this book we take a different approach to data, information, and knowledge by differentiating between these terms as much as possible. For us data is usually some value like numbers, integers, and strings. Information is obtained when some meaning or semantics is associated with the data such as John's salary is 20K. Knowledge is something that you acquire through reading and learning and, as a result, understand the data and information and take actions. Data and information can be transferred into knowledge when uncertainty about the data and information is removed from someone's mind. It should be noted that it is rather difficult to give strict definitions of data, information, and knowledge. Sometimes we will use these terms interchangeably. Our framework for data management discussed in Appendix A helps clarify some of the differences. To be consistent with the terminology in our previous books, we distinguish between database systems and database-management systems. A database-management system is that component which manages the database containing persistent data. A database system consists of both the database and the database-management system.

Final Thoughts

The goal of this book is to explore security issues for the semantic Web and discuss how trustworthy semantic Webs may be applied for Web services, interoperability, and knowledge management, among others. The goal is also to show the breadth of the applications of trustworthy semantic Webs in multiple domains. We have used the material in this book together with the numerous papers listed in the references in each chapter for a graduate level course at the University of Texas at Dallas on *Building Trustworthy Semantic Web*s. In addition to trying out the exercises at the end of each chapter, the students also wrote term papers and carried out a programming project on trustworthy semantic Webs.

One could argue that because the developments in secure semantic Webs are just beginning, this book might be premature. I feel that in many ways it is timely to write such a book so that various viewpoints can be taken into consideration in advancing the field. It is important that appropriate tools and technologies are developed to secure the semantic Web. Security cannot be an afterthought. There-fore, although the technologies for the semantic Web are being developed, it is important to include security at the onset. Furthermore, a lot of progress has been made on data security, and it is important to take advantage of these developments in securing the semantic Web. I believe strongly in taking as much advantage as possible of the knowledge that is out there rather than reinventing the wheel. It was for these reasons that I decided to write this book now.

Acknowledgments

I would like to thank the Administration at the Erik Jonsson School of Engineering and Computer Science at the University of Texas at Dallas for giving me the opportunity to direct the Cyber Security Research Center and teach courses on data and applications security and building trustworthy semantic Webs. I thank all my Ph.D. and M.S. students for giving me many insights and the students who have taken my classes, especially the students who took my class on Building Trustworthy Semantic Webs during the fall semester of 2006. I am especially grateful to my Ph.D. student Alam Ashraful for the many discussions on trustworthy semantic Webs and giving me examples on query modification, RDF and OWL policy specifications, and geospatial ontology for this book. I also thank my M.S. student Yashaswini Harsha Kumar for example documents on XML, RDF, and OWL for this book. I also thank my M.S. student Ganesh Subbiah for his contributions to geospatial semantic Webs.

I would also like to thank many people who have supported my work including the following:

- My husband Thevendra for his continued support for my work and my son Breman for being such a wonderful person and for motivating me.
- Professor C. V. Ramamoorthy at the University of California at Berkeley for his constant encouragement.
- Henry Bayard at MITRE for his continued mentoring and encouragement.
- Prof. Elisa Bertino (Purdue University), Prof. Tim Finin (University of Maryland [Baltimore County]) for leading the fields of XML security and trust for the semantic Web; Prof. Tim Berners Lee (Massachusetts Institute of Technology) for conceiving the idea of the semantic Web; and Prof. Ravi Sandhu (now UTSA) for RBAC/UCON models that have influenced my research on trustworthy semantic Webs.
- Profs. Elena Ferrari, Barbara Carminati, and Anna Cinzia Squicciarini for collaborating with me on various aspects of XML and RDF security.

- My colleagues at the University of Texas at Dallas, especially Prof. Latifur Khan, Prof. Murat Kantarcioglu, Prof. Kevin Hamlen, and Prof. I-Ling Yen for their collaboration on related topics.
- Prof. Latifur Khan as well as students including Alam Ashraful, Ganesh Subbiah, Nathalie Tsublinik, and Ryan Layfield who have been involved in some aspect of my research on secure semantic Webs.
- My colleagues who have collaborated with me, especially during the past three years since I joined the University of Texas at Dallas.
- The sponsors of my research at the University of Texas at Dallas, especially the Air Force Office of Scientific Research, the National Science Foundation, Raytheon Corporation, the National Geospatial Intelligence Agency, and the Texas Enterprise Funds.
- I also thank the sponsors of my research at MITRE and Honeywell on data and applications security including AFRL, CECOM, SPAWAR, NSA, CIA, IRS, and NASA.
- My former colleagues at the National Science Foundation, the MITRE Corporation, and Honeywell Inc. for their encouragement on my work in secure data management.

I hope that we can continue to make progress in building trustworthy semantic Webs so that we not only have agents that understand Web pages, but also ensure the security of operation in carrying out activities on the Web.

The Author

Bhavani Thuraisingham joined the University of Texas at Dallas (UTD) in October 2004 as a Professor of Computer Science and Director of the Cyber Security Research Center in the Erik Jonsson School of Engineering and Computer Science. She is an elected fellow of three professional organizations: the IEEE (Institute for Electrical and Electronics Engineers), the AAAS (American Association for the Advancement of Science), and the BCS (British Computer Society) for her work in data security. She received the IEEE Computer Society's prestigious 1997 Technical Achievement Award for "outstanding and innovative contributions to secure data management." She was quoted by *Silicon India Magazine* as one of the top seven technology innovators of South Asian origin in the United States in 2002.

Prior to joining UTD, Dr. Thuraisingham was an IPA (Intergovernmental Personnel Act) Program Director at the National Science Foundation (NSF) in Arlington, VA, from the MITRE Corporation. At NSF she established the Data and Applications Security Program and cofounded the Cyber Trust theme and was involved in interagency activities in data mining for counterterrorism. She worked at MITRE in Bedford, MA between January 1989 and September 2001, first in the Information Security Center and was later a department head in Data and Information Management as well as Chief Scientist in Data Management in the Intelligence and Air Force centers. She has served as an expert consultant in information security and data management to the Department of Defense, the Department of Treasury, and the intelligence community for over 10 years. Dr. Thuraisingham's industry experience includes six years of research and development at Control Data Corp. and Honeywell Inc. in Minneapolis, MN. While she was in industry and at MITRE, she was an adjunct professor of computer science and a member of the graduate faculty, first at the University of Minnesota and later at Boston University between 1984 and 2001. She also worked as visiting professor soon after her Ph.D., first at the New Mexico Institute of Technology and later at the University of Minnesota between 1980 and 1983.

Dr. Thuraisingham's work in information security and information management has resulted in over 80 journal articles, over 200 refereed conference papers and workshops, and three U.S. patents. She is the author of eight books in data management, data mining, and data security including one on data mining for counterterrorism and another on database and applications. She has given over 40 keynote presentations at various technical conferences and has also given invited talks at the White House Office of Science and Technology Policy and at the United Nations on data mining for counterterrorism. She serves (or has served) on editorial boards of leading research and industry journals including several IEEE and ACM Transactions and currently serves as the Editor-in-Chief of *Computer Standards and Interfaces Journal*. She is also an instructor at the Professional Development Center of the Armed Forces Communications and Electronics Association (AFCEA) since 1998 and has served on panels for the Air Force Scientific Advisory Board and the National Academy of Sciences.

Dr. Thuraisingham is the president of Bhavani Security Consulting, which provides consulting and training in information technology and security. Dr. Thuraisingham promotes mathematics and science to high school students as well as to women and underrepresented minorities and has given featured addresses at conferences sponsored by Women and Technology International (WITI) and the Society for Women Engineers (SWE). Articles on her efforts as well as her vision have appeared in multiple magazines including the *Dallas Morning News*, *D Magazine*, *MITRE Matters*, and the *DFW Metroplex Technology Magazine*. She is dedicated to advising and motivating her several research students pursuing M.S. and Ph.D. degrees in data mining and data security at UTD and mentors assistant and associate professors related to her field at the university.

Dr. Thuraisingham was educated in the United Kingdom, both at the University of Bristol and at the University of Wales.

Chapter 1

Introduction

1.1   Trends

A semantic Web is intelligent and understands and reads Web pages. At present we need the human in the loop to read and understand Web pages and make decisions. The vision of Tim Berners Lee is to develop technologies such as eXtensible Markup Language (XML), Resource Description Framework (RDF), and ontologies so that agents acting on behalf of users can read and understand the Web pages and make decisions.

Although progress has been made on semantic Webs during the past decade, much progress has also been made on trustworthy information systems over the past three to four decades. Such systems include secure systems, high-assurance systems, and high-integrity systems. Until recently much of the focus has been on security (i.e., confidentiality). However, recently there has been work on integrating features such as security, integrity, trust management, fault tolerance, and real-time processing.

One of the major challenges in the development of semantic Webs is to build trustworthy semantic Webs. By trustworthy semantic Webs we mean semantic Webs that are secure, manage trust, have integrity, ensure privacy, and are capable of processing information in a timely manner. In this book we will discuss developments, directions, and challenges for trustworthy semantic Webs.

Trustworthy semantic Webs integrate two major technologies: trustworthy information systems and semantic Webs. In our terminology, trustworthy information includes systems that are secure and dependable. Dependable systems include high-assurance systems that meet timing constraints, recover from faults, and ensure integrity. We have assumed that features of trustworthy systems include security, integrity, privacy, and trust. It is almost impossible to incorporate all these features in designing a system. Therefore, the challenge is to make tradeoffs between the various features and enforce flexible policies.

Our main focus in this book will be on building secure semantic Web technologies with a focus on confidentiality. However, we will also give consideration to other features such as integrity, privacy, trust, and data quality so that we can build trustworthy semantic Webs. Some books and papers have used the terms *trustworthiness* and *dependability* interchangeably. Note that standard definitions of the terms such as trustworthiness and dependability have yet to be developed. Our goal is to focus on the features of trustworthy semantic Webs based on the definition that we have assumed, that is, trustworthy semantic Webs include secure semantic Webs and dependable semantic Webs. Dependable semantic Webs include semantic Webs that ensure privacy, manage trust, have high integrity, meet timing constraints, and recover from faults.

1.2   Organization of This Chapter

Before we begin discussing the contents of this book, we give an overview of where we are with respect to trustworthy semantic Webs and discuss why we embarked on this book. Although a lot of work has gone on in recent years on trustworthy semantic Webs (especially since my invited talk at the EU-US [European Union–United States] meeting on semantic Webs at Sophia Antipolis, France, in October 2001, and my funding efforts on this topic while I was a program director at the National Science Foundation between October 2001 and September 2004), there was no source where one could go to find out what is going on in building trustworthy semantic Webs. Therefore, I first decided to teach a course on this topic at the University of Texas at Dallas in the fall of 2006 and subsequently started writing this book, although I had planned on this book soon after I finished my previous book on *Database and Applications Security* in 2005.

This book is divided into five parts. Each part is summarized in the ensuing sections of this chapter. First, an overview of research products and standards is given in Section 1.3. Section 1.4, which summarizes Part I, discusses trustworthy systems, secure data and information-management systems, and semantic Webs. We have assumed that supporting technologies for trustworthy semantic Webs are trustworthy systems, secure data systems, and the semantic Web. Trustworthy information systems include numerous types of information systems including secure systems, real-time systems, fault tolerance systems, and high-assurance systems.

The components of trustworthy semantic Webs are secure semantic Webs and dependable semantic Webs. Section 1.5, which summarizes Part II, discusses concepts in secure semantic Webs, in particular, secure XML, secure RDF, secure ontologies, and secure rules as well as other security issues such as the inference problem for the semantic Web.

Section 1.6, which summarizes Part III, discusses concepts in dependable semantic Webs. Note that we have focused on security, which we assume to be mainly confidentiality, in Part III. We have used dependability to include other features such as trust management, integrity, and data quality in Part III. In addition, we have included privacy as part of dependability. Therefore, in Section 1.6 we discuss semantic Webs that have to manage trust and ensure data integrity as well as timely processing. Privacy issues including the Platform for Privacy Preferences Project (P3P) are also discussed.

Section 1.7, which summarizes Part IV, discusses various applications for secure and trustworthy semantic Webs. In particular, applications such as secure Web services, secure data management, and secure interoperability are discussed.

Section 1.8, which summarizes Part V, discusses special semantic Webs for different user communities including geospatial Webs, sensor Webs, and Webs for medical and financial communities.

Section 1.9 gives further details on the organization of this book. As with our previous books, this book is also based on a framework for trustworthy semantic Webs. The framework consists of the supporting technologies, core concepts, and applications. Future directions are discussed in Section 1.10.

1.3   Research, Products, and Standards

The major research institution conducting research in trustworthy semantic Webs is the University of Maryland (Baltimore County) under the leadership of Prof. Tim Finin (with Profs. Anupam Joshi and Yelena Yesha). Other institutions include the University of Maryland (Prof. James Hendler, now at Rensselaer Polytechnic Institute), the Massachusetts Institute of Technology (Prof. Tim Berners Lee with Dr. Lalana Kagal and Lawyer Daniel Weitzner among others), and the University of Texas at Dallas (Prof. Bhavani Thuraisingham with Prof. Latifur Khan). Work on policy issues is also being carried out at other universities in the United States and Europe. For example, Purdue University is conducting excellent research on XML-based policy management (Prof. Bertino, formerly at the University of Milan). The University of Como in Italy is conducting research on XML and RDF-based policy management (Profs. Elena Ferrari and Barbara Carminati). George Mason University is conducting research on bringing the Usage Control (UCON) Model into the semantic Web framework (Prof. Ravi Sandhu now at the University of Texas at San Antonio).

At present there is no commercial semantic Web or secure semantic Web product. However, one can develop a semantic Web by putting together technologies such as XML and RDF. Corporations such as International Business Machines Corporation (IBM), Oracle, Microsoft, and SAP among others are developing semantic Web technologies. For example, Oracle has developed a data-management system to manage XML and, more recently, RDF documents. Oracle also is providing security solutions.

With respect to standards, organizations such as the World Wide Web Consortium (W3C) and the Organization for the Advancement of Structured Information Standards (OASIS) are developing semantic Web standards. Whereas W3C is focusing entirely on standards for semantic Webs, OASIS standards are mainly based on XML technologies. Also organizations such as the Open Geospatial Consortium (OGC) are developing standards such as Geography Markup Language (GML) for geospatial data management.

1.4 Trustworthy Information Systems

Part I of this book will discuss the supporting technologies for trustworthy semantic Webs. These supporting technologies are lumped into what we call trustworthy information systems. These systems consist of many aspects including trustworthy systems, secure data and information systems, and semantic Webs.

Trustworthy systems are systems that are secure and dependable. By dependable systems we mean systems that have high integrity, are fault tolerant, and meet real-time constraints. Trustworthy systems may include information systems including data-management systems, information-management systems, and trustworthy networks. In other words, for a system to be trustworthy it must be secure, fault tolerant, meet timing deadlines, and manage high-quality data. However, integrating these features into a system means that the system has to meet conflicting requirements. For example, if the system makes all the access control checks, then it may miss some of its deadlines. The challenge in designing trustworthy systems is to design systems that are flexible. For example, in some situations it may be important to meet all the timing constraints, whereas in other situations it may be critical to satisfy all the security constraints.

Trustworthy systems have sometimes been referred to as dependable systems, whereas in some other cases dependability is considered to be part of trustworthiness. For example, in some papers dependability includes mainly fault-tolerant systems, and when one integrates fault tolerance with security, then one gets trustworthy systems. Regardless of what the definitions are, for systems to be deployed in operational environments, especially for command and control and other critical applications, we need end-to-end dependability as well as security. For some applications not only do we need security and confidentiality, we also need to ensure that the privacy of the individuals is maintained. Therefore, privacy is also another feature of trustworthiness.

For a system to be dependable and trustworthy, we need end-to-end dependability and trustworthiness. Note that the components that comprise a system include

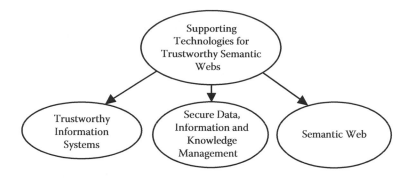

Figure 1.1 Supporting technologies for trustworthy semantic Webs.

the network, operating systems, middleware and infrastructure, data manager, and applications. We need all the components to be dependable and trustworthy.

As stated earlier, other supporting technologies for building trustworthy semantic Webs are secure data, information and knowledge-management systems as well as semantic Webs. Secure data and information systems include secure database systems such as secure relational database systems and secure information systems such as secure multimedia information systems and digital libraries.

The third supporting technology is the semantic Web. As previously stated, the goal of the semantic Web is to ensure that the Web pages are machine understandable. This is the vision of Tim Berners Lee. The idea is to develop common ontologies and specification languages so that agents that act on behalf of the users can read the Web pages and make sense of the data. The ultimate goal is for the system to take actions without the human in the loop. Figure 1.1 illustrates the supporting technologies for trustworthy semantic Webs. Figure 1.2 illustrates the technology stack for the semantic Web as defined by Tim Berners Lee.

1.5   Secure Semantic Webs

As discussed earlier, trustworthy semantic Webs include secure semantic Webs and dependable semantic Webs. Part II discusses technologies for secure semantic Webs. By security we mean confidentiality. For many applications, especially for Command, Control Communications, Computers, Intelligence, Surveillance, and Reconnaissance (C4ISR), the semantic Web has to operate securely. Note that security cannot be considered in isolation. Security cuts across all layers, and this is a challenge; that is, we need security for each of the layers illustrated in Figure 1.3.

For example, consider the lowest layer. One needs secure Transmission Control Protocol/Internet Protocol (TCP/IP), secure sockets, and secure Hypertext Transfer Protocol (HTTP). There are now security protocols for these various lower-layer

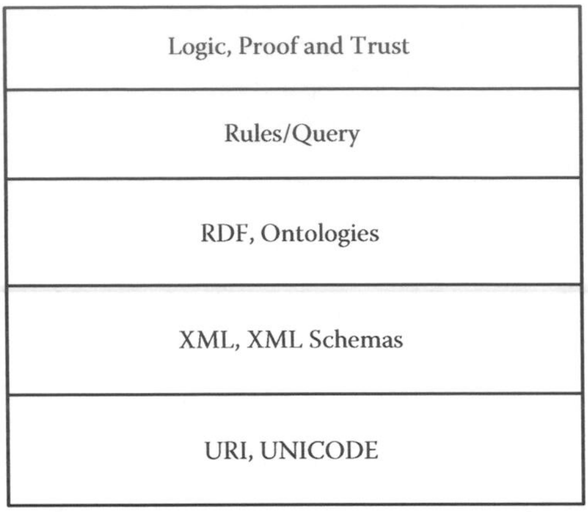

Logic, Proof and Trust
Rules/Query
RDF, Ontologies
XML, XML Schemas
URI, UNICODE

Figure 1.2   Technology stack for the semantic Web.

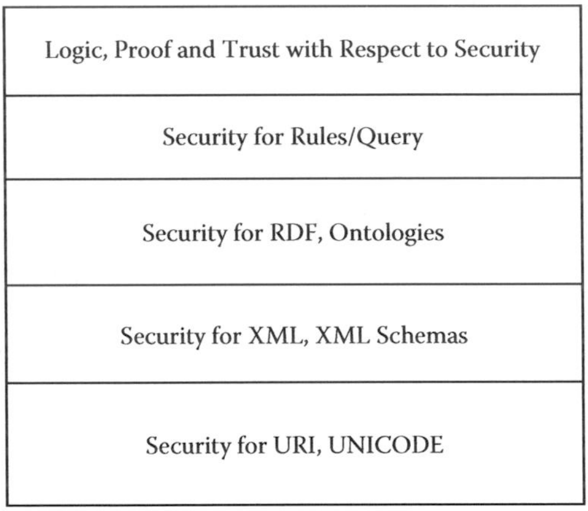

Logic, Proof and Trust with Respect to Security
Security for Rules/Query
Security for RDF, Ontologies
Security for XML, XML Schemas
Security for URI, UNICODE

Figure 1.3   Technology stack for a secure semantic Web.

protocols. One needs end-to-end security; that is, one cannot just have secure TCP/IP built on untrusted communication layers. We need network security. The next layer is XML and XML schemas. One needs secure XML; that is, access must be controlled to various portions of the document for reading, browsing, and modifications. There is research on securing XML and XML schemas. The next step is securing RDF. Now with RDF, not only do we need secure XML, we also need security for the interpretations and semantics. For example, under certain contexts, portions of the document may be unclassified, whereas under certain other contexts the document may be classified. As an example, one could declassify an RDF document once the war is over.

Once XML and RDF have been secured, the next step is to examine security for ontologies and interoperation, that is, ontologies may have security levels attached to them. Certain parts of the ontologies could be secret, whereas certain other parts may be unclassified. The challenge is, how does one use these ontologies for secure information integration? Researchers have done some work on the secure interoperability of databases. We need to revisit this research and then determine what else needs to be done so that the information on the Web can be managed, integrated, and exchanged securely.

Security should not be an afterthought. We have often heard that one needs to insert security into the system right from the beginning. Similarly, security cannot be an afterthought for the semantic Web. However, we cannot also make the system inefficient if we must guarantee 100 percent security at all times. What is needed is a flexible security policy. During some situations we may need 100 percent security, whereas during some other situations 30 percent security may be sufficient. In Part II we discuss secure XML, RDF, and ontologies as well as rules and the inference problem.

1.6 Dependable Semantic Webs

In our definition, trustworthiness consists of security and dependability. By dependable system, we mean systems that have integrity, high assurance, and are fault tolerant and meet real-time constraints. Similarly, a dependable semantic Web is a semantic Web that has integrity; the information is of high quality, is fault tolerant, and meets timing constraints. We have also added privacy, trust management, and rights management as part of dependability. Note that this is not a standard definition; that is, some papers and books have used the terms trustworthiness and dependability interchangeably. Furthermore, some papers have also implied that security includes confidentiality, integrity, and privacy.

Figure 1.4 illustrates aspects of a dependable semantic Web. The challenge is to ensure that the semantic Web has all the features such as privacy, trust, and integrity. Essentially the system has to be flexible. Part III focuses on dependable semantic Webs.

1.7 Applications

A semantic Web is being deployed for many domain applications including medical, financial, and command and control. However, a semantic Web is also a key technology for many other technologies such as Web services, grids, and knowledge management. Therefore, by applications we mean the technical applications such as knowledge management. Domain applications are discussed in Section 1.8.

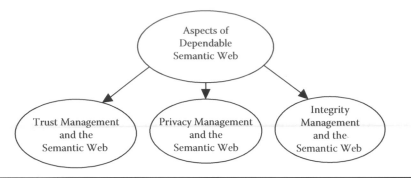

Figure 1.4   Aspects of a dependable semantic Web.

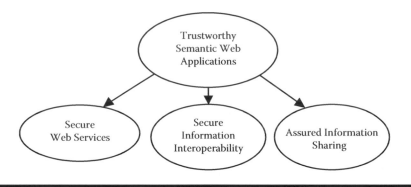

Figure 1.5   Trustworthy semantic Web technology applications.

Web services are the various services that a user can invoke. These services make use of semantic Web technologies such as XML and RDF. Secure semantic Web technologies can be applied to secure Web services. Similarly, secure semantic Web technologies can be applied to secure data, information, and knowledge management. For example, technologies such as RDF and ontologies are useful to capture knowledge, and the reasoning tools could be used to manage the knowledge. Other applications include interoperability and E-business. Figure 1.5 illustrates the technical applications.

1.8   Specialized Trustworthy Semantic Webs

Although much of the research and development about the semantic Web has focused on managing and exchanging text-based and structured data, there is now an urgent need to manage geospatial and sensor data. Languages such as GML and

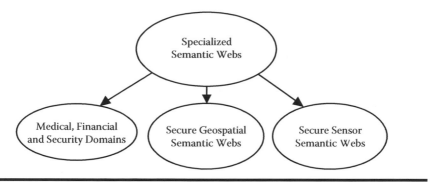

Figure 1.6 Specialized trustworthy semantic Webs.

Sensor Markup Language (SML) are being developed by standards organizations such as OGC. The end result is semantic Webs for geospatial and sensor data.

Very few of the efforts have focused on incorporating security and trust for specialized semantic Webs. Part V of the book discusses these specialized Webs as well as Webs for domains for medical, financial, and defense applications (Figure 1.6).

1.9   Organization of This Book

This book is divided into five parts, each describing some aspect of trustworthy semantic Webs. As mentioned, the major focus of this book will be on security and confidentiality. Other features such as trust management, integrity, data quality, and timely fault-tolerant processing will be addressed for semantic Webs. Applications for trustworthy semantic Webs such as semantic E-business and digital libraries will also be discussed.

Part I discusses concepts in trustworthy information systems. Note that the supporting technologies for trustworthy semantic Webs are trustworthy information systems and semantic Webs. Trustworthy information systems consist of many aspects. We focus on three aspects. Chapter 2 discusses concepts in trustworthy systems including secure systems as well as features such as integrity, trust, and privacy. Chapter 3 discusses secure data, information, and knowledge management. We discuss topics such as secure database systems, secure information systems such as secure multimedia systems, and secure knowledge management. Chapter 4 discusses concepts in semantic Webs.

Part II discusses secure semantic Webs. Note that this part is the heart of the book. In Chapter 5 we provide an overview of secure semantic Web. In Chapter 6 we discuss XML security based on our collaborative research with the University of Milan. In Chapter 7 we discuss RDF security. Security and ontologies including security for Web Ontology Language (OWL) are discussed in Chapter 8. Integrating security into Web rules is the subject of Chapter 9.

Part III discusses dependability of the semantic Web. Note that whereas security (i.e., confidentiality) has been our main focus, we also address other features such as trust management and privacy. Chapter 10 discusses trust management for the semantic Web. We discuss trust policies and describe how automatic trust management may be included in the operation of the semantic Web. Note that trust is already discussed in the definition of the semantic Web by Tim Berners Lee. For example, how can we trust the statements? Logicians are working on proof systems to determine trust. However, the security community has also investigated trust extensively. For example, if A trusts B and B trusts C, then should A trust C? Finin and others have carried out extensive research on trust for the semantic Web at the University of Maryland (Baltimore County). Chapter 11 discusses privacy for the semantic Web. We examine P3P and discuss ways to extend it. We also examine the privacy problems that arise through semantic Web mining and discuss approaches for privacy-preserving semantic Web mining. Chapter 12 discusses integrity and data quality for the semantic Web. How do we ensure that the information that is exchanged is of high quality? Multilevel security for a semantic Web is the subject of Chapter 13. Note that multilevel security is an aspect of confidentiality. However, we decided not to include it in Part II to give that part more focus. Managing the policies is an important aspect. Therefore, policy engineering is discussed in Chapter 14. Finally, in Chapter 15 we elaborate on the developments discussed in Section 1.2. We decided to include this in Part III mainly for completion.

Part IV discusses applications that utilize trustworthy semantic Webs. Chapter 16 discusses secure Web services that utilize semantic Web technologies. Semantic Web technologies for managing secure databases is the subject of Chapter 17. Secure semantic interoperability for heterogeneous information sources is discussed in Chapter 18. Chapter 19 discusses secure E-business applications. Chapter 20 discusses semantic Web for secure digital libraries. Chapter 21 discusses semantic Web technologies for an important application area called assured information sharing.

Part V describes special semantic Webs. In Chapter 22 we discuss domain-specific semantic Webs for financial and medical domains, among others. Trustworthy semantic Webs for geospatial data as well as sensor data are discussed in Chapter 23; in particular the work carried out on GML as well as OGC's interoperability work are studied. Chapter 24 discusses pervasive computing applications including secure mobile-sensor semantic Webs that we will call pervasive semantic Webs.

Each part begins with an introduction and ends with a conclusion. Furthermore, each of Chapters 2 through 24 starts with an overview and ends with a summary and references. Chapter 25 summarizes the book and discusses future directions. We have included three appendices. Appendix A provides an overview of data management and discusses the relationship between the texts we have written. This has been the standard practice with all of our books. Note that although Book 7, *Database and Applications Security*, essentially ends our series of books on data management, it also begins our new series on data security. Our current book is an elaboration of Chapter 25 of Book 7. A summary of *Database and Applications Security* is given in Appendix B to give the reader a better understanding as to where we are coming from. Various standards efforts related to a semantic Web are detailed in Appendix C. This book ends with a bibliography and an index.

We have essentially developed a five-layer framework to explain the concepts better in this book. This framework is illustrated in Figure 1.7. Layer 1 is the supporting technologies layer and consists of trustworthy information systems technologies. Layer 2 is the core technologies layer that consists of the key technologies for secure semantic Webs including secure XML, RDF, ontologies, rules, integrity, privacy, and trust management. Layer 3 is the dependability layer and consists of features for privacy, trust, and integrity. Layer 4 is the applications layer and includes applications such as Web services and semantic interoperability. Layer 5 is the specialized semantic Web layer and consists of trustworthy geospatial semantic Webs and sensor Webs. Each layer uses the technologies of the lower layers. Furthermore, the technologies in Layers 1 through 5 feed into the research, products, and standards that are evolving. Figure 1.8 illustrates how Chapters 2 through 24 in this book are placed in the framework. Essentially the technologies of Parts I through V belong to Layers 1 through 5, respectively.

1.10 Next Steps

This chapter has provided an introduction to the book. We first presented a brief overview of the supporting technologies for a trustworthy semantic Web including trustworthy information systems and semantic Webs. Then we discussed secure semantic Webs and dependable semantic Webs. Applications such as semantic Web services and assured information sharing were discussed next. Finally, we discussed specialized semantic Webs. The organization of this book, detailed in Section 1.9, includes a framework for organization purposes. Our framework is a five-layer framework, and each layer is addressed in one or more parts of this book.

This book provides the information for a reader to become familiar with a secure semantic Web and trustworthy systems. We discuss some topics such as a secure semantic Web in more depth as we have carried out much research on this topic. Some other topics are less concrete such as sensor-based semantic Webs and security. In fact many of the topics we discuss are still in the research stages.

Note that one could argue that semantic Webs are not yet commercially available as a whole and therefore a book on secure semantic Webs may be somewhat premature. We feel that such a book is very timely. Even though the concepts are not mature, we have discussed many issues and solutions so that the reader has some understanding of what needs to be done to develop a secure semantic Web. Further-

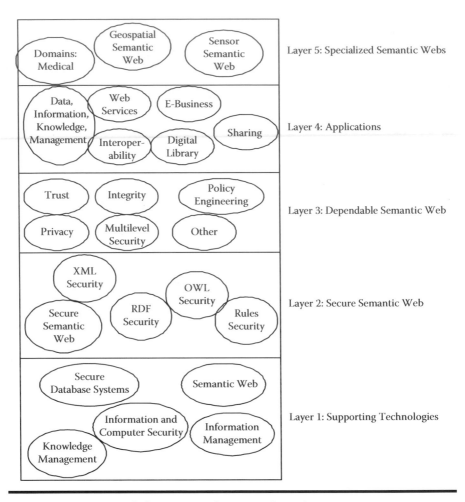

Figure 1.7   Framework for trustworthy semantic Webs.

more, as we have stated, security cannot be an afterthought. It has to be incorporated while the standards for these semantic Webs are being developed by the W3C and others. One of the main contributions of this book is raising the awareness of the importance of security and trustworthiness.

We have also given a set of exercises, intended for those who wish to pursue research in the area, at the ends of Chapters 2 through 24. To be consistent with our previous books, our purpose is to explain, especially to technical managers, what a secure semantic Web is all about. However, because of our fairly extensive research in secure information systems, we have also tried to include technical details that would help the technologists, researchers, and developers.

We provide several references that can help the reader in understanding the details of data security. My advice to the reader is to keep up with the develop-

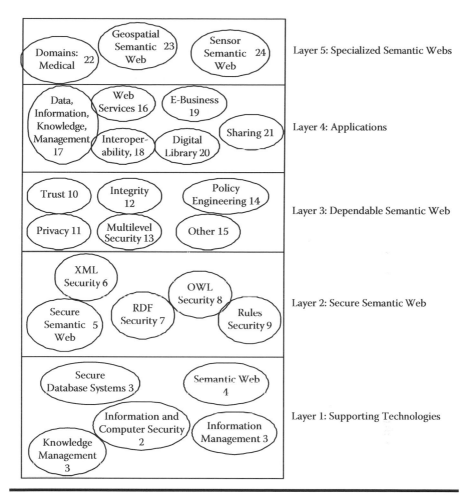

Figure 1.8 Contents of the book with respect to the framework.

ments in semantic Webs as well as in data and applications security, various data and applications security as well as information security-related conferences and workshops that are being held. Most notable is the IFIP11.3 Data and Applications security conference series. Other security conferences include the Institute of Electrical and Electronics Engineers (IEEE) Symposium on Security and Privacy, the Association for Computing Machinery (ACM) Conference on Computers and Communications Security, and the Computer Security Applications Conference. Journals include the *Journal of Computer Security, Computers and Security Journal, ACM Transactions on Information and Systems Security, IEEE Magazine on Security and Privacy, IEEE Transactions on Dependable and Secure Computing,* and the *Journal of Privacy Technologies.* Several semantic Web conferences are also being conducted. These include the International Semantic Web Symposium and the WWW

Conference. Furthermore, there are also journals on semantic Webs. Papers on this topic have also appeared in database and intelligent systems conferences including the Very Large Database Conference, ACM Special Interest Group on the Management of Data (SIGMOD) Conference, and IEEE Data Engineering Conference. We list the references to these conference series and some useful texts in semantic Webs throughout the book. With respect to a secure semantic Web, the relevant conferences are IEEE Policy, ACM Symposium on Access Control Models and Technologies (SACMAT), and the various semantic Web conferences that have emerged over the past decade. The Idea Group's *Journal of Semantic Web* is also a venue for publications. We believe that as progress is made on trustworthy semantic Web technologies, conferences and journals devoted entirely to secure semantic Webs will emerge.

Part I

Supporting Technologies for Trustworthy Semantic Webs

Introduction to Part I

As we have stated, to understand the concepts in trustworthy semantic Webs, we need to understand the concepts in trustworthy systems, secure data and information-management systems, and the semantic Webs, that is, trustworthy systems and semantic Webs are key supporting technologies for trustworthy semantic Webs. Trustworthy information systems include trustworthy systems, secure data and information-management systems, and Web information systems.

Part I will focus on the concepts in trustworthy information systems. It consists of three chapters. In Chapter 2 we discuss various concepts in trustworthy systems including secure systems and dependable systems. Chapter 3 describes concepts in secure data, information, and knowledge-management systems. Chapter 4 describes various semantic Web technologies on which we will base our discussion of trustworthy semantic Webs.

Chapter 2

Trustworthy Systems

2.1   Overview

As we stated in Chapter 1, trustworthy semantic Webs integrate trustworthy information systems and semantic Webs. Trustworthy information systems include trustworthy systems as well as secure data and information-management systems. Trustworthy systems are systems that are secure and dependable. By dependable systems we mean systems that have high integrity, are fault tolerant, and meet real-time constraints. In other words, for a system to be trustworthy it must be secure, be fault tolerant, meet timing deadlines, and manage high-quality data.

This chapter provides an overview of the various developments in trustworthy systems with special emphasis on secure systems. In Section 2.2 we discuss secure systems in some detail. Section 2.3 provides an overview of dependable systems that include trust, privacy, integrity, data quality, high-assurance systems, real-time processing, and fault tolerance. In Section 2.4 we discuss Web security in some detail. Semantic Web security includes securing the Web as well as securing the semantic information technologies. The chapter is summarized in Section 2.5.

2.2   Secure Systems

2.2.1 Overview

Secure systems include secure operating systems, secure data-management systems, secure networks, and other types of systems such as Web-based secure systems and secure digital libraries, among others. This section provides an overview of the various developments in information security.

In Section 2.2.2 we discuss basic concepts such as access control for information systems. Section 2.2.3 provides an overview of the various types of secure systems. Secure operating systems are discussed in Section 2.2.4. Secure database systems are discussed in Section 2.2.5. Network security is discussed in Section 2.2.6. Emerging trends is the subject of Section 2.2.7. The impact of the Web is given in Section 2.2.8. An overview of the steps to building secure systems is provided in Section 2.2.9.

2.2.2 Access Control and Other Security Concepts

Access control models include those for discretionary security and mandatory security. In this section we discuss both aspects of access control and consider other issues. In discretionary access-control models, users or groups of users are granted access to data objects. These data objects could be files, relations, objects, or even data items. Access-control policies include rules such as User U has read access to Relation R1 and write access to Relation R2. Access control could also include negative access control where User U does not have read access to Relation R.

In mandatory access control, subjects that act on behalf of users are granted access to objects based on some policy. A well-known policy is the Bell and LaPadula policy [BELL73] where subjects are granted clearance levels and objects have sensitivity levels. The set of security levels form a partially ordered lattice where Unclassified < Confidential < Secret < Top Secret. The policy has the following two properties:

- ■ A subject has read access to an object if its clearance level dominates that of the object.
- ■ A subject has write access to an object if its level is dominated by that of the object.

Other types of access control include role-based access control. Here access is granted to users, depending on their roles and the functions they perform. For example, personnel managers have access to salary data whereas project mangers have access to project data. The idea here is generally to give access on a need-to-know basis.

Although the early access control policies were formulated for operating systems, these policies have been extended to include other systems such as database systems, networks, and distributed systems. For example, a policy for networks includes policies not only for reading and writing, but also for sending and receiving messages.

Other security policies include administration policies. These policies include those for ownership of data as well as how to manage and distribute the data. Database administrators as well as system security officers are involved in formulating the administration policies.

Security policies also include policies for identification and authentication. Each user or subject acting on behalf of a user has to be identified and authenticated, possibly by using some password mechanisms. Identification and authentication becomes more complex for distributed systems. For example, how can a user be authenticated at a global level?

The steps to developing secure systems include developing a security policy, developing a model of the system, designing the system, and verifying and validating the system [ANDE01]. The methods used for verification depend on the level of assurance that is expected. Testing and risk analysis are also part of the process. These activities will determine the vulnerabilities as well as assess the risks involved. Figure 2.1 illustrates various types of security policies.

2.2.3 Types of Secure Systems

In the previous section we discussed various policies for building secure systems. In this section we elaborate on various types of secure systems. Much of the early research in the 1960s and 1970s was on securing operating systems. Early security policies such as the Bell and LaPadula policy were formulated for operating systems. Subsequently secure operating systems such as Honeywell's SCOMP and MULTICS were developed (see Reference [IEEE83]). Other policies such as those based on noninterference also emerged in the early 1980s.

Although early research on secure database systems was reported in the 1970s, it was not until the early 1980s that active research began in this area. Much of the

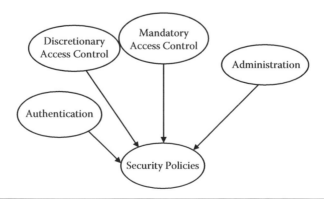

Figure 2.1   Security policies.

focus was on multilevel secure database systems. The security policy for operating systems was modified slightly. For example, the write policy for secure database systems was modified to state that a subject has write access to an object if the subject's level is that of the object. Because database systems enforced relationships between data and focused on semantics, there were additional security concerns. For example, data could be classified based on content, context, and time. The problem of posing multiple queries and inferring sensitive information from the legitimate responses became a concern. This problem is now known as the inference problem. Also, research was carried out not only on securing relational systems, but also on object systems as well as distributed systems, among others.

Research on computer networks began in the late 1970s and throughout the 1980s and beyond. The networking protocols were extended to incorporate security features. The result was secure network protocols. The policies include those for reading, writing, sending, and receiving messages. Research on encryption and cryptography has received much prominence due to networks and the Web. Security for stand-alone systems was extended to include distributed systems. These systems included distributed databases and distributed operating systems. Much of the research on distributed systems now focuses on securing the Web, known as Web security, as well as securing systems such as distributed object management systems.

As new systems emerge, such as data warehouses, collaborative computing systems, multimedia systems, and agent systems, security for such systems has to be investigated. With the advent of the World Wide Web, security is being given serious consideration by not only government organizations, but also commercial organizations. With E-commerce it is important to protect a company's intellectual property. Figure 2.2 illustrates various types of secure systems.

2.2.4 Secure Operating Systems

Work on security for operating systems was carried out extensively in the 1960s and 1970s. Research still continues as new kinds of operating systems such as Windows, Linux, and other products emerge. The early ideas included access-control lists and capability-based systems. Access-control lists are lists that specify the types of access that processes, which are called subjects, have on files, which are objects. The access is usually read or write access. Capability lists are capabilities that a process must possess to access certain resources in the system. For example, a process with a particular capability can write into certain parts of the memory.

Work on mandatory security for operating systems started with the Bell and La Padula security model, which has two properties:

■ The simple security property states that a subject has read access to an object if the subject's security level dominated the level of the object.

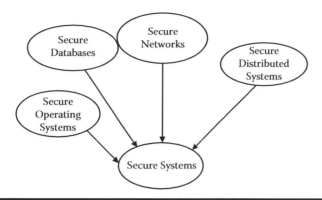

Figure 2.2   Secure systems.

■ The *-property (pronounced star property) states that a subject has write access to an object if the subject's security level is dominated by that of the object.

Since then, variations of this model as well as a popular model called the non-interference model (see Reference [GOGU82]) have been proposed. The noninterference model is essentially about higher-level processes not interfering with lower-level processes.

As stated earlier, security is becoming critical for operating systems. Corporations such as Microsoft are putting in many resources to ensure that their products are secure. Often we hear of vulnerabilities in various operating systems and about hackers trying to break into operating systems especially with networking capabilities. Therefore, this is an area that will continue to receive much attention for the next several years. Figure 2.3 illustrates some key aspects of operating systems security.

2.2.5 Secure Database Systems

Work on discretionary security for databases began in the 1970s when security aspects were investigated for System R at IBM Almaden Research Center. Essentially the security properties specified the read and write access that a user may have to relations, attributes, and data elements. In the 1980s and 1990s, security issues were investigated for object systems. Here the security properties specified the access that users had to objects, instance variables, and classes. In addition to read and write access, method execution access was also specified [FERN81].

Since the early 1980s, much of the focus has been on multilevel secure database-management systems [AFSB83]. These systems essentially enforce the mandatory policy discussed in Section 2.2.2 with the modification described in Section 3.3

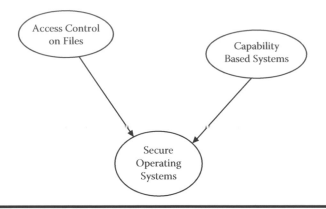

Figure 2.3   Secure operating systems.

(i.e., the policy of read at or below your level and write at your level). Since the 1980s, various designs, prototypes, and commercial products of multilevel database systems have been developed. Ferrari and Thuraisingham give a detailed survey of some of the developments [FERR00]. Example efforts include the SeaView effort by SRI International and the LOCK Data Views effort by Honeywell. These efforts extended relational models with security properties. One challenge was to design a model where a user sees different values at different security levels. For example, at the unclassified level an employee's salary may be 20K and at the secret level it may be 50K. In the standard relational model, such ambiguous values cannot be represented due to integrity properties.

Note that several other significant developments have been made on multilevel security for other types of database systems. These include security for object database systems [THUR89]. In this effort, security properties specify read, write, and method execution policies. Much work has also been carried out on secure concurrency control and recovery. The idea here is to enforce security properties and still meet consistency without having covert channels. Research has also been carried out on multilevel security for distributed, heterogeneous, and federated database systems. Another area that has received a lot of attention is the inference problem. For details on the inference problem we refer the reader to Reference [THUR93]. For secure concurrency control we refer the reader to the numerous algorithms by Atluri et al. (see, for example, Reference [ATLU97]). For information on secure distributed and heterogeneous databases as well as secure federated databases we refer the reader to Reference [THUR91] and Reference [THUR94].

As database systems become more sophisticated, securing these systems will become more and more difficult. Some of the current work focuses on securing data warehouses, multimedia databases, and Web databases (see, for example, *Proceedings of the IFIP* (International Federation for Information Processing) *Database Security Conference Series*). Figure 2.4 illustrates various types of secure database systems [IFIP].

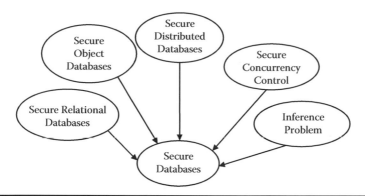

Figure 2.4 Secure database systems.

2.2.6 Secure Networks

With the advent of the Web and the interconnection of different systems and applications, networks have proliferated over the past decade. There are public networks, private networks, classified networks, and unclassified networks. We continually hear about networks being infected with viruses and worms. Furthermore, networks are being intruded on by malicious code and unauthorized individuals. Therefore, network security is emerging as one of the major areas in information security.

Various techniques have been proposed for network security. Encryption and cryptography are still dominating much of the research. For a discussion of various encryption techniques we refer the reader to Reference [HASS00]. Data-mining techniques are being applied for intrusion detection extensively (see Reference [NING04]). There has also been a lot of work on network protocol security where security is incorporated into the various layers of the protocol stack such as the network layer, transport layer, and session layer (see Reference [TANN90]). Verification and validation techniques are also being investigated for securing networks. *Trusted Network Interpretation* (also called the Red Book) was developed back in the 1980s to evaluate secure networks [TNI87]. Various books on the topic have also been published (see Reference [KAUF02]). Figure 2.5 illustrates network security techniques.

2.2.7 Emerging Trends

In the mid-1990s, research on secure systems expanded to include emerging systems. These included securing collaborative computing systems, multimedia computing, and data warehouses. Data mining has resulted in new security concerns. Because users now have access to various data-mining tools and they could make sensitive associations, it could exacerbate the inference problem. On the other hand,

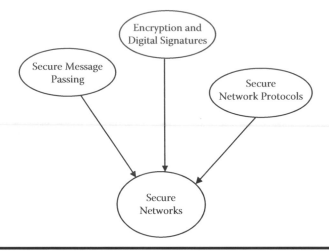

Figure 2.5   Secure networks.

data mining could also help with security problems such as intrusion detection and auditing.

The advent of the Web has resulted in extensive investigations of security for digital libraries and electronic commerce. In addition to developing sophisticated encryption techniques, security research has also focused on securing Web clients as well as servers. Programming languages such as Java were designed with security in mind. Much research has also been carried out on securing agents.

Secure distributed-system research focuses on security for distributed object-management systems. Organizations such as the Object Management Group (OMG) started working groups to investigate security properties (see Reference [OMG]). As a result we now have commercially available secure distributed object-management systems. Figure 2.6 illustrates the various emerging secure systems and concepts.

2.2.8 Impact of the Web

The advent of the Web has greatly impacted security. Security is now part of mainstream computing. Government organizations as well as commercial organizations are concerned about security. For example, in a financial transaction, millions of dollars could be lost if security is not maintained. With the Web, all sorts of information is available about individuals, and therefore privacy may be compromised.

Various security solutions are being proposed to secure the Web. In addition to encryption, focus is on securing clients as well as servers; end-to-end security has to be maintained. Web security also has an impact on electronic commerce; when one carries out transactions on the Web, it is critical that security be maintained.

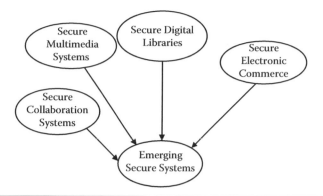

Figure 2.6   Emerging trends.

Information such as credit card numbers and social security numbers has to be protected.

All the security issues discussed in the previous sections have to be considered for the Web. For example, appropriate security policies have to be formulated. This is a challenge, as no one person owns the Web. The various secure systems including secure operating systems, secure database systems, secure networks, and secure distributed systems may be integrated in a Web environment. Therefore, this integrated system has to be secure. Problems having to do with inference and privacy may be exacerbated due to various data-mining tools. Various agents on the Web have to be secure. In certain cases, tradeoffs need to be made between security and other features; quality of service is an important consideration. In addition to technological solutions, legal aspects also have to be examined; lawyers and engineers have to work together. Although much progress has been made on Web security, there is still a lot to be done as progress is made on Web technologies. Figure 2.7 illustrates aspects of Web security. For a discussion of Web security we refer the reader to Reference [GHOS98].

2.2.9 Steps to Building Secure Systems

In this section we outline the steps to building secure systems. Note that our discussion is general and applicable to any secure system. However, we may need to adapt the steps for individual systems. For example, to build secure distributed database systems, we need secure database systems as well as secure networks. Therefore, multiple systems have to be composed.

The first step to building a secure system is developing a security policy. The policy can be stated in an informal language and then formalized. The policy essentially specifies the rules that the system must satisfy. Then the security architecture has to be developed. The architecture should include the security critical compo-

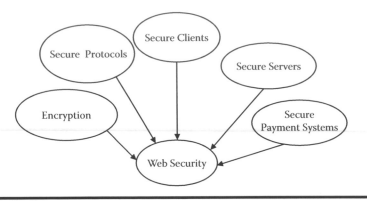

Figure 2.7   Web security.

nents. These are the components that enforce the security policy and therefore should be trusted. The next step is to design the system. For example, if the system is a database system, the query processor, transaction manager, storage manager, and metadata manager modules are designed. The design of the system has to be analyzed for vulnerabilities. The next phase is the development phase. Once the system is implemented, it has to undergo security testing. This will include designing test cases and making sure that the security policy is not violated. Furthermore, depending on the level of assurance expected of the system, formal verification techniques may be used to verify and validate the system. Finally, the system will be ready for evaluation. Note that initially systems were being evaluated using the Trusted Computer Systems Evaluation Criteria [TCSE85]. There are interpretations of these criteria for networks [TNI87] and for databases [TDI91]. There are also several companion documents for various concepts such as auditing and inference control. More recently some other criteria have been developed including the Common Criteria and the Federal Criteria [CC] [FC92].

Note that before the system is installed in an operational environment, one needs to develop a concept of operation of the environment. Risk assessment has to be carried out. Once the system is installed, it has to be monitored so that security violations including unauthorized intrusions are detected. Figure 2.8 illustrates the steps. An overview of building secure systems can be found in Reference [GASS88].

2.3   Dependable Systems

2.3.1 Overview

As discussed earlier, by dependability we mean features such as trust, privacy, integrity, data quality and provenance, and rights management, among others. We have separated confidentiality and included it as part of security. Therefore, essentially trustworthy systems include both secure systems and dependable systems. (Note that this is not a standard definition.)

Whether we are discussing security, integrity, privacy, trust, or rights management, there is always a cost involved. At what cost do we enforce security, privacy, and trust? Is it feasible to implement sophisticated privacy policies and trust-management policies? In addition to bringing lawyers and policy makers together with the technologists, we also need to bring economists into the picture. We need to carry out economic tradeoffs for enforcing security, privacy, trust, and rights management. Essentially what we need are flexible policies for security, privacy, trust, and rights management. For a discussion of the economic impact on security we refer the reader to Reference [NSF03].

In this section we discuss various aspects of dependability. Trust issues are discussed in Section 2.3.2. Digital rights management is discussed in Section 2.3.3. Privacy is discussed in Section 2.3.4. Integrity issues are discussed in Section 2.3.5. Data quality and data provenance are discussed in Section 2.3.6. Fault tolerance and real-time processing are discussed in Section 2.3.7. Figure 2.9 illustrates the dependability aspects.

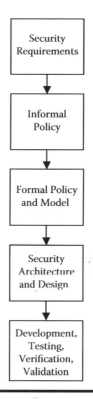

Figure 2.8 Steps to building secure systems.

2.3.2 *Trust Management*

Trust management is all about managing the trust that one individual or group has in another. Even if a user has access to the data, do I trust the user so that I can release the data? The user may have the clearance or possess the credentials, but he may not be trustworthy. Trust is formed by the user's behavior. The user may have betrayed one's confidence or carried out some act that is inappropriate in nature. Therefore, I may not trust that user. Now, even if I do not trust, say, John, Jane may trust John, and she may share her data with John; that is, John may not be trustworthy to me, but he may be trustworthy to Jane.

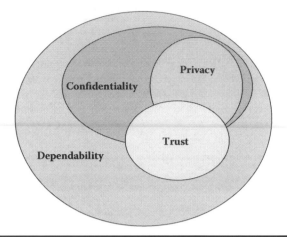

Figure 2.9 Aspects of dependability.

The question is, how do we implement trust? Can we trust someone partially? Can we trust, say, John 50 percent of the time and Jane 70 percent of the time? If we trust someone partially, then can we share some of the information? How do we trust the data that we have received from, say, Bill? If we do not trust Bill, then can we trust the data he gives us? There have been many efforts on trusted management systems as well as trust negotiation systems. Yu and Winslett have carried out extensive work and developed specification languages for trust as well as designed trust negotiation systems (see Referencce [YU03]). The question is, how do two parties negotiate trust? A may share data D with B if B shares data C with A. A may share data D with B only if B does not share this data with F. There are many such rules that one can enforce, and the challenge is to develop a system that consistently enforces the trust rules or policies.

2.3.3 Digital Rights Management

Closely related to trust management is managing digital rights. This whole area has been called digital rights management (DRM). This is especially critical for entertainment applications. Who owns the copyright to a video or an audio record-ing? How can rights be propagated? What happens if the rights are violated? Can I distribute copyrighted films and music on the Web?

We have heard a lot about the controversy surrounding Napster and similar organizations. Is DRM a technical issue or is it a legal issue? How can we bring technologists, lawyers, and policy makers together so that rights can be managed properly? There have been numerous articles, discussions, and debates about DRM. A useful source is Reference [DRM].

2.3.4 Privacy

Privacy is about protecting information about individuals. Furthermore, an individual can specify to a Web service provider the information that can be released about himself or herself. Privacy has been discussed a great deal in the past especially when it relates to protecting medical information about patients. Social scientists as well as technologists have been working on privacy issues.

Privacy has received enormous attention during recent years. This is mainly because of the advent of the Web, the semantic Web, counterterrorism, and national security. For example, to extract information about various individuals and perhaps prevent or detect potential terrorist attacks, data-mining tools are being examined. We have heard much about national security versus privacy in the media. This is mainly due to the fact that people are now realizing that to handle terrorism, the government may need to collect data about individuals and mine the data to extract information. Data may be in relational databases or it may be text, video, or images. This is causing a major concern with various civil liberties unions (see Reference [THUR03]). Therefore, technologists, policy makers, social scientists, and lawyers are working together to provide solutions to handle privacy violations.

2.3.5 Integrity, Data Quality, and High Assurance

Integrity is about maintaining the accuracy of the data as well as its processes. Accuracy of the data is discussed as part of data quality. Process integrity is about ensuring the processes are not corrupted. For example, we need to ensure that the processes are not malicious processes. Malicious processes may corrupt the data due to unauthorized modifications. To ensure integrity, the software has to be tested as well as verified to develop high-assurance systems.

The database community has ensured integrity by ensuring integrity constraints (e.g., the salary value has to be positive) as well as by ensuring the correctness of the data when multiple processes access the data. To achieve correctness, techniques such as concurrency control are enforced. The idea is to enforce appropriate locks so that multiple processes do not access the data at the same time and corrupt the data.

Data quality is about ensuring the accuracy of the data. The accuracy of the data may depend on who touched the data. For example, if the source of the data is not trustworthy, then the data-quality value of the data may be low. Essentially some quality value is assigned to each piece of data. When data is composed, quality values are assigned to the data in such a way that the resulting value is a function of the quality values of the original data.

Data provenance techniques also determine the quality of the data. Note that data provenance is about maintaining the history of the data. This will include information such as who accesses the data for read or write purposes. Then based on this history, one could assign quality values of the data as well as determine when the data is misused.

Other closely related topics include real-time processing and fault tolerance. Real-time processing is about the processes meeting the timing constraints. For example, if we are to get stock quotes to purchase stocks, we need to get the information in real time. It does not help if the information arrives after the trading desk is closed for business for the day. Similarly, real-time processing techniques also have to ensure that the data is current. Getting yesterday's stock quotes is not sufficient to make intelligent decisions. Fault tolerance is about ensuring that the processes recover from faults. Faults could be accidental or malicious. In the case of faults, the actions of the processes have to be redone, the processes aborted, and if needed restarted.

Note that to build high-assurance systems, we need the systems to handle faults, be secure, and handle real-time constraints. Real-time processing and security are conflicting goals, as we have discussed in Reference [THUR05a]. For example, a malicious process could ensure that critical timing constraints are missed. Furthermore, to enforce all the access-control checks, some processes may miss the deadlines. Therefore, what we need are flexible policies that will determine which aspects are critical for a particular situation.

2.4   Web Security

2.4.1 Overview

Because the Web is essential for the semantic Web, we will discuss Web security in more detail. In particular, threats and solutions are discussed. The Web has had a major impact on developments in data-management technologies. However, the Web also causes major security concerns. This is because with the Web, users from all over the world can access the data and information on the Web as well as compromise the security of the data, information, systems, and applications. Therefore, protecting the information and applications on the Web is critical.

This section will review the various threats to information systems on the Web, with a special emphasis on threats to Web databases. Then we will discuss some solutions to managing these threats. Threats include access-control violations, integrity violations, unauthorized intrusions, and sabotage. Solutions include data-mining techniques, cryptographical techniques, and fault-tolerance processing techniques.

The organization of this section is as follows. In Section 2.4.2, we provide an overview of some of the cyber-threats (which are essentially threats to Web security). Much of our focus will be on threats to the public and private databases on the Web. In Section 2.4.3, we discuss potential solutions.

2.4.2 Threats to Web Security

2.4.2.1 Overview

In recent years we have heard a lot about viruses and Trojan horses that disrupt activities on the Web. These security threats and violations are costing several millions of dollars to businesses. Identity thefts are quite rampant these days. Furthermore, unauthorized intrusions, the inference problem, and privacy violations are also occurring. In this section we provide an overview of some of these threats. A very good overview of these threats has also been provided by Ghosh [GHOS98]. We also discuss some additional threats such as threats to Web databases and information systems. Some of the threats and solutions discussed here are also given in Reference [THUR04a].

We have separated the threats into two groups. One group consists of some general cyber-threats, which may include threats to Web databases. The second group consists of threats to Web databases. Note that we have only provided a subset of all possible threats. There are many more threats such as threats to networks, operating systems, middleware, and electronic payment systems including spoofing, eavesdropping, covert channels, and other malicious techniques. Section 2.4.2.2 focuses on some general cyber-threats, whereas section 2.4.2.3 discusses threats specific to Web databases. It should be noted that it is difficult to group threats so that one threat is exclusive for Web databases whereas another is relevant only for operating systems. Threats such as access-control violations are applicable for both databases and operating systems. However, due to complex relationships in databases, access controls are much harder to enforce, whereas for operating systems, access controls are granted or denied at the file level. Another example is natural disasters as well as attacks to infrastructures. These attacks and disasters could damage the networks, databases, and operating systems.

2.4.2.2 General Cyber-Threats

We discuss some general cyber-threats that are applicable to information systems including data-management systems, operating systems, networks, and middleware. Figure 2.10 illustrates threats to Web security.

Authentication violations: Passwords can get stolen, and this could result in authentication violations. One may need to have multiple passwords and additional information about the user to solve this problem. Biometrics and other techniques are also being examined to handle authentication violations.

Nonrepudiation: The sender of a message could very well deny that he has sent the message. Nonrepudiation techniques will ensure that one can track the message to the sender. Today it is not difficult to track the owner of the message. However, it is not easy to track the person who has accessed the Web

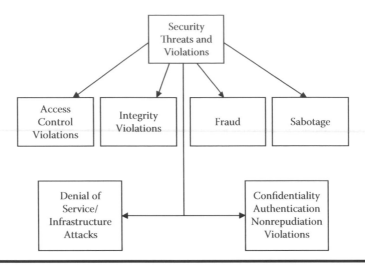

Figure 2.10   Attacks on Web security.

page. Whereas progress has been made to analyze Web logs, it is still difficult to determine the exact location of the user who has accessed a Web page.

Trojan horses and viruses: Trojan horses and viruses are malicious programs that can cause all sorts of attacks. In fact, many of the threats discussed in this section could be caused by Trojan horses and viruses. Viruses can spread from machine to machine and can erase files in various computers. Trojan horses can leak information from a higher level to a lower level. Various virus protection packages have been developed and are now commercially available.

Sabotage: We hear of hackers breaking into systems and posting inappropriate messages. For example, some information on the sabotage of various government Web pages is reported in Reference [GHOS98]. One only needs to corrupt one server, client, or network for the problem to cascade to several machines.

Fraud: With so much business and commerce being carried out on the Web without proper controls, Internet fraud can cause businesses to lose millions of dollars. The intruder can obtain the identity of legitimate users and through masquerading may empty bank accounts.

Denial of service and infrastructure attacks: We hear about infrastructures being brought down by hackers. Infrastructures can be the telecommunication system, power system, and the heating system. These systems are being controlled by computers and often through the Web. Such attacks would cause denial of service.

Natural disasters: In addition to terrorism, computers and networks are also vulnerable to natural disasters such as hurricanes, earthquakes, fire, and other similar disasters. The data has to be protected, and databases have to be recovered from disasters. In some cases the solutions to natural disasters are similar to those for threats due to terrorist attacks. For example, fault-tolerant processing techniques are used to recover databases from damages. Risk-analysis techniques may contain the damage.

2.4.2.3   Threats to Web Databases

This section discusses some threats to Web databases. Note that although these threats are mainly applicable to data-management systems, they are also relevant to general information systems. Figure 2.11 illustrates threats to Web databases.

Access-control violations: The traditional access-control violations can be extended to the Web. Users may access unauthorized data across the Web. Note that with the Web, there is so much data all over the place that controlling access to this data will be quite a challenge.

Integrity violations: Data on the Web may be subject to unauthorized modifications. Also, data can originate from anywhere, and the producers of the data may not be trustworthy. This makes it easier to corrupt the data. Incorrect data could cause serious damages such as incorrect bank accounts, which could result in incorrect transactions.

Confidentiality violations: Security includes confidentiality as well as integrity. Confidential data has to be protected from those who are not cleared. This book has discussed a great deal about multilevel security where users access

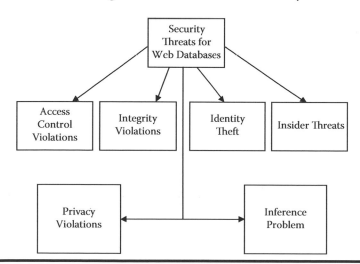

Figure 2.11   Attacks on Web databases.

only the information at or below their clearance levels. Statistical database techniques have also been developed to prevent confidentiality violations.

Authenticity violations: This is a form of data-integrity violation. For example, consider the case of a publisher, subscriber, and owner. The subscriber will subscribe to various magazines, the owner creates the magazines (in electronic form), and the publisher, who is the third party, will publish the magazines. If the publisher is not trusted, he could alter the contents of the magazine. This violates the authenticity of the document. Various solutions have been examined to determine the authenticity of documents (see for example, Reference [BERT04]). These include cryptography and digital signatures.

Privacy violations: With the Web one can obtain all kinds of information collected about individuals. Also, with data-mining tools and other analysis tools one can make all kinds of unauthorized associations about individuals.

Inference problem: Inference is the process of posing queries and deducing unauthorized information from legitimate responses. In fact, we consider the privacy problem to be a form of inference problem. Various solutions have been proposed to handle the inference problem including constraint processing and the use of conceptual structures. We discuss some of them in the next section.

Identity theft: We are hearing a lot about identity theft these days. The thief gets hold of one's Social Security number, and from there can wipe out the bank account of an individual. Here the thief is posing legitimately as the owner, and he now has much of the critical information about the owner. This is a threat that is very difficult to handle and manage. Viable solutions are yet to be developed. Data mining offers some hope, but may not be sufficient.

Insider threats: Insider threats are considered to be quite common and quite dangerous. In this case, one never knows who the terrorists are. They could be the database administrators or any person who may be considered trusted by the corporation. Background checks alone may not be sufficient to detect insider threats. Role-based access controls as well as data-mining techniques are being proposed. We will examine these solutions in the next section.

All the threats and attacks discussed here plus various other cyber-security threats and attacks collectively have come to be known as cyber-terrorism. Essentially cyber-terrorism is about corrupting the Web and all its components so that the enemy or adversary's system collapses. Currently a lot of funds are being invested by various governments in the United States and Europe to conduct research on protecting the Web and preventing cyber-terrorism. Note that terrorism includes cyber-terrorism, bioterrorism, and violations to physical security including bombing buildings and poisoning food and water supplies.

2.4.3 Web Security Solutions

2.4.3.1 Overview

This section will discuss various solutions to handle the threats mentioned in Section 2.4.2. The goals are to prevent as well as detect security violations and mitigate risks. Furthermore, damage has to be contained and not allowed to spread further. Essentially we need effective damage-control techniques. The solutions discussed include securing components, cryptography, data mining, constraint processing, role-based access control, risk analysis, and fault-tolerance processing (see also Reference [THUR04a]).

The organization of this section is as follows. In Section 2.4.3.2 we discuss solutions for some generic threats. These solutions included firewalls and risk analysis. In Section 2.4.3.3 we discuss solutions for some of the threats to Web databases. Note that although the solutions for generic threats are applicable for threats to Web databases, the solutions for threats to Web databases are also applicable for generic threats. For example, risk analysis has to be carried out for Web databases as well as for general information systems. Furthermore, data mining is a solution for intrusion detection and auditing both for Web databases as well as for networks. We have included them in the section on solutions for Web databases, as data mining is part of data management (see also Reference [THUR04b]). Figure 2.12 illustrates potential solutions.

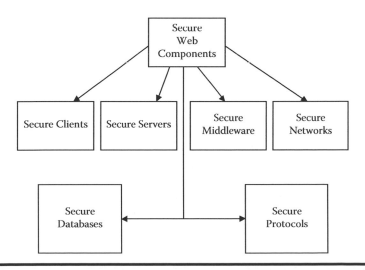

Figure 2.12   Solutions for Web security.

2.4.3.2 Solutions for General Threats

2.4.3.2.1 Securing Components and Firewalls

Various components have to be made secure to get a secure Web. We need end-to-end security, and therefore the components include secure clients, secure servers, secure databases, secure operating systems, secure infrastructures, secure networks, secure transactions, and secure protocols. One needs good encryption mechanisms to ensure that the sender and receiver communicate securely. Ultimately, whether it be exchanging messages or carrying out transactions, the communication between sender and receiver or the buyer and the seller has to be secure. Secure client solutions include securing the browser, securing the Java virtual machine, securing Java Applets, and incorporating various security features into languages such as Java. Note that Java is not the only component that has to be secure. Microsoft has come up with a collection of products including ActiveX, and these products have to be secure also. Securing the protocols includes securing hypertext transfer protocol (HTTP) and the secure socket layer (SSL). Securing the Web server means the server has to be installed securely, and it has to be ensured that the server cannot be attacked. Various mechanisms that have been used to secure operating systems and databases may be applied here. Notable among them are access-control lists, which specify which users have access to which Web pages and data. The Web servers may be connected to databases at the backend, and these databases have to be secure. Finally, various encryption algorithms are being implemented for networks, and groups such as OMG are investigating security for middleware such as Object Request Brokers (ORBs).

One of the challenges faced by Web managers is implementing security policies. One may have policies for clients, servers, networks, middleware, and databases. The question is, how do you integrate these policies? How do you make these policies work together? Who is responsible for implementing these policies? Is there a global administrator, or are there several administrators that have to work together? Security policy integration is an area that is being examined by researchers.

Finally, one of the emerging technologies for ensuring that an organization's assets are protected is the use of firewalls. Various organizations now have Web infrastructures for internal and external use. To access the external infrastructure one has to go through the firewall. These firewalls examine the information that comes into and out of an organization. This way, the internal assets are protected, and inappropriate information may be prevented from coming into an organization. We can expect sophisticated firewalls to be developed in the future.

2.4.3.2.2 Cryptography

Numerous texts and articles have been published on cryptography (see, for example, Reference [DENN82]). In addition, annual cryptology conferences also take place.

Yet cryptography is one of the areas that needs continuous research as the codes are being broken with powerful machines and sophisticated techniques. There are also many discussions on export-import controls on encryption techniques. This section will briefly provide an overview of some of the technical details of cryptography relevant to the Web and therefore to E-commerce. Cryptography is the solution to various threats including authenticity verification as well as ensuring data integrity. It is also useful for ensuring privacy.

The main issue with cryptography is ensuring that a message is sent properly, that the receiver gets the message the way it was intended for him to receive. This means that the message should not be intercepted or modified. The issue can be extended to transactions on the Web also; transactions have to be carried out in the way they were intended. Scientists have been working on cryptography for many decades. We hear about codes being broken during World War II. The study of code breaking has come to be known as cryptanalysis. In cryptography, essentially the sender of the message encrypts the message with a key. For example, he could use the letter B for A, C for B, ... A for Z. If the receiver knows the key, then he can decode this message. So a message with the word COMPUTER would be DPNQVUFS. This code is so simple it will be easy to break. The challenge in cryptography is to find a code that is difficult to break. Number theorists have been conducting extensive research in this area.

Essentially in cryptography, encryption is used by the sender to transform what is called a plaintext message into ciphertext. Decryption is used by the receiver to obtain the plaintext from the ciphertext received. Two types of cryptography are gaining prominence. One type is public key cryptography where there are two keys involved for the sender and the receiver: one key is the public key that is visible to everyone, and the other is the private key. The sender encrypts the message with the recipient's public key. Only the recipient can decode this message with his private key. The second method is private key cryptography. Here both users have a private key. There is also a key distribution center involved. This center generates a session key when the sender and receiver want to communicate. This key is sent to both users in an encrypted form using the respective private keys. The sender uses his private key to decrypt the session key. The session key is used to encrypt the message. The receiver can decrypt the session key with his private key and then use this decrypted session key to decrypt the message.

In the preceding paragraphs we discussed some of the basic concepts in cryptography. The challenge is, how do we ensure that an intruder does not modify the message and that the desirable security properties such as confidentiality, integrity, authentication, and nonrepudiation are maintained? The answer is in message digests and digital signatures. Using hash functions on a message, a message digest is created. If appropriate functions are used, each message will have a unique message digest. Therefore, even a small modification to the message will result in a completely different message digest. This way integrity is maintained. Message digests together with cryptographic receipts, which are digitally signed, ensure that the receiver knows the identity of the sender. The sender may encrypt the message digests with the encryption techniques described in the previous paragraphs. In some techniques, the recipient may need the public key of the sender to decrypt the message. The recipient may obtain this key with what is called a certificate authority. The certificate authority should be a trusted entity and must make sure that the recipient can legitimately get the public key of the sender. Therefore, additional measures are taken by the certificate authority to make sure that this is the case.

2.4.3.3 Risk Analysis

Before developing any computer system for a particular operation, one needs to study the security risks involved. The goal is to mitigate the risks or at least limit and contain them if the threats cannot be eliminated. Several papers have been published on risk analysis, especially at the National Computer Security Conference Proceedings in the 1990s. These risk-analysis techniques need to be examined for cyber-threats.

The challenges include identifying all the threats that are inherent to a particular situation. For example, consider a banking operation. The bank has to employ security experts and risk-analysis experts to conduct a study of all possible threats. Then they have to come up with ways of eliminating the threats. If that is not possible, they have to develop ways of containing the damage so that it is not spread further.

Risk analysis is especially useful for viruses. Once a virus starts spreading, the challenge is how to stop it. If you cannot stop it, then how do you contain it and also limit the damage that is caused? Running various virus packages on one's system will perhaps limit the virus from affecting the system or causing serious damage. The adversary will always find ways to develop new viruses. Therefore, we have to be one step or many steps ahead of the enemy. We need to examine the current state of the practice in risk analysis and develop new solutions to handle the new kinds of threats present in the cyber-world.

2.4.3.4 Biometrics, Forensics, and Other Solutions

Some of the recent developments in computer security have produced tools for biometrics and forensic analysis. Biometrics tools include understanding handwriting and signatures as well as recognizing people from their features and eyes, including the pupils. Although this is a very challenging area, much progress has been made. Voice-recognition tools to authenticate users are also being developed. In the future, we can expect many of us to use these tools.

Forensic analysis essentially carries out postmortems just as in medicine. Once the attacks have occurred, how do you detect these attacks? Who are the enemies and perpetrators? Although progress has been made, there are still challenges. For example, if one accesses Web pages and uses passwords that are stolen, then it will be difficult to determine from the Web logs who the culprit is. We still need a lot of research in the area. Digital forensics also deals with using computer evidence for crime analysis.

Biometrics and forensics are just some of the new developments. Other solutions being developed include smartcards and tools for detecting spoofing and jamming as well as tools to carry out sniffing.

2.4.3.5   Solutions for Threats to Web Databases

Figure 2.13 illustrates solutions for Web database security. These include data mining, security constraint processing, and role-based access control.

2.4.3.5.1   Data Mining

Data mining is the process of posing queries and extracting patterns (often previously unknown) from large quantities of data, using pattern matching or other reasoning techniques (see Reference [THUR98]). In Reference [THUR03], we examined data mining for counterterrorism. We discussed various types of terrorist attacks including information-related terrorism. As mentioned in Reference [THUR03], by information-related terrorism we essentially mean cyber-terrorism. Cyber-security is the area that deals with cyber-terrorism. We listed various cyber-attacks including access-control violations, unauthorized intrusions, and denial of service. We are hearing that cyber-attacks will cost corporations billions of dollars. For example, one could masquerade as a legitimate user and swindle billions of dollars from a bank.

Data mining may be used to detect and possibly prevent cyber-attacks. For example, anomaly-detection techniques could be used to detect unusual patterns and behaviors. Link analysis may be used to trace the viruses to the perpetrators.

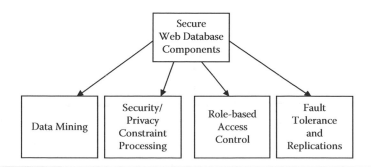

Figure 2.13   Solutions for Web database security.

Classification may be used to group various cyber-attacks and then use the profiles to detect an attack when it occurs. Prediction may be used to determine potential future attacks, depending on information learned about terrorists through e-mail and phone conversations. Also, for some threats non-real-time data mining may suffice, whereas for certain other threats such as for network intrusions we may need real-time data mining.

Many researchers are investigating the use of data mining for intrusion detection. Although we need some form of real-time data mining, that is, the results have to be generated in real-time, we also need to build models in real time. For example, credit card fraud detection is a form of real-time processing. However, here models are built ahead of time. Building models in real-time remains a challenge.

Data mining can also be used for analyzing Web logs as well as analyzing the audit trails. Based on the results of the data-mining tool, one can then determine whether any unauthorized intrusions have occurred and whether any unauthorized queries have been posed. There has been much research on data mining for intrusion detection that was reported at the IFIP Database Security Conferences (see also Reference [NING04]). This is an area in which we can expect to see much progress. Some interesting work on data mining for intrusion detection is given in Reference [LAZA03]. More recently, data-mining techniques are being examined for insider cyber-threat detection. The main question is, can general-purpose data-mining techniques be used for such applications, or do we need special-purpose data-mining techniques? We need a research agenda for data-mining applications in information security. Note that some directions were given in Reference [THUR05a].

2.4.3.5.2 Constraint Processing

We introduced the idea of security-constraint processing for the inference problem and revisit here some of the points. We defined security constraints to assign security levels to the data and then developed a system to process the constraints (see Reference [THUR93]). We have now adapted these techniques for privacy. In a recent paper, we elaborated on privacy-constraint processing [THUR05b]. Essentially, privacy constraints are rules that are enforced on the data. These rules determine the level of privacy of the data (called privacy levels or privacy values). Our definition of privacy constraints follows along the lines of our work on security constraints discussed in Reference [THUR93]. Privacy values of the data can take a range of values including public, semipublic, semiprivate, and private. Even within a privacy value, we can have different levels of privacy including low-privacy, medium-privacy, and high-privacy.

We have defined various types of privacy constraints. We give examples using a medical informatics database. The constraints we have identified include simple constraints, content-based constraints, context- or association-based constraints, release constraints, and event constraints. Although we use a relational database to illustrate the concepts, constraints can be defined on the object as well as on XML databases.

Simple constraints assign privacy values to attributes, relations, or even a database. For example, all medical records are private. Content-based constraints assign privacy values to data, depending on content. For example, all financial records are private except for those who are in public office (e.g., President of the United States). Association-based constraints assign privacy values to collections of attributes taken together. For example, names and medical records are private; individually they are public, that is, one can release names and medical records separately, but one cannot release them together. Furthermore, one has to be careful so that the public user cannot infer medical records for a particular person by posing multiple queries. Event constraints are constraints that change privacy values after an event has occurred. For example, after a patient has been released, some information about him or her could be made public, but while he or she is in the hospital, information about him or her is private. A good example was the sniper shootings that occurred in the Washington, D.C. area in the fall of 2002. After a victim died, information about him or her was released. Until then, the identity of the person was not available to the public. Finally, release constraints assign privacy values to the data, depending on what has already been released. For example, after the medical records have been released, one cannot release any information about the names or social security numbers that can form a link to the medical information.

One could define many more types of privacy constraints. As we explore various applications, we will start defining various classes of constraints. Our main purpose in Reference [THUR05b] was to show how privacy constraints can be processed in a database management system (DBMS). We call such a system a privacy-enhanced database system. Our approach is to augment a DBMS with a privacy controller. Such a DBMS is called a privacy-enhanced DBMS. The privacy controller will process the privacy constraints. The question is, what are the components of the privacy controller, and when do the constraints get processed? We take an approach similar to the approach proposed in Reference [THUR93] for security-constraint processing. In our approach, some privacy constraints are processed during database design, and the database is partitioned according to privacy levels. Then some constraints are processed during database updates. Here, the data is entered at the appropriate privacy levels. Because the privacy values change dynamically, it is very difficult to change privacy levels of the data in the database in real time. Therefore, some constraints are processed during the query operation.

The modules of the privacy controller include the constraint manager, query manager, database design tool, and the update manager. The constraint manager manages the constraints. The database design tool processes constraints during database design and assigns levels to the schema. The query processor processes constraints during the query operation and determines what data is to be released. The update processors process constraints and compute the level of the data [THUR05b].

2.4.3.5.3   Role-Based Access Control

One of the popular access-control techniques is role-based access control. The idea here is that users based on their roles are given access to certain data. For example, the engineer has access to project data, whereas the accountant has access to financial data. The challenges include handling multiple roles and conflicting roles. For example, if one is an engineer and cannot have access to financial data, and if one also happens to be an accountant, then how can the conflict be resolved? Maintaining the consistency of the access-control rules is also a challenge.

Many papers have been published on role-based access control. There is also now a conference devoted entirely to role-based access control called the ACM Symposium on Access Control Models and Technologies (SACMAT). Also, papers relevant to role-based access control on databases have been presented at the IFIP database security conferences. It is also being examined for handling insider threats; that is, by using a combination of data-mining techniques to find out information about employees and granting them roles depending on their trustworthiness, one could perhaps manage the insider-threat analysis problem.

2.4.3.5.4   Fault-Tolerant Processing, Recovery, and Replication

We focus here on handling faults in critical data. The databases could be national databases that contain critical information about individuals or private corporate databases or bank databases that contain financial information. They could also be agency databases that contain highly sensitive information. When such databases are attacked, it is then possible for the enemy to obtain classified information or wipe out bank accounts. Furthermore, even if the enemy does not do anything with the data, just by corrupting the databases, the entire operation could be thwarted. Today computer systems are controlling the operation of manufacturing plants, process control plants, and many critical infrastructures. Corrupting the data could be disastrous.

The fault-tolerance computing community has come up with several algorithms for recovering databases and systems from failures and other problems. These techniques include acceptance testing and checkpointing. Sometimes data is replicated so that there are backup copies. These techniques have to be examined for handling malicious attacks on the databases and corrupting the data. We also need to conduct research on dependable computing where we need security, integrity, fault tolerance, and real-time processing; we need to develop quality-of-service metrics for dependable computing. We also need flexible security policies as the requirements, such as security and real-time processing, may be conflicting.

2.5 Summary and Directions

This chapter has provided a brief overview of the developments in trustworthy systems. We first discussed secure systems including basic concepts in access control as well as discretionary and mandatory policies; types of secure systems such as secure operating systems, secure databases, secure networks, and emerging technologies; the impact of the Web; and the steps to building secure systems. Next we discussed dependable systems including aspects on trust, rights, privacy, integrity, quality, and real-time processing. Then we focused in more detail on aspects of Web security including threats to Web security and secure Web databases.

Development of trustworthy information systems is a major supporting technology for building trustworthy semantic Webs. Furthermore, trustworthy systems and secure information systems are supporting technologies for trustworthy information systems. Therefore, in Chapter 3 we will discuss secure information systems including secure data management and knowledge systems, and in Chapter 4 we will discuss semantic Webs. Chapters 2, 3, and 4 will give us the background information necessary to understand trustworthy semantic Webs.

References

[AFSB83] Air Force Studies Board, Committee on Multilevel Data Management Security. *Multilevel Data Management Security*, National Academy Press, Washington, D.C., 1983.

[ANDE01] Anderson, R., *Security Engineering: A Guide to Building Dependable Distributed Systems*, John Wiley & Sons, New York, 2001.

[ATLU97] Atluri, V., S. Jajodia, and E. Bertino, Transaction processing in multilevel secure databases with kernelized architectures: Challenges and solutions, *IEEE Trans. Knowledge Data Eng.* 9(5): 697–708, 1997.

[BELL73] Bell, D. and L. LaPadula, *Secure Computer Systems: Mathematical Foundations and Model*, M74-244, The MITRE Corporation, Bedford, MA, 1973.

[BERT04] Bertino, E. et al., Selective and authentic third party publication of XML documents, *IEEE Trans. Knowledge Data Eng.* 16 (10): 1263–1278, 2004.

[CC] Common Criteria, www.commoncriteriaportal.org.

[DENN82] Denning, D., *Cryptography and Data Security*, Addison Wesley, Reading, MA, 1982.

[DRM] Digital Rights Management Architectures, http://www.dlib.org/dlib/june01/iannella/06iannella.html.

[FC92] Federal Criteria for Information Technology Security, Fort Meade, MD, 1992.

[FERN81] Fernandez, E. et al., *Database Security and Integrity*, Addison–Wesley, Reading, MA, 1981.

[FERR00] Ferrari E. and B. Thuraisingham, Secure database systems, in *Advances in Database Management*, M. Piatini and O. Diaz, Eds., Artech House, London, UK, 2000.

[GASS88] Gasser, M., *Building a Secure Computer System*, Van Nostrand Reinhold, New York, 1988.

[GHOS98] Ghosh, A., *E-commerce Security, Weak Links and Strong Defenses*, John Wiley & Sons, New York, 1998.

[GOGU82] Goguen, J. and J. Meseguer, Security Policies and Security Models, *Proc. IEEE Symp. on Security Privacy*, Oakland, CA, April 1982.

[HASS00] Hassler, V., *Security Fundamentals for E-commerce*, Artech House, London, UK, 2000.

[IEEE83] *IEEE Computer Magazine*, Special issue on computer security, 16(7), 1983.

[IFIP] *Proc. IFIP Database Security Conf. Series*.

[KAUF02] Kaufmann, C. et al., *Network Security: Private Communication in a Public World*, Prentice Hall, Upper Saddle River, NJ, 2002.

[LAZA03] Lazarevic, A., et al., Data Mining for Computer Security Applications, *Tutorial Proc. IEEE Data Mining Conf.*, Melbourne, FL, 2003.

[NING04] Ning, P., et al., Techniques and tools for analyzing intrusion alerts, *ACM Trans. Inf. Syst. Security*, 7(2), 2004.

[NSF03] *Proc. National Science Found. Cyber Trust Principal Investigators Meeting*, Baltimore, MD, 2004.

[OMG] Object Management Group, www.omg.org.

[TANN90] Tannenbaum, A., *Computer Networks*, Prentice Hall, New York, 1990.

[TCSE85] Trusted Computer Systems Evaluation Criteria, National Computer Security Center, Gaithersburg, MD, 1985.

[TDI91] Trusted Database Interpretation, National Computer Security Center, Gaithersburg, MD, 1991.

[THUR89] Thuraisingham, B., Mandatory Security for Object-Oriented Database Systems, *Proc. ACM OOPSLA* (Object Oriented Programming Systems, Language, and Applications) *Conf.*, New Orleans, October 1989.

[THUR91] Thuraisingham, B., Multilevel Security for Distributed Database Systems, *Comput. Security*, 10(9): 727–747, 1991.

[THUR94] Thuraisingham, B., Multilevel Security for Federated Database Systems, *Comput. Security*, 13(6): 509–525, 1994.

[THUR98] Thuraisingham, B., *Data Mining: Technologies, Techniques, Tools and Trends*, CRC Press, Boca Raton, FL, 1998.

[THUR03] Thuraisingham, B., *Web Data Mining Technologies and Their Applications in Business Intelligence and Counter-Terrorism*, CRC Press, Boca Raton, FL, 2003.

[THUR04a] Thuraisingham, B., *Managing Threats to Web Databases and Cyber Systems, Issues, Solutions and Challenges*, V. Kumar et al., Eds., Kluwer, Dordrecht, The Netherlands, 2004.

[THUR04b] Kargupta, H., et al., Eds., *Data Mining for Counter-Terrorism, Next Generation Data Mining*, AAAI (Association for Advancement of Artificial Intelligence) Press, MA, 2004.

[THUR05a] Thuraisingham, B., *Database and Applications Security: Integrating Data Management and Information Security*, CRC Press, Boca Raton, FL, 2005.

[THUR05b] Thuraisingham, B., Privacy constraint processing in a privacy enhanced database management system, *Data Knowledge Eng. J.*, November 2005.

[THUR93] Thuraisingham, B., W. Ford, and M. Collins, Design and implementation of a database inference controller, *Data Knowledge Eng. J.*, 11(3), 1993.

[TNI87] Trusted Network Interpretation, National Computer Security Center, Gaitherburg, MD, 1987.

[YU03] Yu, T. and M. Winslett, A Unified Scheme for Resource Protection in Automated Trust Negotiation, IEEE Symposium on Security and Privacy, Oakland, CA, May 2003.

Exercises

1. Elaborate on the steps to designing a secure system for a secure database system.
2. Conduct a survey of network security technologies.
3. Select three secure operating system products and examine their features.
4. What are the important developments in database and applications security?
5. Conduct a survey of Web security threats and solutions.

Chapter 3

Secure Data, Information, and Knowledge Management

3.1 Overview

In this section we first discuss secure data, information, and knowledge-management technologies that have influenced the development of the semantic Web. Therefore, we need to examine the security impact on these technologies for building trustworthy semantic Webs. Later, in Part IV, we will discuss the application of semantic Web technologies for secure data, information, and knowledge management.

Data-management technologies include database management, database integration, dataware warehousing, and data mining. Information-management technologies include information retrieval, multimedia information management, collaborative information management, E-commerce, and digital libraries. Knowledge management is about organizations utilizing corporate knowledge to get a business advantage.

The organization of this chapter is as follows. Secure data management is discussed in Section 3.2. Secure information management is discussed in Section 3.3. Secure knowledge management is discussed in Section 3.4. The chapter is summarized in Section 3.5.

3.2 Secure Data Management

3.2.1 Overview

Database security has evolved from database management and information-security technologies. In Chapter 2 we discussed information-security technologies. Therefore, in this section we will discuss secure data management. In particular, we will provide an overview of database management and then discuss the security impact.

Database-systems technology has advanced a great deal during the past four decades from the legacy systems based on network and hierarchical models to relational and object-oriented database systems based on client-server architectures. We consider a database system to include both the database-management system (DBMS) and the database (see also the discussion in Reference [DATE90]). The DBMS component of the database system manages the database. The database contains persistent data, that is, the data is permanent even if the application programs go away.

The organization of this section is as follows. In Section 3.2.2 we will discuss database management. Database integration will be discussed in Section 3.2.3. Data warehousing and data mining will be discussed in Section 3.2.4. Web data management will be discussed in Section 3.2.5. Security impact of data-management technologies will be discussed in Section 3.2.6.

3.2.2 Database Management

We discuss data modeling, function, and distribution for a DBMS.

3.2.2.1 Data Model

The purpose of a data model is to capture the universe that it represents as accurately, completely, and naturally as possible [TSIC82]. Data models include hierarchical models, network models, relational models, entity relationship models, object models, and logic-based models. The relational-data model is the most popular data model for database systems. With the relational model [CODD70], the database is viewed as a collection of relations. Each relation has attributes and rows. For example, Figure 3.1 illustrates a database with two relations: EMP (employee) and DEPT (department). Various languages to manipulate the relations have been proposed. Notable among these languages is the ANSI (American National Standards Institute) Standard Structured Query Language (SQL). This language is used to access and manipulate data in relational databases [SQL3]. A detailed discussion of the relational-data model is given in Reference [DATE90] and Reference [ULLM88].

EMP

SS#	Ename	Salary	D#
1	John	20K	10
2	Paul	30K	20
3	Mary	40K	20

DEPT

D#	Dname	Mgr
10	Math	Smith
20	Physics	Jones

Figure 3.1   Relational database.

3.2.2.2 Functions

The functions of a DBMS carry out its operations. A DBMS essentially manages a database, and it provides support to the user by enabling him or her to query and update the database. Therefore, the basic functions of a DBMS are query processing and update processing. In some applications, such as banking, queries and updates are issued as part of transactions. Therefore, transaction management is also another function of a DBMS. To carry out these functions, information about the data in the database has to be maintained. This information is called the metadata. The function that is associated with managing the metadata is metadata management. Special techniques are needed to manage the data stores that actually store the data. The function that is associated with managing these techniques is storage management. To ensure that the above functions are carried out properly and that the user gets accurate data, there are some additional functions. These include security management, integrity management, and fault management (i.e., fault tolerance). The functional architecture of a DBMS is illustrated in Figure 3.2 (see also Reference [ULLM88]).

3.2.2.3 Data Distribution

As stated by Ceri and Pelagatti [CERI84], a distributed database system includes a distributed database-management system (DDBMS), a distributed database, and a network for interconnection (Figure 3.3). The DDBMS manages the distributed database. A distributed database is data that is distributed across multiple databases. The nodes are connected via a communication subsystem, and local applications are handled by the local DBMS. In addition, each node

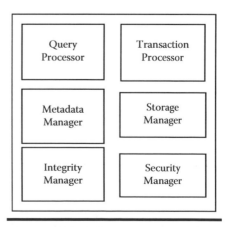

Figure 3.2   Database architecture.

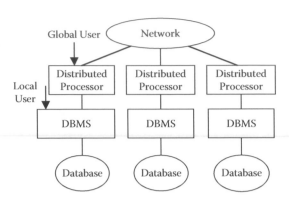

Figure 3.3   Distributed data management.

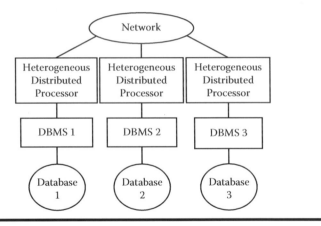

Figure 3.4   Heterogeneous database integration.

is also involved in at least one global application, so there is no centralized control in this architecture. The databases are connected through a component called the distributed processor (DP). Distributed database-system functions include distributed query processing, distributed transaction management, distributed metadata management, and enforcing security and integrity across the multiple nodes. It has been stated that the semantic Web can be considered a large distributed database.

3.2.3 Heterogeneous Data Integration

Figure 3.4 illustrates an example of interoperability between heterogeneous database systems. The goal is to provide transparent access for both users and application programs to query and execute transactions (see, for example, Reference [WIED92]). Note that in a heterogeneous environment, the local DBMSs may be heterogeneous. Furthermore, the modules of the DP have both local DBMS-specific processing as well as local DBMS-independent processing. We call such a DP a heterogeneous distributed processor (HDP). There are several technical issues that need to be resolved for the successful operation between these diverse database systems. Note that heterogeneity could exist with respect to different data models, schemas, query-processing techniques, query languages, transaction-management techniques, semantics, integrity, and security.

Some of the nodes in a heterogeneous database environment may form a federation. Such an environment is classed as a federated data mainsheet environment. As stated by Sheth and Larson [SHET90], a federated database system is a collection of cooperating but autonomous database systems belonging to a federation, that is, the goal is for the DBMSs, which belong to a federation, to cooperate with one another and yet maintain some degree of autonomy. Figure 3.5 illustrates a federated database system. This concept will be elaborated on in a coalition data-sharing environment in Part IV.

3.2.4 Data Warehousing and Data Mining

Data warehousing is one of the key data-management technologies to support data mining and data analysis. As stated by Inman [INMO93], data warehouses are subject oriented. Their design depends to a great extent on the application utilizing them. They integrate diverse and possibly heterogeneous data sources, they are persistent, and the warehouses are very much like databases. They vary with time. This is because as the data sources (from which the warehouse is built) get updated, the changes have to be reflected in the warehouse. Essentially data warehouses provide support for decision support functions of an enterprise or an organization. Although the data sources may have the raw data, the data warehouse may

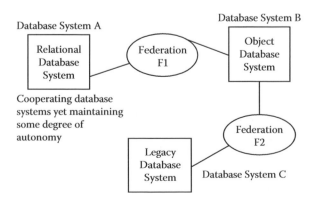

Figure 3.5   Federated data management.

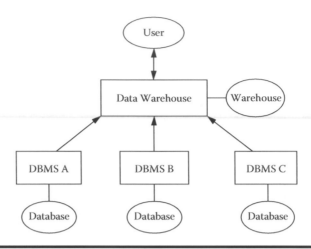

Figure 3.6 Data warehouse.

have correlated data, summary reports, and aggregate functions applied to the raw data.

Figure 3.6 illustrates a data warehouse. The data sources are managed by database systems A, B, and C. The information in these databases is merged and put into a warehouse. With a data warehouse, data may often be viewed differently by different applications; that is, the data is multidimensional. For example, the payroll department may want data to be in a certain format, whereas the project department may want data to be in a different format. The warehouse must provide support for such multidimensional data.

Data mining is the process of posing various queries and extracting useful information, patterns, and trends often previously unknown from large quantities of data possibly stored in databases. Essentially, for many organizations, the goals of data mining include improving marketing capabilities, detecting abnormal patterns, and predicting the future based on past experiences and current trends.

Some of the data-mining techniques include those based on statistical reasoning techniques, inductive logic programming, machine learning, fuzzy sets, and neural networks, among others. The data mining outcomes include classification (finding rules to partition data into groups), association (finding rules to make associations between data), and sequencing (finding rules to order data). Essentially one arrives at some hypothesis, which is the information extracted, from examples and patterns observed. These patterns are observed from posing a series of queries; each query may depend on the responses obtained to the previous queries posed. There have been several developments in data mining. A discussion of the various tools is given in Reference [KDN]. A good discussion of the outcomes and techniques

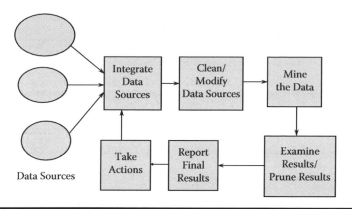

Figure 3.7   Steps to data mining.

is given in Berry and Linoff [BERR97]. Figure 3.7 illustrates their data-mining process.

3.2.5 Web Data Management

A major challenge for researchers and practitioners of Web data management is coming up with an appropriate data-representation scheme. The question is, is there a need for a standard data model for Web database systems? Is it at all possible to develop such a standard? If so, what are the relationships between the standard model and the individual models used by databases on the Web?

Database-management functions for the Web include those such as query processing, metadata management, security, and integrity. In Reference [THUR00], we examined various DBMS functions and discussed the impact of Web database access on these functions. Some of the issues are discussed here. Figure 3.8 illustrates the functions. Querying and browsing are two key functions. First of all, an appropriate query language is needed. Because SQL is a popular language, appropriate extensions to SQL may be desired. XML-QL, which has evolved from XML (eXtensible Markup Language to be discussed later) and SQL, is moving in this direction. Query processing involves developing a cost model. Are there special cost models for Internet database management? With respect to a browsing operation, the query-processing techniques have to be integrated with techniques to follow links, that is, hypermedia technology has to be integrated with database-management technology.

Updating Web databases could entail different things. One could create a new Web site, place servers at that site, and update the data managed by the servers. The question is, can a user of the library send information to update the data at a Web site? An issue here has to do with security privileges. If the user has write privileges,

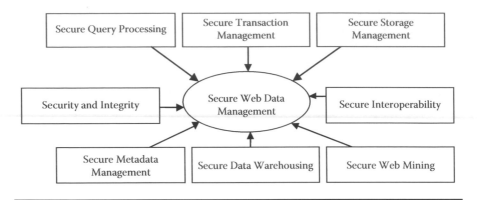

Figure 3.8 Web data management.

then he or she could update the databases that he or she is authorized to modify. Agents and mediators could be used to locate the databases as well as to process the update.

Transaction management is essential for many applications. There may be new kinds of transactions on the Web. For example, various items may be sold through the Internet. In this case, the item should not be locked immediately when a potential buyer makes a bid. It has to be left open until several bids are received and the item is sold. Thus, special transaction models are needed. Appropriate concurrency control and recovery techniques have to be developed for transaction models.

Metadata management is a major concern for Web data management. What is metadata? Metadata describes all the information pertaining to the library. This could include various Web sites, the types of users, access control issues, and policies enforced. Where should the metadata be located? Should each participating site maintain its own metadata? Should the metadata be replicated, or should there be a centralized metadata repository? Metadata in such an environment could be very dynamic, especially because the users and the Web sites may be changing continuously.

Storage management for Web database access is a complex function. Appropriate index strategies and access methods for handling multimedia data are needed. In addition, due to the large volumes of data, techniques for integrating database-management technology with mass storage technology are also needed. Other data management functions include integrating heterogeneous databases, managing multimedia data, and mining. We discussed them in Reference [THUR02a].

3.2.6 Security Impact

Now that we have discussed data-management technologies, we will provide an overview of security impact. With respect to data management, we need to enforce appropriate access-control techniques. Early work focused on discretionary access control; later on, in the 1980s, focus was on mandatory access control. More recently the focus has been on applying some of the novel access-control techniques such as role-based access control and usage control. Extension to SQL to express security assertions as well as extensions to the relational data model to support multilevel security have received a lot of attention. More details can be found in Reference [THUR05].

With respect to data integration, the goal is to ensure the security of operation when heterogeneous databases are integrated. The policies enforced by the individual data-management systems have to be enforced at the coalition level. Data warehousing and data mining result in additional security concerns, and this includes the inference problem. When data is combined, the combined data could be at a higher security level. Specifically, inference is the process of posing queries and deducing unauthorized information from the legitimate responses received. An inference problem exists for all types of database systems and has been studied extensively within the context of multilevel databases. Figure 3.9 illustrates the security impact on data management. Secure data management will be revisited in Chapter 17.

3.3   Secure Information Management

3.3.1   Overview

In this section we discuss various secure information-management technologies. We will first discuss information retrieval, multimedia information management, col-

---

Secure Database Functions

Query processing: Enforce access control rules during query processing; inference control; consider security constraints for query optimization

Transaction management: Check whether security constraints are satisfied during transaction execution

Storage management: Develop special access methods and index strategies that take into consideration the security constraints

Metadata management: Enforce access control on metadata; ensure that data is not released to unauthorized individuals by releasing the metadata

Integrity management: Ensure that integrity of the data is maintained while enforcing security

---

Figure 3.9   Secure data management.

laborative information management, and E-business and digital libraries, and then discuss the security impact. Part IV will give more details when we describe the application of semantic Web technologies for secure information management.

Note that we have tried to separate data management and information management. Data management focuses on technologies of database systems such as query processing, transaction management, and storage management. Information management is much broader than data management, and we have included many topics in this category such as information retrieval and multimedia information management.

Information retrieval is discussed in Section 3.3.2. Multimedia information management is the subject of Section 3.3.3. Digital libraries are discussed in Section 3.3.4. E-commerce technologies are discussed in Section 3.3.5. Security impact is discussed in Section 3.3.6.

3.3.2 Information Retrieval

Information-retrieval systems essentially provide support for managing documents. The functions include document retrieval, document update, and document storage management, among others. These systems are essentially DBMSs for managing documents. There are various types of information-retrieval systems, and they include text-retrieval systems, image-retrieval systems, and audio- and video-retrieval systems. Figure 3.10 illustrates a general-purpose information-retrieval system that may be utilized for text retrieval, image retrieval, audio retrieval, and video retrieval. Such architecture can also be utilized for a multimedia data-management system. We discuss the special features of each type of information-retrieval system (see also Reference [THUR01]).

3.3.2.1 Text Retrieval

A text-retrieval system is essentially a DBMS for handling text data such as books, journals, magazines, etc. One needs a good data model for document representation. A considerable amount of work has gone into developing semantic data models and object models for document management. For example, a document could have paragraphs, and a paragraph could have sections, etc.

The querying of documents could be based on many factors. One could specify keywords and request that doc-

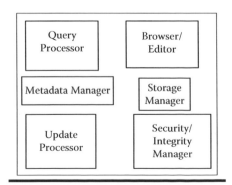

Figure 3.10　Information-retrieval system.

uments be retrieved with keywords. One could also retrieve documents that have some relationships with one another. Recent research on information retrieval is focusing on querying documents based on semantics. For example, "retrieve documents that describe scenic views" or "retrieve documents that are useful to children under ten years" are such types of queries.

Much of the information is now in textual form. This could be data on the Web or library data or electronic books, among others. One of the problems with text data is that it is not structured as relational data. In many cases it is unstructured, and in some cases it is semistructured. Semistructured data, for example, would be an article that has a title, author, abstract, and paragraphs. The paragraphs are not structured, whereas the format is structured.

Information-retrieval systems and text-processing systems have been developed over the past few decades. Some of these systems are quite sophisticated and can retrieve documents by specifying attributes or keywords. There are also text-processing systems that can retrieve associations between documents.

3.3.2.2   Image Retrieval

An image-retrieval system is essentially a DBMS for handling image data. Image data could be X-rays, pictures satellite images, or photographs. One needs a good data model for image representation. Some work has gone into developing semantic data models and object models for image management. For example, an image could consist of a right image and a left image (an example is the X-ray of the lungs).

The querying of images could be based on many factors. One could extract text from images and then query the text. One could tag images and then query the tags. One could also retrieve images from patterns. For example, an image could contain several squares. With a picture of a square, one could query the image and retrieve all the squares in the image. We can also query images depending on content. For example, "retrieve images that illustrate sunset" or "retrieve images that illustrate Victorian buildings" are such types of queries.

Image processing has been around for quite a while. We have image-processing applications in various domains including medical imaging for cancer detection, processing satellite images for space and intelligence applications, and handling hyperspectral images. Images include maps, geological structures, biological structures, and many other entities. Image processing has dealt with areas such as detecting abnormal patterns which deviate from the norm, retrieving images by content, and pattern matching.

3.3.2.3   Video Retrieval

A video-retrieval system is essentially a DBMS for handling video data. Video data could be documents such as books, journals, magazines, etc. There are various issues that need to be considered. One needs a good data model for video representation. Some work has gone into developing semantic data models and object models for video data management (see Reference [WOEL86]). For example, a video object could have advertisements, main film, and coming attractions.

The querying of documents could be based on many factors. One could extract text from the video and query the text. One could also extract images from the video and query the images. One could store short video scripts and carry out pattern matching; that is, "find the video that contains the following script." Examples of queries include "find films where the hero is John Wayne," or "find video scripts that show two presidents shaking hands." Recently there have been some efforts on mining video data.

3.3.2.4 Audio Retrieval

An audio-retrieval system is essentially a DBMS for handling audio data. Audio data could be documents such as books, journals, magazines, etc. One needs a good data model for audio representation. Some work has gone into developing semantic data models and objects models for audio data management (see Reference [WOEL86]). For example, an audio object could have introductory remarks, speech, applause, and music.

The querying of documents could be based on many factors. One could extract text from the audio and query the text. One could store short audio scripts and carry out pattern matching, that is, "find the audio that contains the following script." Examples include, "find audio tapes containing the speeches of President John," or "find audio tapes of poems recited by female narrators." Recently there have been some efforts on audio mining [IEEE03].

3.3.3 Multimedia Information Management

A multimedia data manager (MM-DM) provides support for storing, manipulating, and retrieving multimedia data from a multimedia database [PRAB97]. In a sense, a multimedia database system is a type of heterogeneous database system, as it manages heterogeneous data types. Heterogeneity is due to the multiple media of the data such as text, video, and audio. Because multimedia data also conveys information such as speeches, music, and video, we have grouped this under information management. One important aspect of multimedia data management is data representation. Both extended relational models and object models have been proposed.

An MM-DM must provide support for typical DBMS functions. These include query processing, update processing, transaction management, storage management, metadata management, security, and integrity. In addition, in many cases, the various types of data such as voice and video have to be synchronized for display, and therefore, real-time processing is also a major issue in an MM-DM.

Various architectures are being examined to design and develop an MM-DM. In one approach, the data manager is used just to manage the metadata, and a multimedia file manager is used to manage the multimedia data. There is a module for integrating the data manager and the multimedia file manager. In this case, the MM-DM consists of the three modules: the data manager managing the metadata, the multimedia file manager, and the module for integrating the two. The second architecture is the tight coupling approach. In this architecture, the data manager manages both the multimedia data as well as the metadata. The tight coupling architecture has an advantage because all the data-management functions could be applied on the multimedia database. This includes query processing, transaction management, metadata management, storage management, and security and integrity management. Note that with the loose coupling approach, the DBMS only manages the metadata for the multimedia data unless the file manager performs the DBMS functions.

There are other aspects to architectures, as discussed in Reference [THUR97]. For example, a multimedia database system could use a commercial database system such as an object-oriented database system to manage multimedia objects. However, relationships between objects and the representation of temporal relationships may involve extensions to the DBMS. A DBMS together with an extension layer provides complete support to manage multimedia data. In the alternative case, both the extensions and the database-management functions are integrated so that there is one DBMS to manage multimedia objects as well as the relationships between the objects. Further details of these architectures as well as managing multimedia databases are discussed in Reference [THUR01]. Figure 3.11 illustrates a multimedia information-management system.

3.3.4 *Collaboration and Data Management*

Although the notion of computer-supported cooperative work (CSCW) was first proposed in the early 1980s, it was only in the 1990s that much interest was shown in this topic. Collaborative computing enables people, groups of individuals, and organizations to work together with one another to accomplish a task or a collection of tasks. These tasks could vary from participat-

Figure 3.11 Multimedia information management.

ing in conferences, solving a specific problem, or working on the design of a system (see Reference [ACM91]).

One aspect of collaborative computing of particular interest to the database community is workflow computing. Workflow is defined as the automation of a series of functions that comprise a business process such as data entry, data review, and monitoring performed by one or more people. An example of a process that is well suited for workflow automation is the purchasing process. Some early commercial workflow-system products targeted for office environments were based on a messaging architecture. This architecture supports the distributed nature of current work teams. However, the messaging architecture is usually file based and lacks many of the features supported by DBMSs such as data representation, consistency management, tracking, and monitoring. The emerging workflow systems utilize data-management capabilities.

Figure 3.12 illustrates an example where Teams A and B are working on a geographical problem such as analyzing and predicting the weather in North America. The two teams must have a global picture of the map as well as any notes that go with it. Any changes made by one team should be instantly visible to the other team, and both teams communicate as if they are in the same room.

To enable such transparent communication, data-management support is needed. One could utilize a DBMS to manage the data or some type of data manager that provides some of the essential features such as data integrity, concurrent access, and retrieval capabilities. In the above example, the database may consist of information describing the problem the teams are working on, the data that is involved, and history data, as well as the metadata information. The data manager must provide appropriate concurrency control features so that when both teams simultaneously access the common picture and make changes, these changes are coordinated.

The Web has increased the need for collaboration even further. Users now share documents on the Web and work on papers and designs on the Web. Corporate

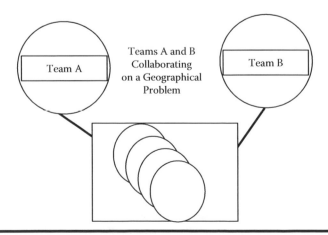

Figure 3.12 Collaborative computing system.

information infrastructures promote collaboration and sharing of information and documents. Therefore, the collaborative tools have to work effectively on the Web. More details are given in Reference [IEEE99].

3.3.5 Digital Libraries

Digital libraries gained prominence with the initial effort by the National Science Foundation (NSF), Defense Advanced Research Projects Agency (DARPA), and National Aeronautical and Space Administration (NASA). The NSF continued to fund special projects in this area, and as a result, the field has grown very rapidly. The idea behind digital libraries is to digitize all types of documents and provide efficient access to these digitized documents.

Several technologies have to work together to make digital libraries a reality. These include Web data management, markup languages, search engines, and question-answering systems. In addition, multimedia information management as well as information-retrieval systems play an important role. This section will review the various developments in some of the digital library technologies. Figure 3.13 illustrates an example of a digital library system.

3.3.5.1 Search Engines

Since the early 1990s, numerous search engines have been developed. They have origins in the information-retrieval systems developed in the 1960s and beyond. Typically, when we invoke a browser such as Netscape or Microsoft's Explorer,

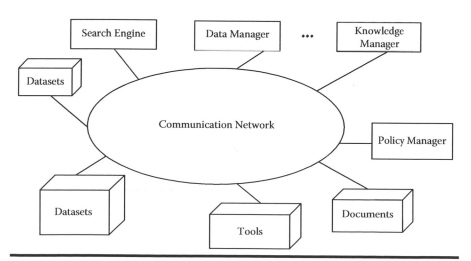

Figure 3.13   Digital libraries.

we have access to several search engines. Some of the early search engines were Altavista, Yahoo, Infoseek, and Lycos. These systems were around in 1995 and were fairly effective for their time. They are much improved now. Since around 1999, one of the popular search engines has been Google. It started off as a Stanford University research project funded by organizations such as the NSF and the Central Intelligence Agency as well as industry, and was later commercialized. Systems such as Google as well as some of the other search engines provide intelligent searches. However, they still have a long way to go before users can get exact answers to their queries.

Search engines are accessed via browsers. When you click on the search engines, you will get a window requesting your search parameters. Then you list the keywords, and the various Web pages are listed. The question is, how does a search engine find the Web pages? It essentially uses information retrieval on the Web.

The rating of a search engine is determined by the speed in which it produces results, and more importantly the accuracy with which it produces the results; that is, does the search engine list the relevant Web pages for the query? For example, when you type a query called "lung cancer", does it provide the relevant information you are looking for with respect to lung cancer? It can, for example, list resources about lung cancer or list information about who has had lung cancer. Usually people want to get resources about lung cancer. If they want to find out who has lung cancer, then they could type in "people with lung cancer".

The problem with many searches, although extremely useful, is that they often provide a lot of irrelevant information. To get accurate results, they have to build sophisticated indexing techniques. They also may cache information from Web servers for frequently posed queries. The search engines have a directory about the various Web servers they have to search. This directory is updated as new servers enter. Then the search engines build indices for the various keywords. When a user poses a query, the search engine will consult its knowledge base, which consists of information about the Web servers and various indices. It also examines the caches, if it has any, and will then search the Web servers for the information. All this has to be carried out in real time.

Web mining enables one to mine the user log and build profiles for various users so that the search can be made more efficient. Note that there are millions of users, and building profiles is not straightforward. We need to mine the Web logs and find out what the preferences of users are. Then we list those Web pages for the user. Furthermore, if a user is searching for some information, from time to time, the search engines can list Web pages that could be relevant to the user's request; that is, search engines will have to dynamically carry out searches depending on what the user wants.

3.3.5.2 Question-Answering Systems

Question-answering systems are sort of the early information-retrieval systems and were developed in the late 1960s. They would typically give yes or no answers. Since then, there have been many advances in information-retrieval systems including text, image, and video systems. However, with the advent of the Web, the question-answering systems have received much prominence. They are not just limited to a yes or no answer. They give answers to various complex queries such as "What is the weather forecast today in Chicago?" or "Retrieve the flight schedules from London to Tokyo that make at most one stop."

The various search engines such as Google are capable of doing complex searches. But they have yet to answer complex queries. The research on question-answering systems is just beginning, and we can expect search engines to have this capability. Question-answering systems integrate many technologies including natural language processing, information retrieval, search engines, and data management.

3.3.6 E-business

Various models, architectures, and technologies are being developed. Business-to-business E-commerce is all about two businesses conducting transactions on the Web. We give some examples. Suppose Corporation A is an automobile manufacturer and needs microprocessors to be installed in its automobiles. It will then purchase the microprocessors from Corporation B who manufactures the microprocessors. Another example is when an individual purchases some goods such as toys from a toy manufacturer. This manufacturer then contacts a packaging company via the Web to deliver the toys to the individual. The transaction between the manufacturer and the packaging company is a business-to-business transaction. Business-to-business E-commerce also involves one business purchasing a unit of another business or two businesses merging. The main point is that such transactions have to be carried out on the Web. Business-to-consumer E-commerce is when a consumer such as a member of the mass population makes purchases on the Web. In the toy manufacturer example, the purchase between the individual and the toy manufacturer is a business-to-consumer transaction.

The modules of the E-commerce server may include modules for managing the data and Web pages, mining customer information, security enforcement as well as transaction management. E-commerce client functions may include presentation management and user interface, as well as caching data and hosting browsers. There could also be a middle tier, which may implement the business objects to carry out the business functions of E-commerce. These business functions may include brokering, mediation, negotiations, purchasing, sales, marketing, and other E-commerce functions. The E-commerce server functions are impacted by the information-management technologies for the Web. In addition to the data-management functions and the business functions, the E-commerce functions also include those for managing distribution, heterogeneity, and federations.

E-commerce also includes nontechnological aspects such as policies, laws, social impacts, and psychological impacts. We are now doing business in an entirely different way; therefore, we need a paradigm shift. We cannot do successful E-commerce if we still want the traditional way of buying and selling products. We have to be more efficient and rely on the technologies a lot more to gain a competitive edge. Some key points for E-commerce are illustrated in Figure 3.14.

3.3.7 Security Impact

Security impact for information-management technologies includes developing appropriate secure data models, functions, and architectures. For example, to develop secure multimedia information-management systems, we need appropriate security policies for text, audio, and video data. The next step is to develop secure multimedia data models. These could be based on relations or objects or a combination of these representations. What is the level of granularity? Should access be controlled to the entire video or video frames? How can access be controlled based on semantics? For digital libraries there is research on developing flexible policies. Note that digital libraries may be managed by multiple administrators under different environments. Therefore, policies cannot be rigid. For collaborative information systems we need policies for different users to collaborate with one another. How can participants trust each other? How can truth be established? What sort of access control is appropriate? There is research in developing security models for workflow and collaboration systems [BERT99].

Secure E-business is receiving a lot of attention. How can the models, processes, and functions be secured? What are these security models? Closely related

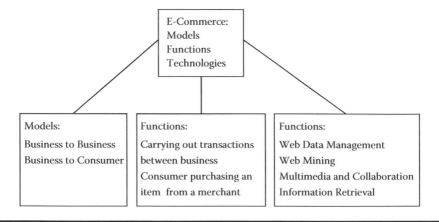

Figure 3.14   E-business components.

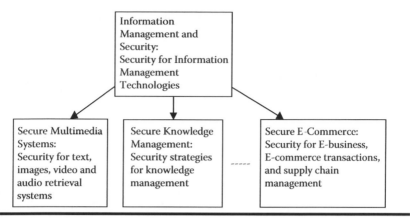

Figure 3.15   Secure information management.

to E-business is supply-chain management. The challenge here is ensuring security as well as timely communication between the suppliers and the customers. Figure 3.15 illustrates the security impact on information-management technologies.

3.4   Secure Knowledge Management

3.4.1 Knowledge Management

Knowledge management is the process of using knowledge as a resource to manage an organization. It could mean sharing expertise, developing a learning organization, teaching the staff, or learning from experiences, as well as collaboration. Essentially knowledge management will include data management and information management. However, this is not a view shared by everyone. Various definitions of knowledge management have been proposed. Knowledge management is a discipline invented mainly by business schools. The concepts have been around for a long time. But the word knowledge management was coined as a result of information technology and the Web.

In the collection of papers on knowledge management by Morey et al. [MORE01], knowledge management is divided into three areas: strategies such as building a knowledge company and making the staff knowledge workers, processes (such as techniques) for knowledge management including developing a method to share documents and tools, and metrics that measure the effectiveness of knowledge management. In the *Harvard Business Review* there is an excellent collection of articles on knowledge management describing a knowledge-creating company, building a learning organization, and teaching people how to learn [HARV96].

Organizational behavior and team dynamics play major roles in knowledge management.

Knowledge-management technologies include several information-management technologies such as knowledge representation and knowledge-based management systems. Other knowledge-management technologies include collaboration tools, tools for organizing information on the Web, as well as tools for measuring the effectiveness of the knowledge gained such as collecting various metrics. Knowledge-management technologies essentially include data-management and information-management technologies as well as decision-support technologies. Figure 3.16 illustrates some of the knowledge-management components and technologies. It also lists the aspects of the knowledge-management cycle. Web technologies play a major role in knowledge management. Knowledge management and the Web are closely related. Although knowledge-management practices have existed for many years, it is the Web that has promoted knowledge management.

Many corporations now have intranets, the single most powerful knowledge-management tool. Thousands of employees are connected through the Web in an organization. Large corporations have sites all over the world, and the employees are becoming well connected with one another. E-mail can be regarded as one of the early knowledge-management tools. Now there are many tools such as search engines and E-commerce tools.

With the proliferation of Web data management and E-commerce tools, knowledge management will become an essential part of the Web and E-commerce. A collection of papers on knowledge-management experiences including strategies, processes, and metrics is given in Reference [MORE01]. Collaborative knowledge management is discussed in Reference [THUR02b].

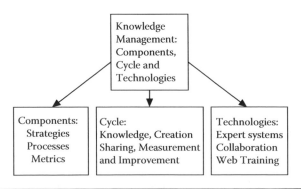

Figure 3.16   Knowledge-management components and technologies.

3.4.2 Security Impact

Secure knowledge management is receiving a lot of attention [SKM04]. One of the major challenges here is to determine the security impact on knowledge-management strategies, processes, and metrics [BERT06]. We will examine each of the components.

Note that an organization's knowledge-management strategy must be aligned with its business strategy; that is, an organization must utilize its knowledge to enhance its business, which will ultimately include improved revenues and profits. Therefore, its security strategy has to be aligned with its business strategy. For example, an organization may need to protect its intellectual property. Whereas patents are one aspect of intellectual property, other aspects include papers and trade secrets. Some of this intellectual property should not be widely disseminated to maintain a competitive edge. Therefore, policies are needed to ensure that sensitive intellectual property is treated as classified material.

With respect to knowledge-management processes, we need to incorporate security into them. For example, consider the workflow management for purchase orders. Only authorized individuals should be able to execute the various processes. This means that security for workflow systems is an aspect of secure knowledge management; that is, the data- and information-management technologies will contribute to knowledge management.

With respect to metrics, security will have an impact. For example, one metric could be the number of papers published by individuals. These papers may be classified or unclassified. Furthermore, the existence of the classified documents may also be classified. This means that at the unclassified level there may be one value for the metric, whereas at the classified level there may be another value. Therefore, when evaluating the employee for his or her performance, both values have to be taken into consideration. However, if the manager does not have an appropriate clearance, then there will be an issue. The organization has to then develop appropriate mechanisms to ensure that the employee's entire contributions are taken into consideration when he or she is evaluated. Figure 3.17 illustrates secure knowledge management.

3.5   Summary and Directions

In this chapter we have provided an overview of secure data, information, and knowledge management. In particular, we have discussed data, information, and knowledge-management technologies and then examined the security impact. Later in Chapter 17, we will discuss the applications of trustworthy semantic Web technologies for data, information, and knowledge management.

As we have stated earlier, data, information, and knowledge management are supporting technologies for building trustworthy semantic Webs. The agents that

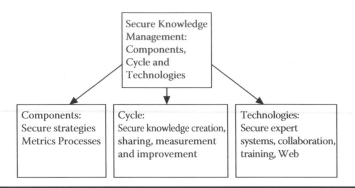

Figure 3.17   Secure knowledge management.

carry out activities on the Web have to utilize the data, extract information from the data, and reuse knowledge so that machine untreatable Web pages can be developed. There are several other aspects of data, information, and knowledge management that we have not covered in this chapter such as peer-to-peer information management and information management for virtual organizations. We will introduce these notions as needed when discussing semantic Web technologies as well as the applications of semantic Web technologies. Various concepts relating to semantic Webs will be introduced in the next chapter.

References

[SIGM01] *ACM SIGMOD Record*, 30(3), 2001.

[BERN87] Bernstein, P. et al., *Concurrency Control and Recovery in Database Systems,* Addison-Wesley, Reading, MA, 1987.

[BERR97] Berry, M. and G. Linoff, *Data Mining Techniques for Marketing, Sales, and Customer Support*, John Wiley & Sons, New York, 1997.

[BERT99] Bertino, E. et al., The specification and enforcement of authorization constraints in workflow management systems. *ACM Trans. Inf. Syst. Security*, 2(1), 1999.

[BERT06] Bertino, E., L. Khan, R. Sandhu, and B. Thuraisingham, Secure knowledge management, *IEEE Trans. Syst. Man Cybern.*, May 2006.

[CERI84] Ceri, S. and G. Pelagatti, *Distributed Databases, Principles and Systems*, McGraw-Hill, New York, 1984.

[CODD70] Codd, E.F., A relational model of data for large shared data banks, *Commn. ACM*, 13(6), 1970.

[IEEE99] Collaborative Computing, *IEEE Comput.*, 32 Special Issue (9), 1999.

[ACM91] Computer supported cooperative work, *Commn. ACM*, Special Issue, December 1991.

[DATE90] Date, C., *An Introduction to Database Systems*, Addison-Wesley, Reading, MA, 1990.

[HARV96] *Harvard Business School Articles on Knowledge Management*, Harvard University, Cambridge, MA, 1996.

[IEEE89] Hurson, A. et al., Eds., *Parallel Architectures for Databases*, IEEE Tutorial, IEEE Computer Society Press, Washington, D.C., 1989.

[IEEE03] *IEEE Comput. Magazine*, Special Issue on Audio Mining, 36, 2003.

[INMO93] Inmon, W., *Building the Data Warehouse*, John Wiley & Sons, New York, 1993.

[KDN] Kdnuggets, www.kdn.com.

[MORE01] Morey, D., M. Maybury, and B. Thuraisingham, Eds., *Knowledge Management*, MIT Press, Cambridge, MA, 2001.

[PRAB97] Prabhakaran, B., *Multimedia Database Management Systems*, Kluwer, Norwell, MA, 1997.

[SKM04] *Proc. Secure Knowledge Management Workshop*, Buffalo, NY, 2004.

[SHET90] Sheth A. and J. Larson, Federated database systems, *ACM Comput. Surveys*, 22(3) 1990.

[THUR97] Thuraisingham, B., *Data Management Systems Evolution and Interoperation*, CRC Press, Boca Raton, FL, 1997.

[THUR98] Thuraisingham, B., *Data Mining: Technologies, Techniques, Tools and Trends*, CRC Press, Boca Raton, FL, 1998.

[THUR00] Thuraisingham, B., *Web Data Management and Electronic Commerce*, CRC Press, Boca Raton, FL, 2000.

[THUR01] Thuraisingham, B., *Managing and Mining Multimedia Databases for the Electronic Enterprise*, CRC Press, Boca Raton, FL, 2001.

[THUR02a] Thuraisingham, B., *XML, Databases and the Semantic Web*, CRC Press, Boca Raton, FL, 2002.

[THUR02b] Thuraisingham, B. et al, Collaborative commerce and knowledge management, *Knowledge Process. Manage. J.*, 9(1): 43–53, 2002.

[THUR03] Thuraisingham, B., *Web Data Mining Technologies and Their Applications in Business Intelligence and Counter-Terrorism*, CRC Press, Boca Raton, FL, 2003.

[THUR05] Thuraisingham, B. *Database and Applications Security: Integrating Data Management and Information Security*, CRC Press, Boca Raton, FL 2005.

[TSIC82] Tsichritzis, D. and Lochovsky, F., *Data Models*, Prentice Hall, New York, 1982.

[ULLM88] Ullman, J. D., *Principles of Database and Knowledge Base Management Systems*, Volumes I and II, Computer Science Press, Rockville, MD, 1988.

[WIED92] Wiederhold, G., Mediators in the architecture of future information systems, *IEEE Comput.*, March 1992.

[WOEL86] Woelk, D. et al., An Object-Oriented Approach to Multimedia Databases, *Proc. ACM SIGMOD Conf.*, Washington, D.C., June 1986.

Exercises

1. Conduct a survey of the various access control policies in databases.
2. Investigate security issues for data warehousing.
3. Investigate security impact on E-commerce applications and supply-chain management.
4. Develop a model for secure workflow management systems.
5. Describe security for multimedia data management systems.
6. Investigate security for knowledge management systems.

Chapter 4

Semantic Web

4.1 Overview

Whereas current Web technologies facilitate the integration of information from a syntactic point of view, there is still a lot to be done to integrate the semantics of various systems and applications. Current Web technologies depend a lot on the "human in the loop" for information integration. Tim Berners Lee, the father of the World Wide Web (WWW), realized the inadequacies of current Web technologies and subsequently strived to make the Web more intelligent. His goal was to have a Web that will essentially alleviate humans from the burden of having to integrate disparate information sources as well as to carry out extensive searches. He then came to the conclusion that one needs machine-understandable Web pages and the use of ontologies for information integration. This resulted in the notion of the semantic Web [LEE01].

A semantic Web can be thought of as a Web that is highly intelligent and sophisticated so that one needs little or no human intervention to carry out tasks such as scheduling appointments, coordinating activities, searching for complex documents as well as integrating disparate databases and information systems. Although much progress has been made toward developing such an intelligent Web, there is still a lot to be done. For example, technologies such as ontology matching, intelligent agents, and markup languages are contributing a lot toward developing the semantic Web. Nevertheless one still needs the human to make decisions and take actions.

Recently there have been many developments on the semantic Web. The WWW Consortium (W3C) is specifying standards for the semantic Web [W3C].

These standards include specifications for eXtensible Markup Language (XML), Resource Description Framework (RDF), and interoperability. However, it is also very important that the semantic Web be secure, that is, the components that constitute the semantic Web have to be secure. The components include XML, RDF, and ontologies. In addition, we need secure information integration. We also need to examine trust issues for the semantic Web. It is therefore important that we have standards for securing the semantic Web including specifications for secure XML, secure RDF, and secure interoperability (see Reference [THUR05]). The main focus of this book is on securing the semantic Web. However, we need to understand the basic concepts about the semantic Web before we discuss trustworthy semantic Webs. Therefore, in this section we will discuss the various components of the semantic Web.

In Section 4.2 we will provide an overview of the layered architecture for the semantic Web as specified by Tim Berners Lee [Lee01]. The components such as XML, RDF, ontologies, and Web rules are discussed in Section 4.3 through Section 4.6. Agents on managing data and activities on the semantic Web are discussed in Section 4.7. Applications of the semantic Web are discussed in Section 4.8. A motivating scenario is discussed in Section 4.9, and the chapter is summarized in Section 4.10. Much of the discussion of the semantic Web is summarized from the book by Antoniou and van Harmelan [ANTO03]. For an up-to-date specification, we refer the reader to Reference [W3C].

4.2 Layered Architecture

Figure 4.1 illustrates the layered architecture for the semantic Web (also illustrated in Chapter 1 of this book). This is the architecture that was developed by Tim Berners Lee. Essentially the semantic Web consists of layers, where each layer takes advantage of the technologies of the previous layer. The lowest layer is the protocol layer, and this is usually not included in the discussion of the semantic technologies. The next layer is the XML layer. XML is a document representation language and will be discussed in Section 4.3. Although XML is sufficient to specify syntax, semantics such as "the creator of document D is John" is hard to specify in XML. Therefore, the W3C developed RDF. RDF uses XML syntax. The semantic Web community then went further and came up with specification of ontologies in languages such as OWL. Note that OWL addresses the inadequacies of RDF. To reason about various policies, the semantic Web community has come up with Web rules language such as semantic Web rules language (SWRL) and rules markup language (RulesML).

The functional architecture is illustrated in Figure 4.2. It is essentially a service-oriented architecture that hosts Web services. The semantic Web technologies are used by the Web services, as we will see in Part IV.

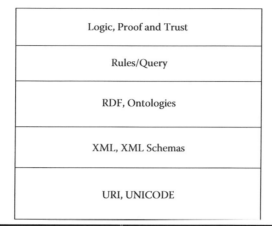

Figure 4.1   Layered architecture for the semantic Web.

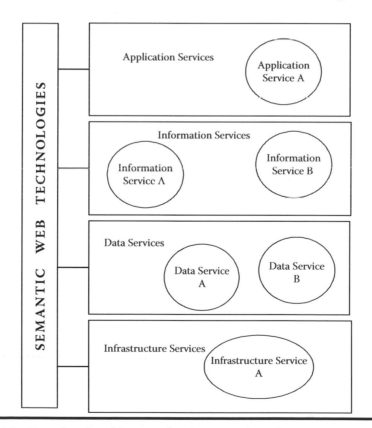

Figure 4.2   Functional architecture for the semantic Web.

4.3 XML

XML is needed due to the limitations of hypertext markup language (HTML) and complexities of standard generalized markup language (SGML). It is an extensible markup language specified by the W3C, designed to make the interchange of structured documents over the Internet easier. The key to XML used to be document type definitions (DTDs), which define the role of each element of text in a formal model. XML schemas have now become critical to specify the structure. XML schemas are also XML documents. This section will discuss various components of XML, including statements, elements, attributes, and schemas. The components of XML are illustrated in Figure 4.3.

4.3.1 XML Statement and Elements

The following is an example of an XML statement that describes the fact that "John Smith is a Professor in Texas." The elements are name and state. The XML statement is as follows:

```
<Professor>
    <name> John Smith </name>
    <state> Texas </state>
</Professor>
```

4.3.2 XML Attributes

Suppose we want to specify that there is a professor called John Smith who makes 60K; then we can use either elements or attributes to specify this. The example below shows the use of attributes Name and Salary.

```
<Professor
    Name = "John Smith", Access = All, Read
    Salary = "60K"
</Professor>
```

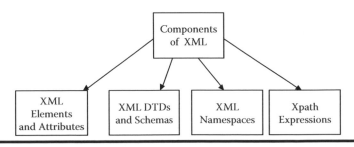

Figure 4.3   Components of XML.

4.3.3 XML DTDs

DTDs essentially specify the structure of XML documents. Consider the following DTD for Professor with elements Name and State. This will be specified as:

```
<!ELEMENT Professor Officer (Name, State)>
<!ELEMENT name (#PCDATA)>
<!ELEMENR state (#PCDATA)>
<!ELEMENT access (#PCDATA).>
```

4.3.4 XML Schemas

Although DTDs were the early attempts to specify structure for XML documents, XML schemas are far more elegant to specify structures. Unlike DTDs, XML schemas essentially use the XML syntax for specification.

Consider the following example:

```
<ComplexType _ name = "ProfessorType">
   <Sequence>
   <element name = "name" type = "string"/>
   <element name = "state" type = "string"/>
   <Sequence>
</ComplexType>
```

4.3.5 XML Namespaces

Namespaces are used for DISAMBIGUATION. An example is given below.

```
<CountryX: Academic-Institution
    Xmlns: CountryX = http://www.CountryX.edu/Instution DTD"
    Xmlns: USA = "http://www.USA.edu/Instution DTD"
    Xmlns: UK = "http://www.UK.edu/Instution DTD"
<USA: Title = College
    USA: Name = "University of Texas at Dallas"
    USA: State = Texas"
<UK: Title = University
    UK: Name = "Cambridge University"
    UK: State = Cambs
</CountryX: Acedmic-Instiution>
```

4.3.6 XML Federations and Distribution

XML data may be distributed, and the databases may form federations. This is illustrated in the following segment.

Site 1 document:

```
<Professor-name>
    <ID> 111 </ID>
    <Name> John Smith </name>
    <State> Texas </state>
</Professor-name>
```

Site 2 document:

```
<Professor-salary>
    <ID> 111 </ID>
    <salary> 60K </salary>
<Professor-salary>
```

4.3.7 XML-QL, XQuery, XPath, XSLT

XML-QL and XQuery are query languages that have been proposed for XML. XPath is used to specify the queries. Essentially, Xpath expressions may be used to reach a particular element in the XML statement. In our research we have specified policy rules as Xpath expressions (see Reference [BERT04]). XSLT is used to present XML documents. Details are given in www.w3c.org as well as in Reference [ANTO03]. Another useful reference is [LAUR00].

4.4   RDF

Although XML is ideal to specify the syntax of various statements, it is difficult to specify the semantics of a statement with XML. For example, with XML, it is difficult to specify statements such as:

- Engineer is a subclass of Employee.
- Engineer inherits all properties of Employee.

Note that the above statement specifies the class and subclass and inheritance relationships. RDF was developed by Tim Berners Lee and his team so that the inadequacies of XML could be handled. RDF uses XML syntax. Additional constructs are needed for RDF, and we discuss some of these constructs. Details can be found in Reference [ANTO03].

RDF is the essence of the semantic Web. It provides semantics with the use of ontologies to various statements and uses XML syntax. RDF Concepts includes the basic model which consists of Resources, Properties, and Statements; and the container model which consists of Bag, Sequence, and Alternative. We discuss some of the essential concepts. The components of RDF are illustrated in Figure 4.4.

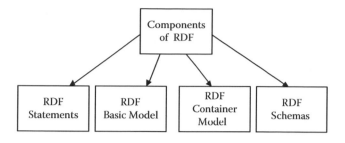

Figure 4.4   Components of RDF.

4.4.1 RDF Basics

The RDF basic model consists of Resource, Property, and Statement. In RDF, everything is a resource such as Person, Vehicle, or Animal. Properties describe relationships between resources such as "brought," "invented," or "ate." Statement is a triple of the form: (Object, Property, Value). Examples of statements are as follows:

- Berners Lee invented the semantic Web.
- Tom ate the apple.
- Mary brought a dress.

Figure 4.5 illustrates a statement in RDF. Here Berners Lee is the Object, Semantic Web is the Value, and invented is the Property.

4.4.2 RDF Container Model

An RDF container model consists of Bag, Sequence, and Alternative as illustrated in Figure 4.6. As described in Reference [ANTO03], these constructs are specified in RDF as follows:

Bag: Unordered container, may contain multiple occurrences

- Rdf: Bag

Seq: Ordered container, may contain multiple occurrences

- Rdf: Seq

Alt: a set of alternatives

- Rdf: Alt

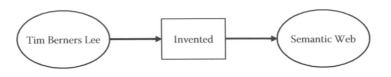

Figure 4.5   RDF statement.

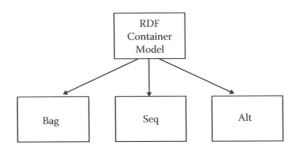

Figure 4.6   RDF container model.

4.4.3 RDF Specification

As stated in Reference [ANTO03], RDF specifications have been given for Attributes, Types, Nesting, Containers, etc. An example is the following:

"Berners Lee is the Author of the book Semantic Web."

The above statement is specified as follows (see also Reference [ANTO03]):

```
<rdf: RDF
     xmlns: rdf = "http://w3c.org/1999/02-22-rdf-syntax-ns#"
     xmlns: xsd = "http:// - - -
     xmlns: uni = "http:// - - - -
<rdf: Description: rdf: about = "949352"
     <uni: name = Berners Lee</uni:name>
     <uni: title> Professor < uni:title>
   </rdf: Description>
<rdf: Description rdf: about: "ZZZ"
     < uni: bookname> semantic Web <uni:bookname>
     < uni: authoredby: Berners Lee <uni:authoredby>
     </rdf: Description>
</rdf: RDF>
```

4.4.4 RDF Schemas

Although XML schemas specify the structure of the XML document and can be considered to be metadata, an RDF schema specifies relationships such as the class and subclass relationships. For example, we need RDF schema to specify statements such as "engineer is a subclass of employee." The following is the RDF specification for this statement.

```
<rdfs: Class rdf: ID = "engineer"
<rdfs: comment>
The class of Engineers
All engineers are employees
<rdfs: comment>
<rdfs: subClassof rdf: resource = "employee"/>
<rdfs: Class>
```

4.4.5 RDF Axiomatic Semantics

First-order logic is used to specify formulas and inferencing. The following constructs are needed:

> Built-in functions (First) and predicates (Type)
> Modus Ponens: From A and If A then B, deduce B

The following example is taken from Reference [ANTI03]:

> Example: All Containers are Resources; that is, if X is a container, then X is a resource.

- Type(?C, Container) → Type(?c, Resource)
- If we have Type(A, Container) then we can infer (Type A, Resource)

4.4.6 RDF Inferencing

Unlike XML, RDF has inferencing capabilities. Although first-order logic provides a proof system, it will be computationally unfeasible to develop such a system using first-order logic. As a result, horn clause logic was developed for logic programming [LLOY87]; this is still computationally expensive. The semantic Web is based on a restricted logic called Descriptive Logic, and details can be found in Reference [ANTO03]. RDF uses if-then rules as follows:

> IF E contains the triples (?u, rdfs: subClassof, ?v)
> and (?v, rdfs: subClassof ?w),

THEN

E also contains the triple (?u, rdfs: subClassOf, ?w).

That is, if u is a subclass of v, and v is a subclass of w, then u is a subclass of w.

4.4.7 RDF Query

Like XML Query, query languages are being developed for RDF. One can query RDF using XML, but this will be very difficult as RDF is much richer than XML. Therefore, RQL has been developed. RQL, an SQL-like language, has been developed for RDF. It is of the form:

Select from "RDF document" where some "condition".

4.5   Ontologies

Ontologies are common definitions for any entity, person, or thing. Ontologies are needed to clarify various terms; therefore, they are crucial for machine-understandable Web pages. Several ontologies have been defined and are available for use. Defining a common ontology for an entity is a challenge as different groups may come up with different definitions. Therefore, we need mappings for multiple ontologies; these mappings map one ontology to another. Specific languages have been developed for ontologies. Note that RDF was developed as XML and is not sufficient to specify semantics such as class and subclass relationship. RDF is also limited as one cannot express several other properties such as union and intersection. Therefore, we need a richer language. Ontology languages were developed by the semantic Web community for this purpose.

OWL (Web Ontology Language) is a popular ontology specification language. It is a language for ontologies and relies on RDF. The Defense Advanced Research Projects Agency (DARPA) developed the early language DARPA Agent Markup Language (DAML). Europeans developed Ontology Interface Language (OIL). DAML+OIL combine both and were the starting point for OWL. OWL was developed by the W3C. OWL is based on a subset of first-order logic, that is, descriptive logic.

OWL features include: Subclass relationship, Class membership, Equivalence of classes, Classification, and Consistency (e.g., x is an instance of A, A is a subclass of B, x is not an instance of B).

There are three types of OWL: OWL-Full, OWL-DL, and OWL-Lite. Automated tools for managing ontologies are called Ontology Engineering.

Below is an example of OWL specification:

Textbooks and Coursebooks are the same.
EnglishBook is not a FrenchBook.
EnglishBook is not a GermanBook.

```
< owl: Class rdf: about = "#EnglishBook">
<owl: disjointWith rdf: resource "#FrenchBook"/>
<owl: disjointWith rdf: resource = #GermanBook"/>
</owl:Class>
<owl: Class rdf: ID = "TextBook">
<owl: equivalentClass rdf: resource = "CourseBook"/>
</owl: Class>
```

Below is an OWL specification for Property.

Englishbooks are read by Students.

```
< owl: ObjectProperty rdf: about = "#readBy">
<rdfs domain rdf: resource = "#EnglishBook"/>
<rdfs: range rdf: resource = "#student"/>
<rdfs: subPropertyOf rdf: resource = #involves"/>
</owl: ObjectProperty>
```

Below is an OWL specification for property restriction.

All Frenchbooks are read only by Frenchstudents.

```
< owl: Class rdf: about = "#"FrenchBook">
<rdfs: subClassOf>
<owl: Restriction>
<owl: onProperty rdf: resource = "#readBy">
<owl: allValuesFrom rdf: resource = #FrenchStudent"/>
</rdfs: subClassOf>
</owl: Class>
```

4.6   Web Rules

RDF is built on XML, and OWL is built on RDF. We can express subclass relationships in RDF, and additional relationships can be expressed in OWL. However, reasoning power is still limited in OWL. Therefore, we need to specify rules and subsequently a markup language for rules so that machines can understand and make inferences.

Below are some examples as given in Reference [ANTI03].

- Studies(X,Y), Lives(X,Z), Loc(Y,U), Loc(Z,U) → DomesticStudent(X). That is, if John Studies at UTDallas and John lives on Campbell Road and the location of Campbell Road and UTDallas is Richardson, then John is a DomesticStudent.
- Note that Person (X) → Man(X) or Woman(X) is not a rule in predicate logic. That is, if X is a person, then X is either a man or a woman cannot be expressed in first-order predicate logic. Therefore, in predicate logic we express the above as if X is a person and X is not a man, then X is a woman; similarly, if X is a person and X is not a woman, then X is a man. In predicate logic, we can have a rule of the form
     Person(X) and Not Man(X) → Woman(X)

However, in OWL we can specify the rule if X is a person, then X is a man or X is a woman.

Rules can be monotonic or nonmonotonic. Below is an example of a monotonic rule:

- → Mother(X,Y)
- Mother(X,Y) → Parent(X,Y)
- If Mary is the mother of John, then Mary is the parent of John
- Rule is of the form:
- B1, B2, ---- Bn → A
- That is, if B1, B2, ---Bn hold then A holds

In the case of nonmonotonic reasoning, if we have X and NOT X, we do not treat them as inconsistent as in the case of monotonic reasoning. For example, as discussed in Reference [ANTO03], consider the example of an apartment that is acceptable to John. In general, John is prepared to rent an apartment unless the apartment has fewer than two bedrooms and does not allow pets. This can be expressed as follows:

- → Acceptable(X)
- Bedroom(X,Y), Y<2 → NOT Acceptable(X)
- NOT Pets(X) → NOT Acceptable(X)

The first rule states that an apartment is, in general, acceptable to John. The second rule states that if the apartment has fewer than two bedrooms, it is not acceptable to John. The third rule states that if pets are not allowed, then the apartment is not acceptable to John. Note that there could be a contradiction. But with nonmonotonic reasoning this is allowed, whereas it is not allowed in monotonic reasoning.

We need rule markup languages for a machine to understand the rules. The various components of logic are expressed in the rule markup language called RuleML developed for the semantic Web. Both monotonic and nonmonotonic rules can be represented in RuleML.

Example representation of Fact Parent(A), which is A is a parent, is expressed as follows:

```
<fact>
        <atom>
    <predicate>Parent</predicate>
      <term>
        <const>A</const>
      </term>
    </atom>
  </fact>
```

4.7   A Note on Agents

Agents are crucial to managing the data and the activities on the semantic Web. Usually agents are not treated as part of semantic Web technologies, although some consider agents as part of the semantic Web. Because the subject of agents is vast and there are numerous efforts on developing agents as well as secure agents, we do not discuss agents as part of this book. However, we mention agents throughout the book as it is these agents that use XML and RDF and make sense of the data and understand Web pages. Agents act on behalf of the users. Agents communicate with each other using well-defined protocols.

Various types of agents have been developed depending on the tasks they carry out. These include mobile agents, intelligent agents, search agents, and knowledge-management agents. Agents invoke Web services to carry out the operations. For details of agents we refer the reader to Reference [HEND01]. Figure 4.7 illustrates the operation of an agent within the context of the semantic Web.

4.8   Applications

As stated in Reference [ANTO03], the problem with the current Web is that the Web pages have high recall and low precision; that is, too many Web pages are returned for a query. Furthermore, results are sensitive to vocabulary. Different words will give different results even if they mean the same entity. The results are single Web pages, and these Web pages are not linked. To address these difficulties,

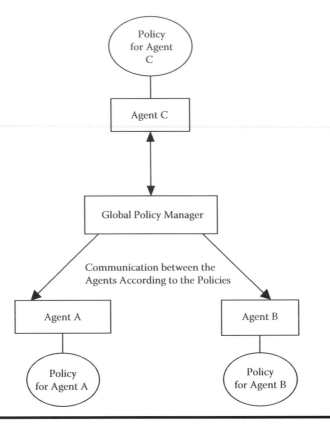

Figure 4.7   Agents.

the semantic Web technologies were developed by Tim Berners Lee and his team. The goal is to have machine-understandable Web pages. Furthermore, it is intended that activities on the Web such as searching should be carried out with little or no human intervention. The semantic Web provides the technologies for applications in knowledge management, E-commerce, and interoperability. Figure 4.8 illustrates these applications, and more details are given in Part IV. In this section we discuss some of the applications.

> **Knowledge management:** As discussed in Chapter 3, there is a need for many corporations to search, extract, and maintain information, uncover hidden dependencies, and view information. The semantic Web technologies such as RDF and ontologies will aid in representing, organizing, and maintaining knowledge, question answering, querying multiple documents, and controlling access to documents. We will discuss semantic Web technologies for secure knowledge management in Chapter 17.

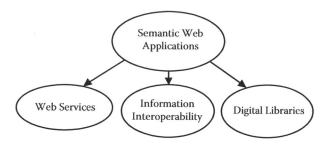

Figure 4.8   Applications.

Business-to-consumer E-commerce: Wrapper technology is currently used to extract information about user preferences for carrying out E-commerce and displaying products to the user. The goal is to develop software agents that can interpret privacy requirements, pricing and product information, and can display timely and correct information to the user as well as to provide information about the reputation of shops. In the future, agents may carry out negotiations on behalf of the user. We will discuss semantic Web technologies for secure E-business in Chapter 19.

Business-to-business E-commerce: Organizations work together in carrying out transactions such as collaborating on a product and automating supply-chain management. With the current Web, there is a lack of standards for data exchange. Use of XML is a big improvement in recent years, but we need to agree on vocabulary. In the future we can expect to use ontologies to agree on meanings and interpretations. We will discuss the application of semantic Web technologies for secure E-business in Chapter 19.

Personal agents: John is a president of a company. He needs to have surgery for a serious but not critical illness. With the current Web, he has to check each Web page for relevant information and make decisions depending on the information provided. With the semantic Web, the agent will retrieve all the relevant information, synthesize the information, ask John if needed, and then present the various options to John and also makes recommendations. In Part IV of this book, we will discuss how semantic Web technologies may be used to understand the data and make decisions.

Web services: Web services are services that are invoked to carry out an operation such as searching and carrying out a transaction; that is, agents invoke Web services. Web services are specified according to a well-defined protocol. They utilize semantic Web technologies to understand and reason about the service. We will discuss semantic Web applications to secure Web services in Chapter 16.

Information interoperability: The information in heterogeneous data sources has to interoperate. Ontologies are needed for common understanding of the data and to handle semantic heterogeneity. The semantic Web for secure information interoperability will be discussed in Chapter 18.

Information sharing: Since September 11, 2001, the need-to-know model has changed to a need-to-share model. Organizations have to share information and at the same time enforce policies. Ontologies are needed for understanding the information. Chapter 21 discusses information sharing.

Digital libraries: Digital libraries are digitized libraries. The goal is to develop storage facilities and indexing as well as query technologies for efficient access. Semantic Web technologies may be used to represent as well as understand the data. Chapter 19 discusses the semantic Web for secure digital libraries.

4.9   Motivating Scenario

Now that we have provided an overview of semantic Web technologies and discussed the applications, we will discuss a motivating semantic that illustrates how semantic Web technologies may be applied in the real world. After we have covered the essential points in describing trustworthy semantic Webs and the applications as in Parts II, III, IV, and V, in the final chapter (that is, Chapter 25), we will revisit this scenario and illustrate how secure semantic Web technologies may be applied.

Consider the scenario where four intelligence organizations (e.g., United States, United Kingdom, Australia, and Canada) have to work together to fight the global war on terror. Each organization maintains its own databases of terrorists and terrorist organizations. Suppose the United Kingdom detects that there is a suspicious activity and wants to warn its partners as well as get more information. Now, all of these organizations have to agree on common terms. Therefore, they will work with each other as well as by themselves to develop ontologies specified possibly in OWL. Furthermore, data may be represented using XML or RDF. In some cases they may have to integrate parts of their databases so that the partners can work with the integrated database. Finally, they may make use of digital library technologies to retrieve information about prior incidents. They also make use of the knowledge they have gathered from their experts for reuse. Furthermore, the organizations will use their reasoning systems to determine whether a future terror attack will occur. An agent will act on behalf of each organization. Agents will communicate with each other using some well-defined protocols. Finally, agents will invoke Web services to carry out an operation such as data integration and information retrieval.

The above example shows how technologies such as XML and RDF may be used. However, at this time we have not discussed security issues. After we complete the discussions in Parts II, III, IV, and V, we will revisit this scenario in Chapter 25 and show how trustworthy semantic Web technologies may be used for this application. Figure 4.9 illustrates the scenario.

4.10   Summary and Directions

This chapter provided an overview of semantic Web technologies. In particular we discussed Tim Berners Lee's technology stack as well as a functional architecture for the semantic Web. Then we discussed XML, RDF, and ontologies as well as Web rules for the semantic Web. Next we discussed agents as well as some applications. Finally, we discussed a motivating scenario that we will revisit toward the end of this book.

Semantic Webs, data, information and knowledge management, and trustworthy systems have to be integrated to develop trustworthy semantic Webs; that is, the supporting technologies for trustworthy semantic Webs are trustworthy systems, data, information and knowledge management as well as semantic Webs. Now that we have provided an overview of these supporting technologies, we are ready to discuss the various details of trustworthy semantic Webs. In particular, Part II will focus on confidentiality aspects. Trust, integrity, and privacy aspects are discussed in Part III. Applications will be elaborated on in Part IV. Some specialized secure semantic Webs will be discussed in Part V. Note that although our focus

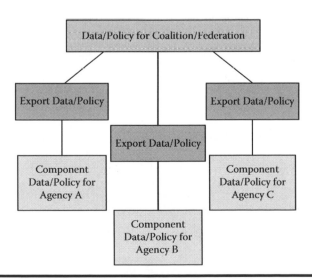

Figure 4.9   Inter-agency collaboration.

is on security issues, in many cases we also discuss some of the basic technologies so that we can then examine the security issues.

References

[ANTO03] Antoniou, G. and F. van Harmelan, *A Semantic Web Primer*, MIT Press, Cambridge, MA, 2003.
[BERT04] Bertino, E. et al., Secure third party publication of XML documents, *IEEE Trans. Knowledge Data Eng.*, 10, 2004.
[HEND01] Hendler, J., Agents and the semantic Web, *IEEE Intelligent Syst. J.*, March 2001.
[LEE01] Lee, T.B, and J. Hendler, The semantic Web, *Sci. Am.*, May 2001.
[LLOY87] Lloyd, J., *Logic Programming*, Springer-Verlag, Heidelberg, 1987.
[LAUR00] St. Laurent, S., *XML: A Primer*, Power Books, London, UK, 2000.
[THUR05] Thuraisingham, B., *Database and Applications Security: Integrating Data Management and Information Security*, CRC Press, Boca Raton, FL, 2005.
[W3C] www.w3c.org.

Exercises

1. Consider the hypothetical scenario described in this chapter. Elaborate on this scenario and specify with examples the use of XML for data sharing.
2. Redo Exercise 1 with RDF specifications.
3. Describe how ontologies may facilitate interoperability in Exercise 1.
4. Show how Web rules may be used to reason across organizations in Exercise 1.

Conclusion to Part I

In Part I, we provided an overview of the various supporting technologies for building trustworthy semantic Webs. Note that the supporting technologies include trustworthy systems, secure data and information management, and semantic Webs. Chapter 2 described various information security technologies including database security and network security. Chapter 3 described various data- and information-management technologies including multimedia, collaboration, and knowledge management. Chapter 4 described semantic Web technologies.

Now that we have provided an overview of the various supporting technologies, we are now ready to embark on a very important topic, and that is building trustworthy semantic Webs. Parts II through V discuss aspects of secure semantic Webs, dependability issues, applications, and specialized systems.

Part II

Secure Semantic Webs

Introduction to Part II

Now that we have provided an overview of the supporting technologies for trustworthy semantic Webs including trustworthy systems, secure data- and information-management systems, and semantic Webs, we are now ready to embark on the main topic of this book, which is building trustworthy semantic Webs. As previously stated, trustworthy semantic Webs include secure semantic Webs and dependable semantic Webs. Part II will focus on secure semantic Webs, and that will be mainly on confidentiality aspects of security.

Part II consists of five chapters. In Chapter 5, we will provide an overview of secure semantic Webs. XML security will be discussed in Chapter 6. RDF security will be discussed in Chapter 7. Security and ontologies will be the subject of Chapter 8. Finally, in Chapter 9 we will discuss security and rules processing.

Chapter 5

Security and the Semantic Web

5.1 Overview

As we have stated earlier, as the demand for data and information-management increases, there is also a critical need for maintaining the security of the databases, applications, and information systems. Data and information have to be protected from unauthorized access as well as from malicious corruption. With the advent of the Web, it is even more important to protect the data and information as numerous individuals now have access to this data and information. Therefore, we need effective mechanisms to secure semantic Web technologies.

In Chapter 4, we provided an overview of the semantic Web. In this chapter we focus on securing the semantic Web with emphasis on confidentiality. In particular, eXtensible Markup Language (XML) security, resource description framework (RDF) security, and securing other components such as secure ontologies and secure Web rules will be discussed. Each of the components of the semantic Web will be elaborated on in Chapters 6, 7, 8, and 9. Other aspects of securing the semantic Web such as privacy and trust will also be discussed. This chapter will also include a discussion of secure applications for the semantic Web such as secure Web services as well as specialized semantic Webs.

The organization of this chapter is as follows. Security for the semantic Web is discussed in Section 5.2. Privacy and trust for the semantic Web is addressed in Section 5.3. Some aspects of secure applications such as Web services are discussed in Section 5.4. Some specialized semantic Webs are discussed in Section 5.5. Note that Sections 5.2, 5.3, 5.4, and 5.5 will be elaborated on in Parts II, III, IV, and V, respectively. This chapter is summarized in Section 5.6.

5.2   Security for the Semantic Web

5.2.1   Overview

We first provide an overview of security issues for the semantic Web and then discuss some details on XML security, RDF security, and secure information integration, which are components of secure semantic Webs. As more progress is made on investigating these various issues, we hope that appropriate standards will be developed for securing the semantic Web. Security cannot be considered in isolation; there is no one layer that should focus on security. Security cuts across all layers, and this is a challenge. We need security for each of the layers illustrated in Figure 5.1.

Consider the lowest layer. One needs secure Transmission Control Protocol/ Internet Protocol (TCP/IP), secure sockets, and secure Hypertext Transfer Protocol (HTTP). There are now security protocols for these various lower-layer protocols. One needs end-to-end security; one cannot just have secure TCP/IP built on untrusted communication layers. We need network security. The next layer is XML and XML schemas. One needs secure XML. Access must be controlled to various portions of the document for reading, browsing, and modifications. There is ongoing research on securing XML and XML schemas. The next step is securing

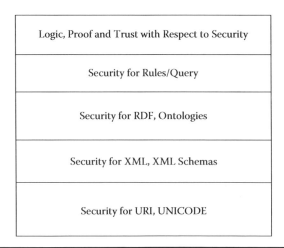

| Logic, Proof and Trust with Respect to Security |
| Security for Rules/Query |
| Security for RDF, Ontologies |
| Security for XML, XML Schemas |
| Security for URI, UNICODE |

Figure 5.1   Layers for the secure semantic Web.

RDF. Now, with RDF not only do we need secure XML, we also need security for the interpretations and semantics. For example, in certain contexts, portions of the document may be unclassified, whereas in certain other contexts, the document may be classified.

Once XML and RDF have been secured, the next step is to examine security for ontologies and interoperation. Ontologies may have security levels attached to them. Certain parts of the ontologies could be secret, whereas certain other parts may be unclassified. The challenge is, how does one use these ontologies for secure information integration? Researchers have done some work on the secure interoperability of databases. We need to revisit this research and then determine what else needs to be done so that the information on the Web can be managed, integrated, and exchanged securely. Logic, proof, and trust are at the highest layers of the semantic Web. How can we trust the information that the Web gives us?

We also need to examine the inference problem for the semantic Web. Inference is the process of posing queries and deducing new information. It becomes a problem when the deduced information is something the user is unauthorized to know. With the semantic Web, and especially with data-mining tools, one can make all kinds of inferences. Recently there has been some research on controlling unauthorized inferences on the semantic Web. We need to continue with such research (see, for example, Reference [FARK04] and Reference [THUR06]).

Security should not be an afterthought. We have often heard that one needs to insert security into the system right from the beginning. Similarly, security cannot be an afterthought for the semantic Web. However, we cannot also make the system inefficient if we must guarantee 100 percent security at all times. What is needed is a flexible security policy. In some situations we may need 100 percent security, whereas in some other situations, 30 percent security (whatever that means) may be sufficient.

5.2.2 XML Security

Various research efforts have been reported on XML security (see, for example, Reference [BERT02]). We briefly discuss some of the key points. The main challenge is whether to give access to entire XML documents or parts of the documents. Bertino et al. have developed authorization models for XML. They have focused on access-control policies as well as on dissemination policies. They also considered push and pull architectures. They specified the policies in XML. The policy specification contains information about which users can access which portions of the documents. In Reference [BERT02], algorithms for access control as well as computing views of the results are presented. In addition, architectures for securing XML documents are also discussed. In Reference [BERT04], the authors go further and describe how XML documents may be published on the Web. The idea is for owners to publish documents, subjects to request access to the documents, and untrusted publishers to give the subjects views of the documents they are authorized to see. We discuss XML security in more detail in Chapter 6.

The World Wide Web Consortium (W3C) is specifying standards for XML security. The XML security project [XML1] is focusing on providing implementation of security standards for XML. The focus is on XML-Signature Syntax and Processing, XML-Encryption Syntax and Processing, and XML Key Management. The W3C also has a number of working groups including XML Signature Working Group [XML2] and XML Encryption Working Group [XML3]. Although the standards are focusing on what can be implemented in the near term, much research is needed on securing XML documents.

5.2.3 RDF Security

RDF is the foundation of the semantic Web. Whereas XML is limited in providing machine-understandable documents, RDF handles this limitation. As a result, RDF provides better support for interoperability as well as searching and cataloging. It also describes contents of documents as well as relationships between various entities in the document. Whereas XML provides syntax and notations, RDF supplements this by providing semantic information in a standardized way.

The basic RDF model has three concepts: they are resources, properties, and statements. Resource is anything described by RDF expressions. It could be a Web page or a collection of pages. Property is a specific attribute used to describe a resource. RDF statements are resources together with a named property plus the value of the property. Statement components are subject, predicate, and object. So, for example, if we have a sentence of the form "John is the creator of xxx", then xxx is the subject or resource; the property or predicate is "creator," and the object or literal is "John." There are RDF diagrams very much like entity relationship (ER) diagrams or object diagrams to represent statements. It is important that the intended interpretation be used for RDF sentences [CHEN76], [FOWL97]. This is accomplished by RDF schemas. A schema is sort of a dictionary and has interpretations of various terms used in sentences.

More advanced concepts in RDF include the container model and statements about statements. The container model has three types of container objects: bag, sequence, and alternative. A bag is an unordered list of resources or literals. It is used to mean that a property has multiple values, but the order is not important. A sequence is a list of ordered resources; here the order is important. An alternative is a list of resources that represent alternatives for the value of a property. Various tutorials in RDF describe the syntax of containers in more detail.

RDF also provides support for making statements about other statements. For example, with this facility one can make statements of the form "The statement A is false," where A is the statement "John is the creator of X." Again, one can use object-like diagrams to represent containers and statements about statements. RDF also has a formal model associated with it. This formal model has a formal grammar. For further information on RDF we refer the reader to the excellent discussion in the book by Antoniou and van Harmelan [ANTO03].

To make the semantic Web secure, we need to ensure that RDF documents are secure. This would involve securing XML from a syntactic point of view. However, with RDF we also need to ensure that security is preserved at the semantic level. The issues include the security implications of the concepts, resources, properties, and statements. How is access control ensured? How can properties and statements be protected? How can one provide access control at a finer degree of granularity? What are the security properties of the container model? How can bags, lists, and alternatives be protected? Can we specify security policies in RDF? How can we resolve semantic inconsistencies for the policies? How can we express security constraints in RDF? What are the security implications of statements about statements? How can we protect RDF schemas? These are difficult questions, and we need to start research to provide answers. XML security is just the beginning. Securing RDF is much more challenging (see also Reference [CARM04]). More details will be given in Chapter 7.

5.2.4 Security and Ontologies

Ontologies are essentially representations of various concepts to avoid ambiguity. Numerous ontologies have been developed. These ontologies have been used by agents to understand Web pages and conduct operations such as the integration of databases. Furthermore, ontologies can be represented in languages such as RDF or special languages such as Web ontology language (OWL).

Ontologies have to be secure. Therefore, access to the ontologies has to be controlled. This means that different users may have access to different parts of the ontology. On the other hand, ontologies may be used to specify security policies, just as XML and RDF have been used to specify policies. Chapter 8 will discuss ontologies and security, and we will describe how ontologies may be secured as well as how ontologies may be used to specify various policies.

5.2.5 Secure Query and Rules Processing
for the Semantic Web

The layer above the Secure RDF Layer is the Secure Query- and Rules-Processing Layer. Whereas RDF can be used to specify security policies (see, for example, [CARM04]), the Web rules language being developed by W3C is more powerful to specify complex policies. Furthermore, inference engines are being developed to process and reason about the rules (e.g., the Pellet engine developed at the University of Maryland). One could integrate ideas from the database inference controller that we have developed (see Reference [THUR93]) with Web rules processing to develop an inference or privacy controller for the semantic Web.

The query-processing module is responsible for accessing heterogeneous data and information sources on the semantic Web. Researchers are examining ways to integrate techniques from Web query processing with semantic Web technologies to locate, query, and integrate heterogeneous data and information sources. We need to examine the security impact of query processing.

5.3 Privacy and Trust for the Semantic Web

5.3.1 Overview

Privacy is about protecting information about individuals. Furthermore, an individual can specify to a Web service provider the information that can be released about him or her. Privacy has been discussed a great deal in the past, especially when it relates to protecting medical information about patients. Social scientists as well as technologists have been working on privacy issues. However, privacy has received enormous attention during the past year. This is mainly because of the advent of the Web, the semantic Web, counterterrorism, and national security. For example, to extract information about various individuals and perhaps prevent or detect potential terrorist attacks, data-mining tools are being examined. We have heard much about national security versus privacy in the media. This is mainly due to the fact that people are now realizing that to handle terrorism, the government may need to collect data about individuals and mine the data to extract information. Data may be in relational databases, or it may be text, video, and images. This is causing a major concern with various civil liberties unions (see Reference [THUR03]). Closely related to privacy is anonymity. Some argue that it is more important to maintain anonymity.

In this section we discuss privacy threats that arise due to data mining and the semantic Web. We also discuss some solutions and provide directions for standards. Section 5.3.2 will discuss issues on data mining, national security, and privacy. Some potential solutions are discussed in Section 5.3.3. Trust management will be discussed in Section 5.3.4. More details will be given in Part III.

5.3.2 Data Mining, National Security, Privacy, and the Semantic Web

With the Web and the semantic Web, there is now an abundance of data information about individuals that one can obtain within seconds. The data could be structured data or could be multimedia data such as text, images, video, and audio. Information can be obtained through mining or from information retrieval. Data mining is an important tool in making the Web more intelligent. Data mining may be used to mine data on the Web so that the Web can evolve into the semantic Web. However, this also means that there may be threats to privacy. Therefore, one needs to enforce privacy controls on databases and data-mining tools on the semantic Web. This is a very difficult problem. In summary, one needs to develop techniques to prevent users from mining and extracting information from data, whether they are on the Web or on networked servers. Note that data mining is a technology that is critical for, say, analysts so that they can extract patterns previously unknown. However, we do not want the information to be used in an incorrect manner. For example, based on information about a person, an insurance company could deny insurance or a loan agency could deny loans. In many cases these denials may not be legitimate. Therefore, information providers have to be very careful in what they release. Also, data-mining researchers have to ensure that privacy aspects are addressed.

Although little work has been reported on privacy issues for the semantic Web, we are moving in the right direction. As research initiatives are started in this area, we can expect some progress to be made. Note that there are also social and political aspects to consider. Technologists, sociologists, policy experts, counterterrorism experts, and legal experts have to work together to develop appropriate data-mining techniques as well as ensure privacy. Privacy policies and standards are also urgently needed. Whereas the technologists develop privacy solutions, we need the policy makers to work with standards organizations so that appropriate privacy standards are developed. The W3C has made a good start with the Platform for Privacy Preferences Project (P3P).

5.3.3 Solutions to the Privacy Problem

The challenge is to provide solutions to enhance national security, but at the same time ensure privacy. There is now research at various laboratories on privacy-enhanced, privacy-sensitive, and privacy-preserving data mining (e.g., Agrawal and Srikant at IBM [AGRA00]; Almaden and Gehrke at Cornell University [GEHR02]; and Clifton et al. at Purdue University [CLIF02]). The idea here is to continue with mining, but at the same time ensure privacy as much as possible. For example, Clifton has proposed the use of the multiparty security policy approach for carrying out privacy-sensitive data mining. Although there is some progress, we still have a long way to go. Some useful references are provided in Reference [CLIF02] and [EVFI02].

We give some more details on an approach we are proposing. Note that one mines the data and extracts patterns and trends. The privacy constraints determine which patterns are private and to what extent. For example, suppose one could extract the names and healthcare records. If we have a privacy constraint that states that names and healthcare records are private, then this information is not released to the general public. If the information is semiprivate, then it is released to those who have a need to know. Essentially the inference-controller approach we have discussed is one solution to achieving some level of privacy. It could be regarded as a type of privacy-sensitive data mining. In our research we have found many challenges to the inference-controller approach we have proposed (see Reference [THUR93]). These challenges will have to be addressed when handling privacy constraints (see also Reference [THUR04b]). Figure 5.2 illustrates privacy controllers for the semantic Web. As illustrated, there are data-mining tools on the Web that mine the Web databases. The privacy controller should ensure privacy-preserving data mining. Ontologies may be used by the privacy controllers. For example, there may be ontology specification for privacy constructs. Furthermore, XML may be extended to include privacy constraints. RDF may incorporate privacy semantics. We need to carry out more research on the role of onotologies for privacy control.

Much of the work on privacy-preserving data mining focuses on relational data. We need to carry out research on privacy-preserving semantic Web data mining. We need to combine techniques for privacy-preserving data mining with techniques for semantic Web data mining to obtain solutions for privacy-preserving semantic Web data mining.

5.3.4 Trust for the Semantic Web

Recently there has been much work on trust and the semantic Web (see the research by Denker et al. [DENK03] and Kagal et al. [KAGA03]). The challenges are as follows: How do you trust the information on the Web? How do you trust the sources? How do you negotiate between different parties and develop contracts? How do you

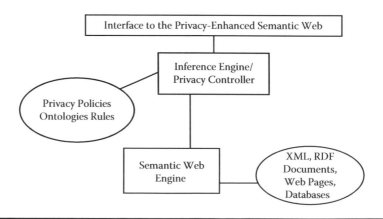

Figure 5.2   Privacy controller for the semantic Web.

incorporate constructs for trust management and negotiation into XML and RDF? What are the semantics for trust management?

Researchers are working on protocols for trust management. Languages for specifying trust-management constructs are also being developed. Also there is research on the foundations of trust management. For example, if A trusts B and B trusts C, then can A trust C? How do you share the data and information on the semantic Web and still maintain autonomy? How do you propagate trust? For example, if A trusts B, say, 50 percent of the time and B trusts C 30 percent of the time, then what value do you assign for A trusting C? How do you incorporate trust into semantic interoperability? What is the quality of service primitives for trust and negotiation? For certain situations one may need 100 percent trust, whereas for other situations 50 percent trust may suffice (see also Reference [YU03]).

Another topic that is being investigated is trust propagation and propagating privileges. For example, if you grant privileges to A, what privileges can A transfer to B? How can you compose privileges? Is there an algebra and calculus for the composition of privileges? Much research still needs to be done here. One of the layers of the semantic Web is logic, proof, and trust. Essentially this layer deals with trust management and negotiation between different agents and examining the foundations and developing logics for trust management.

5.4   Secure Semantic Web Applications

This section will discuss some applications of a secure semantic Web such as Web services and interoperability. More details of some of the applications will be given in Part IV.

5.4.1 Secure Web Services

Web services are services such as resource-management services, directory services, publishing services, subscription services, and various other services that are provided on the Web. There has to be some way to describe the communication on the Web in a structured and organized way. Web Services Description Language (WSDL) does this by defining an XML grammar for describing network services. As described in Chapter 16, the network services are described as a collection of communication endpoints capable of exchanging messages. A WSDL document has various elements including the following: types, which is a container for data type definition; message, which is the data being communicated; operation, which is an action supported by the service; port type, which is a subset of operations supported by the endpoints; binding, which is a concrete protocol and data-format specification for a particular port type; port, which is an endpoint; and service, which is a collection of endpoints.

Whereas WSDL is a Web services-description language, what are Web services? These are services provided by the Web to its users. These could be publishing services, data-management services, information-management services, directory services, etc. Any service that the Web provides is a Web service, and WSDL provides the means to specify the service. Web services is an area that will expand a great deal in the coming years. These services will form the essence of the semantic Web.

These Web services have to be secure. This would mean that we need to ensure that appropriate access-control methods are enforced. We also need to ensure that malicious processes do not subvert the Web services or cause a denial of service. There has been much work these past few years or so on secure Web services (see Reference [BHAT04]). Intrusion-detection techniques are being examined to detect and prevent malicious intrusions. Extensions to WSDL for security are proposed. Details can be found in the standards work by the W3C and the Organization for the Advancement of Structured Information Standards (OASIS).

5.4.2 Secure Information Interoperability

One needs to integrate the diverse and disparate data sources on the Web. The data may not be in databases. It could be in files both structured and unstructured. Data could be in the form of tables or in the form of text, images, audio, and video. Semantic Web technologies such as ontologies are becoming critical for information interoperability (see also Chapter 4).

The challenge for security researchers is, how does one integrate information securely? For example, in Reference [THUR94] and Reference [THUR97], the schema integration work of Sheth and Larson [SHET90] was extended for security policies. Different sites have security policies, and these policies have to be integrated to provide a policy for the federated database system. One needs to examine these issues for the semantic Web. Each node on the Web may have its own policy. Is it feasible to have a common policy for a community on the Web? Do we need a tight integration of the policies, or do we focus on dynamic policy integration? How can ontologies play a role in secure information integration? How do we provide access control for ontologies? Should ontologies specify the security policies? How do we minimize the trust placed on information integrators on the Web? We have posed several questions. We need a research program to address many of these challenges.

5.4.3 Secure Agents and Related Technologies

Agents are processes that carry out specific tasks. Agents for the semantic Web have been investigated extensively by the DARPA Agent Markup Language (DAML) Program at the Defense Advanced Projects Research Agency (DARPA). The goal of this program is to develop a markup language for agents. The idea is for agents to understand Web information and process the information.

Security for agents is essential if the semantic Web is to be secure. Agents that carry out security-critical functions have to be trusted. Furthermore, agents have to communicate with each other through secure agent protocols.

The main question is, how much of the agents should be trusted? Because the Web has several millions of agents, it is impossible to trust all of them. How much of the work can be accomplished by using appropriate encryption and cryptographic techniques? For example, in Reference [BERT04], we have shown that with appropriate encryption techniques we can ensure authenticity and completeness without having to trust publishers who publish XML documents. These publishers may be implemented as agents. There is also work on querying encrypted databases to ensure confidentiality (see Reference [HACI02]) as well as work on mobile agent security. We need to examine all of this research and see how the results can be applied to secure agents for the semantic Web.

5.4.4 Secure Grid and Secure Semantic Grid

Another technology that makes use of the semantic Web is secure semantic grids. A semantic grid essentially integrates grids and semantic Webs. Grid computing is about allocating resources in such a way that high-performance applications can be executed efficiently. There is a lot of interest now on migrating from the grid to the semantic grid. The semantic grid is essentially the grid that uses ontology and intelligent information processes to reason about the resources and the allocation of resources. One can think of the semantic grid as a layer above the grid performing intelligent functions (see also Reference [ROUR04]).

If applications are to be executed securely, the grid has to be secure. This means that the nodes of the grid must have permission to execute various applications. Because applications are executed at different nodes, if there is some malicious code, then the system must ensure that the vulnerabilities are not propagated during application execution. Applications must also possess credentials to utilize various resources. There are many similarities between a grid and the Web. A semantic grid is similar to the semantic Web where knowledge and information management would play a role in allocating resources as well as for application execution. Security for the semantic grid is yet to be investigated. Closely related to the grid is what is known as the cyber-infrastructure. Cyber-infrastructure is essentially providing the data and computing resources for scientists and engineers to carry out their tasks that are computationally intensive (see Reference [ATKI03]). Little work has been reported on security for cyber-infrastructure.

5.5   Specialized Semantic Webs

Whereas Section 5.4 discusses applications of semantic Webs, in this section we provide an overview of specialized semantic Webs that are essentially domain-specific semantic Webs. We consider two types of domains: application domains and technology domains. Application domains are domains that deal with specific applications such as medical, financial, defense, intelligence, and manufacturing, among others. Technology domains are specialized domains dealing with technologies such as geospatial data management, multimedia data management, and sensor data management.

Part V elaborates on the domain-specific semantic Webs. The application domains that we have discussed include defense and intelligence, homeland security, medical, and financial. The technology domains we have considered include geospatial semantic Web and sensor semantic Web. We have also discussed how secure semantic Web technologies may be applied to these specialized domains.

5.6   Summary and Directions

This chapter has provided an overview of the semantic Web and discussed security standards. We first discussed security issues for the semantic Web. We argued that security must cut across all layers. Next we provided some more details on XML security, RDF security, secure information integration, and trust. If a semantic Web is to be secure, we need all its components to be secure. We also described some of our research on access control and dissemination of XML documents. Next we discussed privacy for the semantic Web. This was followed by a brief discussion of security for the grid and the semantic grid.

Much research needs to be done. We need to continue with the research on XML security. We must start examining security for RDF. This is more difficult as RDF incorporates semantics. We need to examine the work on security-constraint processing and context-dependent security constraints and see if we can apply some of the ideas for RDF security. Finally, we need to examine the role of ontologies for secure information integration. We have to address some hard questions: How do we integrate security policies on the semantic Web? How can we incorporate policies into ontologies? We also cannot forget about privacy and trust for the semantic Web. We need to protect the privacy of individuals and at the same time ensure that individuals have the information they need to carry out their functions. Finally, we need to formalize the notions of trust and examine ways to negotiate trust on the semantic Web. We have a good start and are well on our way to building the semantic Web. Security must be considered at the beginning and not as an afterthought.

Standards play an important role in the development of the semantic Web. The W3C has been very effective in specifying standards for XML and RDF. We need to continue with development and try as much as possible to transfer the research effort to the standards efforts. We also need to transfer the research and standards to commercial products. The next step for the semantic Web standards efforts is to examine security, privacy, quality of service, integrity, and other features such as secure-query services. As we have stressed, security and privacy are critical and must be investigated while standards are being developed.

References

[AGRA00] Agrawal, R. and R. Srikant, Privacy-preserving data mining, *Proc. ACM SIG-MOD Conf.*, Dallas, TX, May 2000.

[ANT003] Antoniou, G., and F. Van Harmelen, *A Semantic Web Primer*, MIT Press, Cambridge, MA 2003.

[ATKI03] Atkins, D. et al., Cyber Infrastructure, NSF Report, http://www.community-technology.org/nsf_ci_report/.

[BERT02] Bertino, E. et al., Access control for XML documents, *Data Knowledge Eng.*, 43(3), 2002.

[BERT04] Bertino, E. et al., Secure third party publication of XML documents, *IEEE Trans. Knowledge and Data Eng.*, 10, 2004.

[BHAT04] Bhatty R., E. Bertino, and A. Ghafoor, Trust-based context aware access control models in Web services, *Proc. Web Services Conf.*, San Diego, July 2004.

[CARM04] Carminati, B. et al., Security for RDF, *Proc. DEXA Conf. Workshop on Web Semantics*, Zaragoza, Spain, 2004.

[CHEN76] Chen, P., The entity relationships model—toward a unified view of data, *ACM Trans. Database Syst.*, 1, 1976,

[CLIF02] Clifton, C., M. Kantarcioglu, and J. Vaidya, Defining Privacy for Data Mining, Purdue University, 2002 (see also Next Generation Data Mining Workshop, Baltimore, MD, November 2002).

[DENK03] Denker, G. et al., Security for DAML Web Services: Annotation and Match making, International Semantic Web Conference, Sanibel Island, FL, 2003.

[EVFI02] Evfimievski, A., R. Srikant, R. Agrawal, and J. Gehrke, Privacy preserving mining of association rules, *Proc. Eighth ACM SIGKDD Int. Conf. Knowledge Discovery and Data Mining*, Edmonton, Alberta, Canada, July 2002.

[FARK03] Farkas, C. et al., Inference problem for the semantic Web, *Proc. IFIP Conf. Data Applications Security*, Colorado, August 2003, Kluwer, Dordrecht, The Netherlands, 2004.

[FOWL97] Fowler, M., *UML Distilled: Applying the Standard Object Modeling Language*, Addison-Wesley, Reading, MA, 1997.

[GEHR02] Gehrke, J., Research problems in data stream processing and privacy-preserving data mining, *Proc. Next Generation Data Mining Workshop*, Baltimore, MD, November 2002.

[HACI02] Hacigumus, H. et al., Providing database as a service, *Proc. IEEE Data Engineering Conf.*, San Jose, CA, March 2002.

[KAGA03] Kagal, L., T.W. Finin, and A. Joshi, A Policy Based Approach to Security for the Semantic Web, International Semantic Web Conference, Sanibel Island, FL, 2003.

[ROUR04] Roure D. et al., E-Science, *IEEE Intelligent Syst.*, January/February 2004.

[SHET90] Sheth, A. and J. Larson, Federated database systems, *ACM Comput.Surveys*, 22(3), 1990.

[THUR93] Thuraisingham, B. et al, Design and implementation of a database inference controller, *Data Knowledge Eng. J.* 11(3), 1993.

[THUR94] Thuraisingham, B., Security issues for federated database systems, *Comput. Security*, 13(6), 1994.

[THUR97] Thuraisingham, B., *Data Management Systems Evolution and Interoperation*, CRC Press, Boca Raton, FL, 1995.

[THUR02a] Thuraisingham, B., Data and Applications Security Developments and Directions, *Proc. IEEE Comput. Software and Applications Conf.* (COMPSAC), Oxford, UK, 2002.

[THUR02b] Thuraisingham, B., *XML, Databases and the Semantic Web* CRC Press, Boca Raton, FL, 2002.

[THUR03] Thuraisingham, B., *Web Data Mining and Applications in Business, Intelligence, and Counter-Terrorism*, CRC Press, Boca Raton, FL, 2003.

[THUR06] Thuraisingham, B. et al., Administering the semantic Web, confidentiality, privacy and trust, *J. Inf. Security Privacy*, 2006.

[YU03] Yu, T. and M. Winslett, A Unified Scheme for Resource Protection in Automated Trust Negotiation, IEEE Symposium on Security and Privacy, Oakland, CA., May 2003.

[XML1] http://xml.apache.org/security/.

[XML2] http://www.w3.org/Signature/.

[XML3] http://www.w3.org/Encryption/2001/.

Exercises

1. Describe with examples the need for security for the semantic Web (include confidentiality, privacy, and trust).
2. Conduct a survey of the various efforts on security for the semantic Web.

Chapter 6

Security and XML

6.1 Overview

In Chapter 4 we provided an overview of the semantic Web, and in Chapter 5 we discussed a secure semantic Web. As we have stated earlier, eXtensible Markup Language (XML) has become the standard language for document exchange and, more recently, data and information interoperability. The components of XML include elements, attributes, document-type definitions (DTDs), schemas, and namespaces. We have discussed these concepts in our previous book [THUR02]. For an excellent exposition of XML and the semantic Web we refer to the book by Antoniou and van Harmelan [ANTO03].

In this chapter we will discuss further security issues for XML. Note that there are two aspects: one is securing XML documents, and the other is using XML to specify policies. We will discuss both aspects. We will give examples and show how access-control rules can be enforced on XML documents. We will also discuss security for XML schemas and security for namespaces. Then we will discuss how policies can be expressed in XML. One of the advantages with a specification language such as XML is that one can specify rules in this language. However, because XML represents data, policies specified in XML can only be enforced on data represented in XML.

The organization of this chapter is as follows. In Section 6.2 we give a sample document that we will use in this chapter to discuss security issues. We discuss issues in XML security such as securing XML data, DTDs, schemas, and namespaces in Section 6.3. In Section 6.4, we discuss the specification of security policies in XML. Access control for XML including query modification is discussed in

Section 6.5. Third-party publication of XML documents as discussed in the research by Bertino et al. [BERT04] is discussed in Section 6.6. Secure management of XML databases is the subject of Section 6.7. Distribution of XML documents is the subject of Section 6.8. In Section 6.9, we discuss the standards efforts on secure XML including the work of the World Wide Web Consortium (W3C) and the Organization for the Advancement of Structured Information Standards (OASIS). Finally, the chapter is summarized in Section 6.10.

6.2   Sample XML Document

In this section we give an example of an XML document both in graphical format and XML format. Then we discuss the XML DTD and the XML schema for this document. Our discussion of XML security has been influenced a great deal by the work of Bertino, Carminati, and Ferrari at the University of Milan [BERT02], [BERT04].

6.2.1 XML Specification for the Graph in Figure 6.1

```
<? xml version="1.0" encoding="UTF-16"?>
<Annual-Report Year="2003" Name="UTD">
        <Assets>
            <Asset Dept="CS">
                    <Expenses Total="400" />
                    <Funds>
                        <Fund Date="060103" Type="NSF" Amount="1"
            />
                            .
                            .
                            .
                    </Funds>
            </Asset>
                .
                .
                .
        </Assets>
        <Patents>
        <Patent PID="12345" Date="030704" Dept="UTD" Short-
        desc="This patent deals with Semantic Web Technologies"
        Tech-details="Deals with XML, RDF and OWL technologies"
        Author="Prof XXX" />
        .
        .
        </Patents>
```

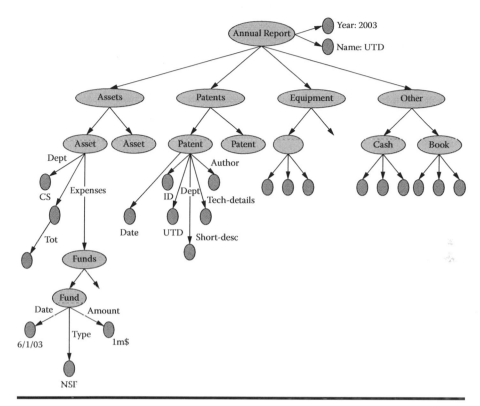

Figure 6.1 Example XML document.

```
<Equipment>
.
.
</Equipment>
<Other>
<Cash />
<Books />
</Other>
</Annual-Report>
```

6.2.2 XML DTD for the Above XML Specification

```
<! ELEMENT Annual-Report (Assets, Patents, Equipment, Others)>
<! ATTLIST Annual-Report
    Year ID #REQUIRED
    Name CDATA #REQUIRED >
<! ELEMENT Assets (Asset *)>
<! ELEMENT Asset (Expenses, Funds)
```

```
<! ATTLIST Asset
    Dept ID #REQUIRED>
<! ELEMENT Expenses>
<! ATTLIST Expenses
    Total CDATA #REQUIRED>
<! ELEMENT Funds (Fund*)>
<! ELEMENT Fund>
<! ATTLIST Fund
    Date CDATA #REQUIRED
    Type CDATA #REQUIRED
    Amount CDATA #REQUIRED>
<! ELEMENT Patents (Patent*)>
<! ELEMENT Patent>
<! ATTLIST Patent
    PID ID
    Date CDATA #REQUIRED
    Dept CDATA #REQUIRED
    Short-desc CDATA #REQUIRED
    Tech-details CDATA #REQUIRED
    Author CDATA #REQUIRED>
<! ELEMENT Equipment>
<! ELEMENT Other (Cash, Books)>
<! ELEMENT Cash>
<! ELEMENT Books>
```

6.2.3 XML Schema for the Above XML Specification

```
<? xml version="1.0" encoding="UTF-16"?>
<element name="Annual-Report" type="reportType"/>
<complexType name="reportType">
    <sequence>
        <element name="Assets" type="assetsType" minOccurs=1
        maxOccurs=1 />
        <element name="Patents" type="patentsType" minOccurs=1
        maxOccurs=1 />
        <element name="Equipment" type="equipmentType" minOc-
        curs=1 maxOccurs=1 />
        <element name="Other" type="otherType" minOccurs=1 maxOc-
        curs=1 />
    </sequence>
</complexType>

<complexType name="assetsType">
    <sequence>
        <element name="Asset" type="assetType" minOccurs=0 maxOc-
        curs="unbounded" />
```

```
      </sequence>
</complexType>

<complexType name="assetType">
    <sequence>
       <attribute name="Dept" type="string" use="required" />
       <element name="Expenses" type="expensesType" minOccurs=1
       maxOccurs=1 />
       <element name="Funds" type="FundsType" minOccurs=1 maxOc-
       curs=1/>
    </sequence>
</complexType>

<complexType name="expensesType">
        <attribute name="Total" type="string" use="required" />
</complexType>

<complexType name="FundsType">
    <sequence
       <element name="Fund" type="fundType" minOccurs=0 maxOc-
       curs="unbounded" />
    </sequence>
</complexType>

<complexType name="fundType">
        <attribute name="Date" type="string" use="required" />
        <attribute name="Type" type="string" use="required" />
        <attribute name="Amount" type="integer" use="required" />
</complexType>

<complexType name="patentsType">
    <sequence>
       <element name="Patent" type="patentType" minOccurs=0 maxOc-
       curs="unbounded" />
    </sequence>
</complexType>

<complexType name="patentType">
        <attribute name="Date" type="string" use="required" />
        <attribute name="ID" type="integer" use="required" />
        <attribute name="Dept" type="string" use="required" />
        <attribute name="Short-desc" type="string" use="required" />
        <attribute name="Tech-details" type="string" use="required" />
        <attribute name="Author" type="string" use="required" />
</complexType>

<complexType name="equipmentType">
    <sequence>
```

```
    </sequence>
</complexType>

<complexType name="otherType">
    <sequence>
       <element name="Cash" type="cashType" minOccurs=1 maxOc-
       curs="1" />
       <element name="Books="booksType" minOccurs=1 maxOc-
       curs="1" />
    /sequence>
</complexType>
```

6.3   Issues in XML Security

In this section we will discuss the various components of XML and examine the security impact. Note that we will discuss only discretionary security. Multilevel security is the subject of Chapter 13.

6.3.1 XML Elements

First, let us consider the following XML statement that John Smith is a professor in Texas. This can be expressed as follows:

```
<Professor>
    <name> John Smith </name>
    <state> Texas </state>
</Professor>
```

Now suppose this data can be read by anyone; then we can augment the XML statement by an additional element called access, as follows:

```
<Professor>
    <name> John Smith </name>
    <state> Texas </state>
    <access> All, Read </access>
</Professor>
```

If only the human resources department can update this XML statement, then we have the following:

```
<Professor>
    <name> John Smith </name>
    <state> Texas </state>
    <access> HR department, Write </access>
</Professor>
```

Note that there are issues with negative authorizations; that is, when an authorization is not specified, then one can assume that the authorization is negative. Furthermore, we have given access to both elements of Professor, and they are name and state. We could have more specialized statements that give access to elements such as name or state. For example, we may not wish for everyone to know that John Smith is a professor, but we can give out the information that this professor is in Texas. This can be expressed as the following:

```
<Professor>
    <name> John Smith, Govt-official, Read </name>
    <state> Texas, All, Read </state>
    <access> HR department, Write </access>
</Professor>
```

Note that in discussing access-control policies we are giving our own opinions and not the standards. Standards will be discussed later on in this chapter. Also some alternative ways to specifying policies in XML are discussed in Section 6.4.

6.3.2 XML Attributes

Next let us examine the concept of attributes in XML. Suppose we want to specify access based on attribute values. One way to specify such access is given below.

```
<Professor
    Name = "John Smith", Access = All, Read
    Salary = "60K", Access = Administrator, Read, Write
    Department = "Security" Access = All, Read
</Professor
```

Here we assume that everyone can read the name John Smith and Department Security. But only the administrator can read and write the salary attribute.

6.3.3 XML DTDs

Next let us examine the notion of DTDs. DTDs essentially specify the structure of XML documents. Consider the following DTD for Professor with elements Name and State. This will be specified as:

```
<!ELEMENT Professor Officer (Name, State)>
<!ELEMENT name (#PCDATA)>
<!ELEMENR state (#PCDATA)>
<!ELEMENT access (#PCDATA).>
```

For a discussion of #PCDATA we refer the reader to Reference [ANTO04]. We can give DTDs for the other examples given in this section such as assigning access to each element. In this case we may need an element within an element to specify access to, say, name and access to state.

6.3.4 XML Schemas

Although DTDs were early attempts to specify structure for XML documents, XML schemas are far more elegant to specify structures. Unlike DTDs, XML schemas essentially use the XML syntax for specification. Consider the following example:

```
<ComplexType = name = "ProfessorType">
    <Sequence>
    <element name = "name" type = "string"/>
    <element name = "state" type = "string"/>
    <element name = "access" type = "strong/>
<Sequence>
</ComplexType>
```

6.3.5 Namespaces

Finally, let us examine namespaces. Note that namespaces are used for disambiguation. Because different groups may come up with different XML specifications for the same concept, namespaces are used to resolve conflicts. Consider the concept of academic institutions. In the United Kingdom they may be called universities and in the United States they may be called colleges. This can be specified using the concept of namespaces as follows:

```
<CountryX: Academic-Institution
    Xmlns: CountryX = "http://www.CountryX.edu/InstitutionDTD"
    Xmlns: USA = http://www.USA.edu/InstituutionDTD"
    Xmlns: UK = http://www.UK.edy/InstitutionDTD
    <USA: Title = College
        USA: Name = "University of Texas at Dallas"
        USA: State = Texas"
    <UK: Title = University
        UK: Name = "Cambridge University"
        UK: State = Cambs
</CountryX: Academic-Institution>
```

One could assign access to the components of the namespaces discussed above as follows:

```
<Country: Academic-Institution
<Access = Government-official, Read </Access>
    Xmlns: CountryX = "http://www.CountryX.edu/InstitutionDTD"
    Xmlns: USA = http://www.USA.edu/InstitutionDTD"
    Xmlns: UK = "http://www.UK.edu/InstitutionDTD"
    <USA: Title = College
       USA: Name = "University of Texas at Dallas"
       USA: State = Texas"
    <UK: Title = University
       UK: Name = "Cambridge University"
       UK: State = Cambs
    </CountryX: Academic-Institution>
```

This means only government officials have read access to the information in the above XML statement. We will revisit this again when we discuss ontologies and interoperability in the ensuing chapters.

6.4 Policy Specification in XML

Whereas XML documents have to be secure, XML can be used to specify the policies. In this section we discuss some sample policies using XML. In particular, we discuss credential specification as well as policy specification.

6.4.1 Credentials

Credentials are certificates that a user may posses to carry out his or her job. For example, if Alice has the credential of a professor then she may grade exams, teach courses, and also advise students. We give examples below.

```
<Professor credID="9" subID = "16: CIssuer = "2">
    <name> Alice Brown </name>
    <university> University of X <university/>
    <department> CS </department>
    <research-group> Security </research-group>
</Professor>

<Secretary credID="12" subID = "4: CIssuer = "2">
    <name> John James </name>
    <university> University of X <university/>
    <department> CS </department>
    <level> Senior </level>
</Secretary>
```

6.4.2 *Policies*

```
<? Xml VERSION = "1.0" ENCODING = "utf-8"?>
  <Policy-base>

    <policy-spec cred-expr = "//Professor[department = 'CS']"
    target =
  "annual_ report.xml" path = "//Patent[@Dept = 'CS']//Node()"
    priv = "VIEW"/>

    <policy-spec cred-expr = "//Professor[department = 'CS']"
    target =
    "annual_ report.xml" path = "//Patent[@Dept = 'EE'] /
    Short-descr/Node() and
    //Patent [@Dept = 'EE']/authors" priv = "VIEW"/>

  <policy-spec cred-expr = - - - -

  <policy-spec cred-expr = - - --

</Policy-base>
```

Explanation: CS professors are entitled to access all the patents of their department. They are entitled to see only the short descriptions and authors of patents of the electrical engineering department

A more complete specification of six policies P1 – P6 as discussed in [BERT04] is described below.

```
<?xml version="1.0" encoding="UTF-8"?>
<policy_base>
...

  <policy_spec ID='P1' cred_expr="//Professor[department='CS']" tar-
  get="annual_report.xml" path="//Patent[@Dept='CS']//node()"
  priv="VIEW"/>
  <policy_spec ID-'P2' cred_expr="//Professor[department='CS']" tar-
  get="annual_report.xml" path="//Patent[@Dept='IST']/Short-descr/node()
  and //Patent[@Dept='IST']/authors" priv="VIEW"/>
  <policy_spec ID='P3' cred_expr="//Professor[department='IST'] " tar-
  get="annual_report.xml" path="//Patent[@Dept='IST']//node()"
  priv="VIEW"/>
  <policy_spec ID='P4' cred_expr="//Professor[department='IST']" tar-
  get="annual_report.xml" path="//Patent[@Dept='CS']/Short-descr/node()
  and //Patent[@Dept='CS']/authors" priv="VIEW"/>
```

```
<policy_spec ID='P5' cred_expr="//secretary[department='CS' and
level='junior']" target="annual_report.xml"
path="//Asset[@Dept='CS']/node()" priv="VIEW "/>
<policy_spec ID='P6' cred_expr="//secretary[department='CS' and
level='senior']" target="annual_report.xml"
path="//Asset[@Dept='IST']/Funds/@Type and
//Asset[@Dept='IST']/Funds/@Funding-Date" priv="VIEW "/>
<policy_spec ID='P7' cred_expr="//secretary[department='IST' and
level='junior']" target="annual_report.xml"
path="//Asset[@Dept='IST']/node()" priv="VIEW "/>
...
</policy_base>
```

6.5 Access Control for XML Documents

Bertino et al. were one of the first to examine security for XML [BERT02],[BERT04]. They first proposed a framework for access control for XML documents and then discussed a technique for ensuring authenticity and completeness of a document for third-party publishing. We will briefly discuss some of the key issues.

In the access-control framework proposed by Bertino et al. [BERT02], security policy is specified depending on user roles and credentials (see Figure 6.2). Users must possess the credentials to access XML documents. The credentials depend on

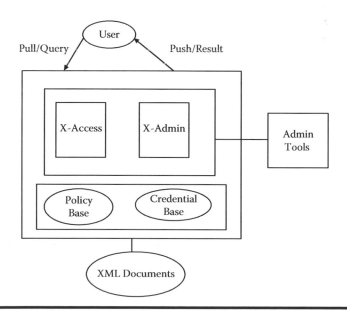

Figure 6.2   Access control for XML documents.

their roles. For example, a professor has access to all the details of students, whereas a secretary has access only to administrative information. XML specifications are used to specify the security policies. Access is granted for an entire XML document or portions of the document. Under certain conditions, access control may be propagated down the XML tree. For example, if access is granted to the root, it does not necessarily mean access is granted to all the children. One may grant access to the DTDs and not to the document instances. One may grant access to certain portions of the document. For example, a professor does not have access to the medical information of students although he has access to student grades and academic information. The design of a system for enforcing access-control policies is also described in Reference [BERT02]. Essentially the goal is to use a form of view modification so that the user is authorized to see the XML views as specified by the policies. More research needs to be done on role-based access control for XML and the semantic Web.

As discussed in Reference [BERT02], the algorithms for access control are as follows:

■ Subjects request access to XML documents under two modes: browsing and authoring
  – With browsing access the subject can read and navigate documents.
  – Authoring access is needed to modify, delete, and append documents.
■ An access-control module checks the policy base and applies policy specifications.
■ Views of the document are created based on credentials and policy specifications.
■ In case of conflict, the least-access privilege rule is enforced.

6.6   Secure Publication of XML Documents

In Reference [BERT04] secure publication of XML documents was discussed (see Figure 6.3). The idea is to have untrusted third-party publishers. The owner of a document specifies access-control polices for the subjects. Subjects get the policies from the owner when they subscribe to a document. The owner sends the documents to the publisher. When the subject requests a document, the publisher will apply the policies relevant to the subject and give portions of the documents to the subject. Now, since the publisher is untrusted, it may give false information to the subject. Therefore, the owner will encrypt various combinations of documents and policies with his or her private key. Using a Merkle signature and encryption techniques, the subject can verify the authenticity and completeness of the document (see Figure 6.3 for secure publishing of XML documents).

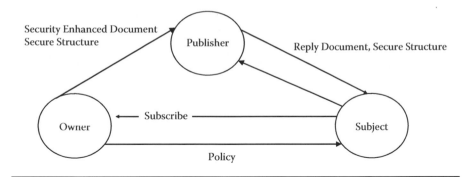

Figure 6.3   Secure XML publishing.

In the work by Bertino et al., the notion of security-enhanced XML documents to ensure the authenticity of a document was defined; that is, the owner of an XML document will develop the security-enhanced version of the document and send it to the publisher with some additional information. When a user queries for a document, the publisher will give the user the document he is authorized to see, together with some other information based on the security-enhanced version of the document. The user then verifies the authenticity of the document. To check for completeness, that is, whether the user has received everything he or she should receive, the owner sends to the publisher the secure structure of an XML document together with the security-enhanced XML document. The publisher sends this secure structure together with the response to the user for a query. The user uses this information and verifies the completeness of the response [BERT04].

6.7   Secure XML Databases

Various commercial vendors of data-management systems such as Oracle are now developing capabilities to manage XML databases. In particular, query, transaction, metadata management, access methods, and indexing algorithms are being developed for XML databases. Data is presented as XML documents. Query languages are being developed including XML-QL and XQuery.

Security has to be incorporated into these XML databases. For example, access-control policies that we have discussed in the previous sections have to be enforced on XML databases. In addition, query modification has to be examined for XML data management. Note that query modification is essentially about modifying the queries according to the security policies. For example, if professors in the computer science department cannot access the trade secrets in the electrical engineering department and if a professor in the computer science department requests the assets in the electrical engineering department, the query is modified to retrieve all the assets, provided these assets are not trade secrets in the electrical engineering department. This example is illustrated below.

Dr. Thuraisingham is a professor of Computer Sciences and requests the folowing query.
select Asset
from {EE} depOnt:hasAssets {Asset}
using namespace
    deptOnt = http://www.example.com/departmentOntology#

New modified query:

select Asset
from {EE} depOnt:hasAsset {Asset}
Where (not {Asset} rdf:type deptOnt:TradeSec)
using namespace
    deptOnt = http://www.example.com/departmentOntology#

Security for XML databases has not received much attention. We need to integrate the research carried out by Bertino and her team into data-management systems such as Oracle.

6.8   Secure Distribution and Federation of XML Documents

6.8.1   Distribution

XML documents may be distributed across sites or used in federated data-management systems for coalition data sharing. Therefore, security has to be provided for secure sharing and distributed XML documents. Whereas we discuss this aspect in more detail in Part IV, when we discuss applications of a secure semantic Web, in this section we discuss some preliminary issues.

Consider the distribution of XML documents. One option to enforce security is to encrypt different portions of the document with different keys and distribute them. For example, if a user, John, should be given read access to the document, then the document is encrypted with the public key of John, Then John can decrypt the document with his private key. This is not efficient because if 10 users are to be given access, then there are 10 different encrypted versions for the document. Another option is to enforce access-control rules across documents. Suppose we have the following document replicated at multiple sites:

```
<Professor>
    <Name> John Smith </name>
    <State> Texas </state>
    <Access> All, Read </access>
</Professor>
```

The rule that everyone can read this document is enforced at each site. Consider more complex rules such as names and salaries cannot be accessed together.

6.8.2 *Rule*

Names and salaries taken together can be accessed only by administrators.

```
<Administrators>
    Only
    <Name> </name>
    <Salary> </salary>
    Together
    <Access> Read </access>
</Administrator>
```

Note that the above specification is quite complex. Therefore, we may need to express such rules using path expressions that we discussed in the previous section.

Furthermore, if names are stored in an XML document in Site 1 and salaries are stored in another XML document in Site 2 as shown below, then the rule is enforced across the sites and it has to be ensured that names and salaries are not displayed together. Essentially the link between names and salaries has to be protected.

6.8.2.1 *Site 1 Document*

```
<Professor-name>
    <ID> 111 </ID>
    <Name> John Smith </name>
    <State> Texas </state>
</Professor-name>
```

6.8.2.2 *Site 2 Document*

```
<Professor-salary>
    <ID> 111 </ID>
    <salary> 60K </salary>
<Professor-salary>
```

Note that we now have ambiguity. The document professor is referred to as Professor-name in Site 1 and Professor-salary in Site 2. We use the XML namespace mechanism for disambiguation.

```
<Site1: Professor
    Xmlns: SiteX = "http://www.SiteX.edu/TeacherDTD"
    Xmlns: Site1 = http://www.Site1.edu/TeacherDTD"
    Xmlns: Site2 = http://www.Site2.edu/TeacherDTD
    <Site1: Title = Professor-Name
        Site1: ID= "111"
        Site1: Name = John Smith
    <Site2: ID = Professor-Salary
        Site2: ID = "111"
        Site2: Salary = 60K
    </SiteX: Professor>
```

6.8.3 Federations

In a heterogeneous and federated environment, each component organization may publish its schema in XML. This way the documents can be exported and integrated at the federation level. In the case of security, each site may enforce its own security policy on the XML documents. The challenge is to integrate these policies to form a consistent set of policies at the federation. We will revisit interoperability and data sharing in Part IV.

6.9 Standards

In this section we discuss some of the major standards for XML security. In particular, we will discuss the developments with W3C and OASIS. A list of some of the developments with these organizations is given in Appendix C (see also Reference [W3C] and Reference [OASIS]).

The W3C has developed three major standards related to security. They are the following: XML Encryption, XML Key Management, and XML Signature. The XML Encryption Working Group has developed a process to encrypt and decrypt digital content, which includes XML documents. This group does not address XML security issues. XML Key Management Working Group has developed a protocol for a client to obtain key information (e.g., value, certificates, etc.) to form a Web service. This group also does not address the security issues. As stated in Reference [W3C], the XML Signature Working Group has developed "an XML-compliant syntax used for representing the signature of Web resources and portions of protocol messages (anything referencable by a URI) and procedures for computing and verifying such signatures." Like the first two groups, this group also does not address XML security issues.

OASIS is the standards organization promoting security standards for Web services. It is a not-for-profit global consortium that drives the development, convergence, and adoption of E-business standards. Two standards provided by OASIS are eXtensible Access Control Markup Language (XACML) and Security Assertion Markup Language (SAML). XACML provides fine-grained control of authorized activities, the effect of characteristics of the access requestor, the protocol over which the request is made, authorization based on classes of activities, and content introspection. SAML is an XML framework for exchanging authentication and authorization information. Part IV provides details on both XACML and SAML, as well as more details on some of the OASIS standards for Web services.

6.10 Summary and Directions

This chapter has provided an overview of XML security. We first discussed issues on securing XML documents including security issues for XML elements, attributes, and schemas. Then we discussed the use of XML for specifying security policies. We also discussed the secure publications of XML documents. Much of our research on XML security is the result of collaboration with Bertino and her team at the University of Milan.

As we have discussed, XML is widely used as it has become not only the desired document representation language for exchange on the Web, but also the schema specification language for integrating heterogeneous databases. XML has been extended for numerous applications in multiple domains. Some of these extensions will be discussed in Parts IV and V.

XML security has also received some attention both in the standards community as well as in the research community. However, the progression of standards for security specifications is lagging behind the research. We need a more effective approach to transfer the research to standards and products. Another issue is the numerous versions of XML floating around. We need to develop some consensus. Whereas organizations such as W3C and OASIS are moving in the right direction, we need better coordination between the diverse groups. Nevertheless, we believe that one of the significant developments in computing during the past decade is the semantic Web in general and XML in particular. Therefore, we need to continue to make enhancements to XML and XML security to realize the ultimate goal of Tim Berners Lee and that is to have machine-readable Web pages.

References

[ANTO03] Antoniou, G. and F. van Harmelan, *A Semantic Web Primer*, MIT Press, Cambridge, MA, 2003.

[BERT02] Bertino, E. et al., Access control for XML documents, *Data Knowledge Eng.*, 43(3), 2002.

[BERT04] Bertino, E. et al., Secure third party publication of XML documents, *IEEE Trans. Knowledge Data Eng.*, October 2004.

[OASIS] Organization for the Advancement of Structured Information Standards. http://www.oasis-open.org/home/index.php.

[THUR01] Thuraisingham, B., *XML, Databases and the Semantic Web*, CRC Press, Boca Raton, FL, 2001.

[W3C] World Wide Web Consortium, www.w3c.org.

Exercises

1. Investigate security issues for XML documents.
2. Specify complex policies in XML.
3. Design an application, and show how secure XML can be used.

Chapter 7

Security and RDF

7.1 Overview

In this chapter we continue with a discussion of the security issues for semantic Web technologies. In particular, we discuss security issues for Resource Description Framework (RDF). As we stated in Chapter 4, RDF uses the syntax of eXtensible Markup Language (XML). Furthermore, whereas XML is not sufficient to express semantics, RDF attempts to address the inadequacies of XML.

Little work has been carried out for securing RDF documents. An early effort is the work of Carminati et al., who discussed a security architecture for RDF [CARM04]. Some further security issues for RDF and the inference problem are discussed in Reference [FARK06]. Whereas standards are being developed for secure XML including the work of the Organization for the Advancement of Structured Information Standards (OASIS) and the World Wide Web Consortium (W3C), little work is reported on standards for securing RDF. In this chapter we attempt to provide a fairly broad overview of what needs to be carried out for securing RDF documents. For a detailed discussion of RDF concepts we refer the reader to Reference [ANTO03].

The organization of this chapter is as follows. We give an example of an RDF document in Section 7.2. In Section 7.3, we discuss security issues for RDF. In particular, we examine each concept in RDF and discuss the security impact. Specification of policies in RDF is discussed in Section 7.4. Access control is the subject of Section 7.5. Managing secure RDF databases is discussed in Section 7.6. The chapter is summarized in Section 7.7.

7.2   Example of an RDF Document

In this section we give an example of an RDF document. The following example illustrates a part of an RDF document describing the books *Building_Trustworthy_ Semantic_Webs* and *Managing_and_Mining_Multimedia_Databases*. They belong to the class "Book" and have properties of author, publisher, year, and ISBN.

7.2.1   RDF Document

```
<?xml version="1.0"?>
<rdf:RDF
xmlns:book="http://www.example.com/book#"
xmlns:owl="http://www.w3.org/2002/07/owl#"
xmlns:rdf="http://www.w3.org/1999/02/22-rdf-syntax-ns#"
xmlns:rdfs="http://www.w3.org/2000/01/rdf-schema#">
<book:Book rdf:ID="Building_Trustworthy_Semantic_Webs">
    <book:author>Bhavani Thuraisingham</book:author>
    <book:publisher>Auerbach Publications</book:publisher>
    <book:year>2007</book:year>
    <book:ISBN>0849350808</book:ISBN>
</book:Book>

<book:Book rdf:ID="Managing_and_Mining_Multimedia_Databases">
    <book:author>Bhavani Thuraisingham</book:author>
    <book:publisher>CRC Press</book:publisher>
    <book:year>2001</book:year>
    <book:ISBN>0849300371</book:ISBN>
</book:Book>
</rdf:RDF>
```

7.2.2   RDF Schema with Policy Specification

For a larger set of RDF properties, refer to http://www.w3.org/TR/rdf-schema/. The RDF schema for the above RDF document is as follows:

```
<?xml version="1.0"?>
<rdf:RDF
    xmlns:owl="http://www.w3.org/2002/07/owl#"
    xmlns:rdf="http://www.w3.org/1999/02/22-rdf-syntax-ns#"
    xmlns:rdfs="http://www.w3.org/2000/01/rdf-schema#"
    xmlns:wsp="http://www.w3.org/2004/08/20-ws-pol-pos/ns#">

    <rdfs:Class rdf:ID="Book">
      <rdfs:comment>Book Class</rdfs:comment>
```

```
        <rdfs:subClassOf rdf:resource="http://www.w3.org/1999/02/22-rdf-
syntax-ns#Resource"/>
    </rdfs:Class>
    <rdf:Property rdf:ID="author">
        <rdfs:Comment>Author of the book</rdfs:Comment>
        <rdfs:domain rdf:resource="#Book"/>
        <rdfs:range rdf:resource="http://www.w3.org/1999/02/22-rdf-
syntax-ns#Literal"/>
    </rdf:Property>

    <rdf:Property rdf:ID="publisher">
        <rdfs:Comment>Publisher of the book</rdfs:Comment>
        <rdfs:domain rdf:resource="#Book"/>
        <rdfs:range rdf:resource="http://www.w3.org/1999/02/22-rdf-
syntax-ns#Literal"/>
    </rdf:Property>

    <rdf:Property rdf:ID="year">
        <rdfs:Comment>Year of first publication of the book</rdfs:Comment>
        <rdfs:domain rdf:resource="#Book"/>
        <rdfs:range rdf:resource="http://www.w3.org/1999/02/22-rdf-
syntax-ns#Literal"/>
    </rdf:Property>

    <rdf:Property rdf:ID="ISBN">
        <rdfs:Comment>ISBN of the book</rdfs:Comment>
        <rdfs:domain rdf:resource="#Book"/>
        <rdfs:range rdf:resource="http://www.w3.org/1999/02/22-rdf-
syntax-ns#Literal"/>
    </rdf:Property>
</rdf:RDF>
```

7.3   Issues in RDF Security

7.3.1 *Basic Concepts*

The basic concepts of RDF are resources, properties, and statements [ANTO03]. In this section we discuss these concepts from a security point of view.

7.3.1.1 *Resources*

Resources are objects such as airplanes, tables, and people. A resource has an identifier called Universal Resource Identifier (URI). The question is, what are the access-control policies for resources? For example, if the book "Semantic Web" is a resource, then who can access the book? Can a person have read access to certain parts of the book? Can a multilevel security policy be enforced for a book? Can different parts of the book have different security levels? Should we control access to the existence of the book? These are the policy questions that need to be answered for a specific application.

7.3.1.2   Properties

Properties are a special kind of resource and describe relationships between resources. The example of a property is "written by". For example, the statement "Semantic Web book is written by Berners Lee" is a property. Essentially it is a relationship between the resources "semantic Web" and "Berners Lee". With respect to security, the question is, can we allow access to the resources and not to the relationship between the resources? For example, John could have access to the resource semantic Web book and also to the resource Berners Lee. But John does not have access to the property "written by."

7.3.1.3   Statements

As discussed in the previous paragraph, a statement asserts the properties of the resources. It is a triple entity (object, attribute, value). Here the object could be the semantic Web book, the attribute is written by, and the value is Berners Lee. As stated in Reference [ANTO03], value could be resources or literals. One would also have a statement "Berners Lee writes the semantic Web book". The security considerations here are granting access to, say, the attribute and not to the object or value. Alternatively, one could grant access to the object and value but not to the attribute. Graphical representations such as semantic models can be used to represent a statement as described in Chapter 4. However, the goal of the semantic Web is to develop machine-readable technologies. Therefore, we can use RDF to specify resources, attributes, and statements. This will be discussed in Section 7.3.2 when we give examples of RDF documents. Figure 7.1 illustrates the classification levels assigned to an RDF statement.

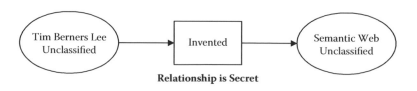

Figure 7.1   Classifying an RDF statement.

7.3.1.4   Reification

This means "a statement about statements," such as, Bhavani believes that Berners Lee is the inventor of the semantic Web. So the security questions are, do we classify what Bhavani believes, or do we classify that she believes in something? If we classify "Bhavani believes," then essentially what we are saying is that someone believes that Berners Lee is the inventor of the semantic Web. If we classify what she believes in, then what we are saying is that Bhavani believes in something, but we do not know what it is. That is, we do not know that she believes in the fact that Tim Berners Lee is the inventor of the semantic Web.

7.3.1.5   Data Types

This is the same notion as data types in languages and systems. How should, say, a literal be considered? Is it an integer or a string? Typed literals are provided through XML schemas. The security considerations for XML schemas apply here also.

7.3.2   Advanced Concepts

In this section we discuss some of the advanced concepts in RDF along with security properties. Below we describe a complex RDF statement and show how it may be classified.

```
<rdf: RDF
    xmlns: rdf = "http://w3c.org/1999/02-22-rdf-syntax-ns#"
    xmlns: uni = "http://www.example.com/universityonto#">

<rdf: Description rdf:about = "949352"
    <uni: name> Berners Lee</uni:name>
    <uni: title> Professor </uni:title>
Level = L1
</rdf: Description>

<rdf: Description rdf: about: "ZZZ">
    <uni: bookname> semantic Web </uni:bookname>
    <uni: authoredby> Berners Lee </uni:authoredby>
Level = L2
</rdf: Description>
</rdf: RDF>
```

7.3.2.1   RDF Schema

Unlike an XML schema that describes an XML document, an RDF schema is used to specify some relationships such as the subclass relationship. The following example classifies the relationship that all engineers are a subclass of employees.

```
<rdfs: Class rdf: ID = "engineer"
<rdfs: comment>
The class of Engineers
All engineers are employees.
<rdfs: comment>
<rdfs: subClassof rdf: resource = "Employee"/>
Level = L
<rdfs: Class>
```

7.4   Policy Specification in RDF

The examples we have discussed in Section 7.2 show how certain policies may be specified for RDF documents. A more detailed example is given below.

```
<?xml version="1.0"?>
<rdf:RDF
xmlns:book="http://www.example.com/book#"
xmlns:owl="http://www.w3.org/2002/07/owl#"
xmlns:rdf="http://www.w3.org/1999/02/22-rdf-syntax-ns#"
xmlns:rdfs="http://www.w3.org/2000/01/rdf-schema#">

<book:Book rdf:ID="Building_Trustworthy_Semantic_Webs">
    <book:author>Bhavani Thuraisingham</book:author>
    Level = Secret
    <book:publisher>Auerbach Publications</book:publisher>
    Level = Confidential
    <book:year>2007</book:year>
    Level = Unclassified
    <book:ISBN>0849350808</book:ISBN>
    Level = Confidential
</book:Book>

<book:Book rdf:ID="Managing_and_Mining_Multimedia_Databases">
    Level = Confidential
    <book:author>Bhavani Thuraisingham</book:author>
    Level = Secret
    <book:publisher>CRC Press</book:publisher>
    Level = Unclassified
    <book:year>2001</book:year>
    Level = Unclassified
    <book:ISBN>0849300371</book:ISBN>
    Level = Unclassified
</book:Book>
</rdf:RDF>
```

Now, in this example, we have specified policies for RDF documents. Can we use RDF to specify policies? For example, how can RDF be used to specify the following policy?

"Only those attending a class from a professor have read access to the lecture notes of the professor."

Below we specify this policy in RDF.

```
</rdf:RDF>
    xmlns:uni=http://www.w3.org/2002/07/universityonto#
    xmlns:policy="http://www.example.com/policyonto#"
    xmlns:rdf="http://www.w3.org/1999/02/22-rdf-syntax-ns#">
<uni:LectureNotes rdf:ID="Data_Quality.doc">
    <uni:Author>Bhavani Thuraisingham</uni:author>
    <policy:AccessBy rdf:resource=http://localhost/bhavani/cs609/>
</rdf:RDF>

<rdf:RDF
    xmlns:uni=http://www.w3.org/2002/07/universityonto#
    xmlns:policy="http://www.example.com/policyonto#"
    xmlns:rdf=http://www.w3.org/1999/02/22-rdf-syntax-ns#>
<uni:Class rdf:ID="cs609">
    <uni:taughtyBy>Bhavani Thuraisingham</book:author>
</rdf:RDF>
```

Now, in XML we used Xpath expressions to specify policies such as:

```
policy_spec ID='P1' cred_expr-"//Professor[department='CS']"
target="annual_report.xml"
path="//Patent[@Dept='CS']//node()" priv-"VIEW"/>
```

Can we use RDF syntax to specify similar policies? Note that RQL (RDF Query Language) has been developed to query RDF documents. Therefore, can one access an RDF data element to use RQL and subsequently specify the policy? Note that Kagal et al. at the University of Maryland (Baltimore County) have developed the RDF-based language Rei to specify policies [KAGA03]. We will give an example of querying RDF documents in a later section.

7.5 Access Control

Carminati et al. were one of the first to discuss access control for RDF documents [CARM04]. They developed security architecture for RDF and designed ways to enforce access-control policies. Subsequently, Farkas has developed access-control enforcement techniques and ways to handle the inference problem for RDF documents [FARK06].

The challenge in access control is to determine the granularity of classification. Should access be given to an RDF document as a whole, or should access be given to parts of the document? Should access be given to the RDF schemas? Should we classify the relationships that are specified using RDF schemas? Again, note that there are two aspects here: one is to control access to RDF documents, and the other is to use RDF to specify policies. Whereas Carminati et al.'s work is to specify access to RDF documents, the work of Kagal et al. focuses on using the RDF-based language Rei to specify policies. Access control for RDF documents is illustrated in Figure 7.2.

The algorithms for access control are similar to the one we proposed for XML.

■ Subjects request access to RDF documents under two modes: browsing and authoring.
  – With browsing access, subjects can read or navigate documents.
  – Authoring access is needed to modify, delete, or append documents.
■ The access-control module checks the policy-based status and applies policy specifications.

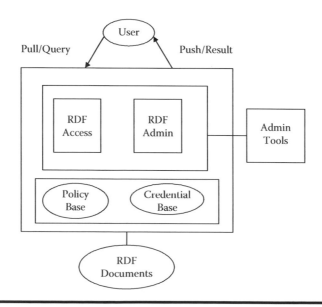

Figure 7.2   Access control for RDF documents.

- Views of the document are created, based on credentials and policy specifications.
- In case of conflict, the least-access privilege rule is enforced.

7.5 Secure RDF Databases

Some commercial data-management vendors such as Oracle are now developing approaches to manage RDF databases. Whereas managing RDF documents is not as widespread as managing XML documents, recent developments are showing a lot of promise. Oracle has query, transaction, metadata management, access methods, and indexing techniques for managing RDF documents. Furthermore, languages such as RQL are gaining prominence in querying RDF documents.

As in the case of XML, security has to be incorporated into these RDF databases. For example, access-control policies that we have discussed in the previous sections have to be enforced in RDF databases. Note that the policies themselves are specified in RDF or in XML. In addition, query modification has to be examined for RDF data. As we have discussed in Reference [THUR05], query modification is essentially about modifying the queries according to the security policies. Below we give an example of query modification in RQL.

7.5.1 Requested Query

```
select Book, NumInStock
from {Book} book:authoredBy {Author}
      . book:Stock {NumInStock}
Where Author Like "Bhavani*"
using namespace
    book = http://www.example.com/book#
```

The requestor does not have access to the number of book copies in stock. Therefore, new modified Query:

```
select Book
from {Book} book:authoredBy {Author}
Where Author Like "Bhavani*"
using namespace
    book = http://www.example.com/book#
```

We need to integrate the research on RDF security with commercial developments with RDF databases such as the products being developed by Oracle Corporation. Note also that the W3C's RFD Data Access Working Group is developing a language called SPARQL for querying RDF documents. We need to examine the expression of security policies in SPARQL.

7.6   Summary and Directions

This chapter has provided an overview of RDF security. We first discussed the issues on securing the components of RDF including RDF statements and schemas. Next we discussed the use of RDF for specifying policies. We also discussed secure RDF databases.

Whereas just a few years ago RDF was not widely heard of, today RDF is gaining popularity, mainly because of the representation of syntax and semantics. Note that XML is still the most widely used language for document interchange on the Web. Because XML has become so popular, it will be more difficult for RDF to replace XML. When XML was introduced, the community was struggling to exchange documents on the Web as well as to integrate heterogeneous databases. Therefore, XML together with ontologies became the solution to these problems. Thus, some believe that RDF's use will be limited. Nevertheless RDF's use is increasing compared to, say, just two years ago.

As RDF is being used, we have to ensure the security of RDF documents. Furthermore, due to the expressiveness of RDF, it can be used to specify more complex policies. Furthermore, the semantics of RDF makes it less difficult to build reasoning engines. Therefore, it is important to examine security for RDF as well to use RDF to specify policies. The works of Finin, Carminati, and Farkas are moving in the right direction. However, we need to express more complex security models such as role-based access control (RBAC) and the Usage Control (UCON) Model and examine RDF-like languages for this purpose [SAND96], [PARK04]. We are beginning collaboration with Finin's group at the University of Maryland (Baltimore County) and Sandhu's team at George Mason University (GMU). Together we believe that we can develop better solutions for RDF security as well as use RDF to specify complex policies based on RBAC and UCON.

References

[ANTO03] Antoniou, G. and F. van Harmelan, *A Semantic Web Primer*, MIT Press, Cambridge, MA, 2003.

[CARM04] Carminati, B. et al, Security for RDF, *Proc. DEXA Conf. Workshop on Web Semantics*, Zaragoza, Spain, 2004.

[FARK06] Farkas, C., Inference problem in RDF, *Proc. ACM SACMAT*, 2006.

[KAGA03] Kagal, L., T.W. Finin, and A. Joshi, A Policy Based Approach to Security for the Semantic Web, International Semantic Web Conference, 2003, 402–418.

[PARK04] Park, J. and R.S. Sandhu, The UCON$_{ABC}$ usage control model, *ACM Trans. Inf. Syst. Secur.*, 7(1), 128–174, 2004.

[SAND96] Sandhu, R., E. Coyne, H. Feinstein, and C. Youman, Role-based access control models, *IEEE Comput.*, 29(2), February 1996.

[THUR05] Thuraisingham, B. *Database and Application Security: Integrating Data Management and Information Security*, CRC Press, Boca Raton, FL, 2005.

Exercises

1. Investigate security issues for RDF documents.
2. Specify complex policies in RDF.
3. Design an application and show how secure RDF can be used.

Chapter 8

Security and Ontologies

8.1   Overview

In this chapter we continue with the discussion of the security issues for semantic Web technologies. In particular, we will discuss security issues for ontologies in general and Web ontology language (OWL) in particular. As stated in Chapter 7, the Resource Description Framework (RDF) uses the syntax of eXtensible Markup Language (XML). Furthermore, whereas XML is not sufficient to express semantics, RDF attempts to address the inadequacies of XML. OWL is an ontology language that has more expressive power and reasoning capabilities than RDF.

Little work has been carried out for securing OWL documents. Furthermore, OWL can be used to specify policies just like XML and RDF. Access-control techniques can be applied to OWL documents. OWL databases need to be secure. This chapter discusses various security issues for OWL.

The organization of this chapter is as follows. An OWL ontology is described in Section 8.2. We discuss security issues for ontologies in Section 8.3. Specification of policies in OWL is discussed in Section 8.4. Access control is the subject of Section 8.5. Managing secure OWL databases is discussed in Section 8.6. Ontologies for policy and data integration are discussed in Section 8.7. The chapter is summarized in Section 8.8. For details of OWL and ontologies we refer the reader to Reference [ANTO03].

8.2   Owl Example

Before we discuss security for OWL and specify policies in OWL, we need to provide an example of an OWL ontology. The following example describes the University Ontology. The different properties shown are DatatypeProperty (hasCredits) and ObjectProperty (hasTaught, isTaughtBy, etc.). Subproperties are also shown ("hasCompleted" is a subproperty of "hasRegistered"). The "disjointWith" property ensures that two classes do not have any individuals in common. For example, an individual from the "Faculty" class cannot be an individual of the "Student" class. Using subproperties, policies can be specified. In the following example, a faculty member can access the "AnnualReports" only if she or he is the dean.

Note that OWL uses RDF and hence XML syntax. Furthermore, OWL has more powerful reasoning capabilities. The following example and subsequent security examples will make this clear.

```
<?xml version="1.0"?>
<!DOCTYPE rdf:RDF [
    <!ENTITY owl "http://www.w3.org/2002/07/owl#" >
    <!ENTITY xsd "http://www.w3.org/2001/XMLSchema#" >
    <!ENTITY rdfs "http://www.w3.org/2000/01/rdf-schema#" >
    <!ENTITY rdf "http://www.w3.org/1999/02/22-rdf-syntax-ns#" >
]>

<rdf:RDF xmlns="http://www.owl-ontologies.com/
Ontology1178660130.owl#"
    xml:base="http://www.owl-ontologies.com/Ontology1178660130.owl"
    xmlns:xsd="http://www.w3.org/2001/XMLSchema#"
    xmlns:rdfs="http://www.w3.org/2000/01/rdf-schema#"
    xmlns:rdf="http://www.w3.org/1999/02/22-rdf-syntax-ns#"
    xmlns:owl="http://www.w3.org/2002/07/owl#" >
    <owl:Ontology rdf:about=""/>
    <owl:Class rdf:ID="AnnualReports">
        <rdfs:subClassOf rdf:resource="#Department"/>
    </owl:Class>
    <owl:ObjectProperty rdf:ID="canAccess">
        <rdfs:domain rdf:resource="#Faculty"/>
        <rdfs:range rdf:resource="#AnnualReports"/>
        <rdfs:subPropertyOf rdf:resource="#isDean"/>
    </owl:ObjectProperty>
    <owl:Class rdf:ID="Course">
        <rdfs:subClassOf rdf:resource="#Department"/>
    </owl:Class>
    <owl:Class rdf:ID="Department"/>
    <owl:Class rdf:ID="Faculty">
        <rdfs:subClassOf rdf:resource="#Department"/>
        <owl:disjointWith rdf:resource="#Student"/>
        <owl:disjointWith rdf:resource="#Staff"/>
```

```
</owl:Class>
<owl:ObjectProperty rdf:ID="hasCompleted">
   <rdfs:subPropertyOf rdf:resource="#hasRegistered"/>
</owl:ObjectProperty>
<owl:DatatypeProperty rdf:ID="hasCredits">
   <rdfs:domain rdf:resource="#Course"/>
   <rdfs:range rdf:resource="&xsd;int"/>
</owl:DatatypeProperty>
<owl:ObjectProperty rdf:ID="hasDean">
   <rdfs:domain>
   <owl:Class>
      <owl:unionOf rdf:parseType="Collection">
         <owl:Class rdf:about="#Course"/>
         <owl:Class rdf:about="#Department"/>
         <owl:Class rdf:about="#Faculty"/>
         <owl:Class rdf:about="#Staff"/>
         <owl:Class rdf:about="#Student"/>
      </owl:unionOf>
     </owl:Class>
   </rdfs:domain>
   <rdfs:range rdf:resource="#Faculty"/>
</owl:ObjectProperty>
<owl:DatatypeProperty rdf:ID="hasName">
   <rdfs:domain>
    <owl:Class>
     <owl:unionOf rdf:parseType="Collection">
         <owl:Class rdf:about="#Department"/>
         <owl:Class rdf:about="#Faculty"/>
         <owl:Class rdf:about="#Staff"/>
         <owl:Class rdf:about="#Student"/>
      </owl:unionOf>
     </owl:Class>
   </rdfs:domain>
   <rdfs:range rdf:resource="&xsd;string"/>
</owl:DatatypeProperty>
<owl:ObjectProperty rdf:ID="hasPrerequisite">
   <rdf:type rdf:resource="&owl;TransitiveProperty"/>
   <owl:inverseOf rdf:resource="#isPrerequisiteOf"/>
</owl:ObjectProperty>
<owl:ObjectProperty rdf:ID="hasRegistered">
   <rdfs:domain rdf:resource="#Student"/>
   <rdfs:range rdf:resource="#Course"/>
</owl:ObjectProperty>
<owl:ObjectProperty rdf:ID="isDean">
   <rdfs:domain rdf:resource="#Faculty"/>
   <rdfs:range rdf:resource="&xsd;boolean"/>
</owl:ObjectProperty>
<owl:ObjectProperty rdf:ID="isPrerequisiteOf">
```

```
        <rdf:type rdf:resource="&owl;TransitiveProperty"/>
        <owl:inverseOf rdf:resource="#hasPrerequisite"/>
    </owl:ObjectProperty>
    <owl:Class rdf:ID="Staff">
        <rdfs:subClassOf rdf:resource="#Department"/>
        <owl:disjointWith rdf:resource="#Student"/>
        <owl:disjointWith rdf:resource="#Faculty"/>
        <rdfs:comment rdf:datatype="&xsd;string"
        >This class represents the nonteaching, nonstudent members of the
    department</rdfs:comment>
    </owl:Class>
    <owl:Class rdf:ID="Student">
        <rdfs:subClassOf rdf:resource="#Department"/>
        <owl:disjointWith rdf:resource="#Staff"/>
        <owl:disjointWith rdf:resource="#Faculty"/>
    </owl:Class>
    <owl:ObjectProperty rdf:ID="taughtBy">
        <rdfs:domain rdf:resource="#Course"/>
        <rdfs:range rdf:resource="#Faculty"/>
        <owl:inverseOf rdf:resource="#teachesCourse"/>
    </owl:ObjectProperty>
    <owl:ObjectProperty rdf:ID="teachesCourse">
        <rdf:type rdf:resource="&owl;InverseFunctionalProperty"/>
        <rdfs:domain rdf:resource="#Faculty"/>
        <rdfs:range rdf:resource="#Course"/>
        <owl:inverseOf rdf:resource="#taughtBy"/>
    </owl:ObjectProperty>
</rdf:RDF>
```

8.3 Securing Ontologies

Ontologies have to be secure; that is, access to ontologies has to be controlled. Access could be based on content, context, or time. As ontologies evolve, access to the ontologies may vary. Below we discuss two examples. In the first example we classify the fact that English books are different from French books and German books at Level L1. In the second example we classify the fact that textbooks and course books are the same at Level L2.

```
< owl: Class rdf: about = "#EnglishBooks">
 <owl: disjointWith rdf: resource "#FrenchBooks"/>
 <owl: disjointWith rdf: resource = #FrenchBooks"/>
Level = L1
</owl:Class>

<owl: Class rdf: ID = "TextBooks">
 <owl: equivalentClass rdf: resource = "CourseBooks"/>
Level = L2
</owl: Class>
```

8.4   Policy Specification in OWL

Now, let us consider the example in Section 8.2. Below we have specified policies for segments of this example.

```
<owl:Ontology rdf:about=""/>
<owl:Class rdf:ID="AnnualReports">
  <rdfs:subClassOf rdf:resource="#Department"/>
 Level = L1
</owl:Class>

<owl:ObjectProperty rdf:ID="canAccess">
  <rdfs:domain rdf:resource="#Faculty"/>
  <rdfs:range rdf:resource="#AnnualReports"/>
  <rdfs:subPropertyOf rdf:resource="#isDean"/>
 Level = L2
</owl:ObjectProperty>
```

In the above example, we specified policies for OWL documents. Now, can we use OWL to specify policies? For example, how can OWL be used to specify the following policy?

"Only those attending a class from a professor have read access to the lecture notes of the professor."

Below we specify this policy in OWL.

```
<owl:Class rdf:ID="BhavaniLectureNotesCS609">
  <rdfssubClassOfrdf:resource="http://localhost/unionto#LectureNotes"/>
</owl:Class>

<owl:Class rdf:ID="CS609Students">
  <rdfs:subClassOf rdf:resource="http://localhost/unionto#Students"/>
</owl:Class>

<owl:ObjectProperty rdf:ID="canAccess">
  <rdfs:domain rdf:resource="#CS609Students"/>
  <rdfs:range rdf:resource=" http://localhost/unionto# BhavaniLec-
tureNotesCS609"/>
</owl:ObjectProperty>
```

8.5   Access Control

Whereas access control for XML has received a lot of attention and there has been some work on securing RDF documents, access control for OWL and ontologies has received little attention. As in the case of XML and RDF, the challenge in access control is to determine the granularity of classification. Should access be given to OWL documents as a whole, or should access be given to parts of the document? Should access be given to OWL schemas? Should we classify the relationships that are specified using OWL schemas? Again note that there are two aspects here: one is to control access to OWL documents (Figure 8.1), and the other is to use OWL to specify policies.

The algorithms for access control are similar to the one we proposed for XML.

- Subjects request access to OWL documents under two modes: browsing and authoring.
  - With browsing access, subjects can read and navigate documents.
  - Authoring access is needed to modify, delete, and append documents.
- Access-control module checks the policy base and applies policy specifications.
- Views of the document are created based on credentials and policy specifications.
- In case of conflict, the least-access privilege rule is enforced.

What makes OWL useful for policy specification is the inherent reasoning capabilities in OWL. Note that OWL is based on descriptive logics. Reasoning engines based on such logics are being developed [MCGU03]. These reasoning

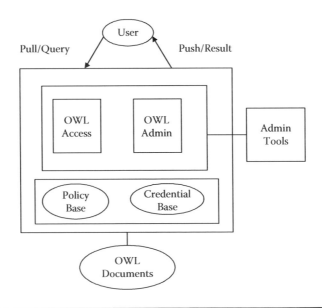

Figure 8.1   Access control for OWL documents.

engines could be used to reason about the security policies. We will describe reasoning in Chapter 9.

8.6   Secure OWL Databases

Some commercial data-management vendors such as Oracle are now developing approaches to manage XML and RDF databases. Although managing RDF documents is not as widespread as managing XML documents, recent developments are showing a lot of promise. However, to our knowledge there is no work on managing OWL databases. We need techniques for query processing, transaction management, and storage management for OWL documents.

As in the case of XML, security has to be incorporated into these OWL databases. For example, access-control policies that we have discussed in previous sections have to be enforced on OWL databases. Note that the policies themselves may be specified in OWL. In addition, query modification has to be examined for OWL data. As we have discussed in [THUR05a], query modification is essentially about modifying the queries according to the security policies.

8.7   Ontology for Policy and Data Integration

Ontologies are becoming common practice for information interoperability including handling data heterogeneity [CAST]. They can also be used to handle policy heterogeneity. We will elaborate on this aspect in Part IV when we discuss applications. We briefly discuss some of these aspects in this section.

Ontologies are specified to define various terms as well as to represent common semantics or to distinguish between different semantics. These ontologies are then used for information interoperability. For example, in our research on a geospatial semantic Web, we are using ontologies specified in RDF-like languages (which we have called GRDF – Geospatial RDF) for handling semantic heterogeneity. These ontologies are then used for semantic interoperability.

With respect to policy integration, each data-management system could use XML or RDF to specify policies, and then we integrate the policies using ontologies to handle semantic differences. Figure 8.2 illustrates the use of ontologies for policy integration.

8.8   Summary and Directions

In this chapter we discussed ontologies and security. We argued that portions of the ontologies may need to be classified for different applications. We also showed how ontologies may be used to specify security policies.

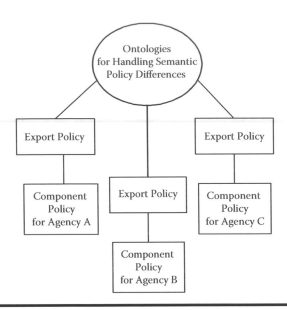

Figure 8.2 Ontologies for policy interoperability.

Ontologies are critical for many applications including information interoperability, Web services, and knowledge management. OWL and DAML+OIL (DARPA Agent Markup Language & Ontology Markup Language) are excellent starting points for specifying ontologies. We need ontologies to be secure. In addition, ontologies may be used to specify policies. Due to the expressiveness of OWL, it can be used to specify more complex policies than, say, XML and RDF. Furthermore, the semantics of OWL makes it a powerful reasoning language. Therefore, it is important to examine security for OWL as well as to use OWL to specify policies. Only recently have we examined security for ontologies and the use of ontologies for policy specification. Much more research needs to be done on the use of ontologies for policy interoperability.

References

[ANTO03] Antoniou, G. and F. van Harmelan, *A Semantic Web Primer*, MIT Press, Cambridge, MA, 2003.

[CAST05] Castano, S., A. Ferrara, and S. Montanelli, Ontology-based Interoperability Services for Semantic Collaboration in Open Networked Systems, University of Milan Report, http://interop-esa05.unige.ch/INTEROP/Proceedings/Interop-ESA-Scientific/PerPaper/I05-1%20400.pdf.

[MCGU03] McGuiness, D. and F. van Harmelan, Ed., Web Ontology Language Overview, http://www.w3c.org/TR/owl-features/, 2003.

[THUR05a] Thuraisingham, B., *Database and Applications Security: Integrating Data Management and Information Security,* CRC Press, Boca Raton, FL, 2005.

[THUR05b] Thuraisingham, B., Security standards for the semantic Web, *Comput. Stand. Interface J.,* 2005.

Exercises

1. Investigate security issues for OWL documents.
2. Specify complex policies in OWL.
3. Design an application and show how ontologies may be used for policy integration.

Chapter 9

Security and Rules

9.1 Overview

The previous three chapters described the three major components of the semantic Web: eXtensible Markup Language (XML), Resource Description Framework (RDF) and Web Ontology Language (OWL). The fourth component is rules. Languages such as Semantic Web Rules Language (SWRL) and RuleML, which are semantic Web rule markup languages, are being developed [W3C], [ANTO03]. This is because rules have more reasoning power than data represented in RDF or OWL. Recently the work of Finin and his team has shown that we can use RDF-based language to specify policies [KAGA03]. We can also use rule-based languages to specify policies. Note that in the end a machine can only understand markup languages. Therefore, representation of rules in first-order logic is not appropriate for agents to understand. We need to convert these rules into markup rules.

In this chapter we will discuss some of our ideas on reasoning with rules. The organization of this chapter is as follows. In Section 9.2 we discuss our prior research on nonmonotonic typed multilevel logic (NTML) for secure data and knowledge-based systems [THUR91], [THUR92]. Our work on rules and security is influenced by NTML. Security issues for rules is discussed in Section 9.3. Specification of policies in languages such as RuleML is discussed in Section 9.4. The inference problem and relationship to rules is discussed in Section 9.5. The chapter is summarized in Section 9.6.

9.2 Nonmonotonic-Typed Multilevel Logic for Secure Data and Knowledge Management

NTML was developed in the 1990s for representing and reasoning about multilevel secure databases. As we will see in Chapter 13, in multilevel data-management systems, a user is cleared at different clearance levels, and the data is assigned different sensitivity levels. Users read data at or below the level assigned and write data at their level. It is assumed that these sets of levels form a particularly ordered lattice with Unclassified < Confidential < Secret < Top Secret. We examined the model and proof-theoretic approaches to deductive database management (see Reference [FROS86]) in the 1980s and subsequently developed both model and proof-theoretic approaches for a secure database using NTML. We also designed a theorem prover for NTML based on a language called NTML-Prolog.

In the proof-theoretic approach, the data and policies are expressed in NTML, and query processing amounts to theorem proving. In the model-theoretic approach, the multilevel database is a model for the policies. We also discussed reasoning, using both the closed-world and open-world assumptions.

NTML also focused on having different facts at different security levels. For example, at the Unclassified Level we could have the fact that the ship is sailing to England, and at the Secret Level we could have the fact that the ship is sailing to India. We also showed that with reasoning NTML could handle problems such as the inference problem.

Note that NTML was developed at a time before the semantic Web, and it was influenced by the developments in logic programming [LLOY87]. Today we have the semantic Web OWL based on descriptive logic, and languages such as RuleML. We also need the capability to carry out nonmonotonic reasoning. Therefore, to successfully integrate semantic Web rule processing with policy reasoning and the inference problem, we need to integrate concepts in NTML with RuleML as well as reasoners such as NTML-Prolog with systems such as Pellet. Research on policy reasoning with semantic Web technologies is just beginning. In the next three sections we will discuss some of our ideas on this problem based on our work and also the discussions on RuleML given in Reference [ANTO03].

9.3 Securing Rules

As we have stated, reasoning power is still limited in OWL. Therefore, the semantic Web community has developed rule-based languages such as Semantic Web Rules Language (SWRL) and reasoning. In this section we will examine the rules we have discussed in Chapter 4 as given in Reference [ANTO03] and examine security issues. Our work is motivated by NTML.

Consider the following rule R1:

Studies(X,Y), Lives(X,Z), Loc(Y,U), Loc(Z,U) → DomesticStudent(X)

> that is, if John Studies at UTDallas and John lives on Campbell Road, and the location of Campbell Road and UTDallas is Richardson, then John is a Domestic student.

Now, we can give a user read access to this rule only if he is an administrator at UTDallas. This can be specified as follows:

Administrator(X, UTDallas) → Read-access(X, R1)

We can also assign security levels atop the rules. If we wish to classify this rule at the Confidential Level, then we can state this as:

→ Level(R1, Confidential)

We can also assign a level next to the rule as follows:

Level(Studies(X,Y), Lives(X,Z), Loc(Y,U), Loc(Z,U) →
DomesticStudent(X), Confidential)

As in the case of NTML, we can have different facts at different levels. For example, at the Unclassified Level we can have a rule that states that John lives in England, but at the Secret Level he is living in Russia. These rules can be specified as follows:

Level(→ Lives(John, England), Unclassified)
Level(→ Lives(John, Russia), Secret)

Now in first-order logic, this is a contradiction, but in NTML it is not a contradiction.

As discussed in Chapter 4, Person (X) → Man(X) or Woman(X) is not a rule in predicate logic.

If X is a person, then X is either a man or a woman cannot be expressed in first-order predicate logic. Therefore, in predicate logic we express the above as if X is a person and X is not a man, then X is a woman; and similarly if X is a person and X is not a woman, then X is a man. Thus, in predicate logic, we can have a rule of the form:

Person(X) and Not Man(X) → Woman(X)

However, in OWL we can specify the rule if X is a person, then X is a man or X is a woman.

In NTML, rules can be monotonic or nonmonotonic. In the semantic Web worlds, a similar assumption is made, as we have seen in Chapter 4.

In the case of nonmonotonic reasoning, if we have X and NOT X, we do not treat them as inconsistent as in the case of monotonic reasoning. For example, as discussed in Reference [ANTO03], consider the example of an apartment that is acceptable to John. In general, John is prepared to rent an apartment unless the apartment has less than two bedrooms and does not allow pets. This can be expressed as follows:

> $\rightarrow$ Acceptable(X)
> Bedroom(X,Y), Y<2 $\rightarrow$ NOT Acceptable(X)
> NOT Pets(X) $\rightarrow$ NOT Acceptable(X)

The first rule states that an apartment is in general acceptable to John. The second rule states that if the apartment has less than two bedrooms, it is not acceptable to John. The third rule states that if pets are not allowed, then the apartment is not acceptable to John. Note that there could be a contradiction. But with nonmonotonic reasoning this is allowed, whereas it is not allowed in monotonic reasoning.

In the same way regarding access control, we can have a general rule that we do not grant access to any piece of data and then give exceptions.

> Administrator(X, UTDallas) $\rightarrow$ NOT (Read-access(X, Y))
> Salary(Y) $\rightarrow$ Read-access(X, Y)

We initially deny the administrator access to all data. Then we state that if Y is a salary value, then the administrator is granted access to that value. In first-order logic such rules are not permitted.

We can also have different data values at different levels even for nonmonotonic rules. This is given in the following example.

> Level ($\rightarrow$ Acceptable(X), Unclassified))
> Level (Bedroom(X,Y), Y<2$\rightarrow$ NOT Acceptable(X), Secret)
> Level (NOT Pets(X) $\rightarrow$ NOT Acceptable(X), TopSecret)

This means that every apartment is acceptable and may be assigned at the Unclassified Level. At the Secret Level, only those apartments that have more than two bedrooms are acceptable. At the TopSecret Level, only those apartments that allow pets are acceptable. Below is another example.

> Level (Country(X) $\rightarrow$ NOT War (X), Unclassified)

Level (→ Country(USA), Unclassified)
Level (→ Country(Nigeria), Unclassified)
Level (→ War (England), Secret)
Level (→ War (Nigeria), TopSecret)

The first rule states that no country is at war at the Unclassified Level. The next two rules state that the USA and Nigeria are both countries at the Unclassified Level. The fourth rule states that the USA is at war at the Secret Level. The fifth rule states that Nigeria is at war at the TopSecret Level.

As stated in Chapter 4, we need rule-markup languages for a machine to understand the rules. The various components of logic are expressed in the rule markup language called RuleML developed for the semantic Web as well as languages such as SWRL. Both monotonic and nonmonotonic rules can be represented in RuleML. Below we state the rule that Nigeria is at war at the TopSecret Level.

Fact "War(Nigeria)," which is, Nigeria is at war at the TopSecret Level

```
<fact>
  <atom>
    <predicate>War</predicate>
      <term>
        <const>Nigeria</const>
      </term>
    </atom>
      Level = TopSecret
  </fact>
```

9.4   Policy Specification Using Rules

Agents understand markup languages such as XML, RDF, OWL, and RuleML. Therefore, ultimately policies have to be expressed in a markup language. In the previous section we showed how the policy "Nigeria is at war is Secret" could be represented in a RuleML-like language. We can express many of the policies below in such a language. For example, consider the following policies that we have taken from our previous research [THUR93].

EMP(X, Y, Z) and Y>50 → Level(EMP) = Secret
EMP(X, Y, Z) → Level(TOGETHER(X,Y) = Secret

The first rule is a content-based policy that classifies the Employee instance if the salary is greater than 50K at the Secret Level.

The second rule states that names and salaries taken together are Secret. Note that we mean EMP is an employee predicate with attribute Name, Salary, and Department.

To explain the representation of policies in a RuleML-like language, we will consider the following rule:

R1: HEALTH-RECORD(X) → Private(X)

The above rule states that all healthcare records are private. This policy may be represented in a markup language as follows:

```
<rule id = R1>
<head>
<atom>
    <predicate>HEATH-RECORD</predicate>
      <term>
        <var> X</var>
       <term>
      </atom>
</head>
<body>
<atom>
    <predicate>Private</predicate>
      <term>
        <var> X</var>
       </term>
      </atom>
</body>
</rule>
```

Note that here we have considered Private to be a predicate. Instead, we could have assumed that Level is a predicate, and the body would have been Level(X, Private), where X is a variable and Private would be a constant. The above representation has to be modified to represent this modified body of the rule.

9.5   Inference Problem and Policy Reasoning

One of the advantages of representing policies as rules is that we can use the reasoning engines (e.g., theorem provers) to reason about the policies. We have designed a reasoning engine for policies expressed in NTML. Reasoning engines such as Pellet are being used for reasoning about policies by Finin and his team as well as the policy-aware Web team at the Massachusetts Institute of Technology. What we need is a combination of NTML theorem provers and reasoning engines such as Pellet to be integrated to develop policy reasoners. These policy reasoners will rea-

---

Policy Management

Specify policies as rules

Rule processing to enforce the access control

Theorem proving techniques to determine if policies are violated

Consistency and completeness checking of policies

Figure 9.1 Policy management.

son about the policies, check for consistency, and also detect security violations via inference (see Figure 9.1). We will discuss policy reasoning under policy engineering in Chapter 14. In this section, we will give some examples. Note that to make it simple we reason with the rule format instead of the RuleML format. Note that research on integrating engines such as Pellet with policies is only just beginning.

The reasoning system that we designed is based on a language we developed called NTML-Prolog. We also developed an algorithm for the resolution principle. If there is a security violation via inference, then the system will arrive at a contradiction. Take the following simple example:

Prescription (John, X) and X = Imitrex $\rightarrow$ Disease(John, Migraine)

$\rightarrow$ Level (Disease(John, Migraine), Private)
$\rightarrow$ Level (Prescription (John, Imitrex), Public)

From the first and third rules we can infer $\rightarrow$ Disease(John, Migraine) at the Unclassified Level. But this contradicts with the rule that John has Migraines at the Private Level. We arrive at a contradiction, and therefore the administrator will then modify the policies. This means that the fact that John is taking Imitrex has to be at least at the Public Level.

Now, note that with nonmonotonic reasoning one could have contradictions; that is, we could classify an entity both at the Secret and Unclassified Levels. Therefore, to be on the safe side, initially we make everything Private or TopSecret and then make exceptions. However, this could also make the reasoning engines more complex. We need to conduct research in this area to understand the problem and develop appropriate solutions. Figure 9.2 illustrates an inference controller for the semantic Web.

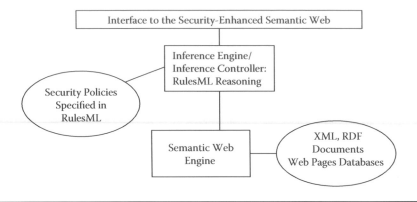

Figure 9.2 Inference controller for the semantic Web.

9.6   Summary and Directions

This chapter has provided an overview of Web rules and security. First we discussed our system based on a logic we developed for secure databases called NTML and then discussed security issues for rules. Then we showed how rules may be used to specify policies. We also discussed the use of rules for handling the inference and privacy problems.

As we have stated, rules have more reasoning power than languages such as RDF and OWL. Furthermore, rules for the semantic Web are nonmonotonic in nature. Therefore, we need to develop descriptive logic-based theorem provers for reasoning about policies. These theorem provers will utilize many of the ideas developed in logic-programming systems. We believe that integrating NTML-Prolog-based systems with Pellet-like systems will be the solution.

References

[ANTO03] Antoniou, G. and F. van Harmelan, *A Semantic Web Primer*, MIT Press, Cambridge, MA, 2003.

[FROS86] Frost, R., *On Knowledge Base Management Systems*, Collins Publishers, London, U.K., 1986.

[KAGA03] Kagal, L., T.W. Finin, and A. Joshi, A Policy Based Approach to Security for the Semantic Web, International Semantic Web Conference, Sanibel Island, FL, 2003.

[LLOY87] Lloyd, J., *Logic Programming*, Springer-Verlag, Heidelberg, 1987.

[THUR91] Thuraisingham, B., A nonmonotonic typed multilevel logic for secure data and knowledge base management systems, *Proc. Comput. Security Foundations Workshop*, 1991.

[THUR92] Thuraisingham, B., A nonmonotonic typed multilevel logic for secure data and knowledge base management systems — II, *Proc. Comput. Security Foundations Workshop*, 1992.

[THUR93] Thuraisingham, B., W. Ford, and M. Collins, Design and implementation of a database inference controller, *Data Knowledge Eng. J.*, 11(3), 1993.

[W3C] www.w3c.org.

Exercises

1. Investigate security issues for RuleML.
2. Specify complex policies in RuleML.
3. Design a policy reasoning engine based on RuleML.

Conclusion to Part II

Part II, consisting of five chapters, discussed secure semantic Webs. In particular we discussed confidentiality aspects. In Chapter 5 we provided an overview of secure semantic Webs. In Chapter 6 we discussed eXtensible Markup Language (XML) security, which included a discussion of securing XML documents as well as using XML to specify policies. In Chapter 7 we discussed Resource Description Framework (RDF) security. Security and ontologies including security for Web Ontology Language (OWL) was discussed in Chapter 8. Integrating security into Web rules was the subject of Chapter 9.

Now that we have provided an overview of the various confidentiality aspects of building trustworthy semantic Webs, we are now ready to discuss dependability aspects. In particular, we will discuss trust, privacy, and integrity for the semantic Web in Part III as well as other topics such as multilevel security, policy engineering, and research and standards developments.

Part III

Dependable Semantic Webs

Introduction to Part III

As we have stated, trustworthy semantic Webs include secure semantic Webs and dependable semantic Webs. Whereas the chapters in Part II focused on confidentiality aspects of security, in this part we will discuss dependability aspects. Furthermore, because confidentiality has been used synonymously with security, we have used the term trustworthy semantic Web to include features such as trust, privacy, and integrity.

Part III consists of six chapters. In Chapter 10 we focus on trust management with respect to the semantic Web. In Chapter 11 we will discuss privacy management, and in Chapter 12 we discuss integrity management. For completion, we discuss multilevel security issues in Chapter 13. Aspects of policy management such as tools for policy specification and evolution are discussed in Chapter 14. This is called policy engineering. Part III concludes with a chapter on developments with respect to research, standards, and products.

Chapter 10

Trust Management and the Semantic Web

10.1 Overview

This chapter focuses on trust management and the semantic Web. Trust has been discussed a great deal in developing secure systems. Much of the early focus has been on trusting the software to develop high-assurance systems. For example, in designing a multilevel system that has to be evaluated at, say, an A1 level according to the Trusted Computer Systems Evaluation criteria (TCSEC), the software has to go through a formal verification process to ensure that there are no covert channels. Such software is called trusted software. However, during the past ten years or so when data and applications security received prominence, the focus has been on trusting the individuals or processes acting on behalf of the individuals. Here, we had to determine the trust that had to be placed on individuals. Furthermore, the data also had to be assigned trust values; that is, data could have a high trust value if it emanated from a trustworthy individual.

The organization of this chapter is as follows. Trust management including trusting individuals as well as data is discussed in Section 10.2. Semantic Web technologies for trust management are the subject of Section 10.3. Trust management for semantic Web technologies is discussed in Section 10.4. Note that trust and risk have a relationship between them, that is, if a person is not trustworthy and if you have to give him or her some data, you are taking a risk. Therefore, some of the developments on correlating trust and risk and the use of semantic Web technologies for this correlation are discussed in Section 10.5. For completion we discuss digital rights management and its relationship to the semantic Web in Section 10.6. The chapter is concluded in Section 10.7.

10.2 Trust Management

Before we discuss aspects of trust management and describe the relationship to semantic Webs, we need to determine what is meant by trust. Trust has been defined by philosophers, and it relates to the amount of value that one can place in another. This value will depend on whether the person can, for example, keep secrets or carry out safe activities. Based on the trust that is placed in a person, the data emanating from that person would also be assigned a trust value. We will address data trust later. First, we will focus on trusting an individual. We can extend the arguments to include not only an individual, but also a group of individuals or even a Web site or an organization.

As stated earlier, work on trust initially focused on the amount of verification or testing necessary to ensure that the software met the specification. If the software had a Trojan horse, then it was not trusted. If the software was trusted, then depending on the techniques used to trust the software (e.g., formal verification versus testing), one could then determine the assurance placed on the software. Later on, with the prominence of data security, trust was assigned to individuals or organizations. In such cases, two approaches were used to define trust; one was based on credentials and the other was based on reputation. Both schools of thought have received attention in the research community working on trust.

Bertino and her team [BERT03] have conducted extensive research in credential-based trust management. The idea here is to exchange credentials between individuals, and depending on the type of credentials, trust is established between two parties. Credentials are obtained initially through some credential authority. Therefore, if John wants to see Jane's personal data, he has to present Jane with credentials given to him by a credential authority. Other noted research on credential-based trust management is the work of Yu and Winslett [YU03] and Winsborough and Li [WINS04], among others. Numerous papers on credential-based trust management have appeared in the proceedings of conferences such as the Association for Computing Machinery (ACM) Symposium on Access Models and Technologies (SACMAT) and IEEE Policy (see also Reference [BERT04]).

In reputation-based systems, trust is assigned based on the reputation of past behavior. For example, if Jane applies for a position as a teacher, then those who have heard about Jane will discuss her reputation, perhaps that she is not reliable and misses classes a great deal of the time. If this is the case, then Jane's reputation as a teacher is not good, and therefore Jane will not be trusted to be given the job. We use reputation all the time in our daily lives; that is, we trust an individual or an organization based on reputation. It is usually very hard to improve reputation. However, it does not take much to ruin one's reputation and, as a result, to decrease trust value. Reputation-based trust systems are discussed in Reference [SHMA06].

Another type of trust is to determine the confidence value that one places on the data. In other words, how much do you trust the data? To give an answer, we need to determine who has produced the data. Who has accessed the data? Has the data gone through an organization that is untrustworthy? We will discuss data trust when we address data quality and data provenance in Chapter 12.

Once trust values are assigned, what does it take to manage trust? This involves exchanging data depending on trust values as well as increasing and decreasing trust values based on credentials received or subtracted or a reputation that has changed. For example, if John is entrusted with some critical data, and if it is known that John has misused the data, the trust value will be decreased. There is research on formalizing the notion of trust and performing operations on trust. Algebras for trust management are also being developed. One important aspect of trust management is trust negotiation. Here two parties may negotiate trust values with each other, and the data to be shared between them. Trust negotiation is an active research area in trust management [WINS04]. Figure 10.1 illustrates various aspects of trust. The trust negotiation process is illustrated in Figure 10.2.

10.3 Semantic Web for Trust Management

What is of interest to us is the use of semantic Web technologies for trust management and negotiation. Whereas several trust policy languages have been developed, a notable system that takes advantage of eXtensible Markup Language (XML) for policy representation is the system developed at the University of Milan and Purdue University by Bertino and her group. The system developed is called Trust-X and is based on XML. It is a credential-based system [BERT04].

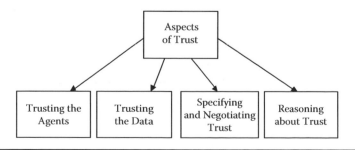

Figure 10.1   Aspects of trust.

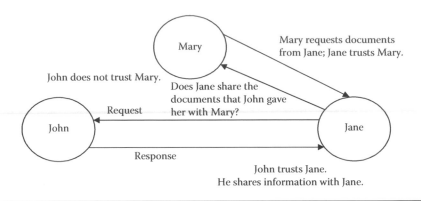

Figure 10.2 Trust negotiation.

Whereas XML is a suitable policy language, it suffers from drawbacks in that it cannot adequately represent semantics. For example, statements such as A trusts B only if B does not trust C, or A trusts B and B trusts C does not mean that A trusts C. It is difficult to express such statements in XML. Note that unlike XML, Resource Description Framework (RDF) can express class-subclass relationships, and languages such as OWL can represent relationships such as union and intersection. Therefore, we need rich policy languages to represent trust. Furthermore, since the 9/11 Commission Report, the environment is migrating from a need-to-know to a need-to-share environment. Therefore, it is important to represent trust relationships in such an environment. We need policy languages to represent statements of the form "in emergency situations, one needs to share all the data, and then determine the consequences of data sharing with respect to trust." Kagal et al. [KAGA03] are investigating the use of languages such as Rei for need-to-share environments.

The advantage of using semantic Web-based policy languages is that one could use reasoning capabilities based on descriptive logic to reason about trust statements and make inferences about trust that are not explicitly specified. Reasoning engines such as Jena and Pellet are also being explored for representing and reasoning about semantic Web-based policy specifications. The policy-aware Web project being carried out at the Massachusetts Institute of Technology (MIT) is also developing specification languages and reasoning engines for trust policies.

Note that one of the layers of the semantic Web is logic, proof, and trust. This type of trust is different from trust as we have discussed in this chapter. The trust layer for the semantic Web is essentially about reasoning about the trustworthiness of statements. For example, how much trust do you place in statements such as "John and James are best friends"? Trusting this statement depends on the source of the statement. We will discuss this type of trust when we discuss data quality and provenance in Chapter 13. We will also revisit this aspect in Section 10.4.

Although there is a lot of research now on specification of policy languages, the advantage of semantic Web languages is that we can utilize the reasoning tools being developed to reason about the policies so that we can check for consistency of the policies. We also want to ensure that trust policies do not divulge sensitive information that is classified or private. Research along these lines is being carried out by Bertino and her group [SQUI06]. Figure 10.3 illustrates a semantic Web for trust management.

10.4 Trust Management for the Semantic Web

In Section 10.3, we discussed the application of semantic Web technologies for trust management. Essentially, the idea here is to use languages such as XML, RDF, and OWL to specify policies and reason about policies based on descriptive logic. In this section we will discuss how trust-management techniques may be applied to a semantic Web. Note that a semantic Web is a collection of technologies that give us machine-understandable Web pages. Therefore, the challenge here is, how do we trust the reasoning that is carried out to obtain machine-understandable Web pages? Furthermore, do we trust the Web pages that are produced? Trust management for a semantic Web is illustrated in Figure 10.4.

As stated in the previous section, one of the layers of a semantic Web is the logic, proof, and trust layer. Here we need technologies to reason about the accuracy of the Web pages. Do we trust the data that is produced? Do we trust the decisions that are made by the agents that carry out the "actives" on behalf of the user? Trusting the Web pages is also determined by who produced the Web pages.

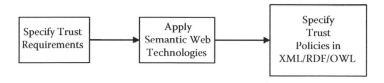

Figure 10.3   Semantic Web for trust management.

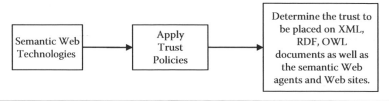

Figure 10.4   Trust for the semantic Web.

If the agents who produced the Web pages are highly trustworthy, then we may place higher trust on the results. We will discuss this aspect under data quality and data provenance in Chapter 13.

The other aspect is trusting the agents that make use of semantic Web technologies such as XML- and RDF-based data and who carry out the activities. Do we trust the answers produced by the agents? Do these agents carry out trust negotiations between themselves? The problem is then reduced to the problem we discussed in Section 10.3; that is, trust established between agents is essentially the trust that is established between people. This trust may depend on credentials or may be based on reputation. For example, in providing a travel service, the agent has to make reservations and book hotels as well as make arrangements for the client to participate in tours. The agent who acts on behalf of the client will read the Web pages in XML or RDF and then contact the agent who is acting on behalf of the airlines and hotels. The trust who the first agent places on the other may depend on the credential or the reputation that the travel agent has [RICH03].

Therefore, when we discuss trust, there are two major aspects. One is the trust placed on the data, and the other is trust placed on the agents. The trust placed on the data will depend on the trust placed on the agent. Similarly an agent who consistently produces trustworthy data can be regarded as having a higher trust value.

10.5 Trust and Risk Management

As stated by Kantarcioglu et al. [MURA06], "to manage risks in data sharing, we need to have a thorough understanding of the underlying risk factors." First of all, although trust and risk are related, they are not one and the same. For example, the more you trust someone the more you share the data with that person. However, there is also the situation where Hospital A trusts Hospital B, but A does not share data with B as B's systems are not secure. One could argue that because B's computers are not secure, then B cannot be trusted. In some cases sharing data with untrustworthy parties may not be risky. For example, a hospital may share its data with a drug company to find a cure, even though the hospital does not trust the company. Here again one could argue that the hospital places some trust that the company will find a cure for the disease even if it may not use the data appropriately. However, if the data is not sensitive, then sharing it may not be an issue. Therefore, one can treat trust and risk as interrelated but different concepts.

Although different models for the relationship between trust and risk have been proposed, the exact relationship between trust and risk in data-sharing applications is yet to be made clear [GEF03]. What we need is an appropriate model to specify trust and risk relationships. As stated by Kantarcioglu, "trust is one, but not the only factor that affects risk." Our research is involved with understanding trust and risk and developing a risk-based trust model. Kantarcioglu states that "in order to create a trust based risk model, we need to capture all the risks associated with trust misjudgments." Furthermore, he states that cost benefit analysis has to be carried out regarding whether to share the data even if the risks are high [MURA06]. Some initial research in this area is being carried out by Finin et al. at the University of Maryland (Baltimore County). We also need to develop an inference engine that can infer trust and risk based on existing values. For example, what are the risks involved in sharing the data? What happens if we do not share the data? What happens if we share the data even if it is risky?

10.6 Digital Rights Management

A digital rights management (DRM) system is composed of information technology components and services along with corresponding law, policies, and business models which enable controlled distribution of content and associated usage rights (see the discussion in Reference [DRM]).Different DRMs must interoperate and standards of the International Standards Organization (ISO) are being specified for interoperation. The relationship between rights management and the semantic Web are the ontologies. An example of such an ontology is the copyright ontology. Copyright ontology is a semantic approach which uses Web ontologies. It is based on OWL. The copyright ontology conceptualization is divided into three parts: creation model, rights model, and action model.

The creation model defines the different forms a creation can take, which are classified depending on three points of view: abstract, object, and process. The rights model follows the World Intellectual Property Organization (WIPO) recommendations to define the rights hierarchy. It includes both economic and moral rights. The most relevant rights in the DRM context are economic rights as they are related to productive and commercial aspects of copyright. Example rights are reproduction, distribution, public performance, fixation, communication, and transformation. The action model corresponds to the primitive actions that can be performed on the concepts defined in the creation model and which are regulated by the rights in the right model. Implementations of the DRM model have used OWL DL and Pellet logic reasoner. Further details can be obtained in Reference [GARC06]. General information on DRM can be found in Reference [DRM].

10.7 Reputation-Based Systems

Trust may be established using what is called a reputation network. As stated in Reference [GOLB03], a reputation-based network is a distributed, Web-based social network. The reputation rating is inferred from one user to another. Individuals are connected to each person they rated and to results in a large interconnected network of users. The only requirement is that the individuals should assert their reputation ratings for one another in the network. Individuals will be controlling their own data. Data is maintained in a distributed fashion. Data can be stored anywhere and integrated through a common foundation.

The Friend-of-a-Friend (FOAF) [RDF] Project illustrates the relationship between the semantic Web and reputation networks. An ontological vocabulary is used for describing people and their relationships. This is extended by providing a mechanism describing the reputation relationships and allows people to rate the reputation or trustworthiness of another person.

Algorithms are being developed to infer reputations. As stated in Reference [GOLB03], recommendations are made to one person (source) about the reputation of another person (sink). Trust and reputation literature contains many different metrics. These metrics are categorized according to the perspective used for making calculations. For example, global metrics calculates a single value for each entity in the network. Local metrics calculates a reputation rating for an individual in the network. In a global system, an entity will always have the same inferred rating. In a local system, an entity could be rated differently, depending on the node for which the inference is made.

An example of a reputation system is TrustMail. It is a message scoring system and adds reputation ratings to the folder views of a message. It helps sort messages according to the user after he or she sees the reputation ratings. It highlights important and relevant messages. Figure 10.5 illustrates a reputation network.

10.8 Summary and Directions

In this chapter we discussed trust management and its connection to the semantic Web. We first discussed aspects of trust management including defining trust and describing trust negotiations. Then we discussed enforcing trust within the context of the semantic Web. Furthermore, we also discussed the use of semantic Web technologies for specifying trust policies. Next we discussed related concepts including risk-based trust management, digital rights management, and reputation networks.

Our goal is to provide a high-level overview of what the challenges are and what is going on in trust related to the semantic Web. Trust management is a fledging research area and several researchers including Bertino at Purdue University, Berners Lee at MIT, Finin at the University of Maryland (Baltimore County), and Winslett at the University of Illinois at Urbana-Champaign among others are conducting extensive research on this topic. For example, Finin et al. have pioneered techniques for specifying and reasoning about trust using a language called Rei. We are collaborating with the University of Maryland (Baltimore County) on trust management in a need-to-share environment. Although numerous trust negotiation approaches have been proposed, we need research on evaluating these approaches and determining which approaches are appropriate and under what

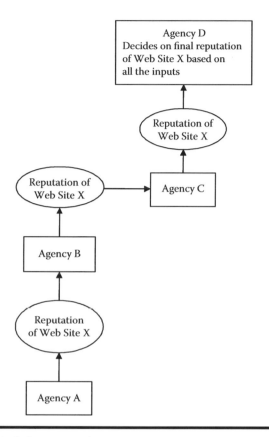

Figure 10.5 Reputation network.

context. Therefore, whereas much has been done on trust management during the past decade, much still remains to be done for specific applications and domains.

References

[BERT03] Bertino, E., E. Ferrari, and A.C. Squicciarini, Trust-Chi: an XML framework for trust negotiations, *Commun. Multimedia Security,* 2003, 146-157.

[BERT04] Bertino, E., E. Ferrari, and A.C. Squicciarini, Trust-X: a peer-to-peer framework for trust establishment, *IEEE Trans. Knowledge Data Eng.* 2004, 16(7): 827-842.

[DRM] http://en.wikipedia.org/wiki/Digital_Rights_Management.

[GARC06] García, R. and R. Gil, An OWL Copyright Ontology for Semantic Digital Rights Management, Workshop on Ontology Content and Evaluation in Enterprise, Montpellier, France, 2006.

[GEF03] Gefen, D. et al., The Conceptualization of Trust and Risk and Their Relationship in Electronic Commerce, Hawaii International Conference on Systems Sciences, Big Island, HI, Jan. 6–9, 2003.

[GOLB03] Golbeck, J., B. Parsia, and J. Hendler, Trust networks on the semantic Web, *Proc. Cooperative Inf. Agents,* August 27-29, 2003, Helsinki, Finland.

[KAGA03] Kagal, L., T. Finin, and A. Joshi, A policy based approach to security for the semantic Web, *Proc. Second Int. Semantic Web Conf.*, Sanibel Island, Florida, 2003, 402-418.

[MURA06] Kantarcioglu, M. et al., Risk-based Access Control, Technical Report, The University of Texas at Dallas, 2006.

[RDF] RDFWeb: FOAF: The Friend of a Friend Vocabulary, http://xmlns.com/foaf/0.1/.

[RICH03] Richardson, M., R. Agrawal, and P. Domingos, Trust management for the semantic Web, *Proc. Second Int. Semantic Web Conf.*, Sanibel Island, Florida, 2003.

[SHMA06] Shmatikov, V. and C. Talcott, Reputation-Based Trust Management, http://www.cs.utexas.edu/~shmat/shmat_rtm.pdf.

[SQUI06] Squicciarini, A.C., E. Bertino, E. Ferrari, and I. Ray, Achieving privacy in trust negotiations with an ontology-based approach, *IEEE Trans. Dependable Sec. Comput.* 2006, 3(1): 13-30.

[WINS04] Winsborough, W.H. and N. Li, Safety in Automated Trust Negotiation, IEEE Symposium on Security and Privacy, Oakland, CA, 2004.

[YU03] Yu, T. and M. Winslett, A Unified Scheme for Resource Protection in Automated Trust Negotiation, IEEE Symposium on Security and Privacy, Oakland, CA, 2003, 110-122.

Exercises

1. Conduct a survey of trust management and trust negotiation techniques.
2. Design an appropriate trust management approach for an application of your choice.
3. Investigate the use of semantic Web technologies for trust management.

Chapter 11

Privacy and the Semantic Web

11.1 Overview

As we have stated, although confidentiality is about the Web site or system releasing data or information only to those who are authorized according to previously specified policies, privacy is about a person determining what information should be released about him. Therefore, if privacy policies of Web sites are not acceptable to the user, then he or she can decide whether he or she wants to give information to the Web site.

Note, however, that although privacy has been discussed a great deal even at the congressional levels, not everyone agrees with this definition. For example, I teach courses at the Armed Forces Communication and Electronics Association in Washington, D.C. on data mining, national security, and privacy at the unclassified level. The students who take my courses mainly work for the Department of Defense and intelligence agencies. For them privacy is not the same as one feels about releasing, say, his or her medical records. It is my understanding that the idea of privacy of the Federal Bureau of Investigation (FBI) is to ensure that the personal information of U.S. citizens does not get into the wrong hands. Even to other agencies, the FBI will release private information only if the agency is authorized to get that information. In a way, privacy becomes more or less like confidentiality for such organizations.

Much work has been carried out on privacy including specification and enforcement of privacy policies, developing techniques for privacy-preserving data mining, and specifying standards for privacy. In this book our interest in privacy is with respect to the semantic Web. One of the significant developments with the World Wide Web Consortium (W3C) is the specification of standards that a Web site can use to specify its privacy polices. This standard is called Platform for Privacy Preferences Project (P3P). Another challenge for the semantic Web is to ensure that private information is not released as a result of semantic Web mining.

The organization of this chapter is as follows. In Section 11.2, we discuss privacy management in general. In Section 11.3, we discuss semantic Web technologies (such as eXtensible Markup Language (XML) and Resource Description Framework (RDF)) for specifying privacy policies. Protecting the private information such as private Web pages is discussed in Section 11.4. P3P is discussed in Section 11.5. Privacy problems via inference including privacy-constraint processing is discussed in Section 11.6. Privacy-preserving semantic Web mining is the subject of Section 11.7. Our prototype implementation is discussed in Section 11.8. The chapter is concluded in Section 11.9.

11.2 Privacy Management

Social scientists have studied privacy for several years, and policy specialists have developed privacy policies for agencies and corporations. However, it is only recently that security specialists have started focusing on privacy. Furthermore, the Terrorism Information Awareness Program at the Defense Advanced Projects Research Agency (DARPA) together with the focus on data mining has resulted in efforts on privacy-preserving data mining and privacy-preserving data management. Today, privacy is an important area of information security. However, it has been difficult to give a precise definition of privacy as each organization and agency has a different view [SWEE04].

So, the question is, what is privacy? The general notion is that a person should decide what personal information should be released about him or her. Such a definition was fine before we had tools for data analysis and data mining and the World Wide Web. Through such tools it may now be possible for someone to infer private information about another person. Therefore, we need to perhaps redefine the notion of privacy. On the other hand, some organizations want to control personal information about the community and decide to whom they should release personal information. For example, as stated earlier, my understanding is that the FBI has information about various individuals; they will determine whether to release the information to, say, the Central Intelligence Agency (CIA). Initially, I argued that this is essentially ensuring confidentiality and not privacy. However, after working more on privacy issues and reading about the subject, I now believe that there can be no universal definition of privacy. Privacy has to be defined by an organization. One organization may define privacy policies as policies protecting its sensitive information. Another organization may define privacy policies to be those that are specified by those who work for the organization as to what information can be released by them. Therefore, whether privacy policies are a subset of confidentiality policies or whether they are separate policies is left to an organization to determine.

Our interest also lies in the relationship between privacy, confidentiality, and trust. As we have discussed in the earlier chapters, we have made the following assumption in our work. Trust is established between, say, a Web site and a user based on credentials or reputations. When a user logs into a Web site to make a purchase, the Web site will specify what its privacy policies are. The user will then determine whether he wants to enter personal information. If the Web site will give out the user's address to a third party, then the user can decide whether to enter this information. However, before the user enters the information, the user has to decide whether he trusts the Web site. This can be based on the credential and reputation. If the user trusts the Web site, then the user can enter his private information if he is satisfied with the policies. If not, he can choose not to enter the information.

We have given a similar reasoning for confidentiality. Here the user is requesting information from the Web site; the Web site checks its confidentiality policies and decides what information to release to the user. The Web site can also check the trust it has on the user and decide whether to give the information to the user. As stated in Chapter 10, one can also determine the quality of the data based on the trust placed on the user or on the Web site.

More details on specific aspects of privacy and the semantic Web will be discussed in the next several sections. In particular, applying semantic Web technologies for privacy management, privacy issues for the semantic Web, the platform for privacy preferences, the privacy problem that occurs via inference, and privacy-preserving semantic Web mining will be discussed. Figure 11.1 illustrates aspects of privacy management.

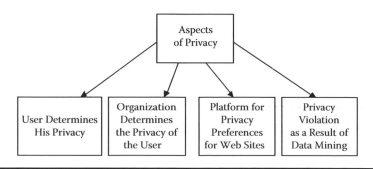

Figure 11.1   Privacy management.

11.3 Semantic Web Applications for Privacy Management

The major contributions of semantic Web technologies for privacy management are in specifying policies in semantic Web technologies. These policies could be specified in XML, RDF, Web Ontology Language (OWL), as shown in Figure 11.2, or related semantic Web languages. Another contribution is the platform for privacy preferences. The W3C community has come up with a framework for Web sites to specify privacy policies. This framework, called the Platform for Privacy Preferences Project (P3P), is discussed in Section 11.5.

As in the case of trust management, one needs to decide the appropriate language to specify privacy polices. XML is becoming a popular language for this purpose. Even the P3P standards initially focused on using RDF for privacy-policy specification and switched to XML. However, if one needs to represent the semantics of the privacy policies and reasoning about privacy, then RDF or OWL would be more appropriate.

In specifying privacy policies, one also needs to determine whether sensitive or private information could be leaked. Appropriate confidentiality or privacy policies may be enforced on the original privacy policies themselves. Therefore, we may want to control access to various parts of the privacy-policy specifications [P3P].

11.4 Privacy for the Semantic Web

Privacy for the semantic Web is essentially about ensuring that private information is not divulged via usage of the semantic Web. Note that the semantic Web is a collection of representation and reasoning technologies. Therefore, the goal is not to reveal private information. For this, we need to ensure that privacy policies are enforced properly on XML and RDF documents as well as OWL ontologies. Furthermore, the goal of the reasoning engines that are developed based on descriptive logics are such that private information cannot be inferred by deduction.

Privacy for semantic Web technologies has received little attention. Bertino et al. [SQUI07] have investigated privacy for XML and also examined aspects of privacy violations that result from trust management based on their Trust-X system.

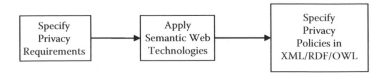

Figure 11.2 Semantic Web for privacy.

Finin et al. are examining privacy for their research on the semantic Web, although their research is focusing mainly on trust management [KAGA03]. In our investigation of confidentiality, privacy, and trust (CPT) for the semantic Web we have privacy enforcement based on what we call the basic system and the advanced system [THUR06a]. Note that the advanced system consists of a privacy engine that will focus on privacy violations via inference. In Section 11.2 we discussed CPT for a general Web environment. With the semantic Web, the idea is for the machine to examine the Web pages and determine whether any private information is revealed. Furthermore, with an ordinary Web, the Web site will display its privacy policies to the user, and the user determines whether to enter his or her private information. However, with semantic Web technologies, the Web site will examine privacy policies and use preferences and give advice to the user as to whether he or she should enter private information.

As stated earlier, one of the significant developments of privacy and the semantic Web lies in the platform for privacy preferences. This will be discussed in Section 11.5. Figure 11.3 illustrates privacy management for the semantic Web.

11.5 Platform for Privacy Preferences

P3P is an emerging industry standard that enables Web sites to express their privacy practices in a standard format. The format of the policies can be automatically retrieved and understood by user agents. It is a product of the W3C [W3C]. As we have stated, the main difference between privacy and security as considered in many domains is the following: the user is informed of the privacy policies enforced by the Web site, or the user is not informed of the security (or confidentiality) policies in general. When a user enters a Web site, the privacy policies of the Web site are conveyed to the user. If the privacy policies are different from user preferences, the user is notified. The user can then decide how to proceed.

Several major corporations are working on P3P standards including Microsoft, IBM, Hewlett Packard, NEC Nokia, and NCR. Several Web sites have also implemented P3P. The Semantic Web group has adopted P3P. An initial version of P3P

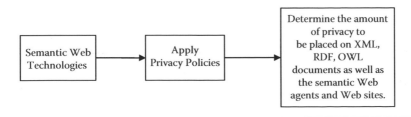

Figure 11.3 Privacy for the semantic Web.

used RDF to specify policies. A recent version has migrated to XML. P3P Policies use XML with namespaces for encoding policies.

Example: Catalog Shopping. Your name will not be given to a third party, but your purchases will be given to a third party.

```
<POLICIES xmlns = http://www.w3.org/2002/01/P3Pv1>
          <POLICY name = - - - -
          </POLICY>
     </POLICIES>
```

P3P has its own statements and data types expressed in XML. P3P schemas utilize XML schemas. XML is a prerequisite to understanding P3P. P3P specification released in January 2005 uses the catalog shopping example to explain concepts. P3P is an international standard and is an ongoing project.

Note that P3P does not replace laws. P3P works together with the law. What happens if the Web sites do not honor their P3P policies? Then appropriate legal actions will have to be taken. Today XML is the technology to specify P3P policies. Policy experts will have to specify the policies. Technologies will have to develop the specifications. Legal experts will have to take actions if the policies are violated.

11.6   Privacy Problem through Inference

We have conducted extensive research on the inference problem for secure databases. Much of our work has focused on security-constraint processing, which has now come to be known as policy management. Policies included those for content and context-dependent constraints as well as dynamic and event-based constraints. For example, the ship's mission becomes classified after the war begins [THUR95]. We have since adapted this approach for privacy-constraint processing where security levels would now become privacy levels (public, private, semipublic, etc.) and the security constraint becomes a privacy constraint such as names and healthcare records taken together. It should be noted that with this approach we are assuming that privacy and confidentiality are one and the same. Now, this agrees with, say, the FBI's notion of privacy where it has to protract the private information of U.S. citizens. But this is not consistent with medical privacy, where in this context, privacy is specified by an individual; that is, an individual determines the information he has to keep private. In this case, the privacy controller is managed by the individual, that is, the client will determine that if it gives out, say, its genetic information, then an insurance company can figure out the illnesses it may be prone to. Therefore, the privacy controller will guide the client as to what information to release about himself or herself.

Figure 11.4 illustrates the privacy controller. Here data represented using semantic Web technologies such as XML, RDF, and ontologies are augmented with infer-

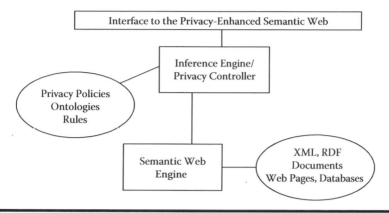

Figure 11.4   Privacy controller.

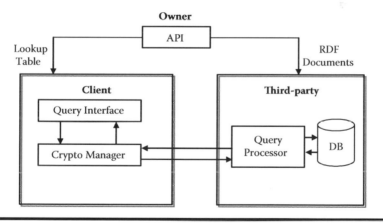

Figure 11.5   Architecture of the prototype system.

ence engines. These engines may carry out rule processing or utilize ontology-based reasoning to deduce new data from existing data. If the new data is private, then it can give advice to the client as to what information should be kept private. Note that under the FBI scenario, the privacy controller is essentially the confidentiality controller (which we have called the inference controller), and therefore it acts on the server side and determines what information it has to release to the client (such as the CIA).

Note that we have proved that the inference problem is unsolvable [THUR90]. We have applied similar techniques to prove that the privacy problem is unsolvable [THUR06b]. Figure 11.5 illustrates the architecture of a privacy controller.

11.7 Privacy-Preserving Semantic Web Mining

In our previous book [THUR05], we discussed privacy-preserving data mining. The idea is as follows. Using data-mining tools, even naïve users can make unauthorized inferences that could be highly sensitive or private. Furthermore, the goal is to hide the private data such as disease of a particular person while giving out general trends and associations. For example, we could give out the information that "people living in California are more prone to asthma" without giving out the fact that John has asthma. Privacy-preserving data-mining techniques work with perturbed or randomized data without revealing the actual data.

Recently there have been reports on semantic Web mining. There are two aspects here. One is to mine the data on the Web using semantic Web technologies such as XML, RDF, and OWL. Note that much of the work has focused on mining relational data. More recently there is work on mining unstructured data such as text, audio, images, and video. The challenge is to mine the databases that store and manage XML and RDF documents. The other aspect is to mine the XML and RDF documents without revealing the actual data, but giving out correlations and trends. The former is an aspect of data mining, whereas the latter is an aspect of privacy-preserving data mining. There is yet a third aspect, and that is to use ontologies to help the mining process. For example, the data-mining tool may need clarifications about the meaning of a Web page. Here, ontologies expressed in OWL may be used to clarify the concepts to facilitate the mining process.

11.8 Prototype Privacy Controller Implementation

Although our goal is to develop a privacy controller using the inference engine approach illustrated in Figure 11.4, we have carried out a preliminary implementation of a privacy controller using products and tools available commercially or as an open source. We have used two enabling technologies, Jena and JCE, to achieve privacy. More information on these tools is given in Appendix C. Details of the implementation are given in Reference [ALAM07].

Jena is a Java-based application programming interface (API) for parsing, querying, and accessing RDF documents and therefore can be thought of as a one-stop source for RDF data processing. JCE is the cryptography extension provided by Sun Java™. Figure 11.4 illustrates the overall framework for privacy-enabling document creation, dissemination, and querying. This programming project implements only the Crypto Manager component. The Crypto Manager is a layered architecture. Figure 11.5 illustrates the architecture, and the interface to the database is illustrated in Figure 11.6. There is a user interface that lets data owners upload their data on the database of the third party. The implementation is done with the assumption that the database is MySQL, although ideally one should go after a dedicated RDF server such as Intellidimension RDF Gateway. But as of the

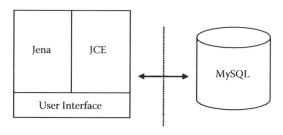

Figure 11.6   Interface to the database.

time when this implementation was done, RDF Gateway lacks full-fledged support for Java clients. On top of that, Jena does not support RDF Gateway driver either, which makes it impossible to go the desired route. There is a workaround to this difficulty: using the native parser of Jena, one can manually manipulate RDF syntax and store the results in any desired database. But for the time being, MySQL suffices to demonstrate the efficiency of our scheme.

There are two main algorithms we have simulated. One is the encryption algorithm to individually encrypt document elements. The other is the decryption algorithm that works in reverse and puts out the original document. There is also a lookup table which is a flat text file that is encrypted with the public key of the client. Our algorithms, the simulation results, and details of the prototype are given in Reference [ALAM07]. We are currently examining ways to extend this prototype to handle privacy violations via inference.

11.9   Summary and Directions

In this chapter we have discussed the various notions of privacy and provided an overview of privacy management. Then we discussed the semantic Web technology applications for privacy management. Privacy for the Web was discussed next. This was followed by a discussion of the standard Platform for Privacy Preferences. Finally, we discussed privacy violations through inference and privacy-preserving semantic Web mining. We also discussed our preliminary prototype implementation.

Much of the discussion in this chapter is in the early stages of research. We have not attempted to discuss the correct definition of privacy. Our goal is to illustrate the connection between privacy management and the semantic Web. As we have mentioned, semantic Web technologies are useful in the specification of privacy policies. Furthermore, data represented by XML and RDF could be mined and privacy violated as a result.

We have stressed in our work that technology alone is not sufficient to protect the privacy of the individuals. We need social scientists, technologists, and policy makers to work together. It is also important to bring in legal specialists. Some have said that it will be impossible to prevent privacy violations and that legal measures are the only viable solution. However, our view is "some privacy is better than nothing." But we have to be careful not to inflict a false sense of privacy or security.

References

[ALAM07] Ashraful, A. and B. Thuraisingham, Design and Implementation of a Privacy Controller.

[BAIN03] Bainbridge, W., Privacy, *Encyclopedia of Community*, Sage Publications, Thousand Oaks, CA, 2003.

[KAGA03] Kaga, L., T.W. Finin, and A. Joshi, A Policy Based Approach to Security for the Semantic Web, International Semantic Web Conference, 2003, 402–418.

[P3P] Platform for Privacy Preferences, www.w3c.org.

[SQUI07] Squicciarini, A.C., E. Bertino, E. Ferrari, F. Paci, and B. Thuraisingham. PP-Trust-X A system for privacy preserving trust negotiations. *ACM TISSEC Tran. Syst. Info. Secur.*, 10, 2007.

[SWEE04] Sweeney, L., Navigating computer science research through waves of privacy concerns: discussions among computer scientists at Carnegie Mellon University, *ACM Comput. Soc.*, 34, 2004.

[THUR90] Thuraisingham, B., Recurison Theoretic Complexity of the Inference Problem, Computer Security Foundations Workshop, 1990 (also Technical Report, The MITRE Corporation MTP-291).

[THUR95] Thuraisingham, B. and W. Ford, Security constraint processing in a multi-level distributed database management system, *IEEE Trans. Knowledge Data Eng.*, 7, 1995.

[THUR05] Thuraisingham, B., *Database and Applications Security: Integrating Data Management and Information Security*, CRC Press, Boca Raton, FL, 2005.

[THUR06a] Thuraisingham, B. et al., Administering the semantic Web, confidentiality, privacy and trust, *J. Inf. Security Privacy*, 2006.

[THUR06b] Thuraisingham, B., On the Complexity of the Privacy Problem, Technical Report, University of Texas at Dallas, 2006.

Exercises

1. Design an application, and describe the privacy requirements.
2. Investigate the applications of semantic Web technologies for privacy management.
3. Design and develop a privacy controller for XML and RDF documents.

Chapter 12

Integrity Management and the Semantic Web

12.1 Overview

In Part II we discussed confidentiality aspects for the semantic Web, and in the earlier chapters of Part III we discussed privacy and trust management aspects. In this chapter we will discuss integrity management for the semantic Web. Integrity includes several aspects. In the database world, integrity includes concurrency control and recovery as well as enforcing integrity constraints. For example, when multiple transactions execute at the same time, the consistency of the data has to be ensured. When a transaction aborts, it has to be ensured that the database is recovered from the failure into a consistent state. Integrity constraints are rules that have to be satisfied by the data. Rules include "salary value has to be positive" and "age of an employee cannot decrease over time." More recently integrity has included data quality, data provenance, data currency, real-time processing, and fault tolerance.

In this chapter we will discuss integrity with respect to semantic Web technologies. For example, how do we ensure the integrity of the data and the processes? How do we ensure that data quality is maintained? Some aspects of integrity are already being investigated by researchers, and some other aspects are yet to be investigated. The organization of this chapter is as follows. In Section 12.2 we discuss aspects of integrity. Semantic Web technologies for integrity management are discussed in Section 12.3. Integrity for the semantic Web is discussed in Section 12.4. Closely related to integrity is data provenance, and this is discussed in Section 12.5. The chapter is concluded in Section 12.6.

12.2 Integrity, Data Quality, and Provenance

As stated in Section 12.1, there are many aspects to integrity. For example, concurrency control, recovery, data accuracy, meeting real-time constraints, data accuracy, data quality, data provenance, fault tolerance, and integrity-constraint enforcement are all aspects of integrity management. This is illustrated in Figure 12.1. In this section we will examine each aspect of integrity.

> **Concurrency control:** In data management, concurrent control is about transactions executing at the same time and ensuring consistency of the data. Therefore, transactions have to obtain locks or utilize time stamps to ensure that the data is left in a consistent state when multiple transactions attempt to access the data at the same time. Extensive research has been carried out on concurrency control techniques for transaction management, both in centralized as well as in distributed environments [BERN87].
>
> **Data recovery:** When transactions abort before they complete execution, the database should be recovered to a consistent state such as its state before the transaction started execution. Several recovery techniques have been proposed to ensure the consistency of the data.
>
> **Data authenticity:** When the data is delivered to the user, its authenticity has to be ensured; that is, the user should get accurate data, and the data should not be tampered with. We have conducted research on ensuring authenticity of XML data during third-party publishing [BERT04].

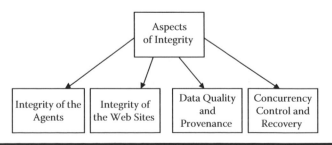

Figure 12.1   Aspects of integrity.

Data completeness: Data that a user receives should not only be authentic, but also be complete; everything that the user is authorized to see has to be delivered to the user.

Data currency: Data has to be current. Data that is outdated has to be deleted or archived, and the data that the user sees has to be current data. Data currency is an aspect of real-time processing. If a user wants to retrieve the temperature, he has to be given the current temperature, not the temperature that is 24 hours old.

Data accuracy: The question is, how accurate is the data? This is also closely related to data quality and data currency. Accuracy depends on whether the data has been maliciously corrupted or whether it has come from an untrusted source.

Data quality: Is the data of high quality? This includes data authenticity, data accuracy, and whether the data is complete or certain. If the data is uncertain, then can we reason with certainty to ensure that the operations that use the data are not affected? Data quality also depends on the data source.

Data provenance: This has to do with the history of the data, that is, from the time the data originated, such as emanating from the sensors, until the present time, such as when it is given to the general user. The question is, who has accessed the data? Who has modified the data? How has the data traveled? This will determine whether the data has been misused.

Integrity constraints: These are rules that the data has to satisfy, such as the age of a person cannot be a negative number. This type of integrity has been studied extensively by the database and artificial intelligence communities.

Fault tolerance: As in the case of data recovery, the processes that fail have to be recovered. Therefore, fault tolerance deals with data recovery as well as process recovery. Techniques for fault tolerance include checkpointing and acceptance testing.

Real-time processing: Data currency is one aspect of real-time processing where the data has to be current. Real-time processing also has to deal with transactions meeting timing constraints. For example, stock quotes have to be given at within, say, five minutes. If not, it will be too late. Missing timing constraints could cause integrity violations.

In the next two sections we will explore the relationships between integrity management and semantic Web technologies.

12.3 Semantic Web for Integrity Management

The previous chapters discussed the use of semantic Web technologies to specify policies for confidentiality, trust, and privacy. For example, in Part II we discussed the use of eXtensible Markup Language (XML) and Resource Description Framework (RDF) to specify confidentiality policies. In Chapter 10 we illustrated how semantic Web technologies may be used to specify privacy policies. Specifying trust policies was discussed in Chapter 11. In this section we will discuss the use of semantic Web technologies for integrity management.

Like confidentiality, privacy, and trust, semantic Web technologies such as XML may be used to specify integrity policies. Integrity policies may include policies for specifying integrity constraints as well as policies for specifying timing constraints, data currency, and data quality. Here are some examples of the policies:

Integrity Constraints: The age of an employee has to be positive. In a relational representation, one could specify this policy as

```
EMP.AGE>0.
```

In XML this could be represented as the following:

```
<Condition Object="//Employe/Age">
  <Apply FunctionId="greater-than">
    <AttributeValue
DataType="http://www.w3.org/2001/XMLSchema#integer">0
    </AttributeValue>
  </Apply>
</Condition>
```

Data Quality Policy: The quality of the data in the employee table is low. In relational resonations this could be presented as

```
EMP.Quality = LOW.
```

In XML this policy could be represented as

```
<Condition Object="//Employe/Quality">
  <Apply FunctionId="equal">
    <AttributeValue
DataType="http://www.w3.org/2001/XMLSchema#string">LOW
    </AttributeValue>
  </Apply>
</Condition>
```

Data Currency: An example is the salary value of the employee (EMP) cannot be more than 365 days old. In a relational representation this could be represented as:

```
AGE(EMP.SAL) <= 365 days.
```

In XML this is represented as:

```
<Condition Object="//Employe/Salary">
  <Apply FunctionId="AGE">
    <Apply FunctionId="less-than-or-equal">
      <AttributeValue
DataType="http://www.w3.org/2001/XMLSchema#integer">365
      </AttributeValue>
    </Apply>
  </Apply>
</Condition>
```

The previous examples have shown how certain integrity policies may be specified. Note that there are many other applications of semantic Web technologies to ensure integrity. For example, to ensure data provenance, the history of the data has to be documented. Semantic Web technologies such as XML are being used to represent, say, the data annotations that are used to determine the quality of the data or whether the data has been misused. The data captured is annotated with metadata information such as what the data is about, when it was captured, and who captured it. Then as the data moves from place to place or from person to person, the annotations are updated so that at a later time the data may be analyzed for misuse. These annotations are typically represented in semantic Web technologies such as XML, RDF, and Web Ontology Language (OWL).

Another application of semantic Web technologies for integrity management is the use of ontologies to resolve semantic heterogeneity. Semantic heterogeneity causes integrity violations. This happens when the same entity is considered to be different at different sites and therefore compromises integrity and accuracy. Through the use of ontologies specified in, say, OWL, it can be expressed that the ship in one site and submarine in another site are one and the same.

Semantic Web technologies also have applications in making inferences and reasoning about uncertainty or miming. For example, the reasoning engines based on RDF, OWL, or, say, Rules may be used to determine whether the integrity policies are violated. We have discussed inference and privacy problems and building inference engines in Part II as well as in the earlier chapters in Part III. These techniques have to be investigated for violation of integrity policies. Figure 12.2 illustrates the use of semantic Web technologies for integrity management.

12.4 Integrity for the Semantic Web

Whereas we discussed the use of semantic Web technologies for integrity management in Section 12.3, in this section we will discuss how integrity may be maintained for semantic Web technologies. Note that in Part II we discussed third-party publications of XML documents while maintaining consistency and completeness.

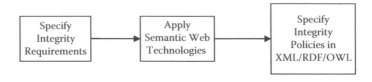

Figure 12.2   Semantic Web for integrity management.

This is one aspect of integrity management for semantic Web technologies. The ideas expressed in our work could be extended to RDF and related documents. Note also that XML, RDF, and OWL documents have to be current, they have to be of high quality, and they have to satisfy the integrity constraints, that is, all of the integrity issues that we discussed in the previous two sections have to be addressed for documents represented in XML and RDF. This is one aspect of integrity for the semantic Web.

As we have discussed in Section 12.3, annotations that are used for data quality and provenance are typically represented in XML or RDF documents. These documents have to be accurate, complete, and current. Therefore, integrity has to be enforced for such documents. Another aspect of integrity is managing databases that consist of XML or RDF documents. These databases have all of the issues and challenges that are present for, say, relational databases; the queries have to be optimized, and transactions should execute concurrently. Therefore, concurrency control and recovery for XML and RDF documents become a challenge for managing XML and RDF databases. This is yet another aspect of integrity for semantic Web documents.

The actions of the agents that make use of the semantic Web to carry out operations such as searching, querying, and integrating heterogeneous databases have to ensure that the integrity of the data is maintained. These agents cannot maliciously corrupt the data. They have to ensure that the data is accurate, complete, and consistent. Finally, when integrating heterogeneous databases, semantic Web technologies such as OWL are being used to handle semantic heterogeneity. These ontologies have to be accurate and complete and cannot be tampered with.

In summary, for the semantic Web technologies to be useful, they have to enforce integrity. Furthermore, semantic Web technologies themselves are being used to specify integrity policies. Figure 12.3 illustrates integrity management for the semantic Web.

12.5   Inferencing, Data Quality, and Data Provenance

Some researchers feel that data quality is an application of data provenance. Furthermore, they have developed theories for inferring data quality. In this section we

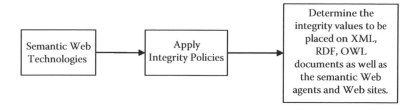

Figure 12.3 Integrity for the semantic Web.

will examine some of the developments, keeping in mind the relationship between data quality, data provenance, and the semantic Web.

Data quality is about accuracy, timeliness, and dependability (i.e., trustworthiness) of the data. It is, however, subjective and depends on the users and the domains. Some of the issues that have to be answered include the creation of the data, that is, where did it come from and why, and how was the data obtained? Data-quality information is stored as annotations to the data and should be part of the data provenance. One could ask the question as to how we can obtain the trustworthiness of the data. This could depend on how the source is ranked and the reputation of the source. Note that we discussed reputation in Chapter 10.

As we have stated, researchers have developed theories for inferring data quality [PON05]. The motivation is due to the fact that data could come from multiple sources, it is shared, and it is prone to errors. Furthermore, data could be uncertain. Therefore, theories of uncertainty such as statistical reasoning, Bayesian theories, and Dempster Schafer Theory of Evidence are being used to infer the quality of the data. With respect to security, we need to ensure that the quality of the inferred data does not violate the policies. For example, at the unclassified level we may say that the source is trustworthy, but at the secret level we know that the source is not trustworthy. The inference controllers that we have developed could be integrated with the theories of interceding developed for data quality to ensure security.

Next let us examine data provenance. For many of the domains including medical, healthcare, and defense where the accuracy of the data is critical for life threating activities, we need to have a good understanding as to where the data came from and who may have tampered with the data. As stated in [SIMM05], data provenance, a kind of metadata, sometimes called "lineage" or "pedigree" is the description of the origins of a piece of data and the process by which it arrived in a database. Data provenance is information that helps determine the derivation history of a data product, starting from its original sources.

Provenance information can be applied for data quality, auditing, and ownership, among others. By having records of who accessed the data, data misuse can be determined. Usually annotations are used to store the present information of the data. The challenge is to determine whether one needs to maintain coarse-grained

Who created the data?

Where has the data come from?

Who accessed the data?

What is the complete history of the data?

Has the data been misused?

Figure 12.4   Data provenance.

provenance data or fine-grained provenance data. For example, in a course-grained situation, the tables of a relation may be annotated, whereas in a fine-grained situation, every element may be annotated. There is, of course, the storage overhead to consider for managing provenance. XML, RDF, and OWL have been used to represent provenance data, and this way the tools developed for the semantic Web technologies may be used to manage the provenance data. Figure 12.4 illustrates annotations to maintain data provenance.

12.6   Summary and Directions

In this chapter we have provided an overview of data integrity which includes data quality and data provenance. We discussed the applications of semantic Web technologies for data integrity as well as discussed integrity for semantic Web technologies. Finally, we provided an overview of the relationship between data quality and data provenance.

Data provenance and data quality, although important, are only recently receiving attention. This is due to the fact that there are vast quantities of information on the Web, and it is important to know the accuracy of the data and whether the data are copies or have been plagiarized. We also need to have answers to questions such as who owns the data. Has the data been misused? Therefore, data provenance is important to determine the security of the data.

Semantic Web technologies provide a way to represent and store data quality and provenance data. As we make progress with these technologies, we will have improved solutions for data quality and data provenance management. Essentially, data quality and data provenance are part of data security, and semantic Web technologies are very useful to manage data quality and data provenance information.

References

[PON05] Pon, R.K. and A.F. Cárdenas, Data quality inference, *Proc. Conf. Inf. Quality Inf. Syst. (IQIS)*, Baltimore, MD, June 2005.

[SIMM05] Simmhan, Y.L., B. Plale, and D. Gannon, A Survey of Data Provenance in e-Science, Indiana University Technical Report.

[BERT04] Bertino, E. et al., Secure third party publication of XML documents, *IEEE Trans. Knowledge Data Eng.*, 10, 2004.

[BERN87] Bernstein, P. et al., *Concurrency Control and Recovery in Database Systems*, Addison-Wesley, Reading, MA, 1987.

Exercises

1. Conduct a survey of data provenance.
2. Design an appropriate data-integrity management approach for an application of your choice.
3. Investigate the use of semantic Web technologies for integrity management.

Chapter 13

Multilevel Security

13.1 Overview

Whereas the previous three chapters discussed trust, privacy, and integrity management for the semantic Web, in this chapter we will discuss aspects of multilevel semantic Webs. In a multilevel secure semantic Web, the data (such as eXtensible Markup Language (XML) and Resource Description Framework (RDF) documents) are assigned multiple security levels and users of the semantic Web (i.e., the agents) have multiple clearance levels. The idea is for users to carry out activities using the semantic Web so that they do not access or infer unauthorized data or information.

To our knowledge, no prior work deals with multilevel semantic Webs. Much of the work on multilevel information systems has focused on multilevel data-management systems where a user is cleared at different clearance levels and the data is assigned different sensitivity levels. Users read data at or below the level and write data at their level. It is assumed that these sets of levels form a particularly ordered lattice, with Unclassified < Confidential < Secret < Top Secret. In this chapter we will discuss multilevel security issues for the semantic Web. We will extend the work on multilevel secure data-management systems to address multilevel security for XML, RDF, and ontologies as well as reason about these different technologies so that security violations via inference does not occur.

The organization of this chapter is as follows. In Section 13.2 we provide some background information on multilevel secure data-management systems. In Section 13.3 we discuss multilevel secure XML, RDF, OWL, and RuleML documents. Reasoning aspects are discussed in Section 13.4. Inference problems for multilevel secure semantic Webs are discussed in Section 13.5. The chapter is summarized in Section 13.6.

13.2 Multilevel Secure Data Management Systems

In a multilevel secure database-management system (MLS/DBMS), users are cleared at different clearance levels such as Unclassified, Confidential, Secret, and TopSecret. Data is assigned different sensitivity levels such as Unclassified, Confidential, Secret, and TopSecret. It is generally assumed that these security levels form a partially ordered lattice. For example, Unclassified < Confidential < Secret < TopSecret. Partial ordering comes from having different compartments. For example, Secret Compartment A may be incomparable to Secret Compartment B.

The early efforts such as the Hinke–Schaefer approach as well as the Air Force Summer Study focused mainly on the relational approach [HINK75], [AFSB83]. Systems such as SeaView, LOCK Data Views, and ASD Views focused on designing multilevel relational data models as well as providing access based on views. These efforts also formulated the notion of polyinstantiation, where users are given different views of an element based on their clearance levels. Other research issues examined in MLS/DBMSs based on the relational data model included secure transaction processing and the inference problem. Security-constraint processing was also explored a great deal. Details are given in our previous book on data and applications security [THUR05].

The most notable hard problem is the inference problem. The inference problem is the process of posing queries and deducing sensitive information from the legitimate responses received. Many efforts have been discussed in the literature on how to handle the inference problem. First of all, we proved that the general inference problem was unsolvable (see Reference [THUR90]). Then we explored the use of security constraints and conceptual structures to handle various types of inferences ([THUR91a]). The aggregation problem is a special case of the inference problem where collections of data elements are sensitive while the individual data elements are Unclassified.

Another hard problem is secure transaction processing. Many efforts have been reported on reducing covert channels when processing transactions in MLS/DBMSs (see, for example, [JAJO90a] and [ATLU95]). A survey of various secure concurrency control efforts in MLS/DBMSs is reported in Reference [KO93]. The challenge is to design MLS/DBMSs that function in a real-time environment; that is, not only do the transactions have to be secure they also have to meet timing constraints.

A third challenging problem is developing a multilevel secure relational data model. Various proposals have been developed including those by Jajodia and Sandhu [JAJO90], the Sea View model [DENN87], and the LOCK Data Views model [STAC90]. SWORD also proposed its own model (see Reference [WISE90]). Thuraisingham has proposed an approach to unify the various models [THUR93]. The problem is due to the fact that different users have different views of the same element. If we use multiple values to represent the same entity, then we are violating the integrity of databases. However, if we do not enforce what is called polyinstantiation, then there is a potential for signaling channels. This is still an open problem.

As technologies emerge, one can examine multilevel security issues for these emerging technologies. For example, as object database systems emerged in the 1980s, we started examining multilevel security for object databases. Today we have many new technologies including data warehousing, E-commerce systems, multimedia systems, and the Web and digital libraries. Only a limited number of efforts have been reported on investigating multilevel security for the emerging data-management systems. This is partly due to the fact that even for relational systems there are hard problems to solve with respect to multilevel security. As the system becomes more complex, developing high-assurance multilevel systems becomes an enormous challenge.

For example, how can one develop usable multilevel secure systems, say, for digital libraries and E-commerce systems? How can we get acceptable performance? How do we verify huge systems such as the World Wide Web? At present we still have a lot to do with respect to discretionary security for such emerging systems. We believe that as we make progress with assurance technologies, and if there is a need for multilevel security for such emerging technologies, then research initiatives will commence on these areas. The next section will discuss some of our ideas on multilevel semantic Webs. Aspects of multilevel secure data management are illustrated in Figure 13.1.

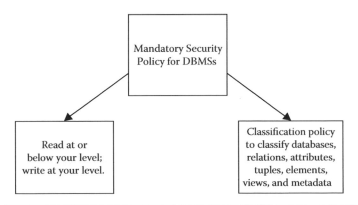

Figure 13.1   Multilevel secure data management.

13.3 Multilevel XML, RDF, OWL, and RuleML Documents

In this section we will discuss multilevel security for semantic Web technologies. In particular, we will examine multilevel security for XML, RDF, OWL, and RuleML. Much of the focus will be on the representation aspects. Reasoning will be discussed in the next section.

First, let us consider multilevel secure XML documents. The main issues here include the granularity of classification and securing XML data-management systems. For example, should the entire XML document be classified, or should portions be classified? How can polyinstantiation be enforced for XML documents? Can we apply the principles for securing relational data for XML data? What policies should we enforce on XML schemas? How can content, context, and dynamic multilevel security policies be enforced? How can query modification and secure-transaction processing be handled for multilevel secure XML databases?

In the case of RDF documents, we need to first secure XML documents and then examine the reasoning aspects. RDF uses XML syntax and has additional semantics. With semantics come additional security concerns. What happens if the conclusion is classified when the antecedents are not classified? Can we arrive at multiple conclusions at different security levels? How can conflicts be handled? How can we classify an RDF statement consisting of a (Object, Property, Value) triple? For example, in the statement "Berners Lee invented the Semantic Web" what are the implications of classifying the fact that Berners Lee invented something at the Unclassified level and the fact that he invented the semantic Web at the Secret level?

With respect to ontologism and OWL, we have to handle all the challenges of RDF and also examine additional issues due to the fact that OWL has additional reasoning and representational capabilities. What happens if multiple ontologies are used at different security levels? Can we link these multiple versions of the same ontology at different levels? What happens if the conclusions are classified whereas the antecedents are not?

With RuleML, there are inherent reasoning capabilities. Therefore, the techniques we have developed for logics such as nonmonotonic typed multilevel logic (NTML) for secure databases [THUR91b] have to be examined for multilevel rules. For example, should we build different reasoning engines at different levels? How can inference and privacy problems be handled?

One major issue for multilevel secure semantic Webs is the trust that we need to place on agents. Note that multiple agents communicate with each other and carry out activities by invoking Web services and other related technologies. Can we have communication between agents at different levels? How do we handle covert channels? How much trust do we place on agents? These are challenging questions. To

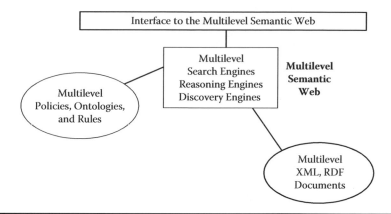

Figure 13.2 Multilevel secure semantic Web (MLS/SW).

date we have yet to see research on multilevel semantic Webs. Figure 13.2 illustrates multilevel secure semantic Webs (MLS/SWs).

13.4 Reasoning and the Inference Problem

In the late 1970s and throughout the 1980s, there were many efforts on designing and developing logic-based database systems. These systems were called deductive databases (see Refences [FROS86] and [ULLM88]). While investigating the inference problem, we designed multilevel secure deductive database systems. These systems were based on a logic called nonmonotonic typed multilevel logic (NTML) that we designed [THUR91b].

NTML essentially provides the reasoning capability across security levels, which are nonmonotonic in nature. Essentially it incorporates constructs to reason about the applications at different security levels. We also designed a Prolog language based on NTML, which is called NTML-Prolog. We investigated both reasoning with the Closed World Assumption as well as with the Open World Assumption.

Due to the fact that there was limited success with logic programming and the Japanese Fifth Generation Project, deductive systems are being used only for a few applications. If such applications are to be multilevel secure, then systems such as those based on NTML will be needed. Nevertheless, there is use for NTML on handling problems such as the inference problem.

Note that we are at present exploring the integration of NTML-like logic with descriptive logics for secure semantic Webs. A discussion of descriptive logics can be found in [MCGU02]. The challenges include, how can we reason across security levels for systems based on descriptive logics? Do we build different reasoning engines? How can we handle policy inconsistency? Figure 13.3 illustrates an inference controller for an MLS/SW.

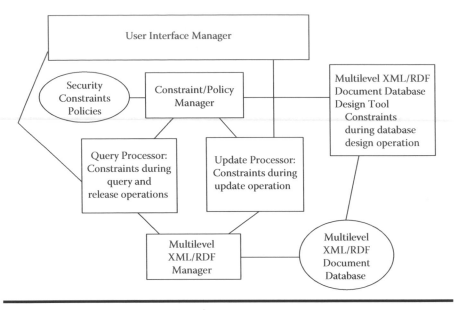

Figure 13.3 Inference controller.

13.5 Summary and Directions

This chapter discussed multilevel security issues with respect to the semantic Web. We first provided an overview of multilevel secure data management. This was followed by a discussion of multilevel security for semantic Web technologies. Next we discussed logics for MLS/SWS and the inference problem.

To our knowledge there is no research on MLS/SWS. However, if these systems are to be used in a highly classified multilevel environment, we need to begin an investigation. Nevertheless, there are many challenges. One is the level of assurance that has to be placed on the system. Should we enforce a policy similar to the Bell and La Padula Policy? How much trust do we place on the agents? Can communication occur between agents at different security levels? Finally, can we combine multilevel security with encryption technologies to ensure that there are no covert channels? We have raised many questions. We need to carry out research to find solutions to the problems.

References

[AFSB] Air Force Studies Board, Committee on Multilevel Data Management Security, National Academy Press, Washington, DC, 1983.

[DENN87] Denning, D. et al., A Multilevel Relational Data Model, IEEE Symposium on Security and Privacy, Oakland, CA, April 1987.

[FROS86] Frost, R., *On Knowledge Base Management Systems*, Collins Publishers, London, U.K., 1986.

[HINK75] Hinke, T. and M. Schaefer, Secure Data Management Systems, System Development Corp., Technical Report RADC-TR-75-266, Nov. 1966.

[JAJO90] Jajodia, S. and R. Sandhu, Polyinstantiation integrity in multilevel relations, *Proc. IEEE Symp. Security Privacy*, Oakland, CA, April 1990.

[KO93] Ko, H. and B. Thuraisingham, Concurrency control for trusted database management system, *ACM SIGMOD Record*, December 1993.

[MCGU02] McGuiness, D. et al., DAML+OIL: An ontology language for the semantic Web, *IEEE Intelligent Syst.*, 17, 2002.

[STAC90] Stachour., P. and B. Thuraisingham, Design of LDV: A multilevel secure relational database management system, *IEEE Trans. Knowledge Data Eng.*, 2(2), 1990.

[THUR90] Thuraisingham, B., Recursion Theoretic Properties of the Inference Problem, presented at the IEEE Computer Security Foundations Workshop, Franconia, NH, June 1990 (also available as MITRE technical Paper MTP291 June 1990).

[THUR91a] Thuraisingham, B., The use of conceptual structures to handle the inference problem, *Proc. IFIP Database Security Conf.*, Shepherdstown, WV, 1991.

[THUR91b] Thuraisingham, B., A Nonmonotonic Typed Multilevel Logic for Secure Data and Knowledge Base Management Systems, *Proc. Comput. Security Found. Workshop*, Franconia, NH, 1991.

[THUR93] Thuraisingham, B., Towards the design of a standard multilevel relational data model, *Comp. Stand. Interface J.*, 1993.

[THUR05] Thuraisingham, B., *Database and Applications Security: Integrating Data Management and Information Security*, CRC Press, Boca Raton, FL, 2005.

[ULLM88] Ullman, J.D., *Principles of Database and Knowledge Base Management Systems*, Volumes I and II, Computer Science Press, Rockville, MD, 1988.

[WISE89] Simon, W., On the problem of security in data bases, *Proc. IFIP Database Security Conf.*, Monterey, CA, 1989.

Exercises

1. Describe design issues for a multilevel secure semantic Web.
2. Develop data models for multilevel XML, RDF, and OWL.

Chapter 14

Policy Engineering

14.1 Overview

In Part II we discussed confidentiality policies for the semantic Web, and in the earlier chapters of Part III we discussed trust, privacy, and integrity policies. Policy research actually began in the 1970s when the data-management research community formulated what they called access control rules. Then in the mid-1980s in the Lock Data Views Project we specified policies, which we called security for classification constraints that assigned security levels to the data based on content, context, and time. Then active research in policies began in the 1990s with the advent of models such as Role-Based Access Control (RBAC), and then in the 2000s with models such as Usage Control (UCON). Our interest in this book has been on policies for the semantic Web. These policies may be expressed in languages such as eXtensible Markup Language (XML), Resource Description Framework (RDF), and Web Ontology Language (OWL). Furthermore, policies may be enforced on documents represented in XML, RDF, and OWL.

One of the major challenges with policy research is the generation, specification, and the management of policies. This area has come to be known as policy engineering. This is similar to software engineering that deals with the specification and management of software, and data engineering that deals with the definition and management of data. In this chapter we will focus on policy engineering as it relates to the semantic Web.

The organization of this chapter is as follows. Now that we have discussed various aspects of policies including confidentiality, trust, privacy, and integrity, we will revisit semantic Web policies in Section 14.2. Much of our discussion on policies has been obtained from the work of Bonatti and his team [BONA04], [BONA05], [BONA06]. In Section 14.3 we discuss policy generation and specification. We utilize some of our earlier research on security-constraints generation and specification to deal with policy engineering. In Section 14.4 we discuss the consistency of policies. Evolution of policies including policy reuse is discussed in Section 14.5. Integration of policies is discussed in Section 14.6. Visualization of policies is discussed in Section 14.7. The chapter is summarized in Section 14.8. Our work on policy engineering with respect to the semantic Web is influenced by the discussions we have had with Finin and his team at the University of Maryland at Baltimore County as well as the developments with ontology engineering as discussed in Reference [ANTO03].

14.2 Revisiting Semantic Web Policies

The previous chapters have discussed semantic Web policies including confidentiality, privacy, trust, and integrity policies. In this section we provide a broad discussion of policies as given in References [BONA04], [BONA05], [BONA06], [BLAZ98].

14.2.1 Policies

There are various types of policies that enhance security, privacy, and usability of distributed services. Bonati and his team have stated that the different policies should be integrated into a single framework. These policies include not only access control, but also privacy policies, business rules, and quality of service among others. Access-control policies protect any system open to the Internet. Privacy policy protects the users while they are browsing the Web and accessing Web services. Business policy specifies the conditions that apply to specific customer Web services. Other policies specify constraints related to quality of service. All these policies make decisions based on the information of the peer or user involved in the transaction. For example, age, nationality, customer profile, identity, and reputation may all be considered both in access control decisions and in determining which discounts are applicable. These kinds of policies need to be integrated to provide a common infrastructure that can be used for decision making and interoperability. Policies can be harmonized and synchronized. There are also policies that require events to be logged called provisional policies.

Policies specify actions to be executed along with the decision process. Policies in these contexts act as both a decision-support system and as declarative behavior systems. An effective approach to policy specification could give common users better control of the behavior of their own system. Achievement of this goal depends on policies' ability to interoperate with rest of the system. Policies make decisions based on properties of the peers interacting with the system. These properties may be strongly certified by cryptographic techniques, or may be reliable to some intermediate degree with lightweight evidence-gathering and validation.

14.2.2 Policy Framework

A flexible policy framework should try to merge these two forms of evidence to meet the efficiency and usability requirements of Web applications. Trust negotiation, reputation models, business rules, and action specification languages have to be integrated into a single framework. Automated trust negotiation plays an important role in trust management. The semantic Web is a large, uncensored system to which anyone may contribute. This raises the question of how much credence to give each source. We cannot expect each user to know the trustworthiness of each source. This is where trust management plays an important role in establishing the trustworthiness of each source.

14.2.3 Trust Management and Negotiation

As we discussed in Chapter 10, two major approaches to managing trust exists and they are policy-based and reputation-based. In a policy-based trust management approach, strong security mechanisms are used to regulate access of the user to Web services. Strong security mechanisms include signed certificates and trusted certification authorities (CAs). Access decisions are based on this mechanism with well-defined semantics and provide strong verification and analysis support. A policy-based approach helps in making a decision about the trustworthiness of the requester. It determines whether the service or resource is allowed or denied to the requester. Reputation-based trust relies on a "soft computational" approach to the problem of trust. In this approach, trust is computed based on the local experience and feedback given by the other entities in the network. For example, online buyers and sellers rate each other after each transaction. The ratings pertaining to a certain seller (or buyer) are aggregated by a Web site reputation system into a number reflecting seller (or buyer) trustworthiness as judged by the Web page community.

The reputation-based approach has been favored for environments such as the peer-to-peer or semantic Web. The existence of certifying authorities cannot always be assumed, but a large pool of individual user ratings is often available. Another common approach is to make the requester commit to contract and copyrights by clicking on the "accept" button. To make decisions in real-life scenarios a combination of these approaches is needed. For example, transaction policies must handle expenses of all magnitudes, from micropayments to credit card payments of one thousand Euro dollars or even more. The cost of the traded goods or services contributes to determine the risk associated with the transaction and, hence, the trust measure required.

Strong evidence is generally harder to gather and verify than lightweight evidence. Sometimes, a "soft" reputation measure or a declaration in the sense outlined above is all one can obtain in a given scenario. Success of trust management depends on the ability of the system to balance trust level and risk level for each task. The following are two important research directions related to the area of trust. How should different forms of trust be integrated? How many different forms of evidence can be conceived? Access control presents difficult problems in a distributed environment. This problem becomes severe when resources and the subject requesting them belong to different security domains.

Common access-control mechanisms provide authorization decisions based on the identity of the requester, which is ineffective. Automated trust negotiation solves this ineffectiveness.

Attribute credentials are exchanged to establish trust among strangers who wish to share a resource. Automated trust negotiation (ATN) is an approach to regulate the exchange of sensitive attribute credentials by using access-control policies. In ATN, peers are able to automatically negotiate credentials according to their own declarative, rule-based policies.

Some of the challenges include, how do negotiations take place between peers? The Web server asks for credentials from the client requesting the resource. The client in turn asks for server credentials to determine the validity of the server. Both are in a symmetrical situation. Each peer decides how to react to the incoming request based on local policy. Local policy is a set of rules written in logic programming. Requests are formulated based on the rules from the policies. Several factors are taken into account while formulating requests. More details on trust management can be found in the policy work of Bonati and his team [BONA04].

14.2.4 Cooperative Policy Enforcement

This involves both machine-machine and human-machine interaction. Machine-machine interaction is handled by various negotiation mechanisms as discussed earlier. Human-machine interaction is more problematic than expected. Most users lack the technical expertise to tailor existing policies to match their own needs, causing easy access to their protected resources. Such lack of knowledge on the part of users also affects privacy protection. Most users are not able to personalize their information-release policies to suit their needs. To make the user understand the meaning of responses better, we bring in cooperative policy enforcement (CPE). This gives users the reasons for negative responses and suggestions for how to avoid such responses in the future.

Greater user awareness and control of policies are the main objectives of CPE. Policies are made user-friendly by using rule-based policy specification language such as controlled natural language and advanced explanation mechanisms. Several novel aspects are described in CPE including tabled explanation structure and suitable heuristics for focusing explanations. Heuristics, a generic, i.e., domain independent, combination of tabling techniques and heuristics, yields a novel method for explaining failure.

Query answering is conceived for the following categories of users: users who try to understand how to obtain access permissions, users who monitor and verify their own privacy policy, and policy managers who verify and monitor their policies. Policy managers must find the right tradeoff between explanation quality and the effort for instantiating the framework in new application domains. Second-generation explanation systems prescribe a sequence of expensive steps, including the creation of an independent domain knowledge base expressly for communicating with the user. This would be a serious obstacle to the applicability of the framework.

14.2.5 Natural Language Policies

Policies should be written by and understandable to users, to let them control behavior of their system. Policies should be formulated based on rules and stated in simple language. The inherent ambiguity of natural language is incompatible with the precision needed by security and privacy specifications.

14.2.6 Next Steps

In summary, policies represent a single body of declarative rules used in many possible ways for negotiations, query answering, and other forms of system behavior control. Transparent interoperation based on ontology sharing will determine the success of trust negotiation. Users have a better understanding and control over the policies that govern their systems with the help of CPE and trust management. Policies will have to handle decisions under a wide range of risk levels and performance requirements.

14.3 Policy Generation and Specification

The first step in policy engineering is generating the policies. The application specialist will specify the application. Together with the policy expert they will come up with the appropriate policies to enforce for the application. This is essentially the policy-generation phase. Once the policies are generated, the next step is to come up with a language to specify the policies.

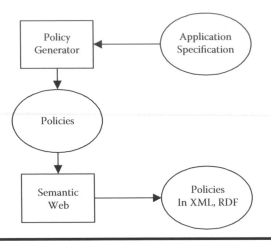

Figure 14.1 Policy generation and specification.

The application specialization will likely specify the policies in natural language. The policy expert will work with the application specialist to refine the policies. However, the policy expert and the application specialist may not have a clear picture of the data. Therefore, based on the policies and the data, the policies will have to be refined further. This will be done with the help of the data engineer.

Note that in the case of ontology engineering, one of the challenges is to generate the ontologies automatically, that is, from the various data sources, the concepts that will form the ontologies have to be generated. For this, data mining has been used; that is, by mining the data concepts, subsequently ontologies are generated. Now, these ontologies may be used to aid in the policy-generation phase.

Once the policies are generated, the next step is to come up with a language to specify the policies. For this we can use the various semantic Web technologies such as XML, RDF, and OWL. There are also several other policy languages that have been generated based on XML and RDF such as the Rei system developed at the University of Maryland, Baltimore County (UMBC) or the XML-based languages developed at the University of Milan and Purdue University. Figure 14.1 illustrates the policy-generation and specification phase.

14.4 Policy Consistency

Once the policies are generated and specified in a language, they have to be refined and made consistent. Consider the following policies, P1 and P2, specified in XML.

```
P1.
<Policy id="P1" Subject="//Professor[department='CS']" Ob-
ject="//ResearchPapers[@Dept='CS']//node()" Action="view" Ef-
fect="permit"/>
```

```
P2.
<Policy id="P2" Subject="//Professor[department='CS']" Ob-
ject="//ResearchPapers[@Dept='CS']//node()" Action="view" Ef-
fect="deny"/>
```

P1 states that the professors in the computer science department have access to the papers written by the professors in their department. P2 states that the professors in the computer science department do not have access to the papers written by professors in their department. These are contradictory policies. We have developed theorem provers in the past for secure systems based on Nonmonotonic Typed Multilevel Logic (NTML), which we developed [THUR91]. More recently, Jim Hendler and his group at the University of Maryland (now at Rensselaer Polytechnic Institute) have developed a system called Pellet that is the reasoning system. Furthermore, reasoning systems such as Jena have been developed for RDF. These systems have to be examined for policy consistency. Research in this direction has been carried out by UMBC, University of Maryland (UMD), and the Massachusetts Institute of Technology (MIT) in the policy-aware Web project.

One of the challenges with reasoning systems is scalability. For example, we can build reasoning systems that can reason about a few policies. However, in the real world, especially with multiple databases, there are numerous policies that have to be handled. Furthermore, the policies may have semantic and syntactic heterogeneity; that is, policy consistency has to be ensured as part of policy integration and interoperability. We will discuss this aspect in a later section. We also have to develop ontologies that will specify the meaning of policies so as to facilitate policy consistency. Figure 14.2 illustrates reasoning systems for policy consistency.

14.5 Policy Evolution and Reuse

Policies, like ontologies, will continue to change. For example, when an administration changes, which is often the case, new policies may be enforced and old policies deleted. Furthermore, policies may be modified. Therefore, an organization needs to ensure that policy changes occur in a smooth fashion.

When policies change, an organization could throw away the old policies and generate a new set of policies from scratch. That means the organization has to go through the policy generation, specification, and consistency-checking phases. On the other hand, the organization may reuse as many policies as possible and introduce additional policies. Furthermore, the organization may want to minimize the number of policies that are modified. This is called policy evolution and reuse.

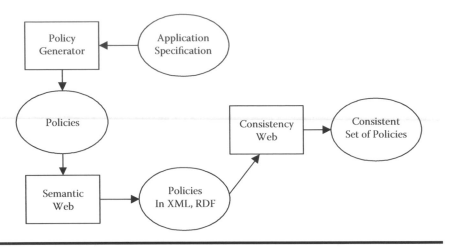

Figure 14.2 Policy consistency checker.

There is a strong analogy between software evolution and reuse as well as ontology and data evolution and reuse. There is still a debate regarding software reuse and redeveloping the software. For example, in the case of legacy applications, do we migrate them to new platforms, or do we throw away the legacy applications and develop new applications?

Up to a certain point, reuse and evolution works. However, when the changes that have to be made are massive, it would be better to redevelop them. In the case of ontologies, we have found that ontology reuse is of immense help. For example, we have developed several geospatial anthologies. However, we have used the ontologies that have been developed by others in many cases and built on top of them. Now, unlike software engineering, ontology engineering is a newer field and therefore reuse may help. But as the field becomes more mature, then there may be a challenge as to whether to reuse the ontologies and build on them or to develop new ontologies.

Policy reuse is even newer than ontology reuse. It is only recently that policy engineering has evolved as a field. Therefore, we need more research on determining how to evolve policies and reuse policies. Figure 14.3 illustrates policy evolution.

14.6 Policy Integration and Interoperability

Until this point we have more or less assumed that policy engineering is with respect to one organization. As we will see in Part IV, organizations work together and form coalitions. Data from multiple organizations and sources have to be integrated. Ontologies are being developed for data integrity. Interoperability issues arise due to heterogeneity. We could have semantic as well as syntactic hetero-

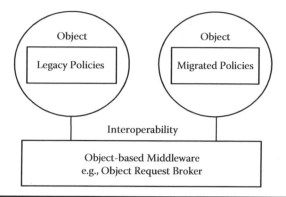

Figure 14.3　Policy evolution.

geneity for data. Ontologies are being used for handling heterogeneity. In Part IV we will discuss secure data interoperability using semantic Web technologies. Although much of the focus has been on data interoperability and integration, the heterogeneous policies have to be integrated. Therefore, in this section we will focus on policy interoperability.

Our recent research has focused on policy interoperability for geospatial technologies. We have developed geospatial ontologies that could be used to handle semantic as well as syntactic heterogeneity with respect to policies. In a coalition environment, heterogeneities have to be resolved to develop global policies. We have developed algorithms that determine the types of heterogeneities and resolve the differences using ontologies and then integrate them to develop a global policy.

Note that policy integration is not new. Our initial work on policy integration was carried out within the context of secure federated data management [THUR94]. This was well before the development of semantic Web technologies. However, today we have policy languages that are based on XML, RDF, and OWL. Furthermore, ontologies show a lot of promise in resolving semantic differences. For the first time we have a good handle on data heterogeneity. Therefore, it is time to examine policy interoperability using semantic Web technologies. Figure 14.4 illustrates policy integration.

14.7　Policy Management, Visualization, and Mining

Whereas policy generation, specification, consistency checking, reuse, and interoperability are all major aspects of policy engineering, we would like to add one other major aspect, and that is policy data management. This encompasses many aspects including policy querying and updating, policy visualization, and policy mining. In this section we will discuss policy management.

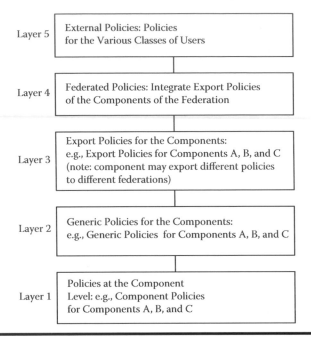

Figure 14.4 Policy integration.

The set of policies can be stored in a database and managed in the same way we manage the data. Therefore, query languages are needed to query the policies. Note that for policies represented in XML, we can use languages such as XML-QL or XQuery, and for policies represented in RDF, we can use RDF Query Language (RQL). Policies also have to be updated, and we can use the policy query language to update the policies.

Policies can be quite complex and difficult to understand. Therefore, graphical resonating languages such as Unified Modeling Language (UML) diagrams have been used for policy representation and merging policies. Furthermore, visualization tools have been developed to visualize the policies and subsequently merge policies. Figure 14.5 illustrates the use of UML diagrams for policy management.

Finally, policies can be mined to extract the nuggets and better understand them. Note that one aspect of policy mining is role mining for role-based access control. Here the user activities are mined so that a consistent set of roles can be defined. Policy mining may go beyond role mining to determine the usage policies as well as role-based policies.

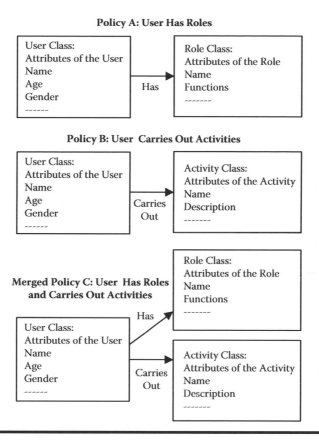

Figure 14.5 Policy merging.

14.8 Summary and Directions

In this chapter we discussed several aspects of policy engineering including policy generation and specification, policy consistency and completeness, policy reuse and evolution, policy integration, and policy management including policy visualization and mining. Like software engineering, data engineering, and ontology engineering, policy engineering is critical for the effective management of policies. UMBC is leading the direction for policy engineering. The research by Bertino, Bonatti, and Winslett is also showing a lot of policy engineering.

Although some progress has been made on policy engineering with languages such as Rei and reasoning systems such as Pellet, there is a lot to be done. One of the directions in which UMBC is working is development of a policy workbench and middleware to integrate the various policy-engineering tools. This is an important direction to pursue. We also need to develop a research program for policy engineering. The discussions in this chapter have provided some of the challenges that need to be addressed.

References

[ANTO03] Antoniou, G. and F. van Harmelan, *A Semantic Web Primer,* MIT Press, Cambridge, MA, 2003.

[BECH04] Becker, M.Y. and P. Sewell, Cassandra: distributed access control policies with tunable expressiveness, in *5th IEEE Intern. Workshop on Policies for Distributed Systems and Networks,* Yorktown Heights, NY, June 2004.

[BLAZ98] Blaze, M., J. Feigenbaum, and M. Strauss, Compliance checking in the policymaker trust management system, in *Proc. 2nd Conf. Financial Cryptography,* Anguilla, British West Indies, February 1998.

[BONA04] Bonatti, P.A., N. Shahmehri, C. Duma, D. Olmedilla, W. Nejdl, M. Baldoni, C. Baroglio, A. Martelli, V. Patti, P. Coraggio, G. Antoniou, J. Peer, and N.E. Fuchs, Rule-Based Policy Specification: State of the Art and Future Work. Technical Report, Working Group I2, EU NoE REWERSE, 2004. http://rewerse.net/deliverables/i2-d1.pdf.

[BONA05] Bonatti, P.A., D. Olmedilla, and J. Peer, Advanced Policy Queries. Technical Report, I2-D4, Working Group I2, EU NoE REWERSE, 2005. http://www.rewerse.net.

[BONA06] Bonatti, P.A., C. Duma, N.E. Fuchs, W. Nejdl, D. Olmedilla, J. Peer, and N. Shahmehri, Semantic Web policies — a discussion of requirements and research issues, European Semantic Web Conference (ESWC), Budva, Montenegro, 712-724, 2006.

[THUR91] Thuraisingham, B., A nonmonotonic typed multilevel logic for secure data and knowledge base management systems, *Proc. Comp. Security Found. Workshop,* Franconia, NH, 1991.

[THUR94] Thuraisingham, B., Security issues for federated database systems, *Comp. Security,* 13(6), 1994.

Exercise

1. Design and develop tools for policy generation, policy consistency checking, and policy integration.

Chapter 15

Research, Standards, Products, and Applications

15.1 Overview

The previous chapters in Parts II and III discussed the various developments, issues, and challenges on securing the semantic Web. In Part II we provided an overview of security issues for XML, RDF, ontologies, and rules. The main focus was on confidentiality issues. We discussed two aspects for each technology such as eXtensible Markup Language (XML) and Resource Description Framework (RDF). One was on expressing policies with semantic Web technologies, and the other was on securing semantic Web technologies such as securing XML documents.

In Part III we discussed trust, privacy, and integrity management for the semantic Web. Here we discussed how trust and privacy policies may be expressed with semantic Web technologies such as XML. We need to ensure that when, say, XML documents are interchanged, trust and privacy policies are enforced. Furthermore, when XML documents are published, their authenticity has to be ensured. We also discussed data quality and provenance aspects for integrity management.

Now that we have discussed various security technologies related to the semantic Web, we next discuss the developments in terms of research, standards, and products. Note that much of the discussion up to now has focused on these developments. In this chapter we essentially summarize what we have discussed thus far and document it with respect to research, standards, and products. The organization of this chapter is as follows. In Section 15.2 we discuss the research developments. Standards are discussed in Section 15.3. Products are discussed in Section 15.4. Application-oriented systems that utilize the secure semantic Web are briefly discussed in Section 15.5. The chapter is summarized in Section 15.6. Note that relevant standards will be elaborated on further in Appendix C, and applications are detailed in Part IV.

15.2 Research

Research on secure semantic Webs is still in the preliminary stages, although there is a lot of research that has been carried out on securing documents such as XML as well as specifying policies in semantic Web languages. To our knowledge one of the earliest proposals for securing the semantic Web was given by Thuraisingham at the European Union-United States workshop on semantic Webs in Sophia Antipolis in October 2001. As program director at the National Science Foundation (NSF) in Information and Data Management (IDM), Thuraisingham discussed some of her initial ideas on securing the semantic Web based on her research with the University of Milan group on XML security. Shortly after that workshop, she initiated a new program at the NSF on data and applications security that funded efforts on XML secretly as well as on a secure semantic Web (e.g., the Policy Aware Web Project at the University of Maryland (UMD) and the Massachusetts Institute of Technology [MIT]).

Following this initial direction, extensive research on trust management for the semantic Web was conducted at the University of Maryland, Baltimore County (UMBC; Tim Finin, Anupam Joshi, Yelena Yesha, Lalana Kagal, et al.). In particular, they developed a language for specifying policies. This language was called Rei. Research on reasoning with Rei was also carried out in early 2000. To date one of the pioneering groups on trust management for the semantic Web is that of Finin at UMBC and Bonatti at the University of Napoli. Furthermore, excellent research on XML security has been carried out by Bertino, Ferrari, and Carminati et al.'s group at the University of Milan and more recently at Purdue University. Around 2004, NSF-funded research on a policy-aware Web was initiated at MIT and the University of Maryland College Park (Hendler, Berners Lee et al.). This effort focused on specifying policies and reasoning about policies. Around the same time Thuraisingham published a paper on security standards for the semantic Web [THUR05]. Since joining the University of Texas at Dallas, Thuraisingham and her students have been conducting research on confidentiality, privacy, and trust (CPT) for the semantic Web as well as starting a new research thrust on securing the geospatial semantic Web (with Latifur Khan et al.). Another notable effort is the research of Farkas et al. at the University of South Carolina, where the focus is on the inference problem that arises due to semantic Web technologies such as RDF.

As noted earlier, although few efforts have focused on securing semantic Webs, several efforts have been reported on securing XML documents. Notable is the research of Bertino, Ferrari, Carminati and others, first at the University of Milan and later at Purdue University. Bertino et al. have come with a comprehensive framework for securing XML documents. Their early research focused on access-control policies. Later they conducted research on secure publishing of XML documents. Trust management based on XML, called Trust-X, as well as privacy issues for XML documents were also carried out by Bertino's group. They have also conducted research on data sharing based on the XML framework. Some initial research on securing RDF documents also was carried out by the Italian researchers in collaboration with Thuraisingham [CARM04].

At present, Thuraisingham is collaborating with Bertino on utilizing secure XML research for trust management based on service-oriented architectures. Furthermore, Thuraisingham and Finin together with Kagal at MIT are conducting research on exploring semantic Web technologies for data sharing in need-to-share environments. Furthermore, the IEEE Policy workshop in 2007 has an entire track on securing a semantic Web related to policy management. Finally, Finin, Sandhu, and Thuraisingham et al. are exploring the use of integrating Finn's Rei with Sandhu's Usage Control (UCON) Model for the semantic Web. Figure 15.1 illustrates the major research efforts on securing the semantic Web.

15.3 Standards

The semantic Web resulted due to standards efforts, that is, the semantic Web is essentially a product of the World Wide Web Consortium (W3C), and as such, it is an effort that resulted from standards. The W3C started developed standards for languages such as XML, RDF, and Web Ontology Language (OWL). These languages contributed to the standards for the semantic Web. The W3C has come up with standards for securing the semantic Web, and these include XML encryption and key management standards. We discuss the standards developed by W3C in more detail in Appendix C. Note that semantic Web standards are also being

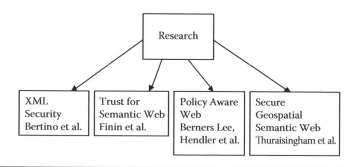

Figure 15.1   Research.

developed by the Organization for the Advancement of Structured Information Standards (OASIS). This group is specifying standards for security assertions such as eXtensible Access Control Markup Language (XACML) and Security Assertions Markup Language (SAML). Both these standards will be discussed in Part IV (Chapter 16). A listing of OASIS standards is also given in Appendix C.

Related standards are also being developed by numerous consortia. For example, the Open Geospatial Consortium (OGC) is developing standards for geospatial markup languages such as GML (Geography Markup Language). XACML and GML have been integrated to provide Geo-XACML [GEO]. Bertino and her group are coming up with standards based on role based access control (RBAC) and geospatial representations, and these specifications are called Geo-RBAC. At the University of Texas at Dallas we have integrated GML and RDF to produce GRDF and Secure GRDF (Geospatial RDF). Other standards being developed include SensorML for making up sensor data, and more recently there are developments with Radio XML for specifying data emanating from cognitive radio devices. Some of these efforts are reported by Bertino et al. [BERT05] and Ashraful and Thuraisingham [ASHR06].

Ontologies are also being standardized for various applications. We believe that these etymologies will contribute toward developing domain-specific semantic Webs as well as semantic Webs for special purpose applications including managing geospatial data as well as operating in pervasive computing environments. These aspects will be discussed in Part V. Figure 15.2 illustrates standards for serving the semantic Web.

15.4 Commercial Products

We have stressed throughout this book that we will not be able to buy a semantic Web product, that is, a semantic Web is just a collection of technologies that agents manipulate to obtain machine-understandable Web pages. We could purchase vari-

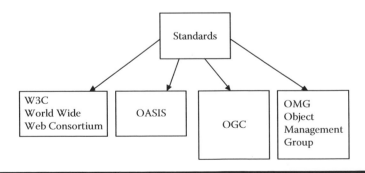

Figure 15.2   Standards.

ous products and put them together to give us the functionality of the semantic Web, which is essentially to have a capability of machine-understandable Web pages. Therefore, semantic Web products may include products for XML and RDF document generation, products for managing XML and RDF documents such as Oracle data-management system and application products, as well as products for developing and managing ontologies.

Security products for the semantic Web currently include products for encryption as well as products for managing secure XML documents. Because securing the semantic Web is still in its infancy, we believe that in the future we can expect to have several products in the marketplace that will secure XML, RDF, and ontologies. Furthermore, policy products such as those for policy specification and engineering can also be expected to be developed in the near future. Figure 15.3 provides a high-level overview of the various classes of products.

15.5 Applications

Several applications are making use of secure semantic Web technologies. These include technology applications as well as domain applications. Technology applications include secure Web services and service-oriented architectures, secure data, information and knowledge management, secure information integration, and assured information sharing. The domain applications include secure geospatial information management, secure information management in medical and financial domains as well as defense and intelligence domains. Figure 15.4 illustrates the applications. We will elaborate on technology applications in Part IV and on domain and specialized applications in Part V.

One major application of semantic Web technologies is with the Department of Defense and that is on Network Centric Enterprise Services (NCES). As stated by DISA (Defense Intelligence Systems Agency), the vision of NCES is the following:

"NCES will enable the secure, agile, robust, dependable, interoperable data-sharing environment for DOD where war fighter, business, and

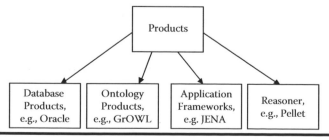

Figure 15.3   Products.

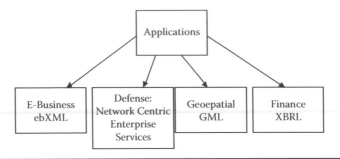

Figure 15.4   Applications.

intelligence users share knowledge on a global network. This, in turn, facilitates information superiority, accelerates decision-making, effective operations and net-centric transformation."

The infrastructure on which NCES is based is the Global Information Grid (GIG) and is based on the service-oriented architecture concept. Semantic Web technologies such as XML and ontologies play a major role. Information assurance for the GIG is a major goal for the National Security Agency. Therefore, the research and development efforts in trustworthy semantic Webs are applicable to NCES and GIG.

15.6 Summary and Directions

In this chapter we have provided a summary of the developments of trustworthy semantic Webs. These include research efforts, standards efforts, products, and applications. Again, trustworthiness includes confidentiality, privacy, trust, and integrity. Although several groups are now working on secure semantic Webs, the pioneering efforts include the trust-management research by Finin et al. at UMBC (in particular Kagal's Ph.D. thesis [KAGA04]) and XML security research by Bertino et al. at the University of Milan and Purdue University (in particular, Carminati's Ph.D. thesis [CARM04]). I would strongly recommend anyone who wants to conduct research in this area to become familiar with the thesis work of Kagal and Carminati.

With respect to standards, the significant work is that of the W3C and the OASIS. In addition, for work on geospatial data representation, OGC is coming up with standards. Furthermore, various groups are now specifying ontologies as well as standards for data representations. As we have stated, semantic Web-based products are increasing in number. It is unlikely that we will have a vendor who will market the semantic Web; that is, we cannot purchase the semantic Web. Instead, we can purchase technologies from multiple vendors (possibly even one vendor) and assemble them together to develop a semantic Web; that is, we believe that semantic Web development will largely be a system engineering and integration effort. With respect to security solutions, we may incorporate them into the technologies we purchase or buy them from a vendor.

Applications utilizing the semantic Web technologies are increasing. Today almost every domain is using its version of XML. Several ontologies are being developed such as cancer ontologism in the medical domain. Perhaps the most significant applications of the semantic Web will be the global information grid being developed by the Department of Defense for NCES.

Although we have seen tremendous progress with respect to semantic Web developments, security has not received much attention. Therefore, it is critical that we start a research program on securing the semantic Web. The information assurance goals of the global information grid are moving in the right direction. We also need other programs utilizing the semantic Web to focus on security. We have provided some direction in Parts II and III of this book. We will focus on applications and domains in Parts IV and V.

References

[ASHR06] Ashraful, A. and B. Thuraisingham, GRDF and Secure GRDF, Technical Report, University of Texas at Dallas, 2006.

[BERT05] Bertino E. et al., GEO-RBAC: a spatially aware RBAC, *Proc. Symp. Access Control Models, Applications and Technologies* (*SACMAT*), 2005.

[CARM04] Carminati, B., Secure Publishing of XML Documents, Ph.D. thesis, University of Milan, Italy, 2004.

[CARM04] Carminati, B., E.A. Ferrari, and B.M. Thuraisingham, Using RDF for Policy Specification and Enforcement, DEXA Workshops 2004, Zaragoza, Spain, 163-167.

[GEO] GEO-XACML, http://www.geoxacml.org/.

[KAGA04] Kagal, L., A Policy-Based Approach to Governing Autonomous Behavior in Distributed Environments, Ph.D. thesis, University of Maryland, Baltimore County, 2004.

[THUR05] Thuraisingham, B., *Database and Applications Security: Integrating Data Management and Information Security*, CRC Press, Boca Raton, FL, 2005.

Exercise

1. Conduct surveys of trustworthy semantic Web research efforts, products, and standards (see also Appendix C).

Conclusion to Part III

In Part III we provided an overview of dependability aspects for the semantic Web. In particular, we focused on trust management, privacy, and integrity for the semantic Web. We also discussed multilevel security, policy engineering, research, standards, and product developments for the semantic Web. Part III consisted of six chapters. In Chapter 10 we discussed trust management with respect to the semantic Web. In Chapter 11 we discussed privacy management, and in Chapter 12 we discussed integrity management. For completion we discussed multilevel security issues in Chapter 13. Aspects of policy management such as tools for policy specification and evolution were discussed in Chapter 14. Part III concluded with a chapter on developments with respect to research, standards, and products (Chapter 15).

Now that we have provided an overview of the various aspects of building trustworthy semantic Webs in Parts II and III, in Parts IV and V we will discuss applications of these semantic Webs and specialized semantic Webs.

Part IV

Applications of Trustworthy Semantic Webs

Introduction to Part IV

The chapters in Parts II and III focused on concepts in trustworthy semantic Webs. In particular, Part II addressed confidentiality aspects, whereas Part III addressed trust, privacy, and integrity aspects. Now that we have provided an overview of the concepts, we are now ready to discuss the applications of these concepts such as Web services and interoperability in Part IV.

Part IV, consisting of six chapters, discusses applications that utilize trustworthy semantic Webs. Chapter 16 discusses secure Web services that utilize semantic Web technologies. Semantic Web technologies for managing secure databases is the subject of Chapter 17. Secure semantic interoperability for heterogeneous information sources is discussed in Chapter 18. Chapter 19 discusses semantic Webs for secure E-business applications. Chapter 20 discusses semantic Webs for secure digital libraries. Chapter 21 discusses semantic Web technologies for an important applications area called assured information sharing.

Chapter 16

Secure Semantic Web Services

16.1 Overview

As stated on the Web site for the Organization for the Advancement of Structured Information Standards (OASIS), Web services refers to the technologies that allow for making connections (see Reference [OASIS]). Services are what you connect together using Web services. For example, Web services could be a query service and a directory service. A service is the endpoint of a connection. Also, a service has some type of underlying computer system that supports the connection offered. The combination of services — internal and external to an organization — make up a service-oriented architecture (SOA).

In this chapter we provide an overview of secure Web services and the application of semantic Web technologies for Web services. The integration of secure Web services with semantic Web technologies is secure semantic Web services. The organization of this chapter is as follows. Web services are discussed in Section 16.2. Secure Web services are discussed in Section 16.3. Standards such as XACML and Security Assertions Markup Language (SAML) are discussed in Section 16.4. The Shibboleth system is discussed in Section 16.5. Application of semantic Web technologies is discussed in Section 16.6. The chapter is summarized in Section 16.7.

16.2 Web Services

An SOA is essentially a collection of services [SOA]. These services communicate with each other. The communication can involve either simple data passing, or it could involve two or more services coordinating some activity such as planning travel. Some means of connecting services to each other is needed. SOAs are not new. The first SOA can be considered to be a distributed component object model (DCOM) and object request brokers (ORBs) based on the common object request architecture (CORBA) specification [OMG]. If an SOA is to be effective, we need a clear understanding of the term *service*. A service is a function that is well-defined, self-contained, and does not depend on the context or state of other services.

The technology of Web services is the most likely connection technology of SOAs. Web services essentially use eXtensible Markup Language (XML) technology to create a robust connection. A service consumer sends a service request message to a service provider. The service provider returns a response message to the service consumer. The request and subsequent response connections are defined in some way that is understandable to both the service consumer and the service provider. A service provider can also be a service consumer. The Web Services Description Language (WSDL) forms the basis for Web services. WSDL uses XML to define messages. The steps involved in providing and consuming a service are the following:

- A service provider describes its service using WSDL. This definition is published to a directory of services. The directory could use Universal Description, Discovery, and Integration (UDDI). Other forms of directories can also be used.
- A service consumer issues one or more queries to the directory to locate a service and determine how to communicate with that service.
- Part of the WSDL provided by the service provider is passed to the service consumer. This tells the service consumer what the requests and responses are for the service provider.
- The service consumer uses the WSDL to send a request to the service provider.
- The service provider provides the expected response to the service consumer.

The UDDI registry is intended to eventually serve as a means of "discovering" Web services described using WSDL. The idea is that the UDDI registry can be searched in various ways to obtain contact information and the Web services available for various organizations. UDDI registry is a way to keep up to date on the Web services your organization currently uses. An alternative to UDDI is ebXML Directory. All the messages are sent using SOAP (SOAP at one time stood for Simple Object Access Protocol; now, the letters in the acronym have no particular meaning). SOAP essentially provides the envelope for sending Web services messages. SOAP generally uses Hypertext Transfer Protocol (HTTP), but other means of connection may be used. Security and authorization is an important topic with Web services. The next section describes security in more detail. Web services architecture is illustrated in Figure 16.1.

16.3 Secure Web Services

Security and authorization specifications for Web services are based on XML and can be found in References [OASIS], [XACML], and [SAML]. Various types of control have been proposed including access control, rights, assertions, and protection. We describe some of them in the next section. The list of specifications includes the following:

- eXtensible Access Control Markup Language (XACML)
- eXtensible Rights Markup Language (XrML)
- Security Assertions Markup Language (SAML)
- Service Protection Markup Language (SPML)
- Web Services Security (WSS)
- XML Common Biometric Format (XCBF)
- XML Key Management Specification (XKMS)

OASIS is the standards organization promoting security standards for Web services. It is a not-for-profit, global consortium that drives the development, convergence, and adoption of E-business standards. Two standards provided by

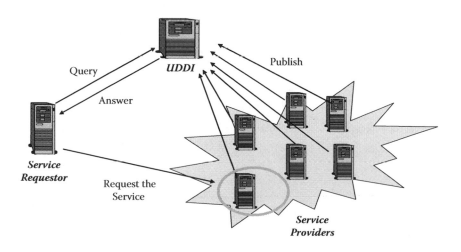

Figure 16.1   Web services architecture.

OASIS are XACML and SAML. XACML provides fine-grained control of authorized activities, the effect of characteristics of the access requestor, the protocol over which the request is made, authorization based on classes of activities, and content introspection. SAML is an XML framework for exchanging authentication and authorization information. The next section gives details of both XACML and SAML. Components of secure Web services are illustrated in Figure 16.2.

16.4 XACML and SAML

SAML provides a single point of authorization. It aims to solve "the Web single sign-on" problem. One identity provider in a group allows access. It has public and private key foundations. Those who are providing SAML in their products are: Microsoft Passport, OpenID (VeriSign), and Global Login System (Open Source). As stated in SAML specifications, its three main components are the following:

- **Assertions:** SAML has three kinds of assertions. Authentication assertions are those in which the user has proven his identity. Attribute assertions contain specific information about the user, such as his spending limits. Authorization decision assertions identify what the user can do, for example, whether he can buy an item.
- **Protocol:** This defines the way that SAML asks for and get assertions, for example, using SOAP over HTTP for now, although using other methods in the future.
- **Binding:** This details exactly how SAML message exchanges are mapped into SOAP exchanges.

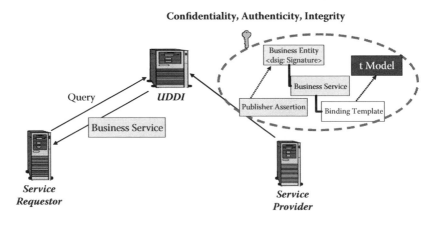

Figure 16.2   Secure Web services architecture.

Outstanding issues for SAML include performance, federations, and handling legacy applications. With respect to performance, there is no support for caching, and it has to be implemented over HTTP protocols using SOAP. Furthermore, it does not specify encryption, and as a result the policies may be compromised. With respect to federations, SAML does not specify authentication protocols. Furthermore, multiple domains cannot be handled. Therefore, OASIS is examining federated identity management. SAML does not work with legacy applications as it is expensive to retrofit.

XACML combines multiple rules into a single policy. It permits multiple users to have different roles, and provides separation between policy writing and application environment. The goal is to standardize access control languages. Some elements of XACML are the following. Users interact with resources. Every resource is protected by an entity known as a policy enforcement point (PEP). This is where the language is actually used and does not actually determine access. PEP sends its request to a policy decision point (PDP). Policies may or may not be actually stored here, but have the final say on access. A decision is relayed to PEP, which then grants or denies access.

Outstanding issues of XACML include distributed responsibility and policy cross-referencing. With respect to distributed responsibility, what happens when the PEP is responsible for multiple objects? What happens when we can compromise the PDP or spoof its communication? How do we guarantee that we reference the right object? Although the system is distributed, a policy is still in only one location. With respect to policy cross-referencing, one policy may access another. Typical issues arise as with inheritance and unions or intersections of related work. The challenge is to deal with conflicts.

Researchers as well as practitioners are working on exchanging both SAML and XACML. In the next section we will discuss Shibboleth, which is a distributed Web resource access-control system that allows federations to cooperate together to share Web-based resources. It uses SAML in its implementation.

16.5 Shibboleth

As stated earlier, Shibboleth is a distributed Web resource access-control system that allows federations to cooperate to share Web-based resources [SHIB]. It defines a protocol for carrying authentication information and user attributes from a home to a resource site. The resource site can then use the attributes to make access-control decisions about the user. This Web-based Middleware layer uses SAML. Access control is carried out in stages. In stage one the resource site redirects the user to its home site and obtains a handle for the user that is authenticated by the home site. In stage two, the resource site returns the handle to the attribute authority of the home site and is returned a set of attributes of the user on which to make an access-control decision.

There are some issues with single sign on with Shibboleth. How does the resource site know the home site of the user? How does it trust the handle returned? The answer is that it is handled by the system-trust model. Authentication procedure is as follows. When the resource site asks for the home site from the user, the user selects it from the list of trusted sites which are already authenticated by certificates. Handles are validated by the SAML signature along with the message. The user selects the home site from the list. The home site authenticates the user if he is already registered. After home server authentication, it returns a message with SAML sign to the target resource site. If the sign matches, the resource site provides a pseudonym (handle) for the user and sends an assertion message to the home page to find out if the necessary attributes are available with the user. To ensure privacy, each time the system provides a different pseudonym for the user's identity. It needs the release attribute policy from the user attributes each time to provide control over the authority attributes in the target site. Agreement attribute release policy is between the user and the administrator.

Trust is the heart of Shibboleth. It completely trusts the target resource site and origin home site registered in the federation. A disadvantage of the existing trust model is there is no differentiation between authentication authorities and attribute authorities. There is a scope of allowing more sophisticated distribution of trust, such as static or dynamic delegation of authority. Another disadvantage in the existing trust model is it provides only basic access-control capabilities. It lacks the flexibility and sophistication that many applications need to provide access-control decisions based on role hierarchies or various constraints such as the time of day or separation of duties.

In the basic Shibboleth, the target site trusts the origin site to authenticate its users and manage their attributes correctly, whereas the original site trusts the target site to provide services to its users. Trust is conveyed using digitally signed SAML messages using target and origin server key pairs. Each site has only one key pair per Shibboleth system. Thus, there is only a single point of trust per Shibboleth system. And there is a need for a finer-grained distributed trust model and being able to use multiple origin authorities to issue and sign the authentication and attribute assertions. Multiple authorities should be able to issue attributes to users, and the target site should be able to verify issuer and user bindings. The target should be able to state, in its policy, which of the attribute authorities it trusts to issue which attributes to which groups of users. The target site should be able to decide independently of the issuing site which attributes and authorities to trust when making its access-control decisions. Not all attribute-issuing authorities need be part of the origin site. A target site should be able to allow a user to gain access to its resources if it has attributes issued by multiple authorities. The trust infrastructure should support dynamic delegation of authority, so that a holder of a privilege attribute may delegate (a subset of) this to another person without having to reconfigure anything in the system. The target site should be able to decide if it really does trust the origin's attribute repository and, if not, be able to demand

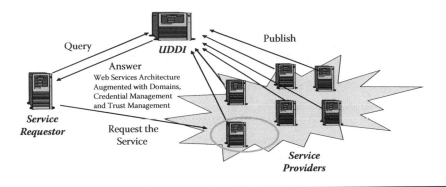

Figure 16.3 Shibboleth architecture.

a stronger proof of attribute entitlement than that conferred by a SAML signature from the sending Web server.

Shibboleth defines various trust models. These models have been implemented using X.509. We can look at trust from two different aspects:

■ Distribution of trust in attribute issuing authorities
■ Trustworthiness of an origin site's attribute repository

Shibboleth architecture is illustrated in Figure 16.3. Further details of the trust models and their implementations as well as authorization and privacy issues are discussed in Reference [TRUST].

16.6 Secure Web Services and the Semantic Web

Integration of the Web services and the semantic Web results in semantic Web services; that is, Web services to the World Wide Web are semantic Web services to the semantic Web. Finin and his team have discussed an architecture for semantic Web services [BURS05]. They have described the inadequacies of Web services and discussed the need for semantic Web services. They state that current technologies allow usage of Web services. In particular, current Web services support syntactic information descriptions as well as syntactic support for service discovery, composition, and execution. They argue that we need semantically marked up content and services and therefore we need to develop semantic Web services. They then define an architecture called the semantic Web service architecture which consists of a set of architectural and protocol abstractions that serve as a foundation for semantic Web service technologies. These technologies support the following: dynamic service discovery, service engagement, service process enactment, community support services, and quality of service.

Service discovery is the process of identifying candidate services by clients. Matchmakers connect the service requesters to the providers. Ontologies may be needed to specify the services. Service engagement specifies the agreements between the requestor and the provider. Therefore, contract negotiation is carried out during this phase. Once the service is ready to be initiated, the service enactment phase begins. As stated in Reference [SHIB], during this phase the requestor determines the information necessary to request performance of service and appropriate reaction to service success or failure. This will also include interpreting the responses and carrying out transitions. Community management services support authentication and security management. Quality of service provides support for negotiation as well as tradeoffs, say, between security and timely delivery of the data.

Security cuts across all these services. Note that the community management service specifically calls for authentication and security management. Security services are needed for service discovery, engine segment, and enactment. For example, not all services can be discovered. This will depend on the sensitivity of the service and the security credentials possessed by the requestor. Therefore, security specifications for XML, RDF, and OWL that we have discussed in Part II have to be examined for semantic Web service descriptions. Figure 16.4 illustrates semantic Web services.

16.7   Summary and Directions

In this chapter we provided an overview of secure Web services and discussed the applications of semantic Web technologies for secure Web services. Web services are the services that are invoked to carry out activities on the Web. A collection of Web services comprise the SOA. We also discussed aspects of XACML, SAML, and Shibboleth which are related to secure Web services.

Web services and SOAs are at the heart of the next-generation Web. They make use of semantic Web technologies to generate machine-understandable Web pages. This is one of the major developments in the late 1990s and early 2000s. Although there are numerous developments on Web services, the application of semantic Web technologies and securing Web services are major challenges. Furthermore, major

Figure 16.4   Secure semantic Web services.

initiatives such as the global information grid and the network-centric enterprise services are based on Web services and SOAs. Therefore, securing these technologies as well as making Web services more intelligent by using the semantic Web will be critical for the next-generation Web.

References

[BURS05] Burstein, M., C. Bussler, M. Zaremba, T. Finin, M.N. Huhns, M. Paolucci, A.P. Sheth, and S. Williams, A semantic Web services architecture, *IEEE Internet Comp.*, September-October, 2005.

[OASIS] OASIS: http://www.oasis-open.org/home/index.php.

[OMG] www.omg.org.

[SAML] OpenSAML: http://www.opensaml.org/.

[SHIB] Shibboleth, http://middleware.internet2.edu/pki05/proceedings/chadwick-distributed-shibboleth.pdf.

[SOA] http://en.wikipedia.org/wiki/Service-oriented_architecture.

[TRUST] www.terena.nl/activities/tf-aace/workshop/presentations/Distributed_trust_model1.ppt.

[XACML] SUN XACML Documentation: http://sunxacml.sourceforge.net/guide.html.

Exercises

1. Conduct a survey of secure Web services.
2. Describe how secure Web services may use semantic Web technologies.
3. Investigate trust management for service-oriented architectures.

Chapter 17

Secure Semantic Data, Information, and Knowledge Management

17.1 Overview

In the previous chapter we discussed the application of semantic Web technologies for secure Web services. In this chapter we will continue with the applications of semantic Web technologies. In particular, we will discuss the applications of semantic Web technologies for secure data, information, and knowledge management.

Note that in Chapter 3 we briefly discussed data, information, and knowledge management and then described some of the security issues. Data is managed by a data manager. Information is extracted from the data, and knowledge is about understanding the information and taking actions. Data-management technologies include database management and data administration. Information-management technologies include multimedia information management and collaborative information management. Knowledge management is about reusing the knowledge and expertise of an organization to improve profits and other benefits. In this chapter we will examine in more detail security issues for data, information, and knowledge management and then discuss how semantic Web technologies may be applied for managing data, information, and knowledge.

The organization of this chapter is as follows. In Section 17.2 we discuss secure data management. In Section 17.3 we discuss secure information management. Note that we focus only on multimedia information and collaborative information management. Other aspects of information management and trustworthy semantic Webs will be discussed in the next three chapters. For example, semantic secure information interoperability will be discussed in Chapter 18. Semantic E-commerce and E-business will be discussed in Chapter 18, and semantic secure digital libraries will be discussed in Chapter 19. In Section 17.4 we discuss secure knowledge management. The applications of semantic Web technologies for secure data, information, and knowledge management are discussed in Section 17.5. The chapter is summarized in Section 17.6.

17.2 Secure Data Management

17.2.1 Discretionary Security

Discretionary security deals with granting access to the data depending on the users, user groups, and other factors such as roles of users. Discretionary security was initially investigated for secure operating systems where access was granted to files, depending on the kinds of processes. The types of access included read and write operations. Then the concept was extended to databases where access was granted, say, to relations, attributes, and elements. Now discretionary security also includes handling complex security policies, granting access to data based on roles and functions, and both positive and negative authorization policies. Figure 17.1 illustrates various types of discretionary access control mechanisms.

17.2.2 Multilevel Security

Numerous developments on multilevel secure database systems were reported throughout the 1980s and during the early 1990s. These systems evolved from

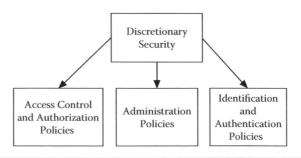

Figure 17.1 Discretionary security.

multilevel secure operating systems. The idea is for users to be granted access to the data depending on the user's clearance level and the sensitivity level of the data. For example, data is assigned sensitivity levels such as Unclassified, Confidential, Secret and TopSecret. Users are also cleared, say, at Confidential, Secret, and TopSecret levels. In addition, there may also be compartments for both data and users. Most policies ensure that users read data at or below their level and write data at their level. The early developments focused on multilevel secure relational database systems. Then the focus was on multilevel object database systems and multilevel distributed database systems. Models, architectures, and functions of multilevel secure data-management systems have been discussed in Reference [THUR05].

17.2.3 Multilevel Relational Data Model

Many of the early developments, especially throughout the 1980s and early 1990s, were on multilevel secure relational data models and systems. For example, after the Air Force Summer Study [AFSB83], various prototypes based on the Integrity Lock approach for relational models were developed at the MITRE Corporation. Then there were the prominent multilevel secure relational database systems such as SeaView at SRI and LOCK Data Views at Honeywell Inc. In the early 1990s there was work at George Mason University on multilevel relational data models. At the same time, multilevel secure relational database systems based on a distributed systems approach were being designed at the Naval Research Laboratory. In Reference [THUR05] we discussed multilevel relational data models, the functions of a multilevel secure relational database system as well as prototype developments and commercial products. In a multilevel relational data model, data may be classified at relation, attribute, or element level. Figure 17.2 illustrates an example of a multilevel relation.

EMP

SS#	Ename	Salary	D#	Level
1	John	20K	10	U
2	Paul	30K	20	S
3	Mary	40K	20	TS

DEPT

D#	Dname	Mar	Level
10	Math	Smith	U
20	Physics	Jones	C

U = Unclassified
C = Confidential
S = Secret
TS = TopSecret

Figure 17.2 Multilevel relation.

17.2.4   Inference Problem

Inference is the process of posing queries and deducing unauthorized information from legitimate responses received. An inference problem exists for all types of database systems and has been studied extensively within the context of multi-level databases. Early developments on the inference problem focused on statistical database security. Then the focus was on security constraint processing to handle the inference problem. Researchers also used conceptual structures to design the database application and detect security violations via inferences during the design time. There are many technical challenges for the inference problem including the insolvability and the complexity of the problem. The developments on the inference problem are illustrated in Figure 17.3. Recently the inference problem is receiving much attention within the context of privacy. Technologies such as data mining are being used extensively for national security. This is causing privacy concerns. The privacy problem is a form of the inference problem, where one deduces highly private information from public information.

17.2.5   Secure Distributed and Heterogeneous Data Management

Security for distributed, heterogeneous, and federated database systems is critical for many operational environments. For example, the individual's data-management systems could enforce their own policies. These policies have to be integrated to form a global policy. Policy integration is a major challenge in heterogeneous and federated data-management systems. Figure 17.4 illustrates policy integration.

17.2.6   Secure Object Data Systems

Object technology is important for many applications including programming languages, design and analysis for applications and systems, interconnection, and

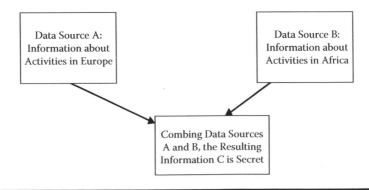

Figure 17.3   Aspects of the inference problem.

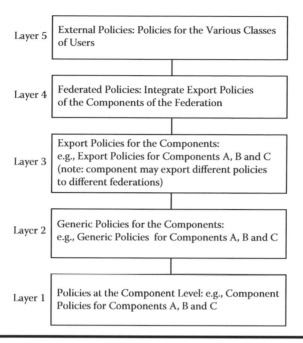

Figure 17.4   Policy integration.

databases. For example, programming languages such as Java are based on objects. Distributed object-management systems connect heterogeneous databases and applications. Databases and applications are modeled using objects. Large systems are created using object components. Finally, object technology is very popular for modeling and design. It is critical that objects be secure; that is, we need secure object programming languages, secure object databases, secure distributed object systems, secure object components, and use of objects to model secure applications. In Reference [THUR05], we discussed various types of secure object technologies relevant to databases and applications. For example, in a secure object model, access may be controlled to the object instances, the attributes, the methods, and the classes. Figure 17.5 illustrates a multilevel object.

17.2.7   Data Warehousing, Data Mining, Security, and Privacy

Many organizations are now developing data warehouses. Warehouses essentially provide different views of the data to different users. For example, a president of a company may want to see quarterly sales figures, whereas a manager of a department may want to see the daily sales numbers. These data warehouses have to be secure. Figure 17.6 illustrates security aspects of data warehouses. For example,

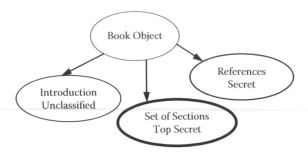

Figure 17.5   Multilevel object.

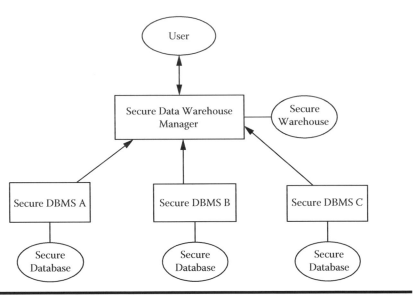

Figure 17.6   Secure data warehousing.

based on the security policies of the individual databases, a policy for the warehouse has to be developed.

In Reference [THUR05], we discussed the relationship between data mining and security. For example, data mining could be used to handle security problems such as intrusion detection and auditing. On the other hand, data mining also exacerbates inference and privacy problems. This is because a user can use the various data-mining tools and combine different pieces of information and deduce new information that may be sensitive and private. This is illustrated in Figure 17.7. Recently there has been much discussion on privacy violations that result from data

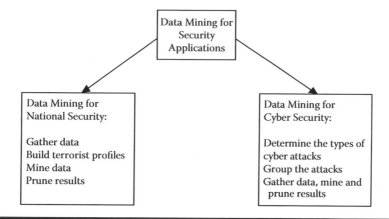

Figure 17.7   Data mining and security.

mining. We discussed privacy issues as well as the notion of privacy preserving data mining in Reference [THUR05].

17.2.8   Secure Web Data Management

We have discussed this extensively in Part I, especially in Chapter 2 where we discussed securing Web databases as well as security threats and solutions to Web data management. The databases on the Web have to be managed and integrated. Access to these databases has to be controlled. Furthermore, the data has to be protected from malicious corruption. In addition, we need to manage secure databases that consist of eXtensible Markup Language (XML) and Resource Description Framework (RDF) documents. Much of the discussion in this book is about secure Web data and information management with respect to the semantic Web.

17.2.9   Emerging Secure Data-Management Technologies

Some emerging secure data-management technologies are illustrated in Figure 17.8. These emerging technologies include secure dependable systems as well as secure sensor and wireless data systems. These technologies are

Some Emerging Security Concerns/Solutions:

Digital identity management
Identity theft management
Biometrics
Digital forensics
Steganography and digital watermarking
Risk and economic analysis

Figure 17.8   Secure emerging data-management technologies.

discussed in Reference [THUR05]. Related topics include data-quality issues as well as topics such as digital identity management and digital forensics for secure databases. Note that emerging security technologies will continue to evolve as new technologies are discovered. Therefore, we encourage the reader to keep up with the developments with technologies and ensure that security is considered at the beginning of the design of a system and not as an afterthought.

17.3 Secure Information Management

We discuss two aspects of secure information management: secure multimedia information management and secure collaborative information management.

17.3.1 Secure Multimedia Information Management

We discuss security policies, secure multimedia data representation, and secure multimedia data-management functions.

17.3.1.1 Security Policy

Security policy essentially specifies the application-specific security rules and application-independent security rules. Application-independent security rules would be rules such as

- The combination of data from two video streams is sensitive.
- A user operating at level L1 cannot read or view data from a text object, image object, audio object, or video object classified at level L2 if L2 is a more sensitive level than L1.

The second rule above is usually enforced for multilevel security (see Chapter 7). In a multilevel secure multimedia database-management system, users cleared at different clearance levels access the multimedia data assigned different sensitivity levels so that the user only gets the data (e.g., video, audio, etc.) he or she can access. For example, a user at the secret level can read all the text at the secret level or below, and a user at the unclassified level can only read the unclassified text.

Now the main question is, how does the policy apply for multimedia data? We could have videocameras operating at different levels. Videocameras operating in the Middle East may be highly classified, whereas videocameras in Europe may be less classified. Classified instruments will gather classified data, whereas unclassified instruments will gather unclassified data. Furthermore, video data may be in the form of streams. Therefore, we need access-control policies for data streams. Within each level, one could enforce application-specific rules.

Application-specific security rules include the following:

- Only law enforcement officials have authorization to examine video streams emanating from videocamera A.
- Data from video streams A and B taken together are sensitive.
- All the data emanating from videocameras in Washington, D.C. federal buildings are sensitive, whereas the data emanating from videocameras in North Dakota federal buildings are not sensitive.

Essentially application-specific rules are specified using security constraints. Note that in addition to video streams, the discussion also applies to document sources, audiotapes, and image data. Another question is, do the multimedia data-collection instruments at different levels communicate with each other? Now, if the Bell and LaPadula policy is to be enforced, a classified instrument cannot send any data to an unclassified instrument. Data can move in the opposite direction. The multimedia network must ensure such communication.

A multimedia data-collection instrument could also be multilevel, that is, an instrument could process data at different levels. Data could be text, video, audio, or imagery. The multilevel data collector can then give data to the users at the appropriate level. For example, a multilevel videocamera may give secret video streams to an intelligence officer, whereas it may give out only unclassified streams or images to a physician. One could also enforce role-based access control where users access data, depending on their roles. A physician may have access to video and audio information about the spread of diseases, whereas he may not have access to video and audio data about potential terrorists.

Granularity of access control could be at different levels for multimedia data. In the case of text, one could grant access at the chapter level or even at the paragraph level. One could also classify the existence of certain chapters or sections. In the case of images, one could grant access depending on the content or at the pixel level. In the case of audio and video, one could grant access at the frame level. For example, John can read frames 1000 to 2000, whereas he can update frames 3000 to 4000. He has no access to any of the other frames (see also Reference [THUR90]).

Security policy integration is a challenge; that is, each multimedia database may enforce its own security policy and have its own constraints. The challenge is to integrate the different policies, especially in distributed and federated environments. For example, in the case of a federation, each federation of multimedia databases may have its own policy, which is derived from the security policies of the individual databases. The policies of the federations will have to be combined to get an integrated policy (see also Chapter 21). Figure 17.9 illustrates access control for multimedia data-management systems.

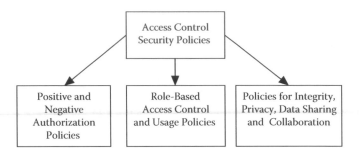

Figure 17.9   Access control.

17.3.1.2 Secure Multimedia Data Representation

We need an appropriate data model for representing multimedia data. Researchers have used both the extended relational model as well as object models for this purpose. Therefore, access-control policies applied for the extended relational data model or object models will be applied to the multimedia data model. More recently, object relational data models are also being used to represent data. We need a secure object relational data model for secure multimedia data.

17.3.1.3 Security Impact on Multimedia Data and Information-Management Functions

Security has an impact on all the functions of a multimedia data manager. Consider the query operation. The query processor has to examine the access-control rules and security constraints and modify the query accordingly. For example, if the fact that the existence of Operation X is classified, then this query cannot be sent to an unclassified multimedia data collector such as a videocamera to film the event. Similarly, the update processor also examines the access-control rules and computes the level of the multimedia data to be inserted or modified. Security also has an impact on multimedia editing and browsing. When one is browsing multimedia data, the system must ensure that the user has the proper access to browse the link or access the data associated with the link. In the case of multimedia editing, when objects at different levels are combined to form a film, then the film object has to be classified accordingly. One may need to classify various frames or assign a high watermark associated with the levels of the individual objects that compose the film. Furthermore, when films are edited (such as deleting certain portions of the film), then one needs to recompute the level of the edited object.

Secure multimedia transaction processing is another issue. First, what does transaction processing mean? One could imagine data being gathered from two different locations (e.g., video streams) and making simultaneous updates to the multimedia database. Both updates have to be carried out as a transaction. This is conceivable if, say, an analyst needs both films to carry out the analysis. So assuming that the notion of a transaction is valid, what does it mean to process transactions securely?

Next consider the storage manager function. The storage manager has to ensure that access is controlled to the multimedia database. The storage manager may also be responsible for partitioning the data according to security levels. The security impact of access methods and indexing strategy for multimedia data are yet to be determined. Numerous index strategies have been developed for multimedia data including for text, images, audio, and video. We need to examine the strategies and determine the security impact. Another issue is the synchronization between storage and presentation of multimedia data. For example, we need to ensure that video is displayed smoothly and that there are no bursts in traffic. There could be malicious programs manipulating the storage and presentation managers so that information is covertly passed from a higher level to lower-level processes.

Metadata management is also another issue. For example, we need to first determine the types of metadata for multimedia data. Metadata may include descriptions about the data, the source of the data as well as the quality of the data. Metadata may also include information such as Frames 100 to 2000 are about the President's speech. Metadata may also be classified. In some cases the metadata may be classified at a higher level than the data itself. For example, the location of the data may be highly sensitive, whereas the data could be unclassified. We should also ensure that one cannot obtain unauthorized information from the metadata.

17.3.2 Secure Workflow and Collaboration

Workflow and collaboration is about organizations or groups working together toward a common goal such as designing a system or solving a problem. Collaboration technologies are important for E-commerce as organizations carry out transactions between each other. Workflow is about a process that must be followed from start to finish in carrying out an operation such as making a purchase. The steps include initiating the agreement, transferring funds, and sending the goods to the consumer. Because collaboration and workflow are part of many operations such as E-commerce and knowledge management, we need secure workflow and secure collaboration. There has been a lot of work by Bertino et al. on this topic. Most notable among the developments is the Bertino, Ferran, and Atluri (BFA) model (see [BERT99]) for secure workflow-management systems. Some work on secure collaborative systems was initially proposed by Demurjian et al. [DEMU93]. Since then, several ideas have been developed (see IFIP Conference Series on Database Security). In this section we will provide an overview of secure workflow and collaboration.

In the case of secure workflow-management systems, the idea is for users to have the proper credentials to carry out a particular task. For example, in the case of making a purchase for a project, only a project leader could initiate the request. A secretary then types the request. Then the administrator has to use his or her credit card and make the purchase. The mailroom has the authority to make the delivery. Essentially what we have proposed is a role-based access-control model for secure workflow. There have been several developments on this topic (see SACMAT Conference Proceedings). Various technologies such as Petri nets have been investigated for a secure workflow system (see [HUAN98]).

Closely related to secure workflow is secure collaboration. Collaboration is much broader than workflow. Whereas workflow is about a series of operations that have to be executed serially or in parallel to carry out a task, collaboration is about individuals working together to solve a problem. Object technologies in general and distributed object-management technologies in particular are being used to develop collaboration systems. Here, the individual and the resources in the environment are modeled as objects. Communications between individuals and resources are modeled as communication between objects. This communication is carried out via object request brokers. Therefore, security issues discussed for object request brokers apply for secure collaboration. For example, should all parties involved be given the same access to the resources? If the access to resources is different, then how can the individuals work together and share data?

Trust and negotiation systems also play an important role in workflow and collaboration systems. For example, how can parties trust each other in solving a problem? If A gives some information to B, can B share the information with C, even if A and C do not communicate with each other? Similar questions were asked when we discussed secure federations. Also, secure data-management technologies are necessary to manage the data for workflow and collaboration applications. Although much progress has been made, there is still a lot to do, especially with the developments on the semantic Web and emerging technologies such as peer-to-peer data management. Figure 17.10 illustrates secure collaboration.

17.4   Secure Knowledge Management

As mentioned in Chapter 4, knowledge management is about corporations sharing resources and expertise as well as building intellectual capital so that they can increase their competitiveness. Although knowledge-management practices have been around for decades, it is only with the advent of the Web that knowledge management has emerged as a technology area. Corporations with intranets promote knowledge management so the employees can learn about various advances in technology, get corporation information, and find expertise in the corporation. Furthermore, when experts leave the corporation through retirement or otherwise, it

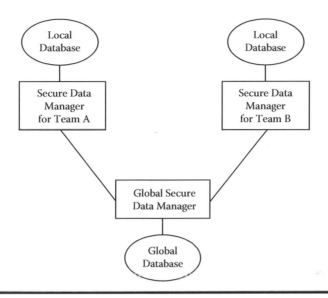

Figure 17.10　Secure collaboration.

is important to capture their knowledge and their practices so that the corporation does not lose valuable information acquired through many years of hard work.

One of the challenges in knowledge management is maintaining security. Now, knowledge management includes many technologies such as data mining, multimedia, collaboration, and the Web. Therefore, security for, say, Web data management, multimedia systems, and collaboration systems contributes toward securing knowledge-management practices. In addition, one needs to protect the corporation's assets such as its intellectual property. Trade secrets have to be kept highly confidential so that competitors do not have any access to them. This means one needs to enforce some form of access control such as role-based access control, credential mechanism, and encryption. Figure 17.11 illustrates the information that must be protected to ensure secure knowledge management.

Secure knowledge management essentially extends the knowledge-management categories discussed in Chapter 4 (see also Reference [MORE01]). To have secure knowledge management, we need to have secure strategies, processes, and metrics [BERT06], that is, metrics must include support for security-related information. Processes must include secure operations. Strategies must include security strategies. When knowledge is created, the creator may specify to whom the knowledge can be transferred. Additional access-control techniques may be enforced by the manager of the knowledge. Knowledge sharing and knowledge transfer operations must also enforce the access control and security policies. Secure knowledge-management architecture may be built around the corporation's intranet. This is an area that has

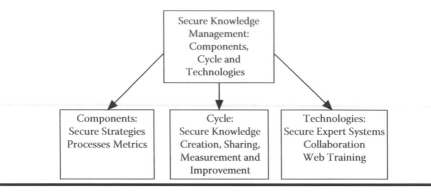

Figure 17.11   Secure knowledge management.

received little attention. A workshop on secure knowledge management was held in Buffalo, New York in September 2004, and this workshop has resulted in many challenging ideas and directions for secure knowledge management [SKM04].

17.5 Applications of the Semantic Web

The semantic Web has applications in secure data, information, and knowledge management. We will examine each of the components below.

17.5.1 Secure Data Management

First of all, the security policies may be expressed in languages such as XML and RDF. This is one of the significant contributions of the semantic Web. Now, databases may also consist of XML and RDF documents. For example, products such as those by Oracle Corporation now have the capability of managing XML and RDF documents. Therefore, we need to apply data-management techniques for managing XML and RDF documents.

Semantic Web technologies have applications in heterogeneous database integration. For example, ontologies are needed for handling semantic heterogeneity. XML is now being used as the common data representation language. With respect to data warehousing, XML and RDF may be used to specify policies. Furthermore, ontologies may be used for data transformation to bring the data into the warehouse. Ontologies have applications in data mining as they clarify various concepts to facilitate data mining. On the other hand, the vast quantities of data on the Web will have to be mined to extract information to guide the agents to understand the Web pages. Semantic Web technologies including the reasoning engines may be applied to handle the inference and privacy problems. For example, languages such as RDF and Web Ontology Language (OWL) may be used to specify policies, and then inference controllers could be developed based on descriptive logic-based engines such as Pellet to determine whether security violations via inference occur.

In summary, in every aspect of secure data management, semantic Web technologies have applications. However, data-management techniques and data-mining techniques can also be applied to manage and mine the data on the Web to facilitate agents to understand the Web pages. We will revisit semantic Web technologies for interoperability in Chapter 18. Figure 17.12 illustrates the relationships between secure data management and the semantic Web.

17.5.2 Secure Information Management

As in the case of data management, semantic Web technologies such as XML, RDF, and OWL can be used to reprint security policies including confidentiality, privacy, and trust policies. Furthermore, the reasoning engines based on, say, descriptive logic such as Pellet can be used to infer unauthorized conclusions via inference. Semantic Web technologies can also be used to represent the data. For example, Synchronized Multimedia Integration Language (SMIL) is a markup language for video, whereas VoiceML is a markup language for audio data. The access-control policies specified in, say, XML, RDF, or a more descriptive language such as Rei can be enforced on video data represented in SMIL. Markup languages such as eBXML (Electronic Business using eXtensible Markup Language) have been developed for E-business. We will discuss this further in Chapter 19.

Semantic Web technologies can also be applied for workflow and collaborative applications. For example, the Workflow Management Coalition has developed two languages: Wf-XML (Workflow XML) and as stated in Reference [WFMC], "Wf-XML extends the ASAP (Asynchronous Service Access Protocol) by the Organization for the Advancement of Structured Information Standards (OASIS) model to include BPM (Business Process Management) and workflow interchange capabilities." This coalition has also developed XPDL (XML Process Definition Language). As stated in Reference [WFMC], "XPDL provides a framework for implementing business process management and workflow engines, and for designing, analyzing, and exchanging business processes."

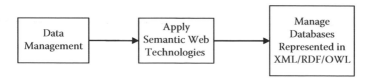

Figure 17.12   Semantic Web for secure data management.

Whereas the markup languages that we have discussed here are comparable to XML for text, these languages have been extended with ontologies to provide semantics for multimedia, workflow, and collaborative computing applications. For example, RDF-based languages have been developed by researchers in Scotland for collaborative and workflow applications [CHEN04].

Whereas trustworthy semantic Webs have applications in information management, information-management technologies have applications in developing semantic Webs. For example, workflow technology can be used to organize semantic Web processes. Furthermore, multimedia technologies can be used by agents to visualize and better understand Web pages. More details on such applications can be found in Reference [MARI02]. Figure 17.13 illustrates the relationships between secure data management and the semantic Web.

17.5.3 Secure Knowledge Management

Semantic Web technologies have many applications in knowledge management. For example, we need ontologies to capture knowledge and reason about the knowledge. In his article on the semantic Web and knowledge management, Warren gives an example of how "a political scientist, Sally, wants to research the extent to which British Prime Minister Tony Blair's stance on Zimbabwe has changed over a year and what factors might have caused that change." He further states that "in the world of the Semantic Web, Sally could search for everything written by Blair on this topic over a specific time period. She could also search for transcripts of his speeches. Information markup wouldn't stop at the article or report level but would also exist at the article section level. So, Sally could also locate articles written by political commentators that contain transcripts of Blair's speeches" [WARR06].

Now, knowledge management also has applications for building the semantic Web. For example, prior knowledge captured as a result of knowledge management can be used by agents to better understand the Web pages. With respect to security, in the example by Warren, confidentiality, privacy, and trust policies will determine the extent to which Sally trusts the articles and has access to the articles in putting together her report on Tony Blair's speeches. Figure 17.14 illustrates the relationship between secure knowledge management and the semantic Web.

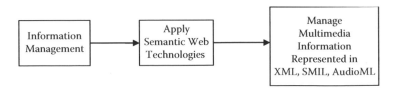

Figure 17.13   Semantic Web for secure information management.

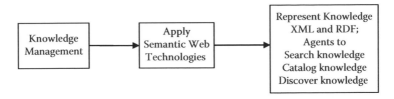

Figure 17.14 Semantic Web for secure knowledge management.

17.6 Summary and Directions

This chapter has discussed secure data, information, and knowledge management and then shown how semantic Web technologies may be applied. We also discussed how data, information, and knowledge management could be used to develop the vision of the semantic Web. Many efforts are under way to develop ontologies and markup languages for different data types and applications. However, security has not received much attention apart from the work of Finin et al., Bertino et al., Berners Lee et al., and Thuraisingham et al. among a few others. Therefore, as we develop various standards, we need to ensure that security issues are addressed thoroughly.

Although there are efforts such as the work of the World Wide Web Consortium (W3C) and OASIS to develop security standards such as eXtensible Access Control Markup Language (XACML) and Security Assertions Markup Language (SAML) specifications, much needs to be done to address numerous security issues including complex confidentiality policies in addition to trust and privacy policies. Furthermore, we cannot forget about data integrity and quality. Therefore, we believe that there are numerous opportunities for research, development, and system-building activities for semantic Web-based data, information, and knowledge management.

References

[AFSB83] Air Force Studies Board, Committee on Multilevel Data Management Security, National Academy Press, Washington, DC, 1983.

[BERT99] Bertino, E. et al., The specification and enforcement of authorization constraints in workflow management systems, *ACM Trans. Inf. Syst. Security*, 2(1), 1999.

[BERT06] Bertino E. et al., Secure knowledge management, *IEEE Trans. Syst. Man Cybernetics*, May 2006.

[CHEN04] Chen-Burger, Y.H, K.Y. Hui, A.D. Preece, P.M.D. Gray, and A. Tate, Supporting Collaboration through Semantic-based Workflow and Constraint Solving, Knowledge Acquisition Modelling and Acquisition Workshop, Whittlebury Hall, UK, October 2004.

[DEMU93] Demurjian, S. et al., Security for collaborative computer systems, multimedia review, *J. Multimedia Comput.*, 5, Summer 1993.

[HUAN98] Huang, W. and V. Atluri, Analyzing the safety of workflow authorization models, *Proc. IFIP Database Security Conf.*, Chalidiki, Greece, July 1998, Kluwer, Dordrecht, 1999.

[WFMC] http://xml.coverpages.org/wf-xml.html.http://www.csd.abdn.ac.uk/~apreece/research/download/ekaw2004.pdf.

[MARI02] Marinescu, D.C., *Internet Based Workflow Management: Towards a Semantic Web*, Wiley Interscience, New York, 2002.

[MORE01] Morey, D., M. Maybury, and B. Thuraisingham, Eds., *Knowledge Management*, MIT Press, Cambridge, MA, 2001.

[SKM04] *Proc. Secure Knowledge Manage. Conf.*, Buffalo, NY, Sept. 2004

[THUR90] Thuraisingham, B., Security for multimedia database systems, *Proc. IFIP Data Security Conf.*, Halifax, UK, 1990.

[THUR05] Thuraisingham, B., *Database and Applications Security*, CRC Press, Boca Raton, FL, 2005.

[WARR06] Warren, P., Knowledge management and the semantic Web: from scenario to technology, *IEEE Intelligent Sys.*, 21(1), 53–59, 2006.

Exercises

1. Describe security issues for data, information, and knowledge management.
2. Describe the use of semantic Web technologies for secure data, information, and knowledge management.

Chapter 18

Secure Semantic Interoperability

18.1 Overview

In this chapter we examine semantic interoperability with emphasis on heterogeneity; that is, we assume that the data sources are not identical. For example, the data manager at Site 1 could be designed based on the relational model, and the data manager at Site 2 could be designed based on the object model. The challenge is, how do the different secure systems interoperate with each other? In addition to data model heterogeneity, the system could enforce different security policies. How do you integrate the heterogeneous security policies? Heterogeneity could also be with respect to query processing and transaction management. What is the security impact, and how can semantic Web technologies help? Note that we are seeing the need for the interoperation of heterogeneous data sources because organizations want to collaborate with each other and yet maintain their autonomy. These organizations have already implemented their own data managers and applications. Therefore, the challenge is to integrate the systems and applications for collaboration and other purposes.

This chapter will examine secure heterogeneous information management and the impact of semantic Web technologies. The organization of this chapter is as follows. Some background on heterogeneous database integration and security is discussed in Section 18.2. Schema and policy integration are discussed in Section 18.3. Semantic heterogeneity is discussed in Section 18.4. The inference problem is revisited in Section 18.5. Application of semantic Web technologies for information interoperability is discussed in Section 18.6. Summary and directions are provided in Section 18.7.

18.2 Background

The earliest effort to investigate security for heterogeneous and federated database systems began around 1991 and was reported in References [THUR92], [THUR94a], and [THUR94b]. In particular, various approaches to designing heterogeneous and federated data managers were examined, and the security impact was investigated. The issues include security for integrating federated schemas as well as handling different ranges of security levels. For example, one system could handle the range from Secret to TopSecret, whereas another system could handle the range from Unclassified to Secret. The work also investigated the integration of multiple security policies where component systems export policies to the federations. Issues on integrating heterogeneous database schemas in a secure environment were also investigated. Much of the work here focused on query-processing issues. In addition, prototype systems were also developed [THUR94b].

Around 1992, the MITRE Corporation began an effort called the Multilevel Secure Transactions (MUSET) database system. This effort focused mainly on transaction management in a heterogeneous database system [BLAU93]. This effort also investigated concurrency control, recovery, and commit protocols for multilevel transactions (see, for example, Reference [JAJO93]). A multilevel transaction is a transaction that can operate at multiple security levels. For example, a subtransaction at one site could operate at the unclassified level, whereas another subtransaction at a different site could operate at the Secret level. The challenge here is to ensure consistency and at the same time minimize covert channels. This is more complex than the single-level transaction approach proposed in Refrerence [THUR91].

Other work on secure distributed data management includes various concurrency control algorithms for transactions. Many of the papers on this topic have been published by Bertino, Jajodia, et al., at various security conferences around the mid-1990s (see, for example, Proceedings of the IEEE Symposia on Security and Privacy and Proceedings of the IFIP Database Security Conference Series). Discretionary security for federated database systems has been investigated by Olivier et al. at the Rand African University and presented at the IFIP conference series (see [OLIV96]). We will discuss some of the key issues in secure heterogeneous and federated database systems in the remaining sections.

In a heterogeneous database environment, we assume that the information sources and data managers are heterogeneous in nature. Heterogeneity could be with respect to data models, security policies, and functions such as query and transaction processing as well as semantics.

18.3 Schema and Policy Integration

There are several aspects to heterogeneity. One is schema heterogeneity where System A is based on a relational system and System B is based on object systems; that is, when two systems are based on different models we need to resolve the conflicts. One option is to have a common data model. This means that the constructs of both systems have to be transformed into the constructs of the common data model. When you consider security properties, we have to ensure that the policies enforced by the individual systems are maintained. Figure 18.1 illustrates the use of a common secure data model to handle data-model heterogeneity. In some cases we may need bidirectional transformation where the constructs of one data model have to be translated into those of another.

Figure 18.2 illustrates the situation where the multiple schemas are integrated to form a federated schema for a secure federated database system. Essentially we have adopted Sheth and Larson's schema of architecture for a secure federated environment [SHET90]. Some of the challenges in integrating heterogeneous schemas are discussed in Reference [THUR94a]. We assume that each component exports certain schema to the federation. Then these schemas are integrated to form a federated policy. In a secure environment, we need to ensure that the security properties of the individual systems are maintained throughout the federation. In the next section we will discuss security policy integration issues.

Next we will focus on policy integration. Initial investigation of security policy integration for federated databases was reported in Reference [THUR94a] and Reference [HOSM96]. Here we assumed that heterogeneous Multilevel Secure Database Management Systems (MLS/DBMSs) had to be integrated to form a Multilevel Secure Federated Database Management System (MLS/FDBMS). We illustrate the policy architecture in Figure 18.3. Our approach is very similar to

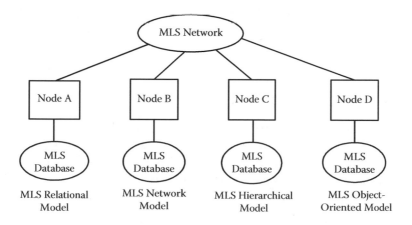

Figure 18.1   Secure data model heterogeneity.

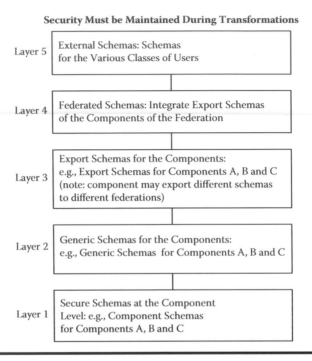

Security Must be Maintained During Transformations

Layer 5	External Schemas: Schemas for the Various Classes of Users

Layer 4	Federated Schemas: Integrate Export Schemas of the Components of the Federation

Layer 3	Export Schemas for the Components: e.g., Export Schemas for Components A, B and C (note: component may export different schemas to different federations)

Layer 2	Generic Schemas for the Components: e.g., Generic Schemas for Components A, B and C

Layer 1	Secure Schemas at the Component Level: e.g., Component Schemas for Components A, B and C

Figure 18.2   Secure schema integration.

the approach taken by Sheth and Larson for schema integration [SHET90]. In the case of policy integration, each system exports security policies to the federation. We assume that the component systems have more stringent access-control requirements for foreign users, that is, export policies may have access-control rules in addition to the rules enforced by the local system. The challenge is to ensure that there is no security violation at the federation level. A view of agencies sharing data and enforcing policies is illustrated in Figure 18.3.

18.4   Semantic Heterogeneity

Semantic heterogeneity occurs when an entity is interpreted differently at different sites or different entities are interpreted to be the same object. For example, the term *speed* could be in miles per hour in Node 1 and in Node 2 it could be kilometers per day. In another example, John Smith could be Smith John at Node 1 and John K. Smith at Node 2. In both cases the same entity is interpreted differently. On the other hand, John Smith at Node 1 could really be John J. Smith, and at Node 2 he is John K. Smith. They are both different people, but mistakenly they are considered to be one and the same.

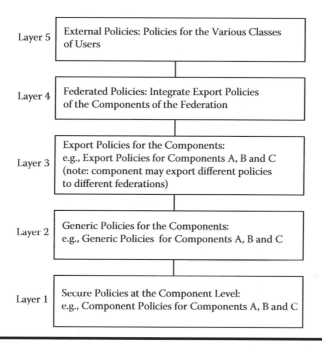

Figure 18.3 Secure policy integration.

Semantic heterogeneity is one of the major challenges for data integration as well as information interoperability. They occur not only in relational databases, but also in object databases, multimedia databases, and even geospatial databases. For example, when heterogeneous geospatial databases are integrated, each database could have different ways of representing the same coordinate system (see also Chapter 23). Various solutions for handling heterogeneity have been proposed since the 1990s, although it is only recently with the use of semantic Web technologies that we have a good handle on the problem. The application of semantic Web technologies for secure information interoperability will be discussed in Section 18.6. Figure 18.4 illustrates semantic heterogeneity.

18.5 Inference Problem

We carried out an extensive investigation of the inference problem for heterogeneous environments in the mid-1990s (see Reference [THUR94b]). Essentially we designed and developed security-constraint processing in a heterogeneous environment. We extended the inference controller discussed in earlier chapters to a distributed and heterogeneous environment.

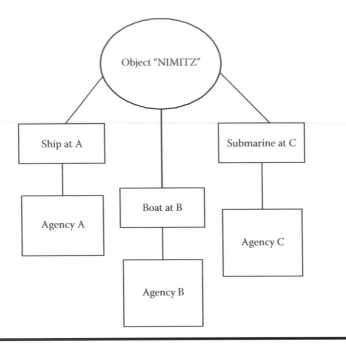

Figure 18.4   Semantic heterogeneity.

Whereas there is little other work reported on inference control in heterogeneous and federated environments, more recently this area is getting attention, especially when agencies have to form federations and coalitions and share information and at the same time enforce inference control and privacy control. We will discuss information sharing in federated and coalition environments in Chapter 21. Figure 18.5 illustrates an inference controller for such an environment.

18.6   Application of Semantic Web

Whereas semantic Web technologies were developed for machine-understandable Web pages, and whereas eXtensible Markup Language (XML) in particular was developed for document exchange on the Web, these technologies have extensive use in information interoperability. Syntactic heterogeneity such as data model heterogeneity was a major issue in the 1990s. Various communities were discussing the development of common object models and extended relational models for common data resonation [THUR97]. However, since the development of XML, XML is the choice language for global data representations. Many organizations including the Department of Defense are using XML and XML schemas to publish the

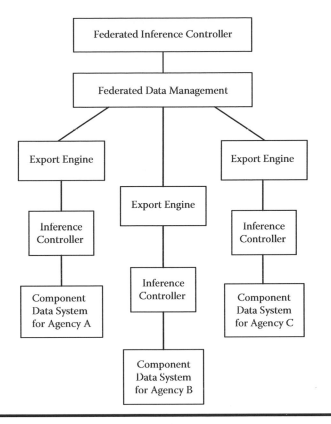

Figure 18.5 Federated inference controller.

metadata for individual databases. This has been a significant development toward a common data model.

Whereas XML is ideal for representing syntax, we have shown in Part II that we need Resource Description Framework (RDF) and Web Ontology Language (OWL)-like languages for representing semantics. Therefore, RDF-based languages are being used to handle semantic heterogeneity. For example, ontologies are specified to define various terms as well as to represent common semantics or to distinguish between different semantics. These ontologies are then used for information interoperability and to understand various terms between different organizations. For example, in our research on geospatial semantic Web we are using ontologism specified in RDF-like languages (which we have called GRDF, or Geospatial RDF) for handling semantic heterogeneity. These ontologies are then used for semantic interoperability.

With respect to policy integration, each data-management system could use XML or RDF to specify policies, and then we integrate the policies using ontologies to handle semantic differences. Integrated policy languages would also be based on XML and RDF. We have explored the use of Geospatial Markup Language (GML) as well as GRDF to integrate policies for geospatial databases (see also Chapter 23). Furthermore, eXtensible Access Control Markup Language (XACML) is being examined for geospatial data, and subsequently GEO-XACML is being developed.

Finally, with respect to the inference problem, we can use descriptive logic-based theorem proverbs such as Pellet to handle such problems. Each data-management system could have an inference controller based on, say, Pellet, and we could have an inference controller operating at the global level. Figure 18.6 illustrates the applications of semantic Web technologies for secure semantic information interoperability.

18.7 Summary and Directions

In this chapter we first discussed security for information integration. We started by providing some background and related work and then discussed schema integration and security policy integration. We also discussed semantic heterogeneity and the inference problem in a federated environment. Finally, we discussed vari-

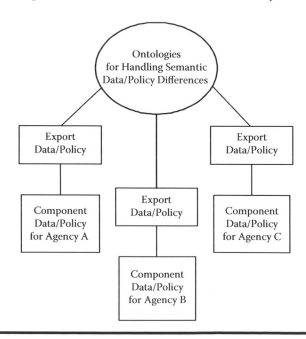

Figure 18.6   Semantic Web for secure information interoperability.

ous semantic Web technologies such as XML, RDF, and OWL for secure semantic interoperability.

It should be noted that much of the work on security for heterogeneous and federated databases is preliminary in nature. However, with information integration on the Web as well as interest in the federated approach for interagency data sharing, there is now a lot more interest. Furthermore, there is also much interest now on trust-negotiation management systems for coalition data sharing. We will discuss more details in Chapter 21.

References

[BLAU93] Blaustein, B., A Model of atomicity for multilevel transactions, *Proc. IEEE Symp. Security and Privacy*, Oakland, California, May 1993.

[HOSM96] Hosmer, H., Availability policies in an adversarial environment, *Proc. New Comput. Security Paradigms Workshop*, Lake Arrowhead, CA, Sept. 1996.

[JAJO93] Jajodia, S. et al, Integrating concurrency control and commit algorithms in distributed multilevel secure databases, *Proc. IFIP Database Security,* Huntsville, Alabama, 1993. North-Holland, Amsterdam, 1994.

[OLIVI96] Olivier, M., Integrity constraints in federated databases, *Proc. IFIP Database Security Conference*, Como, Italy 1996.

[SHET90] Sheth A. and J. Larson, Federated database systems, *ACM Comput. Surveys*, 22(3), 1990.

[THUR91] Thuraisingham, B., Multilevel security issues in distributed database management systems – II, *Comput. Security*, 10(9), 1991.

[THUR94b] Thuraisingham, B., Security issues for federated database systems, *Comput. Security*, 13(6), 1994.

[THUR97] Thuraisingham, B., *Data Management Systems Evolution and Interoperation*, CRC Press, Boca Raton, FL, 1997.

[THUR92] Thuraisingham, B. and Rubinovitz, H., Multilevel security issues for distributed database management systems - III, *Comput. Security*, 11(7), 1992.

[THUR94a] Thuraisingham, B. and H. Rubinovitz, Security Constraint Processing in a Heterogeneous Database System, *Proc. ACM Comput. Conf.*, Phoenix, AZ, March 1994.

Exercises

1. Describe security issues for heterogeneous database integration.
2. Describe the use of ontologies for handling semantic heterogeneity and policy heterogeneity.

Chapter 19

Secure Semantic E-Business

19.1 Overview

E-business (also referred to as E-commerce) is about organizations conducting transactions on the Web. Various models, architectures, and technologies are being developed for E-business. We gave some details of E-business in Chapter 3. We also discussed the security impact on E-business in that chapter. Because we are dealing with critical data such as funds and accounts, when carrying out E-business, confidentiality and privacy of information is crucial. We also have to ensure that the data is not maliciously corrupted.

More recently, semantic Web technologies have been applied to E-business activities. In particular, standards such as eXtensible Markup Language (XML) as well as business-process specifications have been developed for E-business. Furthermore, ontologies are also being developed so that agents can understand the various terms and carry out the transactions on the Web. A new field called semantic E-business has subsequently emerged. This field integrates knowledge management together with business-process management and semantic Web technologies. There is also some research now on incorporating security into semantic E-business [THUR05]. In this chapter we will discuss the developments on secure semantic E-business. We first provide an overview of security issues for E-business applications. Then we will discuss semantic Web technologies for secure E-business.

The organization of this chapter is as follows. In Section 19.2 we discuss secure E-business. Secure semantic E-business, which includes a discussion of XML-based standards, is given in Section 19.3. The chapter is concluded in Section 19.4.

19.2 Secure E-Business

In this section we examine the security impact on E-business processes. As we have stated earlier, E-business is about organizations carrying out business transactions such as sales of goods and business agreements as well as consumers purchasing items from merchants electronically. There have been numerous developments on E-commerce and some discussions on the initial progress were given in Reference [THUR00]. Due to the fact that E-commerce may involve millions of dollars in transactions between businesses or credit card purchases between consumers and businesses, it is important that the E-commerce systems be secure. Examples of such systems include E-payment systems and supply-chain management systems.

There has been some work on secure E-commerce as well as secure supply-chain management (see, for example, Reference [GHOS98] and Reference [ATTA03]). In the case of E-payment systems, the challenges include identification and authentication of consumers as well as businesses as well as tracing the purchases made by consumers. For example, it would be entirely possible for someone to masquerade as a consumer, use the consumer's credit card, and make purchases electronically. Therefore, one solution proposed is for the consumer to have some credentials when he or she makes some purchases. These credentials, which may be some random numbers, could vary with each purchase. This way the malicious process that masquerades as the consumer may not have the credential and therefore may not be able to make the purchases. There will be a problem if the credentials are stolen. Various encryption techniques are being proposed for secure E-commerce (see Reference [HASS00]), that is, in addition to possessing credentials, the information may be encrypted, say, with the public key of the business, and only the business could get the actual data. Similarly the communication between the business and the consumer is also encrypted. When transactions are carried out between businesses, the parties involved will have to possess certain credentials so that the transactions are carried out securely. Figure 19.1 illustrates aspects of secure E-commerce. Note that while much progress has been made on E-commerce transactions as well as secure E-commerce transactions, incorporating techniques for secure database transaction management with E-commerce is still not mature. Some work has been reported in Reference [RAY00].

As we have stated, secure supply-chain management is also a key aspect of secure E-commerce. Here the idea is for organizations to provide parts to other cor-

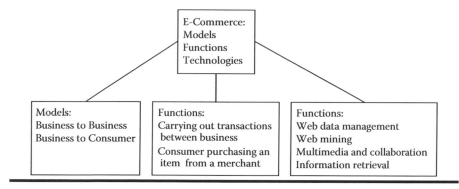

Figure 19.1 Aspects of secure E-business.

porations for manufacturing or other purposes. Suppose a hospital wants to order surgical equipment from a corporation. Then there must be some negotiations and agreements between the hospital and the corporation. Corporation X may request some of its parts from Corporation Y and may not want to divulge the information that it is manufacturing the parts for Hospital A. Such sensitive information has to be protected. Supply-chain management is useful in several areas in manufacturing for many domains including medical, defense, and intelligence. Some of the information exchanged between organizations may be highly sensitive, especially for military and intelligence applications. There needs to be a way to protect such sensitive information. Because the transactions are carried out on the Web, a combination of access-control rules and encryption techniques are being proposed as solutions for protecting sensitive information for supply-chain management.

We have been hearing of E-commerce only since about the mid-1990s, and this has been due to the explosion of the Web. Although much progress has been made on developing information technologies such as databases, data mining, and multimedia information management for E-commerce, there is still a lot to do on security. In addition, the information about various individuals will also have to be kept private. Many of the security technologies we have discussed in this book including secure Web data management and the secure semantic Web will be applicable for secure E-commerce. For example, the semantic Web can be used as a vehicle to carry out E-commerce functions. By having machine-understandable Web pages, E-commerce can be automated without having a human in the loop. This means that it is critical that the semantic Web be secure. If we make progress for secure Web information-management technologies, we can vastly improve the security of E-commerce transactions. The next section will elaborate on semantic Web technologies for E-business. The integration of E-business with the semantic Web has come to be known as semantic E-business.

19.3 Applications of the Semantic Web

The semantic Web has been applied to E-business in two major directions. One is developing specialized markup languages such as Electronic Business using eXtensible Markup Language (ebXML) for E-business applications, and the other is semantic E-business where E-business processes make use of semantic Web technologies. In this section we will discuss both directions and then examine the security impact.

As stated in Reference [WIKI], ebXML "is a family of XML-based standards sponsored by OASIS and UN/CEFACT (between the United Nations Centre for Trade Facilitation and Electronic Business) whose mission is to provide an open, XML-based infrastructure that enables the global use of electronic business information in an interoperable, secure, and consistent manner by all trading partners." The initial goal of this project was to specify XML standards for business processes. These standards include: collaboration protocol agreements, core data components, messaging, registries, and repositories. Some of the ongoing efforts of this project include the following:

- Messaging (ebMS): This is a specialization of Web services for business-to-business applications.
- Business Process and Collaboration (ebBP): This set of specification enables collaboration among business partners.
- Collaboration Protocol Profile and Agreement (CPPA): This effort provides definitions for the sets of information used in business collaborations.
- Registry and Repository: The goal of this effort is to come up with specifications that enable interoperable registries and repositories.
- Core Components (CCTS): This effort focuses on technologies such as context and content assembly.

Ontologies have also been developed for E-commerce applications specified in languages such as Resource Description Framework (RDF), RDF-S, Web Ontology Language (OWL), and OWL-S (see, for example, Reference [ONTO]). For example, in the Obelix project a very good description of E-business and ontologies is provided. The authors state that a problem with E-commerce is the vague ideas that lack precise description. They then discuss their approach which they call E-value, which is based on engineering requirements, and they define ontologies for E-commerce.

More details of this project are given in [OBLE2]. It is stated that "OBELIX is the first ontology-based e-business system of its kind in the world to provide smart, scaleable integration and interoperability capabilities." They also state that this project "incorporates ontology management and configuration, an e-business application server and ontology-based e-application tools as well as an e-business library." OBELIX is a European Commission project, and the goal is to automate

E-business services in a semantic Web environment which has come to be called semantic E-business.

Some interesting efforts on semantic E-business are being carried out by a group at the University of North Carolina at Greensboro. They have stated that semantic E-business is about organizations collaboratively designing business processes that utilize knowledge of the corporation [SING06]. It essentially integrates semantic Web technologies with business process management and knowledge management. The business processes utilize knowledge management to improve their efficiency and utility and use semantic Web technologies such as ontologies for better understanding.

Semantic commerce, which is more or less semantic E-business, is also being investigated. For example, researchers at Hewlett-Packard (HP) Laboratories in Bristol present a life cycle of a business-to-business E-commerce interaction and show how the semantic Web can support a service description language that can be used throughout this life cycle. They show that by using DARPA Agenda Markup Language + Ontology Interface Language (DAML+OIL), they have been able to develop a service description language that is useful not only to represent advertisements, but also implement matchmaking queries, negotiation proposals, and agreements [TRAS].

Like many of the other applications we have discussed in Part IV, although the semantic Web is being applied increasingly for Web services, E-commerce and digital libraries security have not received much attention. There is some work on security for various standards such as Web services. However, trustworthy semantic Web technologies, which include not only confidentiality, but also privacy, trust, and integrity among others, need more examination for the various standards that are evolving. For many of the E-business applications there are complex contracts and negotiations between different organizations, and therefore we need more research on expressing policies and reasoning about the policies. The work of Bertino and Finin on trustworthy semantic Webs and the work of Pernul and his team in Austria and Germany on secure E-commerce is showing a lot of promise (see Reference [ROHM99]). Furthermore, there are also efforts on integrating security into semantic E-business and semantic E-commence [SING06]. However, what we need is to incorporate the research into the standards and specifications so that

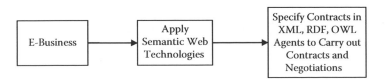

Figure 19.2   Aspects of secure semantic E-business.

products based on these standards can be used in an operational environment. Figure 19.2 illustrates aspects of secure semantic E-business.

19.4 Summary and Directions

This chapter has provided an overview of secure E-business and then discussed various aspects of secure semantic E-business. Semantic E-business essentially integrates semantic Web technologies with business process management and knowledge management. We also discussed some of the key points in ebXML, the XML standard for E-business applications. Finally, we examined the security impact on semantic E-business.

The discussion in this chapter is preliminary because much of the research in semantic E-business in general and secure semantic E-business in particular is in the early stages. We believe that it is important to investigate security while the semantic E-business standards are being developed. As we have discussed, several ontologies for E-business applications are being developed. These ontologies have to be extended to specify various confidentiality, privacy, and trust policies. Business applications will likely have complex policies as transactions are carried out between multiple organizations. Therefore, we need languages to specify the policies and reasoning engines to reason about the policies. We need to examine languages such as the University of Maryland's (Baltimore County) Rei and reasoners such as UMD's Pellet for confidentiality, privacy, and trust policy management of E-business applications.

References

[ATTA03] Atallah, M., et al, Secure supply-chain protocols, *Proc. Int. Conf. Electronic Commerce*, Newport Beach, CA, 2003.

[WIKI] eBXML, http://en.wikipedia.org/wiki/EbXML.

[GHOS98] Ghosh, A., *E-Commerce Security, Weak Links and Strong Defenses*, John Wiley & Sons, New York, 1998.

[OBEL2] http://istresults.cordis.lu/index.cfm/section/news/tpl/article/ID/78390/BrowsingType/Features.

[ONTO] http://www.semantic-Web.at/57.219.219.press.ontologies-for-e-business.htm.

[RAY00] Ray, I. et al., A fair-exchange E-commerce protocol with automated dispute resolution, *Proc. IFIP Database Security Conf.*, Amsterdam, The Netherlands, August 2000, Kluwer, Dordrecht, 2001.

[ROHM99] Röhm, A.W., G. Herrmann, and Pernul, G., A Language for modeling secure business transactions, *Proc. Comput. Security Applications Conf.*, ACSAC, Phoenix, AZ, Dec. 1999.

[SING06] Singh, R. and A.F. Salam, Semantic information assurance for secure distributed knowledge management: a business process perspective, *IEEE Tran. Syst. Man Cybernetics*, May 2006.

[THUR00] Thuraisingham, B., *Web Data Management and Electronic Commerce*, CRC Press, Boca Raton, FL, 2000.

[THUR05] Thuraisingham, B. Security and privacy for semantic E-business, *Commn. Assoc. Comput. Machinery*, 48(12): 71–73, 2005.

[TRAS] Trastour D. et al., Semantic Web Support for the Business-to-Business E-Commerce Lifecycle, http://www2002.org/CDROM/refereed/211/.

Exercises

1. Describe security issues for E-business, and design a secure E-business system.
2. Describe the use of semantic Web technologies for secure E-business.
3. Conduct a survey of secure semantic E-business.

Chapter 20

Secure Semantic Digital Libraries

20.1 Overview

As we have previously stated, digital libraries are essentially about digitizing the libraries. Digital libraries have been developed for various applications including digitizing the British Broadcasting Corporation's content as well as content of the Library of Congress. The early projects were sponsored by the National Science Foundation (NSF), Defense Advanced Research Projects Agency (DARPA), and the National Aeronautical and Space Administration (NASA). As we have stated, several technologies have to work together to make digital libraries a reality. These include Web data management, markup languages, search engines, and question-answering systems. In addition, multimedia information management as well as information retrieval systems play an important role.

In Chapter 3 we discussed digital libraries and provided an overview of the security issues. In this chapter we will elaborate on secure digital libraries so that the reader can understand better some of the challenges and then discuss the application of semantic Web technologies for digital libraries, For example, ontologies, annotations, and inference engines are being applied for digital libraries. However, trustworthy semantic Web technologies including secure eXtensible Markup Language (XML), Resource Description Framework (RDF), and Web Ontology Language (OWL) as well as policy enforcement and reasoning about the policies for digital libraries have received very little attention.

The organization of this chapter is as follows. In Section 20.2 we provide an overview of secure digital libraries. In particular, secure information retrieval, secure search engines, and secure question-answering systems are discussed. The application of semantic Web technologies is discussed in Section 20.3. Directions are given in Section 20.4.

20.2 Secure Digital Libraries

20.2.1 Overview

Our main objective is to describe the application in trustworthy semantic Web technologies for digital libraries. Before we address this topic, we will first give an overview of secure digital libraries. Note that in Chapter 3 we discussed various aspects of digital libraries including Web databases, information retrieval, question answering, and search engines (see also Reference [LESK97]).

In this section we examine each of these techniques and discuss the security impact. Secure information retrieval systems are discussed in Section 20.2.2. Secure markup languages such as secure XML are discussed in Section 20.2.3. Secure search engines are discussed in Section 20.4.5. Finally, in Section 20.2.4 we discuss security for question-answering systems. Various aspects discussed in this chapter are illustrated in Figure 20.1 (see also Reference [SAMA96]).

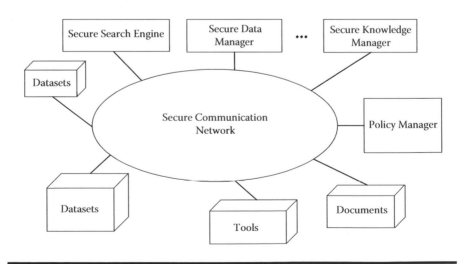

Figure 20.1   Secure digital libraries.

20.2.2 Secure Information Retrieval

In Chapter 3 we discussed information-retrieval systems. These systems include text-retrieval systems, image-retrieval systems, video-retrieval systems, and audio-retrieval systems. We also discussed multimedia data-management systems. In Chapter 17 we discussed security for multimedia data-management systems. In this section we briefly discuss security for information-retrieval systems. Note that information retrieval is a major component of digital libraries; that is, much of the data on the Web is in the form of text. There are also image, video, and audio data. Therefore, secure information retrieval is critical if we are to ensure security for digital libraries.

In Reference [THUR93] we provided some information on multilevel security for information retrieval systems. The challenges include securing the information-retrieval system as well as securing browsers and search engines. Secure search engines are discussed in Section 20.2.3. In this section we identify the issues involved in securing text, images, audio, and video.

When securing text-processing systems, the challenge is to protect certain words, paragraphs, and sentences from unauthorized access. This is far more complex than protecting relational databases where the database is structured. Note that words and paragraphs could appear anywhere in the document. How do you classify certain words and sentences? Do you blank them as we see in physical documents? What sort of metadata do we maintain? Do we have constraints such as "the fifth line in Paragraph 3 of Chapter 6 of Document A is classified"? We may have hundreds of such access-control rules, and therefore, how do we manage these rules?

Similar challenges exist for images and audio and video data. How do we classify pixels? Do we state that the pixel in this particular position is classified? In the case of video and audio, do we classify frames? How can we enforce content-dependent access control? An example of a content-dependent rule is: The user in Group A does not have any access to scenes illustrating terrorist activities.

There have been debates on panels that techniques for securing information-retrieval systems are almost identical to securing relational-database systems. However, with information-retrieval systems, the data to be managed is complex. Therefore, we may have more constraints and more challenges in terms of extracting semantics. Therefore, the challenge is to develop efficient techniques for controlling access to the data such as text, images, video, and audio. In addition, we also need to ensure copyright protection of the documents on the Web as well as ensure data quality. Finally, privacy has to be maintained. Figure 20.2 illustrates secure information retrieval.

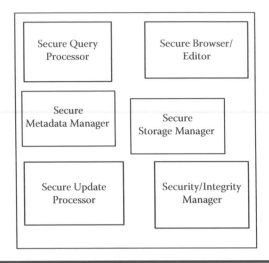

Figure 20.2   Secure information retrieval.

20.2.3   *Secure Search Engines*

In Chapter 3 we provided an overview of search engines and gave some examples of using data mining within search engines so that one can carry out intelligent searching. There are many dependability issues that need to be addressed. These include security, privacy, and data quality. We want to make sure that the search engines list Web pages that can be accessed by the user. Furthermore, they have to ensure that the user's privacy is maintained. Finally, the search engines have to ensure that the information they provide is of high quality.

For example, a Web page may have incorrect information. Then the question is, who is responsible for the information given to the user? There are legal issues involved here. Although there have been discussions on security, privacy, and data quality, there is little work reported. Search engines in general do not enforce access control rules. Essentially access control is maintained by those providing the services. The question is, should the search engines enforce security also? For example, there have been some discussions on protecting children from inappropriate content on the Web (see, for example, the study at the National Academy of Sciences [NAS02]). How can search engines be improved so that they can ensure that children do not get inappropriate material?

There are many questions that need answers, and Web mining is one of the technologies that could help toward finding useful and relevant searches on the Web. Note that while data mining helps solve security problems such as intrusion detection and auditing, there are also privacy concerns. Many Web servers now specify privacy policies enforced by the server. If a user can agree with the policy, then he or she can fill out the various forms. The World Wide Web Consortium (W3C) community is also starting with the Platform for Privacy Preferences Project (P3P) to enforce privacy. We need an active research program on semantic Web security within which we need to examine security for search engines. In Figure 20.3 we illustrate some aspects of secure search engines.

20.2.4 Secure Question-Answering Systems

As we have stated in Chapter 3, the early question-answering systems give just "Yes" or "No" answers. However, more recently question-answering systems have become quite sophisticated and can answer questions such as "Find the directions between New York and Boston where these is no traffic." With more sophisticated technologies there are more problems with respect to security. For example, A may be authorized to get one set of directions, whereas B may be authorized to get another set of directions.

When the question-answering systems were simply Yes or No systems, then the system could analyze as to whether the Yes or No answers have to be given to certain users. Now, with more complex questions and more complex answers, the challenge is to determine what information is to be released to which users. Therefore, secure question-answering systems combine techniques for secure information retrieval, secure search engines, secure Web databases, and secure markup languages. Very little work has been reported on secure question answering. Figure 20.4 illustrates some aspects.

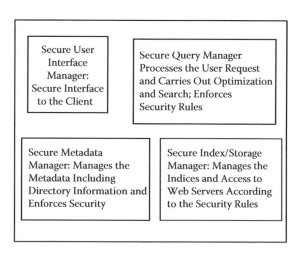

Figure 20.3 Secure search engines.

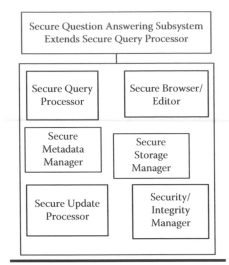

Figure 20.4 Secure question answering.

20.3 Applications of the Semantic Web

Whereas digital libraries have evolved over the past 15 years and the semantic Web has evolved over the past 8 years or so, the two technologies are now converging. Essentially digital libraries have to index, search, and retrieve information from large quantities of data. Semantic Web technologies essentially facilitate machine-understandable Web pages. Therefore, semantic Web technologies will have applications in storing and managing the digital library data.

A significant direction in applying the semantic Web for digital libraries has been provided by Sure and Studer [SURE05] in their article on semantic Web technologies for digital libraries. They state that:

> "Typical usage scenarios for Semantic Technologies in Digital Libraries include among others user interfaces and human-computer interaction (displaying information, allowing for visualization and navigation of large information collections), user profiling (taking into account the overall information space), personalization (balancing between individual and community-based personalization), user interaction."

They describe their SEKT project, which attempts to solve many of the challenges. They further state that whereas there will be several digital libraries, with the use of ontologies and semantic Web technologies, it will be possible to provide a consistent view of the digital libraries. We will summarize some of the prominent semantic Web technologies—ontologies, ontology editors, annotation tools, and inference engines— that Sure and Studer discussed in their paper:

- Ontologies: Onlooker and SHORE are two ontologies. Onlooker developed at the University of Karlsruhe and SHORE developed at the University of Maryland are useful for managing digital libraries.
- Ontology editors: These could be graphics tools to manage the numerous ontologies for digital libraries.
- OntoEdit is one such editor (http://www.ontoprise.com) that has a strong inferencing component.

- Protégé is an academic ontology (http://protege.stanford.edu/).
- KAON (http://kaon.semanticWeb.org) is an open-source ontology as well as an ontology editor and is used for business applications.
- Annotation tools: These tools automate the annotation task, that is, information about the content of a document (e.g., metadata) is annotated. (http://annotation.semanticWeb.org/).
- Annotea (http://www.w3.org/2001/Annotea/) is a Live Early Adoption and Demonstration (LEAD) project and provides support for shared annotations. Note that annotations include comments, notes, and explanations.
- OntoMat-Annotizer (http://annotation.semanticWeb.org/ontomat) is an example of a prominent annotation tool with an associated framework called CREAM.
- KIM (http://www.ontotext.com/kim) provides a knowledge and information management (KIM) infrastructure and supports the annotation and indexing of semistructured data.
- Inference engines deduce information and reason about the information. There are logic-based inferencing methods and special algorithms for problem solving.
- Ontobroker (http://www.ontoprise.com) is a commercial inference engine based on Frame Logic.
- FaCT (http://www.cs.man.ac.uk/~horrocks/FaCT/) is an inference engine based on Description Logic.
- KAON2 (http://kaon2.semanticWeb.org/) is a Description Logic-based inference engine for OWLDL and OWL-Lite reasoning.

As in the case of many other applications of semantic Web, the application of trustworthy semantic Webs for digital libraries has received little attention. Although there has been research on flexible policies for digital libraries by researchers including Bertino, Atluri, and others, the integration of this research with semantic Web technologies has yet to be examined. Now, Bertino and her team have done extensive research on securing XML as well as securing digital libraries. But the application of XML, RDF, and OWL for policy specification and reasoning engines for reasoning about the policies within the framework of digital libraries has to be examined. The question is, how can the technologies that we have discussed in Parts II and III including secure XML, RDF, OWL, RulesML as well as trust management, privacy management, integrity management, annotation management and rights management be applied for secure digital libraries? As we develop more sophisticated digital libraries and semantic Web technologies for digital libraries, we have to investigate the security issues during the early stages and not after the digital libraries are built (see Figure 20.5).

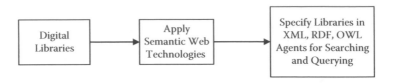

Figure 20-5   Secure semantic digital libraries.

20.4 Summary and Directions

This chapter has discussed secure digital libraries including secure Web databases and secure information-retrieval systems and then described the applications of semantic Web technologies. In particular we have discussed various semantic Web technologies such as ontologies, ontology editors, annotation tools, and inference engines that can be applied to digital libraries. We discussed the need for investigating security for digital libraries and the application of trustworthy semantic Web technologies for digital libraries.

Various research programs are now under way to develop solutions for secure digital libraries. The National Science Foundation had various programs including the Trusted Computing Program and the Data and Applications Security Program. There is now an umbrella theme called Cyber Trust. Other organizations like DARPA, Advanced Research and Development Activity, the National Security Agency, the National Institute of Standards and Technology, and the Department of Defense also have programs in cybersecurity. Although several techniques have been developed, we need to ensure that these techniques scale for very large databases and large numbers of interconnected systems. We need end-to-end security, that is, the clients, the servers, and the infrastructures have to be secure for digital libraries. However, the application of semantic Web technologies for secure digital libraries such as investigating the use of confidentiality, privacy, and trust based on semantic Web for digital libraries needs more investigation.

References

[LESK97] Lesk, M., *Practical Digital Libraries*, Morgan Kaufmann, San Francisco, CA, 1997.

[NAS02] National Academy of Sciences Study Report, *Protecting Children from Inappropriate Content on the Internet*, National Academy Press, Washington, D.C., 2002.

[SAMA96] Samarati, P. et al., An authorization model for a distributed hypertext system, *IEEE Trans. Knowledge Data Eng.*, 8(4), 1996.

[SURE05] Sure, Y. and R. Studer, Semantic Web Technologies for Digital Libraries, Technical Report, University of Karlsruhe, Germany, 2005.

[THUR00] Thuraisingham, B., *Web Data Management and Electronic Commerce*, CRC Press, Boca Raton, FL, 2000.

[THUR93] Thuraisingham, B., W. Ford, and M. Collins, Design and implementation of a database inference controller, *Data Knowledge Eng. J.*, 11(3), 1993.

Exercises

1. Describe security issues for E-digital libraries, and design a secure digital library system.
2. Describe the use of semantic Web technologies for secure digital libraries.

Chapter 21

Assured Semantic Information Sharing

21.1 Overview

This chapter describes issues, technologies, challenges, and directions for assured information sharing (AIS) and in particular the applications of semantic Web technologies for AIS. AIS is about organizations sharing information but at the same time enforcing policies and procedures so that the data is integrated and mined to extract nuggets. For example, data from various data sources at multiple security levels as well as from the military and government agencies including the Air Force, Navy, Army, local, state, and federal agencies have to be integrated so that the data can be mined, patterns and information extracted, relationships identified, and decisions made. The databases would include, for example, military databases that contain information about military strategies, intelligence databases that contain information about potential terrorists and their patterns of attack, and medical databases that contain information about infectious diseases and stockpiles. Data could be structured or unstructured including geospatial or multimedia data. Data also needs to be shared between healthcare organizations such as doctors' offices, hospitals, and pharmacies. Unless the data is integrated and the big picture is formed, it will be difficult to inform all the parties concerned about the incidents that have occurred. Although the different agencies have to share data and information, they also need to enforce appropriate security and integrity policies so that the data does not get into the hands of unauthorized individuals. Essentially the agencies have to share information, but at the same time maintain the security and integrity requirements.

In this chapter we describe AIS that will ensure that the appropriate policies for confidentiality, privacy, trust, release, dissemination, data quality, and provenance are enforced. We discuss technologies for AIS as well as novel approaches based on game theoretical concepts. Our emphasis will be on the application of semantic Web technologies for AIS. In Section 21.2 we provide an overview of organizational and coalition data sharing. The application of service-oriented architectures for AIS is discussed in Section 21.3. Data integration and analysis technologies for AIS are discussed in Section 21.4. Security policy aspects including confidentiality, privacy, and trust policies are discussed in Section 21.5. Integrity and dependability issues such as data provenance, quality, and real-time processing are discussed in Section 21.6. Balancing conflicting requirements including security versus real-time processing is discussed in Section 21.7. Application of semantic Web is the discussion in Section 21.8. The chapter is concluded in Section 21.9.

21.2 Organization Data Sharing

A coalition consists of a set of organizations, which may be agencies, universities, and corporations that work together in a peer-to-peer environment to solve problems such as intelligence and military operations as well as healthcare operations. Figure 21.1 illustrates an architecture for a coalition where three agencies have to share data and information. Coalitions are usually dynamic in nature, that is, members may join and leave the coalitions in accordance with established policies and procedures. A challenge is to ensure the secure operation of a coalition. We assume that the members of a coalition, which are also called its partners, may be trustworthy, untrustworthy, or partially (semi-) trustworthy.

Various aspects of coalition data sharing are discussed in the Markle report [MARK03]. However, security including confidentiality, privacy, trust, integrity, release, and dissemination has been given little consideration. Much of the prior work on security in a coalition environment has focused on secure federated data sharing. Thuraisingham was one of the first to propose multilevel security for federated database systems [THUR94]. Discretionary security was proposed by Olivier [OLIV95].

Little research has been carried out on applying semantic Web technologies for secure data sharing. Confidentiality, privacy, integrity, trust, real-time processing, fault tolerance, authorization, and administration policies enforced by the component organizations via the local agencies have to be integrated at the coalition level. As illustrated in Figure 21.1, each organization may export security policies and data to the coalition. The component systems may have more stringent access-control requirements for foreign organizations. The challenge is to ensure that there is no security violation at the coalition level.

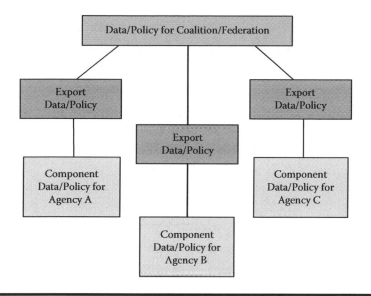

Figure 21.1   Architecture for organizational data sharing.

21.3   Service-Oriented Architectures for Assured Information Sharing

Service-oriented architectures (SOAs) essentially use a collection of Web services to carry out various operations. We briefly discussed SOA and Web services as well as the impact of security in Chapter 16. In this chapter we discuss SOA for AIS.

The framework for AIS could be based on SOA; that is, each organization carries out its operations by involving a collection of Web services. An activity of an organization that is carried out by a Web service could invoke an activity in another organization also carried out by a Web service. Although each organization is based on an SOA, the integration of the multiple organizations that share information may also based on an SOA. Essentially we have a one umbrella SOA that integrates the organization through the use of Web services and carries out data sharing within and across organizations. We illustrate this in Figure 21.2.

21.4   Data Integration and Analysis Technologies

21.4.1   Data Integration

As illustrated in Figure 21.3, data from various data sources at multiple levels such as local, state, and federal levels have to be integrated so that the data can be mined, patterns extracted, and decisions made. Data integration has been attempted for

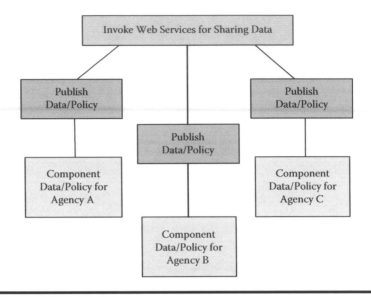

Figure 21.2 SOA for AIS.

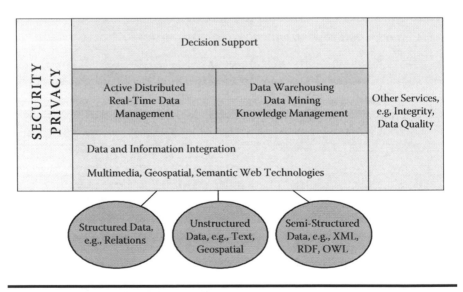

Figure 21.3 Data integration and analysis.

about 20 years. Until recently, brute force integration techniques consisting of translators and gateways were used between multiple data-management systems. Standards such as remote database access (RDA) were developed initially for client-server interoperability. Later, object-base wrappers were used to encapsulate the multiple systems including legacy systems. For example, distributed object-management standards were used to encapsulate systems and applications into objects. However, common representation of the data remained a challenge. It is only recently that we have a good handle on syntactic integration through standards such as eXtensible Markup Language (XML). The idea is as follows: each data system publishes its schema (also called metadata) in XML. Becausee all the systems now represent their schema in XML, the systems can talk to each other in a seamless fashion.

A major challenge for data integration is semantic heterogeneity. Although much progress has been made on syntactic integration, not much work has been reported on semantic integration. For example, multiple systems may use different terms for the same data; the procedure EKG (electrocardiogram) is called ECG in the United Kingdom. Even within the same state, different hospitals may use different terms to mean the same entity. For example, one hospital may use the term influenza while another hospital may use the term flu. In some cases, the same term may be used to represent different entities. Whereas repositories and dictionaries have been built, a satisfactory solution for semantic heterogeneity is still not available. The development of semantic Web technologies including the resource description framework (RDF) language standard shows promise to handle semantic heterogeneity.

21.4.2 Multimedia and Geospatial Data

Data will include structured data as well as unstructured data such as text, voice, video, and audio. Data emanating from multiple data sources including sensor and surveillance data have to be integrated and shared. Managing, integrating, and mining multimedia data remains a challenge. We need efficient indexing techniques as well as XML- and RDF-based representation schemes. Furthermore, the data has to be mined so that patterns and trends are extracted. Video data could be data emanating from surveillance cameras or news feeds such as Cable News Network (CNN) video data. Emergency-response systems have to integrate geospatial data such as maps together with structured data, make sense out of the data, and rapidly produce summaries so that the emergency-response teams can read and understand the data [ASHR06].

21.4.3 Data Mining

Integrated data may be mined to extract patterns for suspicious and unusual behavior. Much of the work in data mining has focused on mining relational and structured databases. Although some work has been reported on text, image, audio, and video data mining, much remains to be done. For example, how can one mine integrated geospatial and multimedia data? How can false positives and false negatives be eliminated or at least reduced? What are the training models used for multimedia data? What are the appropriate outcomes for multimedia data mining? Does it make sense to extract metadata and then mine the metadata? Much remains to be done before operational tools for multimedia and geospatial data mining are developed.

21.5 Security Policy Enforcement

Security policies include policies for confidentiality, privacy, trust, release, dissemination, and integrity. A broader term is dependable systems or trustworthy systems that also include real-time processing and fault tolerance. We will discuss dependability in the next section. By confidentiality we mean that data is only released to individuals who are authorized to get the data. Privacy in general deals with the situation where an individual determines what information should be released about him or her. (Note that different definitions of privacy have been proposed.) Trust policies may add further restriction to privacy and confidentiality policies. For example, a user may be authorized to get the data according to the confidentiality policies, but the system may not trust the individual, in which case the data is not released. Similarly, a person may give permission to release certain private information about him or her, but that person may not trust a particular Web site, in which case the private information is not released to the Web site. Alternatively, one could argue that one needs to establish trust first before establishing the confidentiality and privacy policies. For example, a user's (or Web site's) trust is established before determining that the user (or Web site) can receive confidential (or private) information. Release policies specify rules for releasing data, whereas dissemination policies specify rules for disseminating data. Integrity within the context of security ensures that only authorized individuals can modify the data so that the data is not maliciously corrupted [TSYB06].

Security for relational databases has been studied extensively and standards such as secure Structured Query Language (SQL) have been developed. In addition, several secure data-management system products have been developed. There has been research on incorporating security into next-generation data-management systems. There is also work on data quality as well as trust management. Security has also been investigated for secure object request brokers as well as for secure E-commerce systems. Finally, the World Wide Web Consortium (W3C) is specifying standards for privacy such as the Platform for Privacy Preferences Project (P3P). Although there is research on incorporating security for semantic Webs and heterogeneous data systems, this research is in the early stages. There is an urgent need to develop operational systems that enforce security. Furthermore, security has conflicting requirements with real-time processing. We need to enforce flexible policies and, subsequently, standards for specifying these policies. Security is critical for many of the information technologies we have discussed here. For a discussion of secure data sharing and related standards we refer the reader to Reference [THUR06].

21.5.1 Security Policy Integration

There is a critical need for organizations to share data as well as process the data in a timely manner, but at the same time enforce various security policies. Figure 21.4 illustrates security policy integration in a coalition environment. In this example, A and B form a coalition while B and C form a second coalition. A could be California, B could be Texas, and C could be Oklahoma. California (A) and Texas (B) could form a coalition as part of the larger states in the United States, and Texas (B) and Oklahoma (C) could form a coalition as part of the neighboring states in the southern United States for emergency management. There is also an urgent need for multiple organizations to share data and at the same time enforce security policies. These policies include policies for confidentiality, privacy, and trust. For example, patient data may be shared by multiple organizations including hospitals, levels of government, and agencies. It is important to maintain the privacy of patient data. However, it is also important that there are no unnecessary access controls so that information sharing is prohibited. One needs flexible policies so that during emergency situations all the data is shared so that effective decisions can be made. During normal operations, it is important to maintain confidentiality and privacy. In

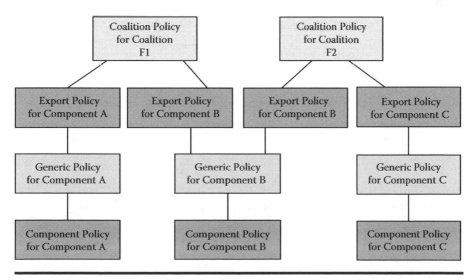

Figure 21.4   Security policy integration and transformation for coalitions.

addition, trust policies ensure that data is shared between trusted individuals. The standards efforts in this area include role-based access control (RBAC) [SAND96] as well as P3P. Our partners at George Mason University (GMU) are examining the use of models such as RBAC and the Usage Control (UCON) model for AIS [SAND96], [PARK04].

21.6 Dependability Aspects

By dependable systems we mean systems that are fault tolerant and meet timing constraints. The time-critical, information-sensitive goals of managing a crisis include actions such as the early confirmation of cases and correct identification of exposed populations over a relevant time period. Early confirmation means that triggers have to be activated when certain situations (such as anomalies) occur. Suppose a hospital is flooded with 30 patients within 15 minutes who are all reporting a temperature of 105 degrees. There has to be a rule such as "If more than 30 patients register at a hospital within 20 minutes with temperature greater than 102 degrees, then alert the emergency-response system". To effectively process a large number of rules, we need active data management. Furthermore, the various parties involved such as federal, state, and local governments have to be informed within a certain time, that is, if the authorities are notified after, say, 2 hours, then it will be difficult to contain the spread of the disease. This means we need real-time data-management capabilities. Some initial research on dependable and secure systems is discussed by Kim and Thuraisingham [KIM06].

Although there are techniques for active real-time data management, the challenge is to develop an integrated system for end-to-end data management. For example, the data manager will ensure that the data is current and the transactions meet the timing constraints. However, in an emergency situation there are numerous dependencies between different data sources. For example, when rule A gets triggered, that would result in rules C, D, and E getting triggered in multiple data-management systems. Such chain-rule processing remains a challenge. We also need end-to-end real-time processing, that is, in addition to the data manager, the infrastructure, the network, and the operating system have to meet timing constraints. This remains a challenge. Incorporating security into real-time processing techniques remains largely unexplored. For example, in an emergency situation, real-time processing and activating triggers may be more critical than enforcing access-control techniques. Furthermore, the system must ensure that the deadlines are not missed due to malicious code and attacks (e.g., denial of service).

Whereas integrity within the context of security implies that the data is not maliciously corrupted, integrity also includes policies for data quality and data-provenance management. Data quality determines the accuracy of the data. This would depend on who updated the data, who owns the data, and what the accuracy is of the source of the data, that is, as data moves from organization to organization, its quality may vary. Some measure to compute the quality of the data is needed. Data provenance is about maintaining the history of the data; that is, information as to who accessed the data from start to finish is needed to determine whether data is misused.

21.7 Balancing Conflicting Requirements

There are two types of conflicting requirements: one is security versus data sharing. The goal of data sharing is for organizations to share as much data as possible so that the data is mined and nuggets obtained. However, when security policies are enforced, then not all of the data is shared. The other type of conflict is between real-time processing and security. The war fighter will need information at the right time. If it is even, say, 5 minutes late, the information may not be useful. This means that if various security checks are to be performed, then the information may not get to the war fighter on time [SON95], [THUR99].

We are conducting research in both areas. For example, we are integrating the data in the coalition databases without any access-control restrictions and applying the data-mining tools to obtain interesting patterns and trends. In particular, we are developing associations between different data entities such as "A and B are likely to be in a location 50 miles from Baghdad." Next, we are using the same tool on the integrated data after enforcing the policies. We can then determine the patterns that might be lost due to enforcing the policies (note that there is some relationship between this work and the research on privacy-preserving data mining).

In addition, we are conducting research on examining the extent to which security affects timing constraints. For example, we enforce timing constraints on the query algorithms. We first process the query using the enforcement algorithms without enforcing any of the policies. Then we enforce the security policies and determine whether the timing constraints can be met. This will determine the extent to which security impacts timely information processing.

Our goal is to develop flexible approaches and balance conflicting requirements. If timely processing of data is critical, then security has to be relaxed. Similarly, say during noncombat operations, security will have to be given full consideration. The same applies for data sharing versus security. If during an emergency operation such as the operation just before, during, or soon after Hurricane Katrina, then several agencies will need the data without any restrictions. However, during non-emergency operations, security policies need to be enforced.

Another aspect of our research on AIS is risk analysis. For example, if the security risks are high and the cost to implement security features is low, then security should be given high consideration. If the risks are low and the cost is high, one needs to evaluate whether it is worth the effort and cost to incorporate security.

21.8 The Role of the Semantic Web

All the applications we discussed in the previous chapters of Part IV are needed for assured information sharing. We need to manage secure data, information, and knowledge; invoke secure Web services; manage secure digital libraries; and carry out secure E-business across organizations. Therefore, the semantic Web applications discussed for secure Web services, secure data, information and knowledge management, secure digital libraries, secure interoperability, and secure E-business apply for secure information sharing. We need to manage XML and RDF documents; use XML, RDF, and OWL for specifying policies; integrate the policies and data using ontologies; utilize knowledge of an organization to share information; use ontologies and XML-based protocols for invoking Web services; and integrate the digital libraries implemented by each organization using ontologies to resolve conflicts.

We are collaborating with the University of Maryland, Baltimore County (UMBC), the Massachusetts Institute of Technology (MIT), and GMU to develop semantic Web technologies in a need-to-share environment. In particular, we are examining the use of Rei to specify policies, utilize UCON for the security model, and reasoning about the policies using reasoning engines such as Pellet. Furthermore, we are also examining accountability for SOAs, and this accountability information is represented using semantic Web languages. Finally, we are examining the use of semantic Web languages for representing and reasoning about annotations for data provenance and quality. Research in this area is just beginning. We believe that semantic Web technologies are critical for AIS applications. Figure 21.5 illustrates the applications of somatic Web technologies for AIS.

21.9 Summary and Directions

In this chapter we have defined AIS and discussed issues, technologies, challenges, and directions for this area. The goal of AIS is for organizations to share data, but at the same time enforce security policies. Security includes confidentiality, privacy, trust, and integrity policies. We discussed approaches for AIS when the partners of a coalition are trustworthy, semitrustworthy, and untrustworthy. In particular, we discussed security policy enforcement and discussed the application of the semantic Web.

As we have stated, all of the applications we discussed in the previous chapters of Part IV are needed for AIS. We need to manage secure data, information, and knowledge; invoke secure Web services; manage secure digital libraries; and carry out secure E-business across organizations. Therefore, the semantic Web applications discussed for secure Web services; secure data, information, and knowledge management; secure digital libraries, secure interoperability, and secure E-business apply for secure information sharing. We believe that semantic Web technologies

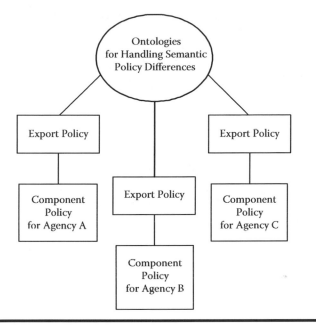

Figure 21.5   Application of the semantic Web.

are critical for AIS. We need to conduct more research in these areas and develop architectures, models, and processes for assured semantic information sharing.

References

[ASHR06] Ashraful, A., G. Subbiah, L. Khan, and B. Thuraisingham, Geospatial Semantic Web, Technical Report, University of Texas at Dallas, 2006.

[KIM06] Kim, J. and B. Thuraisingham, Dependable and secure TMO scheme, *Proc. IEEE ISORC Conf.*, Gyeongju, Korea, April 2006.

[OLIV95] Olivier, M.S., Self-protecting objects in a secure federated database, *Proc. IFIP Database Security Conf.*, New York, August 1995.

[PARK04] Park, J. and R.S. Sandhu, The UCON$_{ABC}$ usage control model, *ACM Trans. Inf. Syst. Secur.*, 7(1): 128-174, 2004.

[SAND96] Sandhu, R., E. Coyne, H. Feinstein, and C. Youman, Role-based access control models, *IEEE Computer*, 29(2), February 1996.

[SON95] Son, S., R. David, and B. Thuraisingham, An adaptive policy for improved timeliness in secure database systems, *Proc.e 9th IFIP Working Conf. Database Security*, New York, August 1995.

[THUR90] Thuraisingham, B., Novel approaches to the inference problem, *Proc. 3rd RADC (Rome Air Development Center) Database Security Workshop*, New York, June 1990.

[THUR94] Thuraisingham, B., Security issues for federated database systems, *Comput. Security,* December 1994.

[THUR99] Thuraisingham, B. and J. Maurer, Information survivability for real-time command and control systems, *IEEE Trans. Knowledge Data Eng.,* January 1999.

[THUR06] Thuraisingham, B., D. Harris, L. Khan, and R. Paul, Standards for secure data sharing across organizations, *Comput. Standards Interfaces J.,* 2005.

[TSYB06] N. Tsyblinik, B. Thuraisingham, and A. Ashraful, CPT: Confidentiality, privacy and trust for the semantic Web, UTDCS-06-06, Technical Report, University of Texas at Dallas, March 2006. *Int. J. Inf. Security Privacy,* 1, 2006.

[MARK03] Vatis, M., Ed., Creating a Trusted Network for Homeland Security, Markle Report, Markle Foundation Publications, New York, 2003.

Exercises

1. Design a data sharing application and show how policies may be enforced across organizations.
2. Investigate the use of semantic Web technologies for assured information sharing.

Conclusion to Part IV

Whereas Parts II and III discussed concepts in trustworthy semantic Webs, Part IV discussed applications that utilize trustworthy semantic Webs. Chapter 16 discussed secure Web services that utilize semantic Web technologies. Semantic Web technologies for managing secure databases was the subject of Chapter 17. Secure semantic interoperability for heterogeneous information sources was discussed in Chapter 18. Chapter 19 discussed semantic Web for secure E-business applications. Chapter 20 discussed semantic Web for secure digital libraries. Chapter 21 discussed semantic Web technologies for an important applications area called assured information sharing.

Now that we have provided an overview of the various applications of trustworthy semantic Webs, we are now ready to discuss specialized semantic Webs. This will be the subject of Part V.

Part V

Specialized Trustworthy Semantic Webs

Introduction to Part V

The chapters in Parts II and III focused on concepts in trustworthy semantic Webs, and the chapters in Part IV focused on the applications of these concepts. Now that we have provided an overview of the concepts and applications, we are ready to discuss some aspects of building specialized semantic Webs for various domains. We discuss both the domain-specific semantic Webs and technology-oriented semantic Webs.

Part V consists of three chapters and describes specialized and domain-specific semantic Webs. In Chapter 22 we discuss domain-specific semantic Webs for defense, financial, and medical domains, among others. Trustworthy semantic Webs for geospatial data are discussed in Chapter 23. In particular the work carried out on Geography Markup Language (GML) as well as the Open Geospatial Consortium's (OGC) interoperability work is discussed. Chapter 24 discusses pervasive computing applications including secure mobile-sensor semantic Webs as well as pervasive semantic Webs.

Chapter 22

Domain-Specific Semantic Webs and Security

22.1 Overview

Whereas Part I discussed supporting technologies for trustworthy semantic Webs, Parts II and III discussed concepts in trustworthy semantic Webs including confidentiality, privacy, and trust management, and Part IV discussed applications of trustworthy semantic Webs, in this part we discuss domain-specific semantic Webs. We consider two types of domains. One is application domain, and the other is technology domain. Application domains are domains that deal with specific applications such as medical, financial, defense, intelligence, and manufacturing, among others. Technology domains are specialized domains dealing with technologies such as geospatial data management, multimedia data management, and sensor data management. This chapter describes application domains, and the next two chapters describe technology domains.

The application domains that we will consider include defense and intelligence, homeland security and border control, medical, and financial. For each domain we will describe how trustworthy semantic Web technologies may be applied. The organization of this chapter is as follows. In Section 22.2 we discuss defense and intelligence domains. In Section 22.3 we discuss homeland security and border patrol. Applications in the medical domain are discussed in Section 22.4. In Section 22.5 we discuss trustworthy semantic Webs for financial domains. It should be noted that semantic Web technologies can be applied to numerous other domains including manufacturing, process control, and entertainment. A discussion of all the domains is beyond the scope of this book. We have selected some domains mainly because they are of interest to us. The chapter is summarized in Section 22.6.

22.2 Defense and Intelligence Domain

One of the earliest domains to utilize semantic Web technologies is the defense domain. Under the management of Jim Hendler, the DARPA Agent Markup Language (DAML) Program at the Defense Advanced Projects Research Agency (DARPA) developed technologies for the Department of Defense (DoD). Although security was not a consideration in that program, the ontology language called DAML was developed. This program worked closely with the World Wide Web Consortium (W3C) to develop technologies for machine-understandable Web pages. DAML was then integrated with the European standard called Ontology Interface Language (OIL) to develop DAML+OIL. Although the United States and Europe together developed DAML+OIL, the W3C developed OWL for ontologies. As we have mentioned earlier, OWL evolved from RDF, DAML, and OIL. In addition to representation of the data, reasoning about the data was also a focus for the DAML program.

About the time the DAML program was carried out in the late 1990s and early 2000s, the DoD was involved with the development of the Global Command and Control System (GCCS) Program. Under this program, the Defense Information Infrastructure Common Operating Environment (DII COE) was developed. DII COE essentially considered several working groups for distributed computing systems, multimedia, and data management. However, with the emergence of Web services, the DoD began to invest heavily in Network Centric Enterprise Services (NCES) for Network Centric Operations. This then led to the development of the global information grid (GIG), which was essentially the infrastructure for NCES. This infrastructure is based on service-oriented architectures. Much of the development is influenced by XML and ontologies. Various communities in the DoD have utilized XML and developed ontologies for their applications. Furthermore, communities of interest have been formed, and these communities have developed common ontologies for their applications.

Although security has been considered critical for the DoD, much of the work has not focused on security. However, more recently there is emphasis on security in general and trust in particular for service-oriented architectures. Furthermore, the National Security Agency is exploring information assurance for the GIG. Furthermore, risk-based access control is considered to be an important aspect of the GIG.

In our research we are applying all of the features discussed in Parts II and III for service-oriented architectures. These include confidentiality, privacy, and trust as well as risk-based access control. Furthermore, we are also exploring accountability for such an environment. Our investigation is not limited to XML. We are working with Finin, Joshi, and Yesha et al. at the University of Maryland, Baltimore County (UMBC) to explore the use of a Resource Description Framework (RDF)-based language they have developed called Rei for specifying the policies for service-oriented architectures. This research is applicable to NCES and the GIG.

Although many of the applications of trustworthy semantic Web technologies have been for defense, there are also efforts with the intelligence community to use these technologies for their applications. The use of eXtensible Markup Language (XML) has become a standard for many of the intelligence applications. The trends are toward incorporating semantics into data representation and reasoning. To our knowledge there appears to be little work on incorporating security into semantic Web technologies for intelligence applications.

We believe that the application of trustworthy semantic Web technologies for defense and intelligence applications is in the beginning stages. As the applications get more complex and there is a need for information sharing across organizations, these technologies as well as policy specification and representation will gain prominence. Figure 22.1 illustrates the semantic Web technologies for defense applications.

22.3 Homeland Security and Border Control

Information management, data mining, and security technologies have many applications in homeland security. One key area is assured information sharing where organizations such as the Immigration and Nationalization Services (INS), the Federal Bureau of Investigation (FBI), and the Central Intelligence Agency (CIA) have to share data about U.S. citizens as well as foreign nationals. Therefore, trustworthy semantic Web technologies are critical for enforcing policies as well as representing the data. We discussed some of the details in Part IV.

Another application of semantic Web technologies for homeland security is in biometrics. The US-Visit program developed by the Department of Homeland Security uses biometric technologies for identification. Now, one of the major issues in biometric data management is interoperability between heterogeneous data sources. Each vendor or organization may use different representations for biometric data. We need standards for common representation to facilitate interoperability. Organizations such as the Organization for the Advancement of Structured Information Standards (OASIS) are coming up with markup languages for biometrics data. As stated in Reference [CBEF], the Common Biometric Exchange

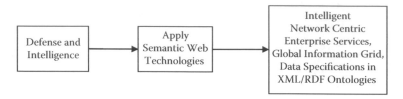

Figure 22.1   Semantic Webs for defense applications.

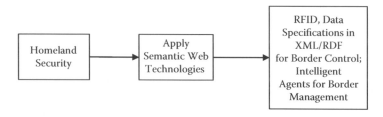

Figure 22.2   Semantic Web for homeland security.

File Format defines a common set of secure XML encoding. In particular, this standard defines cryptographic messages represented in XML for the secure collection, distribution, and processing of biometric information. These messages provide the means of achieving data integrity, authentication of origin, and privacy of biometric data in XML-based systems and applications. Mechanisms and techniques are described for the secure transmission, storage, integrity, and privacy protection of biometric data. Ontologies are also being developed for representing biometric data and resolving ambiguity.

More recently, semantic Web technologies are being used for radio frequency identification (RFID) applications in border control [PALI04]. Nabil Adam and his colleagues at Rutgers University have developed an approach for composing Web services on the semantic Web and use OWL-S for describing these semantics. They have implemented a system to track packages with SAP Auto-ID infrastructure. This system can be used for border-control applications.

Although semantic Web technologies and Web services including service discovery and composition approaches are being applied for homeland security and border control, work on policy enforcement has not received much attention. Essentially there is a lot of data sharing at the border between border personnel and headquarters. Therefore, appropriate policies have to be enforced. Furthermore, data also has to be shared by the immigration authorities from multiple countries. This means trust, confidentiality, and privacy management are critical. Figure 22.2 illustrates homeland security applications.

22.4 Healthcare and Life Sciences

W3C hosted a workshop in October 2004 to bring together researchers in life sciences to determine how semantic Web technologies can be utilized. Today several efforts are focusing on developing ontologies, Web services, and markup languages for healthcare and life sciences applications. For example, ontologies are used to specify drugs and various medical terms. Jonathan Borden, who is part of the W3C Web Ontology Working Group, has specified XML for healthcare applications [BORD01]. He states that his goal is to use ontologies and markup languages to answer questions such as "Of all the patients I operated on for brain tumors between 1996-2000, matching severity of pathology and matching clinical status and who have the P53 mutation, did PCV chemotherapy improve the cure rate at five years?" He then illustrates how XML, RDF, and OWL could be utilized to effectively answer these questions.

Ontologies have been developed for electronic healthcare records as well as for several terms in the life sciences [KREM]. For example, the authors state in Reference [LIFE], that "Contemporary life science research includes components drawn from physics, chemistry, mathematics, medicine, and many other areas, and all of these dimensions, as well as fundamental philosophical issues, must be taken into account in the construction of a domain ontology." They then describe how to go about developing domain ontologies for life sciences.

As in the case of defense and homeland security applications, assured information sharing is key for healthcare applications. Information has to be shared between hospitals, doctors' offices, insurance companies, pharmacies, and healthcare agencies. Therefore, not only will trust and confidentiality play a major rule, it is critical that privacy of the individuals be maintained. For example, genetic information about a person has to be kept highly private and not divulged to, say, insurance companies. Many of the efforts on policy management have focused on healthcare both in the United States and in Europe. Furthermore, XML, RDF, and OWL-based ontologies are being developed for exchanging healthcare-related data. This means that trustworthy semantic Web technologies will have major applications in the healthcare domain.

Another application is data quality and provenance. Genetic data is collected from numerous sources for the human genome project. Much of the data is publicly available. This aspect has to be revisited. Furthermore, the quality of the data is critical if useful results are to be obtained from data analysis. Therefore, data quality and data provenance information have to be maintained and perhaps annotated with the data. The annotation has to answer questions such as, who collected the data, from where did the data originate, how has the data traveled, and has the data been misused? Here again data quality and province for XML- and RDF-based data will play a major role. Figure 22.3 illustrates the application of semantic Web for healthcare and life sciences.

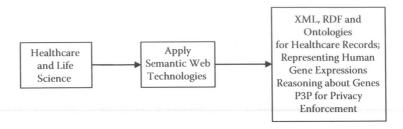

Figure 22.3   Semantic Web for healthcare.

22.5 Financial Domain

The financial domain includes any domain that has to deal with finance including banking and trading, insurance, and investment management. Almost all these activities are now being carried out electronically. We now have electronic trading, electronic banking, and electronic insurance management, among others. In this section we will examine the applications of trustworthy semantic Webs for the financial domain.

Several groups are developing Web services and semantic Web technologies for financial domains. For example, a group in Madrid has done some very good research on applying the semantic "ontology-based platform that provides (a) the integration of contents and semantics in a knowledge base that provides a conceptual view on low-level contents, (b) an adaptive hypermedia-based knowledge visualization and navigation system, and (c) semantic search facilities" [CAST]. Furthermore, they have developed a topology of economic and financial information. Another group in Belgium is developing ontologies for financial security fraud detection. They have used onto-based knowledge engineering in a project to detect financial security fraud. In particular, they have developed a fraud forensic ontology from regulation and laws [ZHAO].

In addition, to specific projects such as the work in Madrid and Belgium to develop ontologies and semantics for financial data management, XML is being used extensively for financial services. There is now a conference normal for finance. As stated in Reference [XML], "the Financial Services industry is creating a variety of standard XML formats to meet their special needs." The list of standards being developed include the following:

Interactive Financial Exchange (IFX) and Open Financial Exchange (OFX) address consumer and other forms of retail banking.

Financial Information eXchange (FIX) is emerging as a standard communications protocol for equity trading data.

FIX Markup Language (FIXML) uses XML to express business messages for the FIX protocol.

Financial Products Markup Language (FpML) is an XML-based interchange format for transactions in financial derivative markets.

Market Data Definition Language (MDDL) is a consortium standard for the definition and communication of market data in XML, including data required to analyze, trade, and account for market value in the handling of financial instruments.

eXtensible Business Reporting Language (XBRL) is an "XML-based specification for the preparation and exchange of financial reports and data." It is developed by a global consortium of organizations and institutions.

As in the case of healthcare applications, security has not received much attention for financial applications with respect to the semantic Web. There are many security concerns such as confidentiality and privacy. We need to ensure that private financial data of a customer is not divulged. Furthermore, assured information sharing is critical for financial applications as data is shared between banks, mortgage companies, employers, and investment bankers. Therefore, appropriate policies have to be developed for data sharing. Furthermore, because semantic Web technologies are gaining prominence in the financial world, we will need trustworthy semantic Web technologies. Figure 22.4 illustrates the application of semantic Web for banking and finance.

22.6 Summary and Directions

In this chapter we have shown how semantic Web technologies, in general, and trustworthy semantic Web technologies, in particular, are being applied to multiple domains including in defense and intelligence, homeland security and border control, healthcare and life sciences, and finance and banking. We also gave examples of projects that are developing these technologies. In general, although semantic Web technologies are gaining a lot of prominence, security is lagging

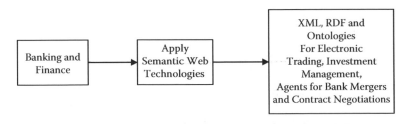

Figure 22.4   Semantic Web for finance.

behind. Therefore, we hope that this book introduces the importance of security to be considered at the beginning of a project. When various specifications of XML are being developed for financial applications, we need to also examine what the security impacts are.

Although this chapter has focused on domain-specific applications, the next two chapters will focus more on technology-related applications. In Chapter 23 we will discuss secure geospatial semantic Web technologies, and in Chapter 24 we will discuss secure sensor semantic Web technologies.

References

[BORD01] Borden, J., XML Healthcare: from ASTM XML DTDs to the Semantic Web, Technical Report, Tufts University, Boston, MA, 2001.

[CAST] Castells, P., B. Foncillas, R. Lara, M. Rico, J.L. Alonso, Semantic Web technologies for economic and financial information management, http://nets.ii.uam.es/aniceto/publications/esws04.pdf.

[CBEF] Common Biometric Exchange File Format (CBEFF), http://www.globalsecurity.org/security/systems/cbeff.htm.

[LIFE] Ontologies for the life sciences, www.jonathanborden-md.com/HealthcareSemWeb.ppt.

[PALI04] Paliwal, A.V., N. Adam, C. Bornhövd, and J. Schaper, Semantic discovery and composition of Web services for RFID applications in border control, http://www.dvs1.informatik.tu-darmstadt.de/staff/bornhoevd/ISWC'04.pdf.

[KREM] Schulze-Kremer, S., and B. Smith, *Encyclopedia of Genetics, Genomics, Proteomics and Bioinformatics, Part 4. Bioinformatics*, Wiley Interscience, New York.

[XML] Thinking XML: A glimpse into XML in the financial services industry, http://www-128.ibm.com/developerworks/xml/library/x-think22.html.

[ZHAO] Zhao, G. et al., Engineering an ontology for financial securities fraud, http://www.ffpoirot.org/Publications/eofsf_20-08-final.pdf.

Exercises

1. Describe security requirements for each of the application areas discussed in this chapter.
2. Conduct a survey of semantic Web technologies for each of the applications discussed in this chapter.
3. Combine Exercises 1 and 2 and subsequently design and develop secure semantic Web technologies for each of the applications discussed in this chapter.

Chapter 23

Secure Geospatial Semantic Web

23.1 Overview

A secure geospatial semantic Web integrates semantic Web technologies with geospatial technologies and security technologies. Geospatial data emanates from numerous devices at multiple sites. Such data is complex and heterogeneous in nature. Geospatial data has to be compressed, fused, and visualized to support the tasks of the analyst for homeland security applications. Furthermore, geospatial information systems have to enforce flexible security policies to address dynamic environments and changing needs of various applications. Although several developments have been made on geospatial data compression, fusion, and visualization, many of the approaches do not take into consideration the complexity and heterogeneity of the data. Furthermore, we need efficient tools to support the analyst. Finally, little work has been reported on developing flexible security policies. Our research is focusing on many aspects of geospatial data management for homeland security. These include developing decision-centric fusion algorithms for geospatial data where we are developing classifiers for each data source and subsequently fusing the outcomes of the local classifiers [LI07], and developing a flexible security policy, model, and architecture that addresses confidentiality and data quality.

Recently we integrated geospatial data management with security and the semantic Web to develop a secure geospatial semantic Web. This chapter describes

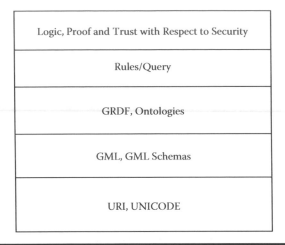

Logic, Proof and Trust with Respect to Security
Rules/Query
GRDF, Ontologies
GML, GML Schemas
URI, UNICODE

Figure 23.1   Layered architecture for geospatial semantic Web.

our work in this area. The organization of this chapter is as follows. We discuss geospatial semantic Web in Section 23.2, including our research on the geospatial semantic Web as well as the Automatic Discovery of Geospatial Information Services (DAGIS) System we developed. The initial version of DAGIS was developed at the University of Texas at Dallas by Alam Ashraful, Ganesh Subbiah, Latifur Khan, and Bhavani Thuraisingham. We discuss secure geospatial data-management issues in Section 23.3. The secure geospatial semantic Web is discussed in Section 23.4. Secure interoperability of geospatial data is discussed in Section 23.5. Some aspects of GeoRSS are given in Section 23.6. The paper is concluded in Section 23.7.

23.2   Geospatial Semantic Web

Secure geospatial semantic Web is an integration of a secure semantic Web and a geospatial semantic Web. We are conducting extensive research on a geospatial semantic Web. Our layered architecture is shown in Figure 23.1. At the bottom layer are the protocols for communication. These would include hypertext transfer protocol (HTTP) and related protocols. eXtensible Markup Language (XML) and XML schemas are replaced by Geography Markup Language (GML) and GML schemas. The Open Geospatial Consortium (OGC) has made tremendous development with GML. We developed Geospatial Resource Description Framework (GRDF) to specify the semantics. Our details of GRDF can be found in Reference [ALAM06]. On top of GRDF we have developed geospatial ontologies. These ontologies are described in Reference [THUR07a]. An example of a GRDF ontology is given in the following. This ontology describes a building.

```
<campusonto:Building rdf:about="#CompScience">
  <grdf:hasSpatialExtent>
    <ogc-gml:Polygon>
     <ogc-gml:exterior_Ring>
      <grdf:LinearRing>
       <grdf:coordinates
        rdf:datatype="&xsd;string">
          0,1 1,0 13,
          0 13,8.5
          0,8.5 0,1
```

Web services and the standards provided by OGC define our approach for a geospatial semantic Web. Web services technologies support interoperable machine-machine interactions over a network. Web services will be developed for the operations to be performed on the different geospatial data sources. Our architecture is as described in Figure 23.2. Each Web service has a high-level service description that is written using GML or OWL-S. OGC specifies geospatial standards that rely on GML as the data layer encoding. OWL-S provides a semantic-rich application level platform to encode the Web service metadata using descriptive logic. The World Wide Web Consortium (W3C) is monitoring innovative ways to integrate these two methods as part of their Geospatial Semantic Web Interoperability experiment. Regardless of the methods, the description generated by them is used for publishing and for discovery of a Web service. Two Web services then bind through the underlying Web Services Description Language (WSDL) layer. WSDL is a specification defining how to describe Web services in a common XML gram-

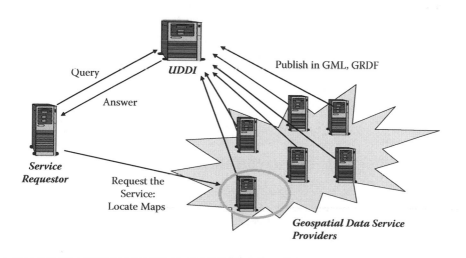

Figure 23.2   Web service architecture for geospatial data.

mar. SOAP is a standard for exchanging XML-based messages over a computer network, normally using HTTP. SOAP forms the foundation layer of the Web services stack, providing a basic messaging framework that more abstract layers can build on.

The client queries the Service Requester Web Service, which handles the GIS (Geospatial/Geographic Information Systems) application. The service requester then discovers the required service provider through the service registry or the matchmaker. The service registry selects the service provider which has already registered with this registry. The service provider can now bind with the service requester to fulfill the service request. The underlying protocol stack is shown in Figure 23.2. In this way two different GIS applications with different heterogeneities can interoperate with each other using Web services.

The ultimate goal is to integrate the work of OGC and the World Wide Web to develop a semantic Web for geospatial data. Although there are efforts to develop languages such as GRDF (e.g., the work at the University of Texas at Dallas), a comprehensive approach to developing a semantic Web such as integration of the various ontologies, GRDF, and GML are yet to be carried out.

Our team (Thuraisingham, Ashraful, Subbiah, and Khan) has developed a system called DAGIS that reasons with the ontologies and answers queries. This system is described in Reference [THUR07a]. It is a framework that provides a methodology to realize the semantic interoperability both at the geospatial data encoding level and also for the service framework. DAGIS is an integrated platform that provides the mechanism and architecture for building geospatial data exchange interfaces using the OWL-S service ontology. Coupled with the geospatial domain-specific ontology for automatic discovery, dynamic composition, and invocation of services, DAGIS is a one-stop platform to fetch and integrate geospatial data. The data encoding is in GRDF and provides the ability to reason about the payload data by DAGIS or client agents to provide intelligent inferences. DAGIS at the service level and GRDF at the data-encoding layer provide a complete unified model for realizing the vision of geospatial semantic Web. The architecture also enhances the query response for the client queries posed to DAGIS interface. The system architecture for DAGIS is illustrated in Figure 23.3.

23.3 Secure Geospatial Data Management

Before we discuss security for geospatial semantic Web, we will provide an overview of some of the challenges in securing geospatial data. Much of our discussion has been influenced by our collaborative research with Bertino at Purdue University and Gertz at the University of California Davis [THUR07b]. This research is also influenced by some of our earlier research on security-constraint processing and securing multimedia data [THUR95], [THUR90]. Atluri has also done

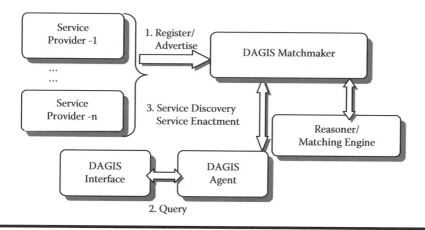

Figure 23.3 DAGIS architecture.

some interesting research on geospatial data management and security [ATLU04], [DAMI07].

Geospatial data are more complex than relational data. For example, we can classify the pixels as well as classify the points and lines that make up the geospatial data. We can define policies based on content, context, and time. For example, the location and the image taken together could be classified, whereas individually they could be unclassified. Furthermore, the location and image could be classified until a particular time and after that it could be declassified. For example, satellite imagery taken over, say, Iraq could be classified for six months from the day the image was captured and unclassified after that. Bertino and her team have developed policy languages for geospatial data and developed a security model which they call Geo-RBAC which integrates role-based access control (RBAC) with geospatial data.

Although there is a clear need for enforcing confidentiality policies for geospatial data, privacy remains a challenge. What does it mean to preserve privacy for geospatial data? Today we have the capability to carry out surveillance as well as capture the images in, say, Google maps. Therefore, we cannot expect the image of our house to remain private as the image is out there. However, the fact that it is my house could be private. We need to study the issues on privacy management for geospatial data. For our semantic Web research, our goal is to develop geospatial Web services that can utilize representation technologies such as GML and GRDF so that we get machine-understandable Web pages. However, to secure a geospatial semantic Web, we need to integrate geospatial semantic Web technologies with secure geospatial data management technologies. This will be the subject of the next section. Figure 23.4 illustrates security for geospatial data management.

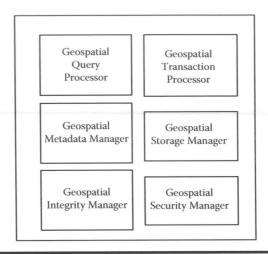

Figure 23.4   Secure geospatial data management.

23.4 Secure Geospatial Semantic Web

We are developing a set of policies for geospatial information systems. Data representation will be based on GML developed by OGC. The policy will include access control such as role-based and usage control, as well as trust, integrity, temporal constraints, data currency, data quality, and data provenance. Subsequently, we are designing and developing secure geospatial Web services that demonstrate the interoperability with respect to security; we will examine security violations via inference for geospatial information systems. For example, inferencing techniques for intelligent data fusion have been developed. By fusing the data, security constraints may be violated. We are adapting various techniques proposed to handle security for relational fused images. Data ownership and the need for profitability require an organization to safeguard its information bank from others. The technical complexity increases severalfold when the organizational domain consists of data that is more than text or numbers. One such instance is geospatial Web services that cater to queries that need information security beyond the level of a traditional RBAC mechanism. Safeguarding geospatial data requires fine granularity of access privileges, which makes RBAC a nonoptimal solution. Our goal is to harness the axiomatic framework provided through Web Ontology Language (OWL) to define policy assertions for potential clients and let the inference engine do the housekeeping. The layered framework for a secure geospatial semantic Web is illustrated in Figure 23.5.

Not all data housed by the geospatial agencies are considered public in nature. For instance, the data might contain critical information about people, exposure of

Figure 23.5　Secure geospatial semantic Web.

which would jeopardize their privacy. The problem is exacerbated in a data integration environment because of a lack of a coherent security framework. If the trend toward on-the-fly data integration continues, Web service providers would very soon perform complicated services that require embedding or combining geospatial data with other kinds of data. However, without appropriate security architecture in place, there will be reluctance by clearinghouses to serve data liberally. In turn, the quality and effectiveness of the data is affected as clients procure only partial information.

We have distinguished between two kinds of security most prevalent in Web services and that form the foundations of semantic Web services architecture as well. The first kind deals with the general authorization procedures of Web service users and any subsequent execution of over-the-wire security criteria. The current set of standardized protocols for this kind of data security includes encryption methods, digital signature verification, certification generation, Web services secure exchange, and so on. The second kind involves organizational protection of data from intruders or bona fide clients without proper access privileges. The most widely used defensive mechanism employed in this regard is various forms of access-control languages. We are developing a semantic-rich, ontology-based, access-control solution for geospatial data that can have a beneficial bearing on the surge in geospatial data integration around the world.

The security for geospatial data can be compartmentalized into different logical segments based on the layer of application. Our work concentrates on secure access of geospatial resources by clients or other Web services in the context of dynamic composition. In line with the vision of the semantic Web, we are developing a modular access control in a language that makes development of reasoning-enabled enforcement engines feasible. In contrast to the XML-based standards and first-order logic-based access controls, we define the axioms in OWL-DL and the emphasis on policy reuse. In our previous experience with policy-centric access control languages, it was observed that defining policies for resources on an individual basis is not well suited for integrated GIS applications. If fine-grained resource access is allowed, it amasses policies in policy files that must be navigated by the decision or enforcement module, thus degenerating overall query-processing time. Our architecture is illustrated in Figure 23.6.

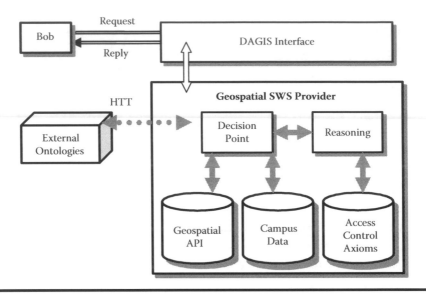

Figure 23.6   Secure DAGIS.

To improve policy decision time, our access-control language keeps the collection of asserted rules as a separate unit. Then the client identities can link to appropriate rules to be applied to the client. The modular use of policies by referencing them minimizes rule duplications. Another important characteristic is the shifting of rule navigation from policies to client identities. The geospatial semantic Web service agent in our framework accepts users with established identities or anonymous users.

To develop a secure geospatial semantic Web, we need to incorporate security across the entire semantic Web technology framework. We illustrate this in Figure 23.7. Organizations such as OGC are examining security assertions to be specified in GML. In addition, organizations such as the Organization for the Advancement for Structured Information Standards (OASIS) are developing Geo-XACML. We are developing security assertions to be specified in GRDF which we call Secure GRDF. We are focusing on extending the secure DAGIS framework into a secure geospatial semantic Web. DAGIS also has a responding component that is based on GRDF and can reason about security policies.

23.5 Secure Interoperability with GRDF

Although organizational resources can be protected with a semantic access-control system, geospatial data protection in a distributed environment can present a lot of

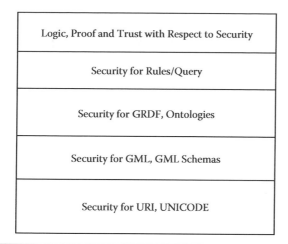

Figure 23.7   Technology stack for secure geospatial semantic Web.

difficulties beyond providing or denying access. Geospatial data is unique in that the same piece of data has varying levels of granularity depending on the context. For instance, raster images could be processed in different resolutions, scale, and accuracy. Even vector data is available at differing scales, depending on the particular data collection agency. For this reason, when data from multiple agencies is integrated, access control of the aggregated geospatial data becomes a potential security trap. For instance, if a multilayered view is presented to users with each layer belonging to a different source provider, it is not clear how a user from one particular agency will see the aggregated view. The special traits make it unfeasible for generic semantic access control such as semantic access control to govern over geospatial data.

Thus far, we have defined two types of constructs. The first type provides alternative abstract elements for vector data, and the second type constitutes ontology for subject and action roles. Subjects are classified based on their functional criteria. Currently, defined top-level classes for various categories of subjects are "Administrator," "Manager," "Regular Professional," "Facility Personnel," and "Guest." The actions defined thus far are "Read," "Write," "Save," and "Execute." In an ideal circumstance, all parties in a distributed system have an agreed-on set of measures to combine their policies or resolve them in case of a failure. However, the pre-arrangement is not always possible, and in such cases, our security constructs would allow a semantic access control processor to interpret the role and action definitions and combine the corresponding policies. Our research is focusing on policy integration algorithms. We have developed a technology for developing partial responses at the same time as ensuring security. This research will be discussed in our future papers. Our policy integration framework is illustrated in Figure 23.8.

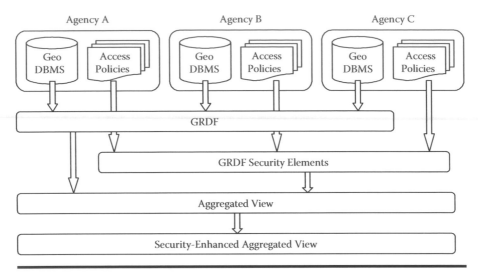

Figure 23.8 Security policy integration framework for geospatial data.

23.6 Geo-RSS

In this section we will discuss an application of geospatial semantic Web technologies, that is, GeoRSS. As stated in Reference [OGC], GeoRSS is a simple proposal for geoenabling, or tagging, "really simple syndication" (RSS) feeds with location information. GeoRSS proposes a standardized way in which location is encoded with enough simplicity and descriptive power to satisfy most needs to describe the location of Web content. GeoRSS is also intended to be a lightweight way to express geography in other XML-based formats, including XHTML.

RSS is a family of XML formats for exchanging news, especially news about Web pages or other Web content. Many dynamic Web sites, especially "blogs," now provide RSS "feeds" of their new or changed content. RSS is a simple, brief, and structured XML format that includes key descriptive elements like author, date, title, narrative description, and hypertext link elements that help the reader decide what source materials are worth examining in more detail. This concise, structured format has also proven useful for publishing all kinds of small, time-sensitive nuggets of information, including Flickr's photo journals, Craigslist classifieds, and local events.

GeoRSS essentially combines RSS with geospatial data. Location needs to be described in an interoperable manner so that applications can request, aggregate, share, and map geographically tagged feeds. GeoRSS has two encodings: GeoRSS GML and GeoRSS Simple. GeoRSS GML is a formal GML application profile and supports a greater range of features than an ably coordinate reference system.

GeoRSS Simple, the simple serialization of GeoRSS, is designed to be concise, but it is limited in expressive power.

The GeoRSS model must be expressed in a concrete form such as in XML or Resource Description Framework (RDF). The core concepts of GeoRSS are CRS, Geometry, Tags, and Elevation. The geometric shapes which can be used to represent location in GeoRSS are the point that contains a single coordinate pair. The coordinate pair contains a latitude value and a longitude value *in that order*. A line contains two or more coordinate pairs. Each pair contains a latitude value and a longitude value *in that order*. Pairs are separated from each other by a *space*. A box contains exactly two coordinate pairs. Each pair contains a latitude value and a longitude value *in that order*. Pairs are separated from each other by a *space*. The first coordinate pair (lower corner) must be a point further west and south of the second coordinate pair (upper corner), and the box is always interpreted as not containing the 180- (or -180)-degree longitude line other than on its boundary and not containing the north or south pole other than on its boundary. In RDF, the content and meaning of Simple GeoRSS can be stated in a few words:

georss:point, georss:line, georss:polygon, georss:box.

The resulting language that integrated geospatial concepts with RDF is Geo-RDF and competes with GRDF.

GeoRSS is limited in security. Therefore, the work that we have carried out on incorporating security into the semantic Web can be integrated with the GeoRSS work. Essentially although there has been work on geospatial data management and building geospatial semantic Webs, security has received little attention. We believe that our research as well as the work of Bertino, Gertz, and Atluri sets the stage for research on secure geospatial semantic Web.

23.7 Summary and Direction

This chapter has provided an overview of geospatial data management and the geospatial semantic Web and then discussed the security impact. In particular, we have focused on our research in building secure geospatial semantic Webs. We also discuss the work on GeoRSS.

Our work has examined mainly the confidentiality aspect of security for geospatial data. We also need to examine privacy, trust, and data-quality issues for geospatial data. As we have stated, much of the research on geospatial data management has focused on the data issues and not on policy issues. Our research sets the direction for policy research in geospatial data. We believe that secure geospatial semantic Webs will be critical for integrating heterogeneous geospatial data sources as well as for geospatial Web services and knowledge management. This will also provide the directions for managing complex data such as voice and video data in this semantic Web environment. For many of the applications that deal with geospatial data, security is critical. Therefore, we need to start a program in secure geospatial semantic Web and data management.

References

[ALAM06] Alam, A. and B. Thuraisingham, GRDF and Secure GRDF, Technical Report, The University of Texas at Dallas, 2006.

[ATLU04] Atluri, V. et al., Secure geospatial data management, *IEEE Trans. Dependable Secure Comput.*, December 2004.

[DAMI07] Damiani, M.L., E. Bertino, B. Catania, and P. Perlasca, GEO-RBAC: A spatially aware RBAC, *ACM Trans. Inf. Syst. Secur.*, 10(1), 2007.

[[LI07] Li, C. et al., Geospatial data mining, *Proc. ISI Conf.*, New Brunswick, NJ, 2007.

[OGC] OGC White Paper, An introduction to GeoRSS: A standards based approach for geo-enabling RSS feeds, http://www.opengeospatial.org/.

[THUR90] Thuraisingham, B., Security for Multimedia Database Systems, IFIP Data Security Conference, 1990.

[THUR95] Thuraisingham, B. and W. Ford, Security constraint processing in a multilevel distributed database management, *IEEE Trans. Knowledge Data Eng.*, April 1995.

[THUR07a] Thuraisingham, B. et al., DAGIS Architecture, Technical Report, University of Texas at Dallas, 2007.

[THUR07b] Thuraisingham, B. et al., Secure geospatial semantic Web, Technical Report, University of Texas at Dallas, 2007.

Exercises

1. Describe a geospatial application and discuss the security requirements.
2. Design semantic Web technologies for geospatial data.
3. Combine Exercises 1 and 2 and subsequently design and develop secure geospatial semantic Web technologies.

Chapter 24

Secure Semantic Sensor Web and Pervasive Computing

24.1 Overview

Sensors are everywhere, and they have become part of our daily lives. These sensors are continually monitoring the environment, events, activities, people, vehicles, and many other objects, gathering data from these objects, aggregating the data, then making sense out of the data, and finally taking actions based on the analysis of the data. For example, we have sensors to monitor periodically the temperature of a manufacturing plant, and if the temperature exceeds a certain value, then an alarm should be raised. At the other extreme, we now have sensors monitoring the activities of people, and if these activities are considered to be suspicious, law enforcement officials are notified. We need sensors to be intelligent; that is, sensors must not only be able to monitor the situation, they must also be able to rapidly analyze the data gathered and make decisions. This is because there is a lot of data out there, and sensors must process certain critical data and discard other data and perhaps store a third set of data for future analysis. Furthermore, sensors are limited in their storage capabilities. Therefore, the challenge is to develop algorithms for sensors to manage the data and information under massive resource and timing constraints. Essentially we need semantic Web technologies to develop what has come to be known as a Web of sensors or a sensor Web.

Recently data-management system researchers have been focusing on developing data-management techniques for managing sensor databases. Although much progress has been made on sensor database management, there is still a lot to be done. For example, very little consideration has been given to security and privacy for sensor databases. Sensors are often operating in an open environment and are vulnerable. The data managed by sensors may be compromised. We need security techniques to ensure that the sensor data is protected. We must also ensure that the data is not maliciously corrupted. Furthermore, privacy is an added consideration. People may want the information collected about them to be private. This clearly illustrates the need for applying trustworthy semantic Web technologies to develop a secure semantic sensor Web.

Closely related to sensor information management is wireless information management pervasive computing. The wireless and mobile devices have embedded sensors and processors. These processors have to communicate with each other to solve problems and carry out activities; that is, we need to apply semantic Web technologies for wireless and pervasive computing environments. This chapter provides a discussion of the issues involved in developing a secure semantic sensor Web. In particular, we discuss various types of security mechanisms, policies, and markup languages for sensor data management.

The organization of this chapter is as follows. In Section 24.2 we discuss security for sensor data management. A note on wireless information management and security is discussed in Section 24.3. Security for moving data systems is discussed in Section 24.4. A secure sensor semantic Web is discussed in Section 24.5. Pervasive computing and the semantic Web are discussed in Section 24.6. The chapter is summarized in Section 24.7. Our view of a sensor Web is illustrated in Figure 24.1. In this network, sensor data managers are connected through some communication subsystem. Background information in data management, sensor networks, and sensor data managers are given by Carney et al. [CARN03].

24.2 Security for Sensor Data Systems

Security policy essentially specifies the application-specific security rules and application-independent security rules. Application-independent security rules are rules such as the following:

- The combination of data from two sensors is always sensitive.
- A sensor operating at Level L1 cannot read data from a sensor operating at Level L2 if L2 is a more sensitive level than L1.

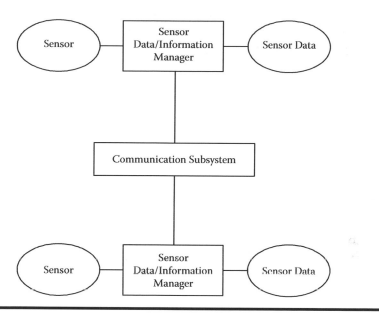

Figure 24.1   Sensor network.

The second rule is usually enforced for multilevel security. Now the main question is, how does the policy for secure data management apply to sensor data? We could have sensors operating at different levels. Sensors in the Middle East may be highly classified, whereas sensors in Europe may be less classified. Classified sensors will gather classified data, whereas unclassified sensors will gather unclassified data. Furthermore, sensor data may be in the form of streams. Therefore, we need access-control policies for data streams. Within each level, one could enforce application-specific rules. Application-specific security rules include the following:

- Only law enforcement officials have authorization to examine data emanating from Sensor A.
- Data from Sensors A and B taken together are sensitive.
- All the data emanating from sensors in Washington, D.C. federal buildings is sensitive, whereas the data emanating from sensors in North Dakota federal buildings is not sensitive.

Essentially application-specific rules are specified using security constraints. We discuss security constraint processing in a later section.

Security policy integration is a major challenge. Each sensor may enforce its own security policy and have its own constraints. The challenge is to integrate the different policies especially in distributed and cluster environments. For example, in the case of a cluster, each cluster of sensors may have its own policy, which is derived from the security policies of the individual sensors. The policies of the clusters will have to be combined to get an integrated policy.

Security has an impact on all the functions of a sensor data manager. Consider the query operation. The query processor has to examine the access-control rules and security constraints and modify the query accordingly. For example, if the fact that the existence of Operation X is classified, then this query cannot be sent to an unclassified sensor node to monitor the situation. Similarly, the update process also examines the access control rules to see if the data coming from a particular sensor can be inserted into the sensor database, that is, for example, data coming from a sensor that manages an operation in the Middle East may not be entered into a sensor data manager in Southeast Asia. Secure sensor transaction processing is another issue. First, what does transaction processing mean? One could imagine a sensor at Site A and a sensor at Site B, monitoring the environments and making simultaneous updates to the sensor database. Both updates have to be carried out as a transaction. This is conceivable if both, say, temperature values depend on the final computation of some parameter. So, assuming that the notion of a transaction is valid, what does it mean to process transactions securely? There has been a lot of work on secure transaction processing both for single-level and multiple-level transactions. In the case of a single-level transaction, it is assumed that the transaction is processed at a single security level. In the case of multilevel transactions, the transaction may operate at multiple security levels. The main challenge is to ensure that information does not flow covertly from a higher level to a lower level. Sensor transaction processing will also have similar challenges. We need to examine the techniques from secure transaction processing and real-time transaction processing to see if we can develop techniques specific for dependable sensor transaction processing (see also Reference [THUR04a] and Reference [THUR04b]).

Next consider the storage manager function. The storage manager has to ensure that access is controlled for the sensor database. The storage manager may also be responsible for partitioning the data according to security levels. The security impact of access methods and indexing strategy for sensor data are yet to be determined. Metadata management is also another issue. For example, we need to first determine the types of metadata for sensor data. Metadata may include descriptions about the data, the source of the data as well as the quality of the data. Metadata may also be classified. In some cases the metadata may be classified at a higher level than the data itself. For example, the location of the data may be highly sensitive, whereas the data could be unclassified. We should also ensure that one cannot obtain unauthorized information from the metadata. Figure 24.2 illustrates the security impact on the query and update operations of sensor databases.

Figure 24.3 illustrates architecture for an inference controller. Because a lot of data has to be aggregated and fused in a shared sensor data processing environment, there could be a potential for inference problems; that is, the aggregated data from sensor nodes A, B, and C could be highly sensitive. For example, one sensor could

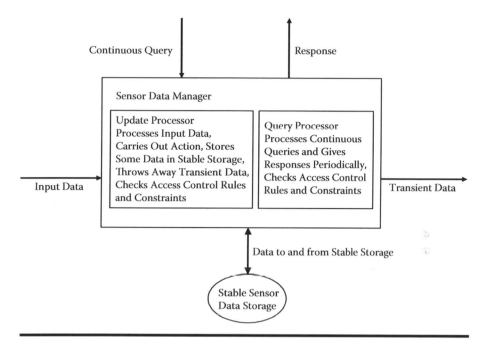

Continuous Query

Response

Sensor Data Manager

Update Processor
Processes Input Data,
Carries Out Action, Stores
Some Data in Stable Storage,
Throws Away Transient Data,
Checks Access Control Rules
and Constraints

Query Processor
Processes Continuous
Queries and Gives
Responses Periodically,
Checks Access Control
Rules and Constraints

Input Data

Transient Data

Data to and from Stable Storage

Stable Sensor
Data Storage

Figure 24.2   Functions of a secure sensor data manager.

monitor the situation in the Middle East, and another sensor could monitor the situation in Asia, and the combined sensed information could be highly sensitive. The inference controller has to examine the constraints and prevent such sensitive information from being released to individuals who are not authorized to acquire this information.

Sensors are especially vulnerable to attacks as they function in an open environment; that is, sensors could be anywhere in the world, and the sensor data managers could be compromised and the results aggregated. As a result the most private information could be divulged. The sensors could monitor, say, people in a shopping mall, and the activities of the people may be monitored by law enforcement agencies as well as hackers who have hacked into the sensor system. Furthermore, based on the events monitored, the law enforcement agencies could arrest innocent individuals, especially if the analysis tools do not give accurate information.

There has been some work recently on privacy-preserving sensor surveillance by Mehrotra et al. [MEHR04]. The idea here is for users to wear radiofrequency identification tags (RFIDs), and these tags are detected by sensors. If it is a tag that the sensor can recognize, then the person's identity is hidden. If the sensor cannot recognize the tag, then the person is displayed, and privacy is not maintained.

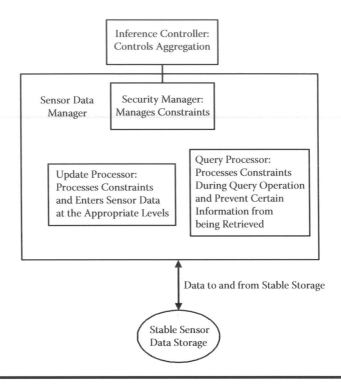

Figure 24.3 Sensor data inference controller.

Note that as stated in a recent special issue of *IEEE Spectrum Magazine* (see Reference [IEEE04]), RFID technology raises many interesting security and privacy questions. Furthermore, it is stated that sensor and wireless technology will revolutionize information technology. Some research on security and surveillance is also reported by Thuraisingham et al. [THUR06] and Chaitanya and Thuraisingham [CHAI06].

24.3 Secure Wireless Data Management

Wireless devices include telephones, personal digital assistants (PDAs), and, more recently, laptop computers. These devices have sensors embedded in them. Therefore all the security issues discussed for sensor data and information management apply for wireless information management. There are also additional considerations for wireless information management.

An excellent introduction to security in wireless networks was given recently by Perrig et al. [PERR04]. The authors state that these networks are susceptible to various attacks including denial of service, node capture, and physical tampering.

These networks are used for various applications including for monitoring building safety and earthquakes as well as for military applications. Various security solutions including encryption, authentication, and privacy are discussed by Perrig et al. [PERR04]. In addition, challenges for secure group communication as well as intrusion detection are discussed.

In the case of secure data management for wireless networks, the challenges include secure query processing, transaction management, storage management, and metadata management. For example, how can queries be optimized efficiently? The users of the mobile devices may not stay in one location, and therefore the query response has to be routed to the user's location. Is the user authorized to see the response? How can access control be enforced? How can the user be authenticated? How can the aggregation problem be handled? As stated by Perrig et al. [PERR04], the sensor data has to be aggregated before being sent to the base station so that the base station is not flooded with data. Does the user have access to the aggregated data?

In the case of transaction management, we need to first define the notion of a transaction. Multiple users may be updating the data managers both attached to the wireless nodes as well as to the base stations. Do the transactions have to be able to be serialized? Can we live with weak ability to be serialized? Can access control be enforced during transaction processing?

Storage management issues include managing the storage attached to the wireless nodes as well as to the base stations. The wireless nodes may have limited storage capability. In addition, they also have limited power capability. Therefore, the challenge is, what data should be maintained by the wireless node, and what data should be stored at the base station? How can replicated copies be kept consistent? How can the integrity and security constraints be enforced? What is the security impact on access methods and index strategies?

Finally, in the case of metadata management, we need to first define what metadata is for wireless networks. Typically, metadata for wireless networks would include information about the nodes, their capacity, power consumption-related information as well as security policies enforced. Storing and managing the metadata is a challenge. If the data storage is limited at the wireless nodes, then where is the metadata to be stored? Is it feasible to store the metadata at the base stations and retrieve it each time it is needed?

Other attacks include intrusions, denial of service, eavesdropping, and spoofing. Although we need security solutions for wireless networks, are there additional challenges for data management? Many organizations including university campuses have gone wireless. Therefore, building security solutions both for wireless networks and data managers as well as other information-management technologies are critical. For an overview of security for wireless sensor networks we refer the reader to Perrig et al. [PERR04].

24.4 Secure Mobile and RFID Data Management

Recently there have been many efforts on developing moving data management. For example, RFID tags on people and objects may be moving from place to place. Any data-management system that manages such tags should have the capability to manage moving data. First of all, we need to develop secure query-processing strategies. In mobile databases, users are moving continuously, and data may also be migrating. Therefore, we need dynamic query-processing strategies as the size of the databases as well as communication distances may vary from time to time. We also need special techniques to handle the movement of data and users. Special transaction-processing techniques are also needed. We may have to sacrifice strict ability of transactions to be serialized, as the data is dynamic in nature. Furthermore, we need to examine security for transaction management in a mobile environment.

Much of the algorithms will depend on the security policies enforced. For example, what are the application-specific security constraints? How can we handle missing information? How can we enforce flexible security policies? How can we securely route the information to the mobile users? How do we handle data that migrates from place to place? Some directions are provided by Lubinski [LUBI98].

24.5 Secure Semantic Sensor Web

The sensor nodes in a network have to interoperate with each other, enforce various security policies, and carry out activities in real-time. Therefore, there is now much interest in integrating sensor networks with semantic Web technologies. In this section we will discuss some of the directions, and in the next section we will go beyond sensor Webs and discuss how the semantic Web is integrated with pervasive computing infrastructures.

In the recent workshop on Semantic Sensor Networks in Athens, Georgia [SSN06], there were discussions on the use of semantic Webs to address sensor networking applications using RFID technologies as well as complex, cross-jurisdictional, heterogeneous, dynamic information systems. As stated in the workshop objective, the goal was "to develop an understanding of the ways semantic Web technologies, including ontologies, agent architectures, and semantic Web services, can contribute to the growth, application, and deployment of large-scale sensor networks."

Hendler and his team at the University of Maryland have developed techniques for the interactive composition of Web services that can be used in a sensor network environment. They state that "as Web services become more prevalent, tools will be needed to help users find, filter, and integrate these services." Therefore, they have developed ways to compose existing Web services that include "presenting matching services to the user at each step of composition, filtering the possibilities by using semantic descriptions, and directly executing the services through WSDL (Web service discription language)" [SIRI03].

A significant development connecting the semantic Web with senior technologies is SensorML standard of the Open Geospatial Consortium (OGC). As stated in Wikipedia [WIKI], "SensorML is an Open Geospatial Consortium standard markup language (using XML schema) for providing descriptions of sensor systems. By design it supports a wide range of sensors, including both dynamic and stationary platforms and both in situ and remote sensors." It supports many features including sensor discovery, sensor geolocation, processing of sensor observations, a sensor programming mechanism, and subscription to sensor alerts.

Although there is much progress, we need to develop ontologies, Web services, and sensor Resource Description Framework (RDF) so that we have the capability to automate machine-understandable sensor data and Web pages. Furthermore, very little research on incorporating security into sensor Webs has been reported. The policies that we have discussed in earlier sections can be expressed in languages like SensorML. Furthermore, we need to build reasoning systems to reason about the policies as well as making deductions and learning. The University of Maryland (Baltimore County) is leading the way for such research. We discuss some of their work in connecting semantic Webs with pervasive computing in the next section. Figure 24.4 illustrates the integration of sensor Web with semantic Web and security.

24.6 Pervasive Computing and the Semantic Web

Pervasive computing is essentially about a collection of sensors, wireless devices, and embedded processes, all interacting with each other to carry out various activi-

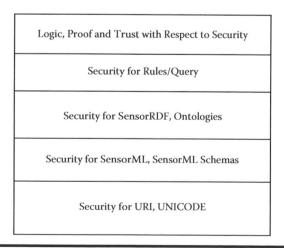

Figure 24.4   Secure sensor semantic Web.

ties such as video surveillance, detecting supplies in registers, automatic washing machine operation, and monitoring the heartbeats of patients. Semantic Web technologies are being integrated with pervasive computing to understand the data and carry out various pervasive computing operations.

Kagal and others at the University of Maryland (Baltimore County) have examined semantic framework for a sensor Web [KAGA]. Their solution is based on Web services and distributed trust management. The key to their architecture is the service manager (SM) that acts as a mediator between the services and the users. All clients of the system, whether they are services or users, have to register with an SM in what they call the "Smart Space." The SM is responsible for processing client registration and deregistration requests, responding to registered client requests for a listing of available services, for brokering subscribe and unsubscribe and command requests from users to services, and for sending service updates to all subscribed users whenever the state of a particular service is modified. They state that the SM is arranged in a tree-like hierarchy, and messages are routed through to other service managers through this tree. The essential points of their trust-management approach are as follows. Each client establishes trust with its SM, and SMs across the hierarchy establish trust among them; hence, trust is now a concept that is transparent between all clients in the system. They have also defined a security agent that carries out the security activities. Semantic Web technologies are utilized for policy specification as well as reasoning by the security agent.

Some of the early work on integrating pervasive computing with a semantic Web was carried out at Nokia research laboratories by Lassila [LASS02]. In his presentation on "pervasive computing meets the semantic Web", Lassila introduced the notion of "semantic gadgets" that combine a semantic Web with ubiquitous computing. He states that device capabilities and service functionality are explicitly represented, that everything is addressable (using URIs), and a semantic Web is the basis for "semantic interoperability." In his approach, agents will discover services and carry out reasoning as well as learn and plan. Lassila also introduced the notion of device coalitions where all devices advertise their services and a device extends its functionality by discovering missing functionality offered by another device and contracting the use of the service. He further states that everything can be discovered including reasoning services and planning services. One needs to integrate the work, say, by Lassila with the work by Kagal to integrate the trustworthy semantic Web and ubiquitous computing.

In other work, researchers at Fujitsu's laboratories introduced the notion of task computing as the technology to integrate the semantic Web with pervasive computing. They state that task computing shifts the focus to what users want to do as opposed to the specific means of users doing the task. They then state that task computing offers device manufacturers an incentive to incorporate semantic Web technologies into their devices. They have implemented a task computing environment using semantic Web technologies such as RDF and Web Ontology Language (OWL) [MASU03].

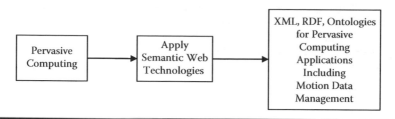

Figure 24.5   Pervasive semantic Web.

There is also now research on integrating sensor Webs with RFID technologies and semantic Webs. For example, Adam and his team at Rutgers have developed techniques for the composition of Web services for RFID data management and interoperability for border patrol [PALI04]. As we have discussed in Chapter 22, this is an area that is critical for homeland security. In summary, although there is now research on integrating the semantic Web with pervasive computing and RFID data management, we need to focus on security issues as well. As we have stated, policies could be expressed in semantic Web languages. Furthermore, we need to develop reasoning engines that can reason about the policies and handle problems like inference and privacy problems. Figure 24.5 illustrates the integration of pervasive computing with the semantic Web and security.

24.7   Summary and Directions

We have discussed a number of security issues for sensor data management and also have given privacy some consideration. We also discussed secure wireless information management. Much of our focus has been on access control. We then discussed the integration of semantic Web technologies with sensor and pervasive computing technologies.

There are several areas for future research. First, we need to develop appropriate policies for sensor data and represent these policies in a suitable language. SensorML is a start. We need to develop languages comparable to RDF such as Sensor. We also need to build reasoning engines to reason with sensor data and policies. Finally, we need to integrate pervasive computing with the semantic Web, the sensor Web, and security.

References

[CARN03] Carney, D. et al., Operator Scheduling in a Data Stream Manager, *Proc. 29th Int. Conf. Very Large Data Bases*, Berlin, Germany, 2003.

[CHAI06] Chaitanya, S. and B. Thuraisingham, Automatic Face Detection for Privacy Preserving Surveillance, Technical Report, University of Texas at Dallas, 2006.

[IEEE04] *IEEE Spectrum*, July 2004.

[KAGA] Kagal, L. et al., A Security Architecture Based on Trust Management for Pervasive Computing Systems, http://ebiquity.umbc.edu/_file_directory_/papers/15.pdf.

[LASSI02] Lassila, O., Semantic Gadgets: Pervasive Computing Meets the Semantic Web, http://www.lassila.org/publications/2002/lassila-nist-pervasive-2002.pdf.

[LUBI98] Lubinski, A., Security Issues in Mobile Database Access, *Proc. IFIP Database Security Conf.*, Chalcidici, Greece, July 1998, Kluwer, Dordrecht, 1999.

[MASU03] Masuoka, R., B. Parsi, and Y. Labrou, Task Computing — the Semantic Web Meets Pervasive Computing, http://www.flacp.fujitsulabs.com/~rmasuoka/papers/Task-Computing-ISWC2003-202-color-final.pdf.

[MEHR04] Mehrotra, S. et al., Privacy Preserving Surveillance, Demonstration, University of California, Irvine, 2004, http://en.wikipedia.org/wiki/SensorML.

[PALI04] Paliwal, A.V., N. Adam, C. Bornhövd, and J. Schaper, Semantic Discovery and Composition of Web Services for RFID Applications in Border Control, http://www.dvs1.informatik.tu-darmstadt.de/staff/bornhoevd/ISWC'04.pdf.

[PERR04] Perrig, A. et al., Security in wireless sensor networks, *Commn. ACM*, 2004.

[SIRI03] Sirin, E., J. Hendler, and B. Parisa, Interactive Composition of Semantic Web Services, http://www2003.org/cdrom/papers/poster/p232/p232-sirin/p232-sirin.html.

[SSN06] *Proc. Semantic Sensor Networks Workshop*, Athens, GA, Nov. 2006.

[THUR04a] Thuraisingham, B., Secure sensor information management, *IEEE Signal Processing*, May 2004.

[THUR04b] Thuraisingham, B., Security and privacy for sensor databases, sensor letters, *Am. Sci.*, Inaugural Issue, March 2004.

[THUR06] Thuraiisngham, B. et al., Access Control for Video Surveillance, *Proc. Symp. Access Control Models Applications and Technologies (ACM SACMAT)*, 2006.

[WIKI] SensorML http://en.wikipedia.org/wiki/SensorML.

Exercises

1. Give a detailed discussion of security for sensor data management.
2. What are the security challenges for wireless and moving data management?
3. Discuss privacy issues for surveillance technologies.
4. Develop a suite of trustworthy semantic Web technologies such as SensorML, SensorRDF, and ontologies for sensor information management.

Conclusion to Part V

Part V described specialized and domain-specific semantic Webs. In Chapter 22 we discussed domain-specific semantic Webs for defense, financial, and medical domains, among others. Trustworthy semantic Webs for geospatial data were discussed in Chapter 23. In particular, the work carried out on Geography Markup Language (GML) as well as the Open Geospatial Consortium's (OGC) interoperability work were discussed. Chapter 24 discussed pervasive computing applications including secure mobile-sensor semantic Webs as well as pervasive semantic Webs.

This brings us to the end of Part V and essentially to the end of the technical aspects of the book. We have addressed a variety of topics in semantic Web security. We started with a discussion of supporting technologies and then discussed confidentiality for the semantic Web. Next we addressed trust, privacy, and integrity management, followed by a discussion of the applications of the trustworthy semantic Web concepts. Finally, we provided an overview of some of the specialized semantic Webs. Chapter 25 will conclude the book.

Chapter 25

Summary and Directions

25.1 About This Chapter

This chapter brings us to the close of *Building Trustworthy Semantic Webs*. We discussed several aspects including supporting technologies for trustworthy semantic Webs, secure semantic Webs, dependable semantic Webs, applications of trustworthy semantic Webs, and specialized semantic Webs. Supporting technologies include semantic Webs, information security, and data, information, and knowledge management. In the area of secure semantic Webs we discussed eXtensible Markup Language (XML), Resource Description Framework (RDF), ontologies, and rules security. Dependability included trust, privacy, and integrity management. Applications included Web services, interoperability, digital libraries, and E-business. Specialized semantic Webs included geospatial and sensor semantic Webs. This chapter provides a summary of the book as well as gives directions for trustworthy semantic Webs.

The organization of this chapter is as follows. In Section 25.2 we give a summary of this book. We have taken the summaries from each chapter and formed a summary of this book. We revisit the scenario discussed in Chapter 4 in Section 25.3. In Section 25.4, we discuss directions for trustworthy semantic Webs. In Section 25.5 we give suggestions as to where to go from here.

25.2 Summary of This Book

We summarized the contents of each chapter essentially taken from the summary and directions section of each chapter. Chapter 1 provided an introduction to the

331

book. We first provided a brief overview of the supporting technologies for trustworthy semantic Webs which included information security; data, information, and knowledge management; and the semantic Web. Then we discussed various topics addressed in this book including secure semantic Webs, a dependable semantic Web, applications of a semantic Web, and specialized semantic Webs such as domain-specific semantic Webs and geospatial semantic Webs. Our framework is a five-layer framework, and each layer was addressed in one part of this book. This framework, illustrated in Figure 1.8, is replicated here (see Figure 25.1).

The book is divided into five parts. Part I, which described the supporting technologies for database and applications security, consisted of Chapters 2, 3, and 4. Chapter 2 provided a brief overview of the developments in trustworthy systems. We first discussed secure systems including basic concepts in access control as well as discretionary and mandatory policies, types of secure systems such as secure operating systems, secure databases, secure networks, and emerging technologies, the impact of the Web, and the steps to building secure systems. Next we discussed dependable systems including aspects on trust, rights, privacy, integrity, quality, and real-time processing. Then we focused in more detail on aspects of Web security including threats to Web security and secure Web databases.

Chapter 3 provided an overview of secure data, information, and knowledge management. In particular, we discussed data, information, and knowledge-management technologies and then examined the security impact. Chapter 4 provided an overview of semantic Web technologies. In particular we discussed Tim Berners Lee's technology stack as well as a functional architecture for the semantic Web. Then we discussed XML, RDF, and ontologies, as well as Web rules for the semantic Web. Next we discussed agents as well as some applications. Finally, we discussed a motivating scenario that we will revisit in Section 25.3.

Part II, which described secure semantic Webs, consisted of Chapters 5, 6, 7, 8, and 9. Chapter 5 provided an overview of the semantic Web and discussed security standards. We first discussed security issues for the semantic Web. We argued that security must cut across all the layers. Furthermore, we need to integrate the information across the layers securely. Next we provided some details on XML security, RDF security, secure information integration, and trust. If the semantic Web is to be secure, we need all its components to be secure. We also described some of our research on access control and dissemination of XML documents. Next we discussed privacy for the semantic Web.

Chapter 6 provided an overview of XML security. We first discussed issues on securing XML documents including security issues for XML elements, attributes, and schemas. Then we discussed the use of XML for specifying security policies. We also discussed the secure publications of XML documents. Chapter 7 provided an overview of RDF security. We first discussed securing the components of RDF including RDF statements and schemas. Next we discussed the use of RDF for specifying policies. We also discussed secure RDF databases. Chapter 8 discussed ontologies and security. We argued that portions of the ontologies may

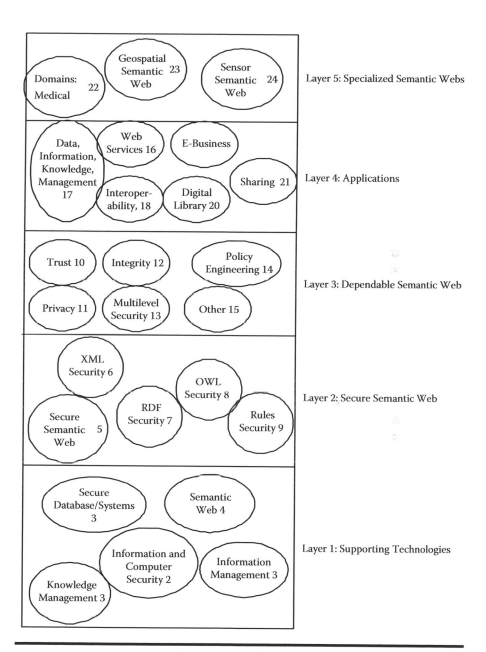

Figure 25.1 Components addressed in this book.

need to be classified for different applications. We also showed how ontologies may be used to specify security policies. Chapter 9 provided an overview of Web rules and security. First we discussed the security issues for rules based on our research on nonmonotonic typed multilevel logic. Then we showed how rules may be used to specify policies. We also discussed the use of rules for handling inference and privacy problems.

Part III, which described dependable semantic Webs, consisted of Chapters 10, 11, 12, 13, 14, and 15. Chapter 10 discussed trust management and its connection to the semantic Web. We first discussed aspects of trust management including defining trust and also describing trust negotiations. Then we discussed enforcing trust within the context of the semantic Web. Furthermore, we discussed the use of semantic Web technologies for specifying trust policies. Next we discussed related concepts including risk-based trust management, digital rights management, and reputation networks.

Chapter 11 discussed the various notions of privacy and provided an overview of privacy management. Then we discussed the semantic Web technology applications for privacy management. Privacy for the Web was discussed next. This was followed by a discussion of the standard Platform for Privacy Preferences Project (P3P). Finally we discussed privacy violations through inference and privacy-preserving semantic Web mining.

Chapter 12 provided an overview of data integrity, which includes data quality and data provenance. We discussed the applications of semantic Web technologies for data integrity as well as integrity for semantic Web technologies. Finally, we provided an overview of the relationship between data quality and data provenance. Chapter 13 discussed multilevel security issues with respect to the semantic Web. We first provided an overview of multilevel secure data management. This was followed by a discussion of multilevel security for semantic Web technologies. Next we discussed logics for multilevel secure semantic Webs and the inference problem.

Chapter 14 discussed several aspects of policy engineering including policy generation and specification, policy consistency and completeness, policy reuse and evolution, policy integration, band policy management including policy visualization and mining. Chapter 15 provided a summary of the developments of trustworthy semantic Webs. These include the research efforts, standards efforts, products, and applications.

Part IV, which described applications of trustworthy semantic Webs, consisted of Chapters 16, 17, 18, 19, 20, and 21. Chapter 16 provided an overview of secure Web services and discussed the applications of semantic Web technologies for secure Web services. Web services are the services that are invoked to carry out activities on the Web. A collection of Web services comprise the service-oriented architecture. We also discussed aspects of eXtensible Access Control Markup Language (XACML), Security Assertions Markup Language (SAML), and Shibboleth, which are related to secure Web services. Chapter 17 discussed secure data, information, and knowledge management and then showed how semantic Web technologies may be applied. We also discussed how data, information, and knowledge management could be used to develop the vision of the secure semantic Web.

Chapter 18 discussed security for information integration. We started by providing some background and related work and then discussed schema integration and security policy integration. We also discussed semantic heterogeneity and the inference problem in a federated environment. Finally, we discussed various semantic Web technologies such as XML, RDF, and Web Ontology Language (OWL) for secure semantic interoperability. Chapter 19 provided an overview of secure E-business and then discussed various aspects of secure semantic E-business. Semantic E-business essentially integrates semantic Web technologies with business-process management and knowledge management. We also discussed some of the key points in ebXML, the XML standard for E-business applications. Finally, we examined the security impact on semantic E-business.

Chapter 20 discussed secure digital libraries including secure Web databases and secure information-retrieval systems and then descried the applications of semantic Web technologies. In particular we discussed the various semantic Web technologies such as ontologies, ontology editors, annotation tools, and inference engines that can be applied to digital libraries. We discussed the need for investigating security for digital libraries and the application of trustworthy semantic Web technologies for digital libraries.

Chapter 21 defined assured information sharing (AIS) and discussed issues, technologies, challenges, and directions for this area. The goal of AIS is for organizations to share data, but at the same time enforce security policies. Security includes confidentiality, privacy, trust, and integrity policies. We discussed approaches for AIS when the partners of a coalition are trustworthy, semitrustworthy, and untrustworthy. In particular, we discussed security-policy enforcement and discussed the application of the semantic Web.

Part V, which described specialized semantic Webs, consisted of Chapters 22, 23, and 24. Chapter 22 showed how semantic Web technologies, in general, and trustworthy semantic Web technologies, in particular, are being applied to multiple domains including defense and intelligence, homeland security and border control, healthcare and life sciences, and finance and banking. We also gave examples of projects that are developing these technologies. Chapter 23 provided an overview of geospatial data management and the geospatial semantic Web and then discussed the security impact. In particular we have focused on our research in building secure geospatial semantic Webs. We also discussed the work on GeoRSS. Chapter 24 discussed a number of security issues for sensor data management and also gave privacy some consideration. We also discussed secure wireless information management. Much of our focus has been on access control. We then discussed the integration of semantic Web technologies with sensor and pervasive computing technologies.

As we have stressed, there are many developments in the field, and it is impossible for us to list all of them. We have provided a broad, fairly comprehensive overview of the field. The book is intended for technical managers as well as technologists who want to get a broad understanding of the field. It is also intended for students who wish to pursue research in data and applications security in general and secure semantic Webs in particular.

25.3   Revisiting the Scenario

Now that we have provided an overview of trustworthy semantic Web technologies and discussed the applications, we will discuss a motivating scenario that illustrates how trustworthy semantic Web technologies may be applied in the real world. Essentially we have taken the scenario of Chapter 4 and discussed the security impact.

Consider the scenario where four intelligence organizations (e.g., United States, United Kingdom, Australia, and Canada) have to work together to fight the global war on terror. Each organization maintains its own database of terrorists and terrorist organizations. Suppose the United Kingdom detects a suspicious activity and wants to warn its partners as well as get more information. Now, all of these organizations have to agree on common terms. Therefore, they will work with each other as well as within their countries to develop ontologies specified, possibly, in OWL. Now, one of the ontologies may be about a particular operation, and this operation may only be available to the United States and the United Kingdom. Therefore, we would need policies that do not grant access to this ontology to Canada and Australia.

As we have stated in Chapter 4, data may be represented using XML or RDF, and policies may be enforced on this data. For example, the United States may enforce a policy on its XML documents where access is granted to the United Kingdom only if the United Kingdom does not collaborate with, say, France. So the question is, how can this access be propagated? That is, if the United Kingdom has made a copy of this XML document, then can it give access to Australia? Should it enforce a policy that the document can be shared with Australia only if Australia doe not share this document with France? Another point is that the United States may share this document with the United Kingdom only if it trusts the United Kingdom not to make a copy of this document.

In some cases they may have to integrate parts of their databases so that the partners can work with the integrated database. Therefore, the United States, the United Kingdom, Australia, and Canada may form one coalition, and the United Kingdom, France, and Germany may form another coalition. This means the United Kingdom shreds certain data with the first coalition and retains other data with the second coalition. The challenge is to come up with policies that specify what data to share with whom when multiple data sources are integrated.

Organizations may make use of digital library technologies to retrieve information about prior incidents. They also make use of the knowledge they have gathered from their experts for reuse. Furthermore, the organizations will use their reasoning systems to determine whether a future terror attack will occur. An agent will act on behalf of each organization. Agents will communicate with each other using some well-defined protocols. Finally, agents will invoke Web services to carry out an operation such as data integration and information retrieval. Now, in this case, the question is, what are the policies enforced during the digital library retrieval operation? How can unauthorized inference be controlled across the organizations? That is, the United Kingdom may get some data from the United States and some other data from France and make unauthorized inferences that the United States and France have a secret pact between them. Therefore, the United States and France will have to collaborate with each other and determine the data to be released to the United States. Here again the organization may use XML to specify the policies and ontologies to specify the secret pact.

A more specific example related to coalition data sharing is the following. We assume that Alice Brown is a general in the U.S. Air Force working at the Defense Information Systems Agency (DISA), and John James is a captain at the junior level from the U.S. Army working at the Communication Electronics Command (CECOM).

```
<General credID="9" subID = "16: CIssuer = "2">
<name> Alice Brown </name>
<country> USA <country/>
<department> AF </department>
< group> DISA </ group>
</General>
<Captain credID="12" subID = "4: CIssuer = "2">
<name> John James </name>
<country> USA <country/>
<department>Army </department>
< group> CECOM </ group>
<level> Junior </level
</Captain>
```

Next we illustrate how policies may be specified in XML. In the following example, we assume the following: Policies P1 and P2 state that an Air Force general can read all the intelligence reports on Operation Iraqi Freedom (OIF) produced by the Air Force, whereas he can only read the short descriptions of the report produced by the Army. Policies P5 and P6 state that a senior captain in the Air Force department can read all the asset details in the intelligence report produced by the Air Force, whereas he can only read certain information from assets in the intelligence report produced by the army.

```
<?xml version="1.0" encoding="UTF-8"?>
<policy_base>
    <policy_spec ID='P1' cred_expr="//General[department='CS']"
target="intelligence_report.xml" path="//OIF[@Dept='AF']//
node()" priv="VIEW"/>
```

```
    <policy_spec ID='P2' cred_expr="//General[department='AF']"
target="intelligence_report.xml" path="//OIF[@Dept='ARMY']/
Short-descr/node() and //OIF[@Dept='ARMY']/authors"
priv="VIEW"/>
    <policy_spec ID='P3' cred_expr="//General[department='ARMY'] "
target="intelligence_report.xml" path="//OIF[@Dept='ARMY']//
node()" priv="VIEW"/>
    <policy_spec ID='P4' cred_expr="//General[department='ARMY']
" target="intelligence_report.xml" path="//OIF[@Dept='AF']/
Short-descr/node() and //OIF[@Dept='AF']/authors"
priv="VIEW"/>
    <policy_spec ID='P5' cred_expr="//Captain[department='AF'
and level='senior']" target="intelligence_report.xml" path="//
Asset[@Dept='AF']/node()" priv="VIEW "/>
    <policy_spec ID='P6' cred_expr="//Captain[department='AF'
and level='senior']" target="intelligence_report.xml" path="//
Asset[@Dept='ARMY']/Funds/@Type and //Asset[@Dept='ARMY']/
Funds/@Funding-Date" priv="VIEW "/>
    <policy_spec ID='P7' cred_expr="//Captain[department='ARMY'
and level='junior']" target="intelligence_report.xml" path="//
Asset[@Dept='ARMY']/node()" priv="VIEW "/>
</policy_base>
```

The above examples show how semantic Web technologies together with security technologies such as policy specification enforcement and trust negotiation may be used for data sharing. Figure 25.2 illustrates assured information sharing across the organizations.

25.4 Directions for Trustworthy Semantic Webs

There are many directions for database and applications security. We discuss some of them for each topic addressed in this book. Figure 25.3 illustrates the directions and challenges. Our vision for the semantic Web is illustrated in Figure 25.4.

Supporting technologies: To develop trustworthy semantic Webs we need to continue to make progress in the semantic Web, information security, and data, information, and knowledge management. For example, we need to develop semantic Web technologies that have powerful representation capabilities as well as reasoning power. We also need to make advances in policy enforcement and knowledge management. In addition, efficient techniques for searching and indexing multimedia data are also needed.

Secure semantic Web: We need to develop tools and techniques to ensure the security of operation of the semantic Web. We need languages to express policies as well as agents to securely carry out various activities on the Web. In addition, we need techniques for securing semantic Web technologies such as XML, RDF, and

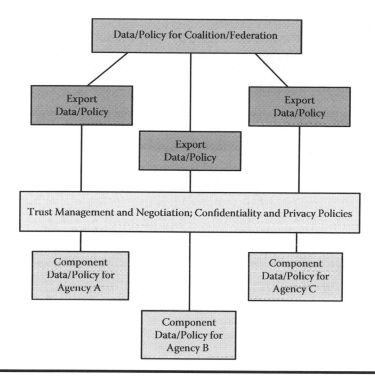

Figure 25.2   Assured information sharing.

OWL documents. We also need a better handle on the inference problem using semantic Web technologies.

Dependable semantic Web: We have assumed that dependability includes trust, privacy, and integrity. We have also included multilevel security as part of dependability. We need trust management and negotiation techniques that take advantage of semantic Web technologies. We need to examine standards such as P3P and develop appropriate technologies to enforce the various privacy policies. When agents carry out activities on the Web, we need to ensure that the data is of high quality. We need a better annotation system that manages data provenance. With respect to multilevel security, we need to ensure that agents at multiple levels communicate with each other securely.

Applications: Applications such as Web services and knowledge management make use of semantic Web technologies. However, much of the work here is preliminary. We need to better integrate the semantic Web technologies with data, information, and knowledge management as well as digital libraries management, integrating heterogeneous data sources, as well as E-business operations.

Specialized domains: Much of the developments on semantic Web technologies focus on textual data. We need to develop specialized semantic Webs for other

Supporting Technologies:	Secure Semantic Web	Dependable Semantic Web
Novel Data, Information and Knowledge Management Techniques for Emerging Applications, New Security Paradigms, Semantic Web Technologies	New Models and Mechanisms for Securing XML, RDF, Ontologies and Rules; Reasoning Engines	New Models and Techniques for Trust Management and Negotiation, Privacy Management, Multilevel Security, and Policy Management

Applications	Specialized domains
Novel Ways for Applications Such as Web Services and Information Integration to Make Use of Semantic Web Technologies	Semantic Webs for Domains such as Medical, Security and Finance; Novel Technologies for Geospatial and Sensor Semantic Webs

Figure 25.3 Directions and challenges in trustworthy semantic Webs.

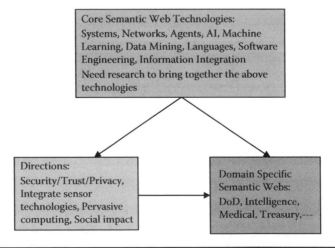

Figure 25.4 Vision for the semantic Web.

types of data such as geospatial and sensor streams. We also need to develop semantic Webs to manage multimedia data. In addition, we need better domain-specific semantic Webs for applications such as healthcare, finance, and security, among others.

25.5 Where Do We Go from Here?

This book has discussed a great deal about trustworthy semantic Webs. We have stated the many challenges in this field in Section 25.4. We need to continue with research and development efforts if we are to make progress in this very important area.

Where do we go from here? First of all, those who wish to work in this area must have a good knowledge of the supporting technologies including semantic Webs, information security, and data, information, and knowledge management. For example, it is important to understand the technologies that comprise the semantic Web and how they are used. Furthermore, one also needs to understand the various information-retrieval and query-management strategies as well as knowledge-management techniques. Next, because the field is expanding rapidly and there are many developments in the field, the reader has to keep up with the developments including reading about the standards and commercial products. We also encourage the reader to work on the exercises we have given in this book. Finally, we encourage the reader to experiment with the products and also develop security tools. This is the best way to become familiar with a particular field; that is, work on hands-on problems and provide solutions to get a better understanding. Although we have not given any implementation exercises in this book, our design problems could be extended to include implementation. The Web will continue to have a major impact on securing these semantic Webs as well as the secure integration of heterogeneous data sources. Ontologism will be critical for many of the developments. In addition, we believe that XML and RDF will continue to evolve for various domains. Therefore, it is important to keep up with all these developments. Furthermore, one cannot overemphasize the importance of Web security for securing the semantic Web.

We need research and development support from the federal and local government funding agencies such as the National Security Agency; the U.S. Army, Navy, Air Force, and the Defense Advanced Research Projects Agency; and funding research in semantic Web technologies as well as in assured information sharing. It is important to continue with this funding and also focus on interacting security with this semantic Web. The Cyber Trust Theme at the National Science Foundation is an excellent initiative to support some fundamental research in securing the semantic Web. We also need commercial corporations to invest research and development dollars so that progress can be made in industrial research as well as to transfer the research to commercial products. We also need to collaborate with the international research community to solve problems and promote standards that are not only of national interest, but also of international interest.

Bibliography

Information Security

Anderson, R., *Security Engineering: A Guide to Building Dependable Distributed Systems*, John Wiley & Sons, New York, 2001.

Bishop, M., *Computer Security: Art and Science*, Addison-Wesley, Reading, MA, 2002.

Castano, S. et al., *Database Security*, Addison-Wesley, Reading, MA, 1995.

Denning, D., *Cryptography and Data Security*, Addison-Wesley, Reading, MA, 1982.

Fernandez, E. et al., *Database Security and Integrity*, Addison-Wesley, Reading, MA, 1981.

Gasser, M., *Building a Secure Computer System*, Van Nostrand Reinhold, New York, 1988.

Ghosh, A., *E-Commerce Security, Weak Links and Strong Defenses*, John Wiley & Sons, New York, 1998.

Hassler, V., *Security Fundamentals for E-Commerce*, Artech House, London, UK, 2000.

Thuraisingham, B., *Database and Applications Security*, CRC Press, Boca Raton, FL, 2005.

Data Management

Bernstein, P. et al., *Concurrency Control and Recovery in Database Systems*, Addison-Wesley, Reading, MA, 1987.

Berry, M. and Linoff, G., *Data Mining Techniques for Marketing, Sales, and Customer Support*, John Wiley & Sons, New York, 1997.

Cattel, R., *Object Data Management Systems*, Addison-Wesley, Reading, MA, 1991.

Ceri, S. and Pelagatti, G., *Distributed Databases, Principles and Systems,* McGraw-Hill, New York, 1984.

Date, C., *An Introduction to Database Systems*, Addison-Wesley, Reading, MA, 1990.

Frost, R., *On Knowledge Base Management Systems*, Collins, London, UK, 1986.

Inmon, W., *Building the Data Warehouse*, John Wiley & Sons, New York, 1993.

Korth, H. and Silberschatz, A., *Database System Concepts*, McGraw Hill, New York, 1986.

Lloyd, J., *Foundations of Logic Programming*, Springer-Verlag, Heidelberg, 1987.

Maier, D., *Theory of Relational Databases*, Computer Science Press, Rockville, MD, 1983.

Prabhakaran, B., *Multimedia Database Systems*, Kluwer, Norwell, MA, 1997.

Thuraisingham, B., *Data Management Systems Evolution and Interoperation*, CRC Press, Boca Raton, FL, 1997.

Thuraisingham, B., *Data Mining: Technologies, Techniques, Tools and Trends*, CRC Press, Boca Raton, FL, 1998.

Thuraisingham, B., *Web Data Management and Electronic Commerce*, CRC Press, Boca Raton, FL, 2000.

Thuraisingham, B., *Managing and Mining Multimedia Databases for the Electronic Enterprise*, CRC Press, Boca Raton, FL, 2001.

Thuraisingham, B., *Web Data Mining Technologies and Their Applications in Business Intelligence and Counter-terrorism*, CRC Press, Boca Raton, FL, 2003.

Tsichritzis, D. and Lochovsky, F., *Data Models*, Prentice Hall, Upper Saddle River, NJ, 1982.

Ullman, J.D., *Principles of Database and Knowledge Base Management Systems, Volumes I and II*, Computer Science Press, Rockville, MD, 1988.

Semantic Web

Antoniou, G. and van Harmelan, F., *A Semantic Web Primer,* MIT Press, Cambridge, MA, 2003.

Lee, T. B., *Weaving the Web*, Harper Collins, San Francsico, 1999.

St. Laurent, S., *XML: A Primer*, Power Books Publishing, London, UK, 2000.

Thuraisingham, B., *XML, Databases and The Semantic Web*, CRC Press, Boca Raton, FL, 2002.

Appendix A

Data Management Systems: Developments and Trends

A.1   Overview

In this appendix we provide an overview of the developments and trends in data management as discussed in our previous book *Data Management Systems Evolution and Interoperation* [THUR97]. Because database systems are an aspect of data management, and database security is an aspect of database systems, we need a good understanding of data management issues for data and applications security.

As stated in Chapter 1, recent developments in information-systems technologies have resulted in computerizing many applications in various business areas. Data have become a critical resource in many organizations, and therefore efficient access to data, sharing the data, extracting information from the data, and making use of the information have become urgent needs. As a result, there have been several efforts on integrating various data sources scattered across several sites. These data sources may be databases managed by database-management systems, or they could simply be files. To provide the interoperability between the multiple data sources and systems, various tools are being developed. These tools enable users of one system to access other systems in an efficient and transparent manner.

We define data-management systems to be systems that manage the data, extract meaningful information from the data, and make use of the information extracted. Therefore, data-management systems include database systems, data warehouses, and data-mining systems. Data could be structured data such as that found in relational databases, or it could be unstructured such as text, voice, imagery, and video. There have been numerous discussions in the past to distinguish between data, information, and knowledge. We do not attempt to clarify these terms. For our purposes, data could be just bits and bytes, or it could convey some meaningful information to the user. We will, however, distinguish between database systems and database-management systems. A database-management system is that component which manages the database containing persistent data. A database system consists of both the database and the database-management system.

A key component to the evolution and interoperation of data-management systems is the interoperability of heterogeneous database systems. Efforts on the interoperability between database systems have been reported since the late 1970s. However, it is only recently that we are seeing commercial developments in heterogeneous database systems. Major database-system vendors are now providing interoperability between their products and other systems. Furthermore, many of the database-system vendors are migrating toward an architecture called the client-server architecture, which facilitates distributed data-management capabilities. In addition to efforts on the interoperability between different database systems and client-server environments, work is also directed toward handling autonomous and federated environments.

The organization of this appendix is as follows. Because database systems are a key component of data-management systems, we first provide an overview of the developments in database systems. These developments are discussed in Section A.2. Then we provide a vision for data-management systems in Section A.3. Our framework for data-management systems is discussed in Section A.4. Note that data mining and warehousing as well as Web data management are components of this framework. Building information systems from our framework with special instantiations is discussed in Section A.5. The relationship between the various texts that we have written (or are writing) for Taylor & Francis is discussed in Section A.6. This appendix is summarized in Section A.7. References are given at the end of the appendix.

A.2   Developments in Database Systems

Figure A.1 provides an overview of the developments in database-systems technology. Whereas the early work in the 1960s focused on developing products based on the network and hierarchical data models, much of the developments in database systems took place after the seminal paper by Codd describing the relational model [CODD70] (see also Reference [DATE90]). Research and development

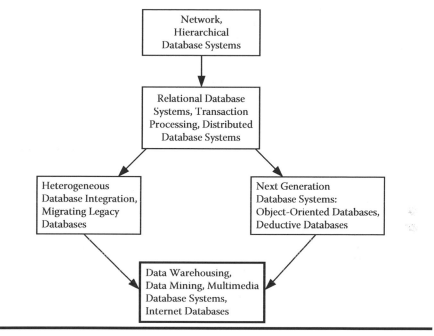

Figure A.1   Developments in database systems technology.

work on relational database systems was carried out during the early 1970s, and several prototypes were developed throughout the 1970s. Notable efforts include International Business Machine Corporation's (IBM)System R, and the University of California at Berkeley's INGRES. During the 1980s, many relational database-system products were being marketed (notable among these products are those of Oracle Corporation, Sybase Inc., Informix Corporation, INGRES Corporation, IBM, Digital Equipment Corporation, and Hewlett Packard Company). During the 1990s, products from other vendors emerged (e.g., Microsoft Corporation). In fact, to date numerous relational database-system products have been marketed. However, Codd has stated that many of the systems that are being marketed as relational systems are not really relational (see, for example, the discussion in Reference [DATE90]). He then discussed various criteria that a system must satisfy to be qualified as a relational database system. Although the early work focused on issues such as data model, normalization theory, query processing and optimization strategies, query languages, and access strategies and indexes, later the focus shifted toward supporting a multiuser environment. In particular, concurrency control and recovery techniques were developed. Support for transaction processing was also provided.

Research on relational database systems as well as on transaction management was followed by research on distributed database systems around the mid-1970s. Several distributed database-system, prototype development efforts also began around the late 1970s. Notable among these efforts include IBM's System R*, Distributed Database Testbed System (DDTS) by Honeywell Inc., SDD-I and Multibase by Computer Corporation of America (CCA), and Mermaid by System Development Corporation (SDC). Furthermore, many of these systems (e.g., DDTS, Multibase, Mermaid) function in a heterogeneous environment. During the early 1990s several database-system vendors (such as Oracle Corporation, Sybase Inc., Informix Corporation) provided data-distribution capabilities for their systems. Most of the distributed relational database-system products are based on client-server architectures. The idea is to have the client of Vendor A communicate with the server database system of Vendor B. In other words, the client-server computing paradigm facilitates a heterogeneous computing environment. Interoperability between relational and nonrelational commercial database systems is also possible. The database-systems community is also involved in standardization efforts. Notable among the standardization efforts are the ANSI/SPARC 3-level schema architecture, the Information Resource Dictionary System (IRDS) standard for Data Dictionary Systems, the relational query language Structured Query Language (SQL), and the Remote Database Access (RDA) protocol for remote database access.

According to the Lagunita report published as a result of a National Science Foundation (NSF) workshop in 1990 (see Reference [NSF90] and Reference [SIGM90]), relational database systems, transaction processing, and distributed (relational) database systems are stated as mature technologies. Furthermore, vendors are marketing object-oriented database systems and demonstrating the interoperability between different database systems. The report goes on to state that as applications are getting increasingly complex, more sophisticated database systems are needed. Furthermore, because many organizations now use database systems, in many cases of different types, the database systems need to be integrated. Although work has begun to address these issues and commercial products are available, several issues still need to be resolved. Therefore, challenges faced by the database-systems researchers in the early 1990s were in two areas. One was next-generation database systems, and the other was heterogeneous database systems.

Next-generation database systems include object-oriented database systems, functional database systems, special parallel architectures to enhance the perfor-

Another significant development in database technology is the advent of object-oriented database-management systems. Active work on developing such systems began in the mid-1980s, and they are now commercially available (notable among them include the products of Object Design Inc., Ontos Inc., Gemstone Systems Inc., and Versant Object Technology). It was felt that new-generation applications such as multimedia, office information systems, CAD/CAM, process control, and software engineering have different requirements. Such applications utilize complex data structures. Tighter integration between the programming language and the data model is also desired. Object-oriented database systems satisfy most of the requirements of these new-generation applications [CATT91].

mance of database system functions, high-performance database systems, real-time database systems, scientific database systems, temporal database systems, database systems that handle incomplete and uncertain information, and intelligent database systems (also sometimes called logic or deductive database systems). Ideally, a database system should provide the support for high-performance transaction processing, model complex applications, represent new kinds of data, and make intelligent deductions. Although significant progress was made during the late 1980s and early 1990s, there is much to be done before such a database system can be developed.

Heterogeneous database systems have been receiving considerable attention during the past decade [ACM90]. The major issues include handling different data models, different query-processing strategies, different transaction-processing algorithms, and different query languages. Should a uniform view be provided to the entire system, or should the users of the individual systems maintain their own views of the entire system? These are questions that have yet to be answered satisfactorily. It is also envisaged that a complete solution to heterogeneous database-management systems is a generation away. Although research should be directed toward finding such a solution, work should also be carried out to handle limited forms of heterogeneity to satisfy customer needs. Another type of database system that has received some attention lately is a federated database system. Note that some have used the terms heterogeneous database system and federated database system interchangeably. Although heterogeneous database systems can be part of a federation, a federation can also include homogeneous database systems.

The explosion of users on the Web as well as developments in interface technologies has resulted in even more challenges for data-management researchers. A second workshop was sponsored by the NSF in 1995, and several emerging technologies were identified to be important as we go into the 21st century [NSF95]. These include digital libraries, managing very large databases, data-administration issues, multimedia databases, data warehousing, data mining, data management for collaborative computing environments, and security and privacy. Another significant development in the 1990s was the development of object-relational systems. Such systems combine the advantages of both object-oriented database systems and relational database systems. Also, many corporations are now focusing on integrating their data-management products with Web technologies. Finally, for many organizations there is an increasing need to migrate some of the legacy databases and applications to newer architectures and systems such as client-server architectures and relational database systems. We believe there is no end to data-management systems. As new technologies are developed, there are new opportunities for data-management research and development.

A comprehensive view of all data-management technologies is illustrated in Figure A.2. As shown, traditional technologies include database design, transaction processing, and benchmarking. Then there are database systems based on data models such as relational and object-oriented models. Database systems may depend

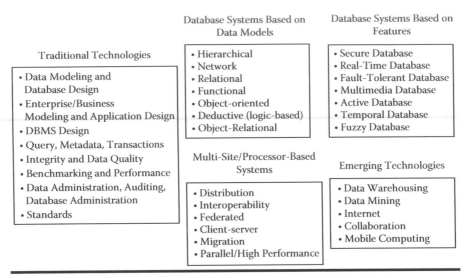

Figure A.2 Comprehensive view of data-management systems.

on features they provide such as security and real time. These database systems may be relational or object-oriented. There are also database systems based on multiple sites or processors such as distributed and heterogeneous database systems, parallel systems, and systems being migrated. Finally, there are the emerging technologies such as data warehousing and mining, collaboration, and the Web. Any comprehensive text on data-management systems should address all these technologies. We have selected some of the relevant technologies and put them in a framework. This framework is described in Section A.5.

A.3 Status, Vision, and Issues

Significant progress has been made on data-management systems. However, many of the technologies are still stand-alone technologies, as illustrated in Figure A.3. For example, multimedia systems have yet to be successfully integrated with warehousing and mining technologies. The ultimate goal is to integrate multiple technologies so that accurate data, as well as information, is produced at the right time and distributed to the user in a timely manner. Our vision for data and information management is illustrated in Figure A.4.

The work discussed by Thuraisingham [THUR97] addressed many of the challenges necessary to accomplish this vision. In particular, integration of heterogeneous databases, as well as the use of distributed object technology for interoperability, was discussed. Although much progress has been made on the system aspects of interoperability, semantic issues still remain a challenge. Different databases have

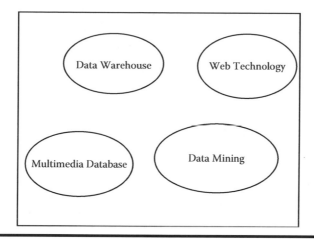

Figure A.3 Stand-alone systems.

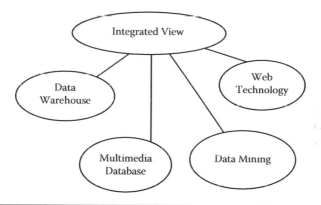

Figure A.4 Vision.

different representations. Furthermore, the same data entity may be interpreted differently at different sites. Addressing these semantic differences and extracting useful information from the heterogeneous and possibly multimedia data sources are major challenges. This book has attempted to address some of the challenges through the use of data mining.

A.4 Data Management Systems Framework

For the successful development of evolving interoperable data-management systems, integration of heterogeneous database systems is a major component. However, there are other technologies that have to be successfully integrated with each other to develop techniques for efficient access and sharing of data as well as for the extraction of information from the data. To facilitate the development of data-management systems to meet the requirements of various applications in medical, financial, manufacturing, and military fields, we have proposed a framework, which can be regarded as a reference model, for data-management systems. Various components from this framework have to be integrated to develop data-management systems to support the various applications.

Figure A.5 illustrates our framework, which can be regarded as a model, for data-management systems. This framework consists of three layers. One can think of the component technologies, which we will also refer to as components, belonging to a particular layer to be more or less built on the technologies provided by the lower layer. Layer I is the Database Technology and Distribution Layer. This layer

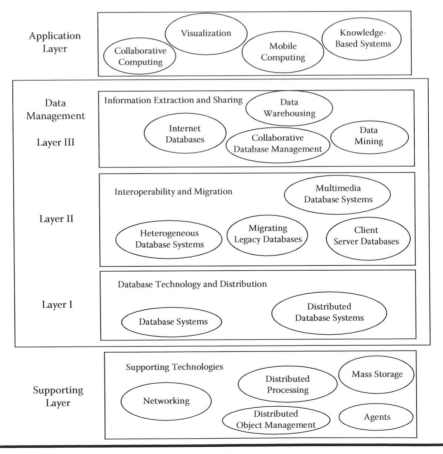

Figure A.5   Data management systems framework.

consists of database systems and distributed database-systems technologies. Layer II is the Interoperability and Migration Layer. This layer consists of technologies such as heterogeneous database integration, client-server databases, and multimedia database systems to handle heterogeneous data types, and migrating legacy databases. Layer III is the Information Extraction and Sharing Layer. This layer essentially consists of technologies for some of the newer services supported by data-management systems. These include data warehousing, data mining [THUR98], Web databases, and database support for collaborative applications. Data-management systems may utilize lower-level technologies such as networking, distributed processing, and mass storage. We have grouped these technologies into a layer called the Supporting Technologies Layer. This supporting layer does not belong to the data-management systems framework. This supporting layer also consists of some higher-level technologies such as distributed object management and agents. Also shown in Figure A.5 is the Application Technologies Layer. Systems such as collaborative computing systems and knowledge-based systems that belong to the Application Technologies Layer may utilize data-management systems. Note that the Application Technologies Layer is also outside the data-management systems framework.

The technologies that constitute the data-management systems framework can be regarded as some of the core technologies in data management. However, features like security, integrity, real-time processing, fault tolerance, and high-performance computing are needed for many applications utilizing data-management technologies. Applications utilizing data-management technologies may be medical, financial, or military, among others. We illustrate this in Figure A.6, where a three-dimensional view relating data-management technologies with features and

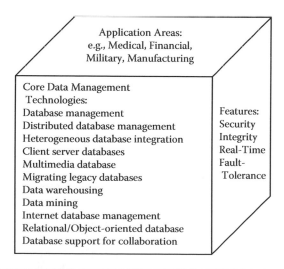

Figure A.6   A three-dimensional view of data management.

applications is given. For example, one could develop a secure distributed database-management system for medical applications or a fault-tolerant multimedia database-management system for financial applications.

Integrating the components belonging to the various layers is important to developing efficient data-management systems. In addition, data-management technologies have to be integrated with the application technologies to develop successful information systems. However, at present, there is limited integration between these various components. Our previous book, *Data Management Systems Evolution and Interoperation,* focused mainly on the concepts, developments, and trends belonging to each of the components shown in the framework. Furthermore, our current book on Web data management, which we also refer to as Web data management, focuses on the Web database component of Layer III of the framework of Figure A.5.

Note that security cuts across all the layers. Security is needed for the supporting layers such as agents and distributed systems. Security is needed for all of the layers in the framework including database security, distributed database security, warehousing security, Web database security, and collaborative data-management security. This is the topic of this book. We have covered all aspects of data and applications security including database security and information-management security.

A.5 Building Information Systems from the Framework

Figure A.5 illustrated a framework for data-management systems. As shown in that figure, the technologies for data management include database systems, distributed database systems, heterogeneous database systems, migrating legacy databases, multimedia database systems, data warehousing, data mining, Web databases, and database support for collaboration. Furthermore, data-management systems take advantage of supporting technologies such as distributed processing and agents. Similarly, application technologies such as collaborative computing, visualization, expert systems, and mobile computing take advantage of data-management systems.

Many of us have heard of the term information systems on numerous occasions. These systems have sometimes been used interchangeably with data-management systems. In our terminology, information systems are much broader than data-management systems, but they do include data-management systems. In fact, a framework for information systems will include not only the data-management system layers, but also the supporting technologies layer as well as the application technologies layer; that is, information systems encompass all kinds of computing systems. It can be regarded as the finished product that can be used for various applications;

that is, although hardware is at the lowest end of the spectrum, applications are at the highest end.

We can combine the technologies of Figure A.5 to put together information systems. For example, at the application technology level, one may need collaboration and visualization technologies so that analysts can collaboratively carry out some tasks. At the data-management level, one may need both multimedia and distributed database technologies. At the supporting level, one may need mass storage as well as some distributed processing capability. This special framework is illustrated in Figure A.7. Another example is a special framework for interoperability. One may need some visualization technology to display the integrated information from the heterogeneous databases. At the data-management level, we have heterogeneous database-systems technology. At the supporting technology level, one may use distributed object-management technology to encapsulate the heterogeneous databases. This special framework is illustrated in Figure A.8.

Finally, let us illustrate the concepts that we have described above by using a specific example. Suppose a group of physicians and surgeons wants a system where they can collaborate and make decisions about various patients. This could be a medical videoteleconferencing application, that is, at the highest level, the application is a medical application and, more specifically, a medical videoteleconferencing application. At the application technology level, one needs a variety of technologies including collaboration and teleconferencing. These application technologies will make use of data-management technologies such as distributed database systems and multimedia database systems, that is, one may need to support multimedia data such as audio and video. The data-management technologies in turn draw on lower-level technologies such as distributed processing and networking. We illustrate this in Figure A.9.

Collaboration,
Visualization

Multimedia Database,
Distributed Database Systems

Mass Storage,
Distributed Processing

Figure A.7   Framework for multimedia data management for collaboration.

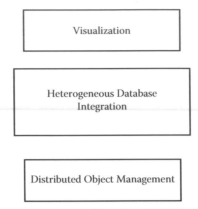

Figure A.8 Framework for heterogeneous database interoperability.

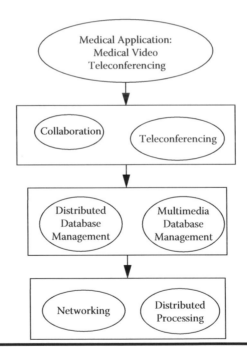

Figure A.9 Specific example.

In summary, information systems include data-management systems as well as application-layer systems such as collaborative computing systems and supporting-layer systems such as distributed object-management systems.

Although application technologies make use of data-management technologies, and data-management technologies make use of supporting technologies, the

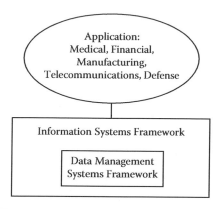

Figure A.10   Application-framework relationship.

ultimate user of the information system is the application itself. Today numerous applications make use of information systems. These applications are from multiple domains such as medical, financial, manufacturing, telecommunications, and defense. Specific applications include signal processing, electronic commerce, patient monitoring, and situation assessment. Figure A.10 illustrates the relationship between the application and the information system.

A.6   Relationship between the Texts

We have published seven books on data management and mining and currently are writing one more. These books are *Data Management Systems Evolution and Interoperation* [THUR97], *Data Mining Technologies, Techniques, Tools and Trends* [THUR98], *Web Data Management and Electronic Commerce* [THUR00], *Managing and Mining Multimedia Databases for the Electronic Enterprise* [THUR01], *XML, Databases and the Semantic Web* [THUR02], *Web Data Mining Technologies and Their Applications in Business Intelligence and Counter-terrorism* [THUR03], and *Database and Applications Security: Integrating Data Management and Information Security* [THUR05]. Our current book has evolved from Chapter 25 of our seventh book [THUR05]. All these books have evolved from the framework that we illustrated in this appendix and address different parts of the framework. The connection between these texts is illustrated in Figure A.11.

Note that security was addressed in all of our previous books. For example, we discussed security for multimedia systems in *Managing and Mining Multimedia Databases for the Electronic Enterprise* [THUR01]. Security and data mining was discussed in *Data Mining Technologies, Techniques, Tools and Trends* [THUR98]. Secure data interoperability was discussed in *Data Management Systems Evolu-*

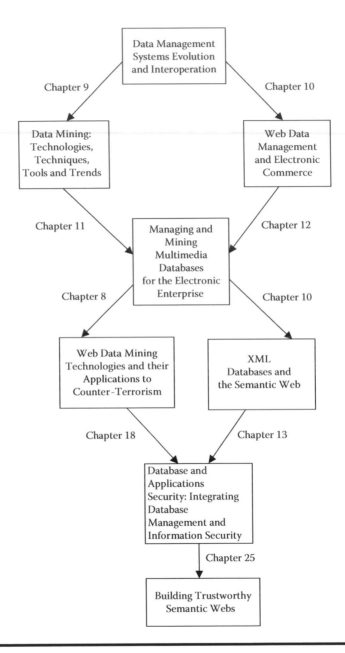

Figure A.11   Relationship among texts.

tion and Interoperation [THUR97]. Essentially our latest book integrates all the concepts in security discussed in our previous books. In addition, we have also addressed many more topics in *Database and Applications Security* [THUR05].

A.7   Summary and Directions

In this appendix we have provided an overview of data management. We first discussed the developments in data management and then provided a vision for data management. Then we illustrated a framework for data management. This framework consists of three layers: a database systems layer, an interoperability layer, and an information extraction layer. Web data management belongs to Layer III. Finally, we showed how information systems could be built from the technologies of the framework.

Let us repeat what we mentioned in Chapter 1 now that we have described the data-management framework we introduced in *Data Management Systems Evolution and Interoperation* [THUR97]. The chapters in that book discuss security which cuts across all the layers. Many of the technologies discussed in the framework of Figure A.5 need security. These include database systems, distributed database systems, data warehousing, and data mining.

We believe that data management is essential to many information technologies including data mining, multimedia information processing, interoperability, and collaboration and knowledge management. This appendix stresses data management. Security is critical for all data-management technologies.

References

[CATT91] Cattell, R., *Object Data Management Systems*, Addison-Wesley, Reading, MA, 1991.

[CODD70] Codd, E.F., A relational model of data for large shared data banks, *Commn. ACM*, 13(6), June 1970.

[DATE90] Date, C.J., *An Introduction to Database Management Systems*, 6th ed., Addison-Wesley, Reading, MA, 1995.

[NSF90] *Proc. Database Systems Workshop*, Report published by the National Science Foundation, 1990 (also in *ACM SIGMOD Record*, December 1990).

[NSF95] *Proc. Database Systems Workshop*, Report published by the National Science Foundation, 1995 (also in *ACM SIGMOD Record*, March 1996).

[SIGM90] Next generation database systems, *ACM SIGMOD Record*, December 1990.

[ACM90] Special issue on heterogeneous database systems, *ACM Comput. Surveys*, September 1990.

[THUR97] Thuraisingham, B., *Data Management Systems Evolution and Interoperation*, CRC Press, Boca Raton, FL, 1997.

[THUR98] Thuraisingham, B., *Data Mining: Technologies, Techniques, Tools and Trends*, CRC Press, Boca Raton, FL, 1998.

[THUR00] Thuraisingham, B., *Web Data Management and Electronic Commerce*, CRC Press, Boca Raton, FL, 2000.

[THUR01] Thuraisingham, B., *Managing and Mining Multimedia Databases for the Electronic Enterprise*, CRC Press, Boca Raton, FL, 2001.

[THUR02] Thuraisingham, B., *XML, Databases and the Semantic Web*, CRC Press, Boca Raton, FL, 2002.

[THUR03] Thuraisingham, B., *Web Data Mining Technologies and Their Applications in Business Intelligence and Counter-terrorism*, CRC Press, Boca Raton, FL, 2003.

[THUR05] Thuraisingham, B., *Database and Applications Security: Integrating Data Management and Information Security*, CRC Press, Boca Raton, FL, 2005.

Appendix B

Secure Data Management

B.1   Overview

Before one designs a secure system, the first question that must be answered is, what is the security policy to be enforced by the system? A security policy is essentially a set of rules that enforce security. Security policies include mandatory security policies and discretionary security policies. Mandatory security policies are the policies that are "mandatory" in nature and should not be bypassed. Discretionary security policies are policies that are specified by the administrator or anyone who is responsible for the environment in which the system will operate. Because much of this book has focused on discretionary security, we will focus only on discretionary security for data management in this appendix.

The most popular discretionary security policy is the access-control policy. Access-control policies were studied for operating systems back in the 1960s and then for database systems in the 1970s. The two prominent database systems, System R and INGRES, were two of the first to investigate access control for database systems (see Reference [GRIF76] and Reference [STON74]). Since then, several variations of access-control policies have been reported. Other discretionary policies include administration policies. We also discuss identification and authentication under discretionary policies.

By policy enforcement, we mean the mechanisms to enforce the policies. For example, back in the 1970s, the relational database-system products such as System R and INGRES developed techniques such as the query-modification mechanisms for policy enforcement (see, for example, [GRIF76] and [STON74]). The query language Structured Query Language (SQL) has been extended to specify security policies and access-control rules. More recently languages such as eXtensible Markup Language (XML) and Resource Description Framework (RDF) have been extended to specify security policies (see, for example, Reference [BERT02] and Reference [CARM04]).

The organization of this appendix is as follows. In Section B.2 we provide an overview of access-control policies. Other types of policies are discussed in Section B.3. Policy enforcement is discussed in Section B.4. The appendix is concluded in Section B.5. For more details we refer the reader to [FERR00].

B.2   Access Control Policies

B.2.1   Overview

As stated in the previous section, access-control policies were first examined for operating systems. The essential question here is, can a process be granted access to a file? Access could be read access or write access. Write access could include access to modify, append, or delete. These principles were transferred to database systems such as Ingres and System R. Since then, various forms of access-control policies have been studied. Notable among those are the role-based access control policies that are now implemented in several commercial systems. Note that access-control policies also include mandatory policies. Such policies are discussed in Part III. In this section we discuss only discretionary access-control policies.

The organization of this section is as follows. In Section B.2.2 we provide an overview of authorization-based access-control policies. These are the most common form of policies studied. Then in Section B.2.3 we discuss role-based access-control policies. Many commercial products are now implementing role-based access control. Such policies are also being enforced for a variety of applications including knowledge management and collaboration. Figure B.1 illustrates the various access-control policies.

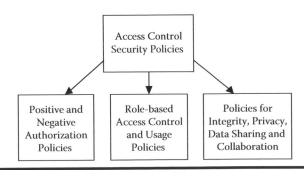

Figure B.1   Access control security policies.

B.2.2 Authorization Policies

Many of the access-control policies are based on authorization policies. Essentially what this means is that users are granted access to data based on authorization rules. In this section we will discuss various types of authority rules. Note that in the appendix to the book by Ferrari and Thuraisingham [FERR00], a detailed discussion of authorization policies is discussed.

- **Positive authorizations:** Early systems focused on what is now called positive authorization rules. Here user John is granted access to relation EMP (employee), or user Jane is granted access to relation DEPT (department). These are access-control rules on relations. One can also grant access to other entities such as attributes and "-tuples", or set of elements. For example, John has read access to attribute salary and write access to attribute name in relation EMP. Write access could include append, modify, or delete access.

- **Negative authorization:** The question is, if John's access to an object is not specified, does this mean John does not have access to that object? In some systems any authorization rule that is not specified is implicitly taken to be a negative authorization, whereas in other systems negative authorizations are explicitly specified. For example, we could enforce rules such as John does not have access to relation EMP or Jane does not have access to relation DEPT.

- **Conflict resolutions:** When we have rules that are conflicting, how do we resolve the conflicts? For example, we could have a rule that grants John read access to relation EMP. However, we can also have a rule that does not grant John read access to the salary attribute in EMP. This is a conflict. Usually a system enforces the least privilege rule, in which case John has access to EMP except for the salary values.

- **Strong and weak authorization:** Systems also enforce strong and weak authorizations. In the case of strong authorization, the rule holds regardless of conflicts. In the case of weak authorizations, the rule does not hold in case of conflict. For example, if John is granted access to EMP and it is a strong authorization rule and the rule where John is not granted access to salary attribute is a weak authorization, there is a conflict. This means the strong authorization will hold.

- **Propagation of authorization rules:** The question here is, how do the rules get propagated? For example, if John has read access to relation EMP, then does it automatically mean that John has read access to every element in EMP? Usually this is the case unless we have a rule that prohibits automatic propagation of an authorization rule. If we have a rule prohibiting the automatic propagation of a rule, then we must explicitly enforce authorization rules that specify the objects to which John has access.

■ **Special rules:** In our work on mandatory policies, we have explored extensively the enforcement of content- and context-based constraints. Note that security constraints are essentially the security rules. Content- and context-based rules are rules where access is granted depending on the content of the data or the context in which the data is displayed. Such rules can be enforced for discretionary security also. For example, in the case of content-based constraints, John has read access to "-tuples" only in DEPT D100. In the case of context- or association-based constraints, John does not have read access to names and salaries taken together; however, he can have access to individual names and salaries. In the case of event-based constraints, after the election, John has access to all elements in relation EMP.

■ **Consistency and completeness of rules:** One of the challenges here is ensuring the consistency and completeness of constraints; that is, if the constraints or rules are inconsistent, then do we have conflict resolution rules that will resolve the conflicts? How can we ensure that all the entities (such as attributes, relations, elements, etc.) are specified in access-control rules for a user? Essentially what this means is, are the rules complete? If not, what assumptions do we make about entities that do not have either positive or negative authorizations specified on them for a particular user or class of users?

We have discussed some essential points with respect to authorization rules. Some examples are given in Figure B.2. In the next section we will discuss a very popular access-control policy called role-based access control, which is now implemented in commercial systems.

B.2.3 Role-Based Access Control

Role-based access control (RBAC) has become one of the more popular access-control methods (see Reference [SAND96]). This method has been implemented in commercial systems including Trusted Oracle. The idea here is to grant access to users depending on their roles and functions.

---

* John has read access to employee
  relation
* John does not have write access to
  department relation
* Jane has read access to name values
  in employee relation
* Jane does not have read access to
  department relation

Figure B.2   Authorization rules.

The essential idea behind RBAC is as follows. Users need access to data depending on their roles. For example, a president may have access to information about his or her vice presidents and the members of the board, whereas the chief financial officer may have access to the financial information and information on those who report to him. A director may have access to information about those working in his division, whereas the human resources director will have information on personal data about the employees of the corporation. Essentially RBAC is a type of authorization policy that depends on the user role and the activities that go with the role.

Various research efforts on role hierarchies have been discussed in the literature. There is also a conference series called *Symposium on Access Control Models and Technologies* (SACMAT) that evolved from RBAC research efforts. For example, how does access get propagated? Can one role subsume another? Consider the role hierarchy illustrated in Figure B.3. If we grant access to a node in the hierarchy, does the access propagate upward? If a department manager has access to certain project information, does that access get propagated to the parent node, which is a director node? If a section leader has access to employee information in his or her section, does the access propagate to the department manager who is the parent in the role hierarchy? What happens to the child nodes? Does access propagate downward? For example, if a department manager has access to certain information, then do his subordinates have access to that information? Are there cases where the subordinates have access to data that the department manager does not have? What happens if an employee has to report to two supervisors, one his department manager and the other his project manager? What happens when the department

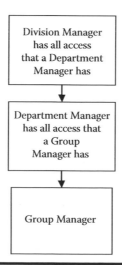

Figure B.3   Role hierarchy.

manager is working on a project and has to report to his project leader who also works for him?

RBAC has been examined for relational systems, object systems, distributed systems, and now some of the emerging technologies such as data warehouses, knowledge-management systems, semantic Web, E-commerce systems, and digital libraries. Furthermore, object models have been used to represent roles and activities (see, for example, *Proceedings of the IFIP Database Security Conference Series*). This is an area that will continue to be discussed, and the *ACM SACMAT* is a venue for publishing high-quality papers on this topic.

More recently Sandhu et al. [SAND96] have developed yet another access-control-like model, and that is the Usage Control Model, which he refers to as UCON (see, for example, the work reported by Park and Sandhu [PARK04]). The UCON model attempts to integrate three policies: trust management, access control, and rights management. The idea is to provide control on the usage of objects. Although the ideas are somewhat preliminary, this model shows a lot of promise.

B.3   Other Policies

B.3.1   Administration Policies

Although access-control policies specify access that specific users have to the data, administration policies specify who is to administer the data. Administration duties would include keeping the data current, making sure the metadata is updated whenever the data is updated, and ensuring recovery from failures and related activities.

Typically the database administrator (DBA) is responsible for updating, say, the metadata, the index, and access methods, and also ensuring that the access-control rules are properly enforced. The System Security Officer (SSO) may also have a role, that is, the DBA and SSO may share the duties between them. The security-related issues might be the responsibility of the SSO, whereas the data-related issues might be the responsibility of the DBA. Some other administration policies being considered include assigning caretakers. Usually owners have control of the data that they create and may manage the data for its duration. In some cases, owners may not be available to manage the data, in which case they may assign caretakers.

Administration policies get more complicated in distributed environments, especially in a Web environment. For example, in Web environments, there may be multiple parties involved in distributing documents including the owner, the publisher, and the users requesting the data. Who owns the data? Is it the owner or the publisher? Once the data has left the owner and arrived at the publisher, does the publisher take control of the data?

There are many interesting questions that need to be answered as we migrate from a relational database environment to a distributed and perhaps a Web environment. These also include managing copyright issues, data quality, data provenance, and governance. Many interesting papers have appeared in recent conferences on administration policies. Figure B.4 illustrates various administrations policies.

B.3.2 Identification and Authentication

For the sake of completion, we discuss identification (ID) and authentication as part of our discussion on discretionary security. By ID we mean users must identify themselves with their user ID and password. Authentication means the system must then match the user ID with the password to ensure that this is indeed the person he or she is purporting to be. A user may also have multiple identities depending on his or her roles. Identity management is receiving a lot of attention lately (see Reference [BERT04]).

Numerous problems have been reported with the password-based scheme. One is that hackers can break into the system and get the passwords of users and then masquerade as a user. In a centralized system, the problems are not as complicated as in a distributed environment. Now, with the World Wide Web and E-commerce applications, financial organizations are losing billions of dollars when hackers masquerade as legitimate users.

More recently biometrics techniques are being applied. These include face-recognition and voice-recognition techniques to authenticate the user. These techniques are showing a lot of promise and are already being used. We can expect widespread use of biometric techniques as face-recognition technologies advance.

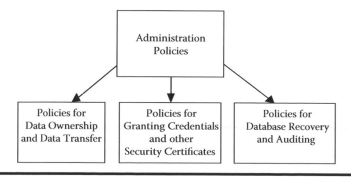

Figure B.4 Administration policies.

B.3.3 Auditing a Database System

Databases are audited for multiple purposes. For example, they may be audited to keep track of the number of queries posed, the number of updates made, the number of transactions executed, and the number of times the secondary storage is accessed so that the system can be designed more efficiently. Databases can also be audited for security purposes. For example, have any of the access-control rules been bypassed by releasing information to the users? Has the inference problem occurred? Has privacy been violated? Have there been unauthorized intrusions?

Audits create a trail, and the audit data may be stored in a database. This database may be mined to detect any abnormal patterns or behaviors. There has been a lot of work in using data mining for auditing and intrusion detection. Audit-trail analysis is especially important these days with E-commerce transactions on the Web. An organization should have the capability to conduct an analysis and determine problems like credit card fraud and identity theft.

B.3.4 Views for Security

Views as a mechanism for security have been studied a great deal both for discretionary security and mandatory security. For example, one may not want to grant access to an entire relation, especially if it has, say, 25 attributes such as healthcare records, salary, travel information, personal data, etc. Therefore, the DBA could form views and grant access to the views.

Views have problems associated with them, including the view update problem (see Reference [DATE90]); that is, if the view is updated, then we need to ensure that the base relations are updated. Therefore, if a view is updated by John and John does not have access to the base relation, then can the base relation still be updated? Do we create different views for different users, and then have the DBA merge the updates on views as updates on base relations? Figure B.5 illustrates views for security.

B.4 Policy Enforcement and Related Issues

B.4.1 SQL Extensions for Security

This section discusses policy specification. Although much of the focus will be on SQL extensions for security policy specification, we will also briefly discuss some of the emerging languages. Note that SQL was developed for data definition and data manipulation for relational systems. Various versions of SQL have been developed including SQL for objects, SQL for multimedia, and SQL for the Web. SQL has influenced data manipulation and data definition a great deal over the past 20 years (see Reference [SQL3]).

V1: VIEW EMP (D# = 20)

SS#	Ename	Salary
2	Paul	30K
3	Mary	40K
4	Jane	20K
1	Michelle	30K

EMP

SS#	Ename	Salary	D#
1	John	20K	10
2	Paul	30K	20
3	Mary	40K	20
4	Jane	20K	20
5	Bill	20K	10
6	Larry	20K	10
1	Michelle	30K	20

V2: VIEW EMP (D# = 10)

SS#	Ename	Salary
1	John	20K
5	Bill	20K
6	Larry	20K

Rules:
John has Read access to V1
John has Write access to V2

Figure B.5   Views for security.

As we have stated, SQL is a data definition and data manipulation language. Security policies could be specified during data definition. SQL has GRANT and REVOKE constructs for specifying grant and revoke access to users; that is, if a user John has read access to relation EMP, then one could use SQL and specify something like "GRANT JOHN EMP READ," and if the access is to be revoked, then we need something like "REVOKE JOHN EMP READ." SQL has also been extended with more complex constraints such as granting John read access to a "-tuple" in a relation and granting Jane write access to an element in a relation.

In Thuraisingham and Stachour [THUR89], we specified SQL extensions for security assertions. These assertions were for multilevel security. We could use similar reasoning for specifying discretionary security policies. For example, consider the situation where John does not have read access to names and salaries in EMP taken together, but he can read names and salaries separately. One could specify this in SQL-like language as follows.

GRANT JOHN READ

EMP.SALARY

GRANT JOHN READ

EMP.NAME

NOT GRANT JOHN READ

Together (EMP.NAME, EMP.SALARY).

If we are to grant John read access to the employees who earn less than 30K, then this assertion is specified as follows.

GRANT JOHN READ

EMP

where EMP.SALARY < 30K.

Note that the assertions we have specified are not standard assertions. These are some of our ideas. We need to explore ways of incorporating these assertions into the standards. SQL extensions have also been proposed for RBAC. In fact, products such as Oracle's Trusted database product enforce RBAC. The access-control rules are specified in an SQL-like language. Note that there are many other specification languages that have been developed. These include XML, RDF, and related languages for the Web and the semantic Web.

B.4.2 Query Modification

Query modification was first proposed in the INGRES project at the University of California at Berkeley (see [STON74]). The idea is to modify the query based on the constraints. We have successfully designed and implemented query modification for mandatory security (see [DWYE87], [THUR87], [THUR93]). However, much of the discussion in this section will be on query modification based on discretionary security constraints. We illustrate the essential points with some examples.

Consider a query by John to retrieve all "-tuples" from EMP. Suppose that John only has read access to all the "-tuples" where the salary is less than 30K and the employee is not in the security department. Then the query

Select * from EMP

will be modified to

Select * from EMP

where salary < 30K, Dept is not Security, and where we assume that the attributes of EMP are, say, Name, Salary, Age, and Department.

Essentially what happens is that the "where" clause of the query has all the constraints associated with the relation. We can also have constraints that span across multiple relations. For example, we could have two relations EMP and DEPT joined by Dept #. Then the query is modified as follows:

Select * from EMP

where EMP.Salary < 30K,

and EMP.D# = DEPT.D#,

and DEPT.Name is not Security.

We have used some simple examples for query modification. The detailed algorithms can be found in Reference [DWYE87] and Reference [STON74]. The high level algorithm is illustrated in Figure B.6.

B.4.3 Discretionary Security and Database Functions

In the previous section we discussed query modification, which is essentially processing security constraints during the query operation. Query optimization will also be impacted by security constraints, that is, once the query is modified, then the query tree has to be built. The idea is to push selections and projection down in the query tree and carry out the join operation later.

Other functions are also impacted by security constraints. Let us consider transaction management. Bertino et al. [BERT89] have developed algorithms for integrity-constraint processing for transactions management. We have examined their techniques for mandatory security-constraint processing during transaction management. The techniques may be adapted for discretionary security constraints. The idea is to ensure that the constraints are not violated during transaction execution.

Constraints may be enforced on the metadata. For example, one could grant and revoke access to users to the metadata relations. Discretionary security constraints for metadata could be handled in the same way they are handled for data.

```
Input: Query, Security Constraints
Output: Modified Query

For Constraints that are Relevant to the
Query, Modify the where Clause of
the Query via a Negation

For Example: If Salary should not be Released to
Jane and if Jane Requests Information from Employee,
then Modify the Query to Retrieve Information from
Employee where Attribute is not Salary

Repeat the Process Until all Relevant Constraints
are Processed
The End Result is the Modified Query
```

Figure B.6 Query modification algorithm.

Secure Database Functions:

Query Processing: Enforce access control rules during query processing; inference control; consider security constraints for query optimization

Transaction management: Check whether security constraints are satisfied during transaction execution

Storage management: Develop special access methods and index strategies that take into consideration the security constraints

Metadata management: Enforce access control on metadata; Ensure that data is not released to unauthorized individuals by releasing the metadata

Integrity management: Ensure that integrity of the data is maintained while enforcing security

Figure B.7 Security impact on database functions.

Other database functions include storage management. The issues in storage management include developing appropriate access methods and index strategies. One needs to examine the impact of the security constraints on the storage-management functions; that is, can one partition the relations based on the constraints and store them in such a way so that the relations can be accessed efficiently? We need to develop secure indexing technologies for database systems. Some work on secure indexing for geospatial information systems is reported in Reference [ATLU04].

In an earlier section, we discussed auditing and views for security; databases are audited to determine whether any security violation has occurred. Furthermore, views have been used to grant access to individuals for security purposes. We need efficient techniques for auditing as well as for view management.

In this section we have examined the impact of security on some of the major database functions including query management, transaction processing, metadata management, and storage management. We also need to investigate the impact of security on other functions such as integrity-constraint processing and fault-tolerant computing. Figure B.7 illustrates the impact of security on the database functions.

B.4.4 Visualization of Policies

As we have mentioned, there are three aspects to policy enforcement. One is policy specification, another is policy implementation, and the third is policy visualization. Policy visualization is especially useful for complex security policies.

Visualization tools are needed for many applications including for geospatial applications as well as Web-based applications so that the users can better understand the data in the databases. Visualization is also useful for integrating security policies. For example, if multiple systems from multiple organizations are to be merged, then their policies have to be visualized and merged so that the administrator can have some idea of the integrated policy. There are now tools available for policy visualization (see, for example, Reference [SMAR]).

Policy visualization is also helpful for dynamic policies. When policies change often, visualizing the effects would be quite useful in designing secure systems. In some of our work we have used graphic structures to specify constraints instead of simple rules. This is because graphs enable us to visualize what the rules look like. Furthermore, policies may be linked to one another, and with graphic structures one can analyze the various links to obtain the relationships between the policies.

The area of policy visualization is a relatively new research area. There are some research programs at the Defense Advanced Research Projects Agency (DARPA) on policy visualization. This is an area that needs work, especially in a Web environment where organizations collaborate with each other and carry out E-business. Policy visualization is also important for homeland security applications where various agencies have to work together and share information and yet maintain their autonomy.

B.4.5 Prototypes and Products

We now discuss discretionary security as implemented in System R and Oracle. Note that System R is a prototype and Oracle is a product. Both are based on the relational model. Note that information on prototypes and products will be changing continually as technology progresses. Therefore, in many cases information about the prototypes and products may be soon outdated. Our purpose in discussing prototypes and products is to explain the concepts. Up-to-date information on prototypes and products can be obtained from the vendor and possibly from the Web.

System R was one of the first systems to introduce various discretionary security concepts (see Reference [GRIFF76]). In this system, objects to be protected are represented by tables and views. Subjects can enforce several privileges on the security objects. Privileges supported by the model include select (select "-tuples"), update (modify "-tuples"), insert (add "-tuples"), delete (delete "-tuples"), and drop (delete table). The model also supports decentralized administration facilities. A subject can grant privileges it has to other subjects. The model also enforces recursive revocation; that is, when Subject A revokes an authorization on a table to Subject B, Subject B in turn revokes authorization of the table to which Subject C had previously been granted access.

System R model has been extended in many directions. These include group management where access is granted and revoked to groups of users, distributed database management where authorization is extended for System R*, which is the distributed version of System R, and negative authorizations. Note that much of the research carried out for System R on security has been transferred to the DB2 commercial product. A detailed discussion of the System R authorization model and its extensions can be found in Reference [FERR00].

In the Oracle Database Server, privileges can be granted to either users or roles. Roles are hierarchically organized. A role acquires all the privileges that are in lower positions of the hierarchy. A user can be authorized to take on several roles, although there is a limit. A role can be enabled or disabled at a given time. With each role, a password may be assigned to ensure only authorized use of privileges is granted to the role.

The privileges can be divided into two categories: system privileges and object privileges. System privileges allow subjects to perform systemwide action on a particular type of object. Examples of system privileges are the privileges to delete the "-tuples" of any table in a database or create a cluster. Object privileges allow subjects to perform a particular action on a particular object. Examples include "insert or delete '-tuples' from a particular table." Other issues such as cascading privileges and revocation of privileges are discussed in detail in Reference [FERR00].

B.5   Summary and Directions

In this appendix we have provided an overview of discretionary security policies in database systems as well as policy-enforcement issues. We started with a discussion of access-control policies including authorization policies and role-based access control. Then we discussed administration policies. We briefly discussed identification and authentication. Next we discussed auditing issues as well as views for security.

The major issues in policy enforcement are policy specification, policy implementation, and policy visualization. We discussed SQL extensions for specifying policies and provided an overview of query modification. We also briefly discussed how policy visualization might be used to integrate multiple policies. Finally, we discussed some prototypes and products that implement discretionary security. We focused mainly on relational database systems.

There is still a lot of work to be done. For example, much work is still needed on RBAC for emerging technologies such as digital libraries and the semantic Web. We need administration policies to mange multiparty transactions in a Web environment. Finally, we need biometric technologies for authenticating users. Digital identity is becoming an important research area, especially with wireless communication and mobile devices.

Security-policy enforcement is a topic that will continue to evolve as new technologies emerge. We have advanced from relational- to object- to multimedia- to Web-based data-management systems. Each system has some unique features that are incorporated into the security policies. Enforcing policies for the various systems will continue to be a major research focus. We also need to carry out research on the consistency and completeness of policies. Policy visualization may help toward this. There is still a lot to be done.

References

[ATLU04] Atluri, V. and S. Chun, An authorization model for geospatial data, *IEEE Trans. Dependable Secure Comput.*, 1, 2004.

[BERT89] Bertino, E. and D. Musto, Integrity constraint processing during transaction processing, *Acta Informat.*, 1989.

[BERT02] Bertino, E. et al., Access control for XML documents, *Data Knowledge Eng.*, 34(3), 2002.

[CARM04] Carminati, B., et al., Security for RDF, *Proc. DEXA* (Database and Expert Systems Applications) *Conf. Workshop on Web Semantics*, Zaragoza, Spain, August, 2004.

[DATE90] Date, C., *An Introduction to Database Systems*, Addison-Wesley, Reading, MA, 1990.

[DWYE87] Dwyer, P. et al., Multilevel security for relational database systems, *Comput. Security*, 6(3), 1987.

[FERR00] Ferrari E. and B. Thuraisingham, Secure database systems, in *Advances in Database Management*, M. Piatini and O. Diaz, Eds., Artech House, London, UK, 2000.

[GRIF76] Griffiths P. and B. Wade, An authorization mechanism for a relational database system, *ACM Trans. Database Syst.*, 1(3), 1976.

[PARK04] Park, J. and R. Sandhu, The UCON usage control model, *ACM Trans. Inf. Syst. Security*, 7(1), 2004.

[SAND96] Sandhu R. et al., Role-based access control models, *IEEE Comput.*, 29(2), 1996.

[SMAR] Smart Center Management, http://www.unipalm.co.uk/products/e-security/check-point/$smartcenter-management.cfm.

[SQL3] SQL3, American National Standards Institute, Draft, 1992.

[STON74] Stonebraker, M. and E. Wong, Access control in a relational data base management system by query modification, *Proc. ACM (Association for Computing Machinery) Annual Conf.*, ACM Press, New York, 1974.

[THUR87] Thuraisingham, B., Security checking in relational database management systems augmented with inference engines, *Comput. Security*, 6(6), 1987.

[THUR89] Thuraisingham, B. and P. Stachour, SQL extensions for security assertions, *Comp. Stand. Interface J.*, 11(1), 1989.

[THUR93] Thuraisingham, B., W. Ford, and M. Collins, Design and implementation of a database inference controller, *Data Knowledge Eng. J.*, 11(3), 1993.

Appendix C

Developments with Standards, Products, and Tools

C.1 Overview

This book has discussed various concepts, directions, and challenges in building trustworthy semantic Webs. As we have stated throughout this book, although the developments with the semantic Web have progressed a great deal, security has not received much attention. However, to provide security, we need to make progress with the technologies. Therefore, in this appendix we will describe the various standards, products, and tools that are emerging for the semantic Web.

As we have discussed, the semantic Web itself is a standard produced by the World Wide Web Consortium (W3C). Portions of semantic Web technologies such as eXtensible Markup Language (XML) are being standardized by various organizations. The Organization for the Advancement of Structured Information Standards (OASIS) is specifying security standards such as eXtensible Access Control Markup Language (XACML) and Security Assertions Markup Language (SAML). Furthermore, organizations such as the Open Geospatial Consortium (OGC) are developing standards for geospatial data.

The organization of this appendix is as follows. Section C.2 describes the various standards organizations working on topics related to the semantic Web. Section C.3 briefly describes the products. Section C.4 describes the various tools.

C.2   Standards

C.2.1 World Wide Web Consortium

In this section we will specify some of the key standards of the W3C that are relevant to this book. Note that in many ways all the standards are relevant as they are interrelated. We strongly urge the reader to keep up with these developments. Much of the information in this section has been obtained from the W3C Website [W3C]. We have used quotes in places where we have duplicated the sentences from Reference [W3C].

- The **Document Object Model** is a "platform and language-neutral interface that will allow programs and scripts to dynamically access and update the content, structure, and style of documents."
- **Hypertext Markup Language (HTTP)** is language for publishing hypertext on the Web. It uses tags to structure text into headings, paragraphs, and lists, among others.
- **Extensible Markup Language (XML)** is a text format derived from SGML (Generalized Markup Language which is an ISO standard). It is crucial for document exchange on the Web.
- **SOAP** is a stateless, one-way message-exchange paradigm and uses XML for its messages.
- The **Resource Description Framework (RDF)** uses XML as an interchange syntax and integrates a variety of applications.
- **Web Ontology Language (OWL)** is used to specify ontologies and builds on RDF.
- The **Rules Interchange Format (RIF) Working Group** is developing a "core rule language plus extensions which together allow rules to be translated between rule languages and thus transferred between rule systems."
- The **Semantic Web** "provides a common framework that allows data to be shared and reused across application, enterprise, and community boundaries." It is based on RDF.
- The **Synchronized Multimedia Integration Language (SMIL**, pronounced "smile") enables simple authoring of interactive audiovisual presentations.
- **MathML** is a low-level specification for describing mathematics as a basis for machine-to-machine communication.

- The **Platform for Privacy Preferences Project (P3P)** "enables Websites to express their privacy practices in a standard format that can be retrieved automatically and interpreted easily by user agents."
- **XML Encryption Working Group** has developed a process to encrypt and decrypt digital content which includes XML documents. This group does not address XML security issues.
- **XML Key Management Working Group** has developed a protocol for a client to obtain key information (e.g., value, certificates, etc.) from a Web service. This group also does not address security issues.
- **XML Signature Working Group** has developed "an XML compliant syntax used for representing the signature of Web resources and portions of protocol messages (anything referencable by a URI) and procedures for computing and verifying such signatures." Like the first two groups, this group also does not address XML security issues.

C.2.2 *Organization for the Advancement of Structured Information Standards*

In this section we will discuss some of the relevant standards of OASIS. The information in this section has been obtained from the OASIS Website [OASIS].

- **Application Vulnerability Description Language (AVDL):** "The goal of AVDL is to create a uniform format for describing application security vulnerabilities."
- **Common Alerting Protocol (CAP)** "provides an open, nonproprietary digital message format for all types of alerts and notifications."
- **Digital Signature Service (DSS):** Two XML-based request and response protocols have been developed. The client and server communicate through these protocols. One is a signing protocol, and the other is a verifying protocol. As stated in the documentation, "through these protocols a client can send documents (or document hashes) to a server and receive back a signature on the documents; or send documents (or document hashes) and a signature to a server, and receive back an answer on whether the signature verifies the documents."
- **The Directory Services Markup Language (DSML)** "provides a means for representing directory structural information as an XML document."
- **Electronic Business using eXtensible Markup Language (ebXML)** is a collection of XML-based standards that enable organizations to interoperate with each other and carry out E-business activities.
- **Extensible Access Control Markup Language (XACML):** As stated in the documentation, "The XACML is a collection of core XML schema for representing authorization and entitlement policies."

- **Reference Model for Service Oriented Architecture (SOA):** "The goal of this reference model is to define the essence of service oriented architecture, and emerge with a vocabulary and a common understanding of SOA."
- **Security Assertions Markup Language (SAML)** is an XML-based framework for communicating user authentication, entitlement, and attribute information.
- **Universal Description, Discovery, and Integration (UDDI)** is a platform-independent, XML-based registry. This registry is used by everyone to register themselves on the Web.
- **Web Service Resource specification (WS-Resource)** is a specification that describes the relationship between a Web service and a resource in the WS-Resource Framework.
- **Web Services Resource Framework** specifies a generic and open framework for modeling and accessing stateful resources using Web services.
- **Web Services Security (WSS):** As stated in the documentation, WSS specification proposes a standard set of SOAP extensions that can be used when building secure Web services to implement message content integrity and confidentiality.

C.3   Products

We have mentioned in this book that we cannot purchase a semantic Web. What we can do is purchase a collection of products from different vendors and assemble them together and put together a semantic Web. In this section we will discuss the various products that have been developed for the semantic Web. Much of the information has been obtained from the Web (see Reference [PROD]). The products Web page is maintained by the W3C semantic Web staff and the semantic Web community.

- **Aduna's Metadata Server:** This product automatically extracts metadata from information sources; http://aduna.biz/products/metadataserver/index.html.
- **Altova SemanticWorks™** 2006 is a visual RDF/OWL editor; http://www.altova.com/products_semanticworks.html.
- **Franz Inc's Allegrograph:** As stated in the product documentation, "SPARQL, the W3C standard RDF query language, gives native object, RDF, and XML responses to queries. Query over sockets, HTTP, Lisp, or a Java API. Also supports OWL DL, RDF Prolog, SWRL, and simple inferencing;" http://www.franz.com/products/allegrograph/.
- **IBM's IODT:** This is a toolkit for ontology-driven development; http://www.alphaworks.ibm.com/tech/semanticstk.

- **Intellidimension's RDF Gateway, InferEd:** "RDF Gateway is a platform for the development and deployment of Semantic Web applications. InferEd is a powerful authoring environment that gives you the ability to navigate and edit RDF (Resource Description Framework) documents;" http://www.intellidimension.com/.
- **Ontotext's OWLIM:** This is a "high-performance semantic repository, packaged as a Storage and Inference Layer (SAIL) for the Sesame RDF database;" http://www.ontotext.com/owlim/.
- **OpenLink's Semantic Web Data Spaces Platform:** This is a distributed platform that creates "semantic Web presence from Wewbv 2.0 application profiles" such as Weblogs and Wikis, and uses an RDF based metadata model with shared ontologies (such as FOAF).
  - Open Source Project Page: http://virtuoso.openlinksw.com/wiki/main/Main/OdsIndex/.
- **OpenLink's Virtuoso Object-Relational Database:** This is an Object-Relational Database Management System (ORDBMS) that includes SQL, XML, and RDF, together with Web content management.
  - Main Product Site: http://virtuoso.openlinksw.com.
  - Open Source Project Page: http://virtuoso.openlinksw.com/wiki/main/.
- **Oracle's 10.2 Database:** As stated in the documentation, "Oracle Spatial 10g introduces the industry's first open, scalable, secure, and reliable RDF management platform. Based on a graph data model, RDF triples are persisted, indexed, and queried, similar to other object-relational data types. The Oracle 10g RDF database ensures that application developers benefit from the scalability of Oracle 10g to deploy scalable and secure semantic applications;" http://www.oracle.com/technology/tech/semantic_technologies/index.html.
- **Thetus Publisher:** This product provides knowledge discovery capabilities so that organizations can describe, search, and structure the information. It provides machine-readable metadata (RF/OWL) for semantic interoperability; http://www.thetus.com/.

C.4 Tools

This section describes tools as provided in Reference [TOOL]. The tools Web page is maintained by the semantic Web community. They are essentially for programming and development and are RDF- and OWL-based tools. The Web page groups these tools depending on their category (e.g., Java developers, C developers, Perl developers, etc.).

- **Amilcare:** University of Sheffield's Amilcare is an adaptive information extraction tool designed to support document annotation for the semantic Web.

- **DERI Ontology Management Environment (DOME)** comprises tool support for editing and browsing, versioning and evolution as well as mapping and merging.
- **Graphl:** This is a tool for collaborative editing and visualization of RDF graphs.
- **GrOWL:** This is a graphical browser and an editor of OWL ontologies that can stand alone or be embedded in a Web browser.
- **IBM's Web Ontology Manager:** This is a Web-based tool for managing ontologies expressed in Web Ontology Language (OWL).
- **IBM's Semantic Layered Research Platform (SLRP):** This is a family of open-source semantic Web software components including an enterprise RDF store, query engine, Web application framework, RCP development libraries, and more.
- **OWL verbalizer:** This is an online tool that verbalizes OWL ontologies in (controlled) English.
- **Stanford's Protégé:** Stanford University's general Protégé 2000 ontology editor tool has a plug-in architecture that enables the development of a number of semantic Web-related tools.
- **SWOOP:** This tool is from the University of Maryland and is a Hypermedia-based Ontology Editor.
- **Boca enterprise RDF store** is a "Java-based store and client libraries which feature named, graph-based RDF storage, access controls, versioning, replication, and local persistence for offline access, and notifications to distributed clients." It is part of IBM's Semantic Layered Research Platform (SLRP).
- **D2RQ and D2R Server:** D2RQ is a Java library that provides access to the content of relational databases through SPARQL, the Jena API, and the Sesame API. D2R Server is a SPARQL and RDF server based on D2RQ.
- **RDFStore** is an RDF storage with Perl and C API-s and SPARQL facilities.
- **SemWeb for .NET** supports persistent storage in MySQL, Postgres, and Sqlite; has been tested with 10 to 50 million triples; supports SPARQL.
- **Euler** is an inference engine supporting logic-based proofs. It is a backward-chaining reasoner enhanced with Euler path detection.
- **Jena Java RDF API and toolkit** is a Java framework to construct semantic Web applications. It provides a programmatic environment for RDF, RDFS, OWL, and SPARQL and includes a rule-based inference engine.
- **OWLJessKB** is a description logic reasoner for OWL. The semantics of the language are implemented using **Jess** (the Java Expert System Shell).
- **Sesame** is an open-source RDF database with support for RDF schema inferencing and querying.
- **Closed World Machine (CWM)** is a data manipulator, rules processor, and query system mostly using the Notation 3 textual RDF syntax.
- **KAON2** is an infrastructure for managing OWL-DL, SWRL, and F-Logic ontologies.

- **Pellet** is an open-source Java-based OWL DL reasoner. It can be used in conjunction with both Jena and OWL API libraries.
- **Disco** is primarily a server-side semantic Web browser developed at the Free University of Berlin, Germany.

C.5. Summary and Directions

In this appendix we have provided an overview of the various standards, products, and tools relevant to the semantic Web and at the same time of interest to us. Note that numerous products and tools as well as standards are emerging for semantic Web development. We refer the reader to the various Web pages that we have listed in this chapter for more information. Several links can also be found in W3C's main Web page.

We have utilized some of the tools including the Oracle product and Jena as well as the Pellet reasoner in our research on secure semantic Webs. We strongly encourage the reader to experiment with these tools as well as build on the ontologies that are out there. It should be noted that security has received little attention. We need to develop tools for handling the inference problem and manage policies as well as reason about the policies. We have discussed various techniques for building semantic Webs. We now need to design and develop the tools to build trustworthy semantic Webs.

References

[OASIS] Organization for the Advancement of Structured Information Standards, http://www.oasis-open.org/home/index.php.

[PROD] Commercial Products for the Semantic Web, http://esw.w3.org/topic/CommercialProducts.

[TOOL] Tools for the Semantic Web, http://esw.w3.org/topic/SemanticWebTools.

[W3C] World Wide Web Consortium, www.w3c.org.

Index